SEMANTICS AND NECESSARY TRUTH

Semantics and Necessary Truth

AN INQUIRY INTO THE FOUNDATIONS

OF ANALYTIC PHILOSOPHY

by Arthur Pap

with a Foreword by Brand Blanshard

NEW HAVEN AND LONDON: YALE UNIVERSITY PRESS

© 1958 by Yale University Press, Inc.
Second printing, January 1966.
Set in Baskerville type and
printed in the United States of America by
The Carl Purington Rollins Printing-Office of
the Yale University Press, New Haven, Connecticut.
Library of Congress catalog card number: 58–6543

FOREWORD

THIS BOOK seems to me the most thorough study of its subject in the English language. That the subject is technical and exacting will be conceded by anyone who sits down to the book seriously. Is the problem worth the effort on the part of the writer and the reader? It is undoubtedly. Philosophers have come to see more clearly than ever before that the problem is central not only to logic and the theory of knowledge, but to metaphysics also. It may be well to develop this a little, not for the sake of the specialist, but for the sake of students who may approach the problem without previous acquaintance with it.

Speculative philosophers of the past have placed their chief reliance on a faculty or process called "reason." It was supposed to provide an insight different in type from perception or common sense or natural science, and to be far greater in sweep and certainty. Indeed it made philosophy possible. The thinker who had command of it was in need of nothing more except a limited experience and an armchair. It was true that instruments and experiments were necessary if one were to enter the world of science, but if one wanted the fundamental truth even about that—about how it came into being, what stuff it was made of, what was the ultimate pattern on which it was put together, how our minds were related to it—the right course was to sit down with such knowledge as one had and use one's "reason" on it. That knowledge was of course fragmentary, but by reason we could interpret it and round it out into a consistent whole of theory.

The great metaphysicians all did this. St. Thomas saw, or thought he saw, that given the frame of things disclosed by common experience, it must have been created by a Deity with such and such attributes. Descartes held that from the existence of his own thought he could infer with certainty the nature of man, the world, and God. Spinoza, starting with the belief in substance, undertook to spin out in Euclidian fashion a complete metaphysical system; and Hegel, Bradley, Royce, and McTaggart repeated the cosmic deduction, each in his own way. They all relied on necessary truths and necessary reasoning.

v

And by a necessary truth they meant more than one that was merely true; it *had* to be true; we could see that it *could* not be other than true. That is what made it so compelling. Crows might, for all we could see, have been flamingo-colored; hydrogen sulphide might have had the odor of gardenias; but two and two *could* not have been anything but four. If philosophy would only hold itself on the straight track of necessity, proceeding from necessary starting points through necessary deductions to conclusions that were therefore necessary, it could arrive at a view of the world that would have the clearness and cogency of a mathematical demonstration.

That we do possess occasional insights of this kind seems clear enough. But there is something mysterious about our having them at all. Why it is that in some matters a thousand unbroken instances of A's being B still leaves us less than sure that it will be so tomorrow, while in others a single case will give us certainty? We cannot be wholly sure that the sun will rise tomorrow; it is quite conceivable that it should explode or that some meteor should abolish the earth before there is any morrow. But we do know with certainty that whether we have a morrow or not, any two planets and any other two will still make four. How do we come by this certainty about times and places that outrun our experience?

Philosophers have been puzzled by this problem for more than two thousand years. Readers of the Platonic dialogues will recall that Socrates was already aware both of the existence of such knowledge and of the difficulty of accounting for it. The most dramatic demonstration on record of the existence of a priori knowledge is the familiar incident in the *Meno* in which Socrates, on a walk by the seaside, calls to an unlettered slave boy and, with the aid of a figure drawn in the sand and a little timely nudging, gets him to establish a geometrical theorem that he had never learned or heard of. Socrates suggested—how much in earnest it is hard to say—that such insight must be accounted for through the retention of knowledge gained in an earlier life. But this only puts the problem one step back, for the puzzle would still remain: how in this earlier existence could we have arrived at certainty from a limited experience?

In philosophic history there have been five important attempts, curiously diverse from each other, to explain our possession of necessary knowledge. Perhaps the simplest is that of the traditional rationalist. His theory is that we grasp necessity because it is there to grasp;

things in nature are actually connected by logical and mathematical relations, and we can apprehend these relations as clearly as we can shapes or motions. It is true that we cannot sense a necessary relation; when we say we *see* that two and two make four, we cannot mean that we see this with our eyes. But we do see it in the sense of apprehending it as necessarily true, and we must assume the existence in us of whatever organ or faculty is required for this apprehension—call it intelligence, understanding, reason, or what you will. The law of contradiction, for example, is not merely a "law of thought"; it is a law that governs the structure of everything that exists. That is why Bradley could use it as the base for a large metaphysical edifice.

Empiricists have always been suspicious of this kind of knowledge and have often tried to explain it away. The most uncompromising of these attempts, which is the second on our list of theories, was made by John Stuart Mill. With great boldness he argued that all apparently necessary truths were really empirical generalizations. If A and B are presented together often enough and with no exceptions, we come in time to lose the power of separating them even in thought. "Two straight lines do not enclose a space." Whenever we have seen two straight lines, either parallel to each other or converging at the corner of a table or a street, this negative property has accompanied them, of not enclosing a space; it is confirmed hourly with never an exception, so that we have reached the point of thinking that it goes with such lines necessarily. Does it really? Mill said No. What links the ideas is psychological association, and this, however often confirmed, always falls short of logical necessity. Such necessity is a fiction.

This theory has not stood up well. It carried with it the implication that "necessary truths," even though we had never known an exception, might have one tomorrow; all we could say was that this was very unlikely. But is it not more than unlikely; is it not plainly impossible? We do not really believe that in some remote bank a case may occur in which two pennies and two others go on strike and perversely make three or five. Of course some weary teller may suppose they do, but this is because he is sleepy or drunk or drugged. We somehow know that two and two could never under any circumstances make anything but four, which means that we possess the knowledge which Mill denied.

The third theory was that of Kant. Unlike Mill, he admitted that we have insight that is both necessary and universal; these were the two marks of a priori knowledge, and he held that we had a remarkable range of such knowledge, extending from logic and mathematics to physics and even ethics. How are we to account for it? He devoted his first and greatest Critique to answering that question, and the answer was a long one, since it involved nothing less than a Copernican revolution in philosophy. To put the answer with an almost brutal brevity, the reason why we can be sure that if we ever reach the moon or Mars we shall find lines and numbers behaving as they do here is that we manufacture them ourselves, whether we know it or not. The frames of logic and arithmetic, space and time, are imposed on experience from within; they are like spectacles grown to our noses, lenses through which we look out at the world; and since they would still be there on our noses if we went to the moon or Mars, we can be sure beforehand how in general things would look. They would look that way because we make them that way. Can we say, as the rationalists do, that such a priori knowledge tells us what the world is really like? Unfortunately not, said Kant. It can tell us what the world is bound to *seem* like, but after all, the world we see through the "categories" is only a world of seeming, a realm of "phenomena," and we have no way of removing the spectacles and looking at things directly. Our certainty about the world of phenomena is bought at the price of an invincible ignorance about things in themselves.

Kant's theory was elaborated with an ingenuity and thoroughness that has given it a vast influence. Yet few philosophers and fewer scientists today accept it. Two discoveries, made since Kant wrote, have gone far toward discrediting it. The first was the discovery of non-Euclidian geometries. Kant accepted the view of Euclid that the whole of traditional geometry consisted of necessary truth; self-evident theorems were self-evidently demonstrated from axioms self-evidently true. But early in the nineteenth century the Russian mathematician Lobachevski began to have doubts about the self-evidence of some Euclidian starting points, notably the postulate of parallels, which states that through a point outside a given line only one parallel to that line is possible. He tried the experiment of assuming that more than one parallel could be drawn and found that with that assumption he could still construct a consistent geometry. Euclid's geometry was not, then, as Kant thought, the only possible one.

Kant might have replied that it was at any rate the only one that applied to nature. But on this point too his theory encountered trouble; it had the great misfortune of running afoul of Einstein. In working out the implications of his theory of relativity, Einstein was able to calculate where a certain star should be seen during a solar eclipse on the assumptions first that the galaxies were arranged on a Euclidian pattern and then on a non-Euclidian. The observation confirmed the latter. Kant's theory never looked the same again.

A fourth theory is of more recent appearance, though one of its proponents, F. C. S. Schiller, maintained that it was in substance as old as Protagoras. This is the pragmatic theory. In an essay on "Axioms as Postulates," Schiller argued for it in an extreme form, but other and more plausible forms have been offered by Henri Poincaré, John Dewey, C. I. Lewis, and Ernest Nagel. Its contention is that even those ultimate principles that have been accepted because they seemed self-evidently necessary are really adopted because they are the most efficient means to ends. Why, for example, do we accept the law of contradiction? Because of its necessity? No, but because of its usefulness. We find that by using it in our intellectual practice we can make our knowledge more precise, coherent, and systematic, which we very much want it to be.

But this pragmatic line of argument always seems to sag down under pressure. *Why* should we want our ideas to be more precise, or more coherent, or more systematically organized? Suppose someone announced that he was not interested in these things, and personally preferred vagueness, incoherence, and chaos. We should regard such a person as excessively foolish if not unbalanced, and the reason is plain enough: It is that precision, coherence, and order are not themselves the end of the line; we want them because we want something else to which they are means. We want them because they are aids to truth, because only as thought embodies them can we see things as they are. Conformity to the law of contradiction is the accepted condition of conformity to fact. That, not its practical usefulness, is the reason why we cling to it.

All of these theories have in recent years been pushed off into the shadow by a fifth theory, "logical empiricism." It agrees with Kant and the rationalists in holding that we do have necessary knowledge, inexplicable by any run of sense experiences. But having made this clear, the logical empiricists turn round on the rationalist and say that this knowledge, far from revealing the nature of things, reveals nothing but our own intentions. They argue for this view in three ways which converge to the same conclusion. Necessary truths, they maintain, are linguistic, conventional, and analytic.

First they are linguistic. This means that they are merely statements of how we propose to use words. When we say, "A straight line is the shortest distance between two points," we are saying that we use the phrase "straight line" only of those lines that are the shortest between their ends, and never of others; the statement thus explains our usage. Now usage is plastic to our preferences; we can define our terms differently if we care to, even the fundamental ones. Hence, secondly, these necessary statements are conventions. "It is perfectly conceivable that we should have employed different linguistic conventions from those which we actually do employ," said A. J. Ayer; "the rules of language are in principle arbitrary," said Moritz Schlick; even the postulates and rules of logical inference, said Carnap, "may be chosen quite arbitrarily." But if the principles of logic reflect our changeable preferences, they cannot also reflect the enduring structure of things; we are deluded if we try to make laws of nature out of mere human conventions. That these necessary truths are really conventions is confirmed if we note, thirdly, that they are all analytic, all attempts to set out, in whole or part, what we mean. Why is it that we refuse to call straight any line that is not the shortest one? Surely because being the shortest is part of what we mean by "straight," so that to deny that it is the shortest would be self-contradiction. To say that two and two are four is to say that what we *mean* by these phrases is identical. That is why we remain unmoved if anyone tries to point out that there are instances to the contrary, that two wolves and two lambs, or two drops of water and two others, sometimes do not make four. We should reply that we are not talking about events in nature, but about what we *mean* by two and two. We know very well what we mean, and we know that it is quite independent of any such events.

Of course if this theory is true, it has far-reaching philosophical consequences. The instrument that philosophers have called "reason," the tool on which they have mainly relied in building their cosmic constructions, will be for this purpose discredited. Rationalists have always assumed that the more severely logical their thinking, the more likely they were to arrive at the truth about the world. But if the very statements they take to report most faithfully the nature of things report only their own meanings and tell them nothing about existence, their major tool turns out to be a broken reed.

No one saw this more clearly than Arthur Pap. Without ignoring the other theories, he plainly regards this last as the really formidable one, which philosophy must now reckon with. He devotes the larger part of his book to stating it, reviewing the various forms of it, qualifying, amending, and criticizing it, and refuting with devastating force some of its more popular forms. He was often considered a logical empiricist himself, and that he belongs in the camp of analysis rather than that of speculative philosophy is abundantly clear. But the theory that emerges after running the gauntlet of this long examination is a very chastened empiricism indeed. Here I shall leave him to tell his own highly competent story.

There is a personal side to this story which he would not have cared to tell, but which those who read and admire this book may wish to know. I shall allow myself a concluding word about it.

Arthur Pap was born in Zürich, in German-speaking Switzerland, the son of a successful businessman of that city. He lived there till he was nineteen, with German as his native language, and harboring thoughts of two very different but very German careers. One was a career in music; he was a sensitive musician and an accomplished pianist. The other was in philosophy, and with none other than Hegel as his master. Both dreams were halted abruptly when his family, finding the backwash of Hitlerism unbearable, even in Switzerland, emigrated to America.

Arthur Pap had to start out over again in a foreign country and with an alien language. It did not take him long to find himself here. He took a degree at Columbia, spent a year with Cassirer at Yale, and returned to the Columbia graduate school to win the Woodbridge prize for his doctoral thesis on "The A Priori in Physical Theory," which was in a sense a preliminary study for the present book. He taught for brief periods at Chicago University, City College, the University of Oregon, Lehigh, and Yale. To his delight he was invited to serve in the year 1953–54 as Fulbright lecturer in Vienna, where he presented in his lectures an evaluation of the historic movement initiated by "the Vienna Circle" a quarter-century before. During his teaching years at Yale, he wrote, taught, and thought with a singular intensity—the intensity of a man whose true life was among ideas. In the same year the university gave him a promotion and the Yale Press published this book. After a long and stony path toward recognition, he seemed to have turned a corner and to be looking down an avenue of assured success. Then suddenly he was struck down. In the spring of the following year he suffered an attack of the kind of nephritis for which there is no known cause or cure. He died in September 1959, at the age of thirty-eight, leaving a wife and four young children.

His achievement in the less than twenty years he spent in his new country was far greater in quality and quantity than most philosophers manage in a lifetime. He wrote five books of notable subtlety and technical proficiency, besides a long list of articles in professional journals, contriving to throw them off while carrying a full load of teaching. If he had lived, he would no doubt have revised this book for its new edition and made it even better than it is. He would also have taken his place as one of the leading philosophers of our time; indeed many readers of this book will feel that he was already there. He has taken as its theme one of the central recurring issues of the theory of knowledge and explored it with a thoroughness and acuteness that are apparent on every page. It is hoped that this new edition of his book will make his name, his quality, and his achievement more widely known.

BRAND BLANSHARD

PREFACE

THE DISTINCTIONS between a priori knowledge and empirical knowledge ("necessary truth" and "contingent truth") and between analytic and synthetic propositions lie at the very heart of modern epistemology. One of the most important and apparently interminable controversies in contemporary, semantically oriented epistemology is whether all necessary truth is "verbal." Even within the—fortunately ever increasing—camp of the analytic philosophers there is lively disagreement about the meaning of necessary truth, the connection between logical necessity and linguistic conventions, the precise meaning of analytic truth, the existence or even possibility of synthetic a priori propositions, etc. It is not even clear whether what is called "analytic philosophy" is an attempt to acquire a special kind of empirical knowledge, viz. knowledge about linguistic usage, or whether analytic philosophers are hunting after necessary truths—though by a method distinctly different from the methods of traditional metaphysicians—or, indeed, whether Schlick was right in saying that analytic philosophy is an activity of clarification of meanings which does not terminate in the assertion of distinctively "philosophical" propositions. However, it would be unwise to belittle an activity because those who are engaged in it are not clear about what they are doing. Great mathematicians may have nothing illuminating to say about the nature of mathematical proof, great physicists may be poor methodologists of physics; similarly it must be admitted that astounding progress has been made in analytic philosophy since the beginning of this century (the very best papers in this field written some fifty years ago may fail to meet the standards of acceptability imposed by leading journals of analytic philosophy today), although there is still great unclarity as to what philosophical analysis is. And there is nothing paradoxical about the fact that a great deal of clarification of concepts has been achieved with the help of the distinction between necessary and contingent propositions even though that distinction itself still needs clarification very badly.

The purpose of this book can be stated without ceremony, quite briefly: to clarify this distinction, even if the outcome of such clarification should be that there is no sharp but only a vague distinction, and thereby to clarify the nature of analytic philosophy itself. Since modern discussions of this problem have been intimately bound up with semantics, this book could also be characterized as an examination of the basic concepts of modern (" philosophical ") semantics. The historical part was added, not only because of its intrinsic interest for historically minded analytic philosophers (an as yet somewhat rare species), but also because I feel that, after the revolution has victoriously taken place (in some parts of the globe), it is time for analytic philosophers to pay a little more attention to their ancestry. It is not that the ancients solved long ago the problems that we despair of solving without their help; such ancestor worship is as incompatible with progress in philosophy as it is incompatible with progress in science. Rather it ought to console our fathers and forefathers to see that, with all our technical equipment, we are still entangled in some (if not all) of the confusions that survived them through the printed word.

It will hardly escape the reader's notice that very few definitive conclusions are reached in this book, that perhaps more problems have been formulated than have been solved. I would not deny that my not solving a problem is mainly due to my not knowing the solution. But I would plead, on the other hand, that from the viewpoint of the analytic philosopher, philosophical progress consists in piecemeal clarification of specific conceptual muddles, rather than in grand proofs of general theses. It seems to me that the history of analytic philosophy in the last half century has shown that where analytic philosophers attempted the latter, they have not been much more successful than the metaphysical system-builders against whom they reacted. I have in mind particularly such theses of logical empiricism as the verifiability theory of meaning, physicalism, the emotive theory of ethical judgment, and the linguistic theory of necessary truth. One of the main criticisms running through this book is, indeed, directed at the latter theory. No doubt I have failed in this enterprise in many ways, but for the stated reason I do not consider it a failing to be unable to replace the criticized thesis by a clear-cut and equally sweeping alternative. The inability to satisfy such requests as to define necessity, possibility, time, mind, etc. is no cause for distress to a philosopher who realizes, unlike the freshman student, that fundamental concepts cannot be clarified by giving simple definitions.

Thus it would be naive to think that a definition like "a necessary proposition is a proposition which cannot be conceived to be false" amounts to great philosophical clarification. For is the meaning of " it is *impossible* to believe the contradictory of *p* " any clearer than the meaning of " it is *necessary* that nobody believes the contradictory of *p* "? Indeed, lest the reader embark on the study of this book with expectations that are bound to remain unfulfilled, I might as well state at the outset that several of my strands of reasoning lead to the conclusion that the concept of necessity involved in such statements as " the conclusion of a valid syllogism follows necessarily from the premises " and " the relation of temporal succession is necessarily—not contingently—asymmetrical " is not analyzable at all. It is a conceptual tool without which the analysis of concepts could not take a single step. We can, of course, characterize the relevant meaning of " necessary " by enunciation of axioms describing its relations to other concepts—such as contingency, probability, possibility, truth—but such " axiomatic definitions " could be given even for such simples as " red " and " hot." I have emphasized especially the shortcomings of attempted analyses in terms of *linguistic concepts*, like " syntactic rule," " semantic rule," " definition," and " conventional usage," because it is widely held in contemporary analytic philosophy that such an analysis is possible, and indeed imperative in order to take the mystical flavor out of traditional conceptions of a priori insight. To say that temporal succession is necessarily asymmetrical because to deny it is to change the conventional meanings of such terms as " earlier " and " later," that the *ponendo ponens* principle is necessarily valid because to deny it is to change the conventional meaning of " if, then," only provokes the question: on what ground is the inference from denial to misinterpretation, or violation of linguistic rules, itself necessary? And if the answer is that it is necessary because it is impossible to believe the contradictories of the propositions conventionally expressed by the relevant sentences, then necessity has of course in no sense been " reduced " to linguistic convention.

Since a major part of this book is occupied with questions *about* analysis, as may be surmised from the subtitle, it is unlikely that readers who have made no prior contact with analytic philosophy will feel a strong urge to master it. Nevertheless, the improbable happens sometimes, and it is in order to help such brave uninitiated readers that I have appended a glossary of technical terms of logic and semantics that are used in the book. Had I defined all technical terms whenever they were first used so as to make them intelligible to laymen, it would be tedious reading indeed for professionals. The glossary, therefore, is a sort of compromise measure.

The bulk of this book was written, at intervals, between 1950 and 1953 at the University of Oregon, though I continued rewriting, as well as adding and deleting material, off and on until the fall of 1956. (Circumstances beyond my control prevented me from taking acount of more recent publications dealing with the problems of this book.) Since I spent the years at the University of Oregon in comparative isolation from analytic philosophers interested in the same problems, I must accept sole responsibility for either the virtues or the shortcomings of the book. Obviously I have been greatly influenced by several outstanding contemporary analytic philosophers in England and in America, but I find it impossible to say who influenced me most (though I would guess that Russell and Carnap have taught me more than all the rest). Above all, I owe a great debt to various brilliant students of mine whose questions and criticisms turned my teaching of analytic philosophy into a creative enterprise.

A few chapters were read and helpfully commented on by Professors A. F. Smullyan, University of Washington, and A. Kaplan, University of California at Los Angeles; I herewith extend my thanks to them. To Mr. David H. Horne of the Yale University Press I wish to express my appreciation for a careful and judicious job of editing the typescript.

Grateful acknowledgement is made to the following for permission to quote: the University of Chicago Press, for R. Carnap, " Logical Foundations of the Unity of Science," in *International Encyclopedia of Unified Science, 1*, No. 1, 1938; the Columbia University Press, for Y. H. Krikorian, ed., *Naturalism and the Human Spirit*, New York, 1944; the Open Court Publishing Company, La Salle, Ill., for C. I. Lewis, *An Analysis of Knowledge and Valuation*, 1946; and the editor of *Philosophy of Science*, Vols. *3, 18*.

ARTHUR PAP

New Haven, Connecticut
May 1957

CONTENTS

PART ONE

The Concept of Necessary Truth in
Traditional Epistemology

*I*N *Leibniz' philosophy we find a central preoccupation with the distinction between " truths of reason " and " truths of fact." This distinction does not, however, coincide with Kant's distinction between analytic and synthetic propositions, since " truths of fact," or even the broader class of empirical propositions, constitute according to Kant only a proper subclass of synthetic propositions. Although Leibniz, like Hume, did not explicitly distinguish the pairs a priori— empirical and analytic—synthetic, one may impute to him the theory that all a priori truth is analytic. In this respect he is, in spite of his usual classification as a " rationalist " (a word of most uncertain significance), an ancestor of contemporary logical empiricism. The disinclination to admit " intuition " as a source of a priori knowledge is, indeed, something which he has in common with logical empiricists of the present, though the latter are of course diametrically opposite to him in other respects. It seems, therefore, highly relevant to re-examine Leibniz' theory of a priori truth in a book which is centrally concerned with the epistemology of logical empiricism. It turns out that some of the difficulties in Leibniz' theory which Russell already brought to daylight in his early book on Leibniz (connected with the notion of " simple " concepts) reappear in Carnap's recent work in pure semantics and inductive logic.*

Kant's definition of the analytic—synthetic distinction, and his doctrine of the synthetic a priori character of geometry and arithmetic, have been much criticized, and much of the criticism has been just. However, as against the tendency on the part of many of the logical empiricists who fought the battle against Kant (for which, undoubtedly, they are to be thanked) to relapse into a new kind of " dogmatic slumber," it is important to become aware of difficulties which modern analytic philosophy still has in common with Kant. They all turn, in my opinion, around the notion of analysis. Kant's definition of " analytic " is justly blamed for obscurity, since it speaks of " the " definition of a concept. But insofar as the analytic-synthetic distinction is of epistemological interest, a distinction must somehow be made between an arbitrary definition and a correct analysis of a meaning antecedently entertained. And if we permit ourselves to use the notion of "correct analysis" without being able to analyze it, we should not be too contemptuous of Kant for having suffered from the same weakness. Again, Kant is accused of "psychologism," on the ground that the definition of "necessity" in terms of "what cannot be conceived, or imagined, to be otherwise" is couched in psychological terms whereas what is to be defined is a logical concept. But (as is shown particularly in Chapter 13 of this book) modern analytical philosophers are then equally "psychologistic" when they ask logically, or at any rate formally, undecidable questions of the form "Is p self-contradictory? Is q entailed by r?" in the attempt to judge proposed analyses of a concept. If we condemn such questions as meaningless, as some "systematic" analysts are inclined to do (see chapter 14, below), we even deny ourselves the right to affirm the logicist thesis of the reducibility of arithmetic to logic and hence the right to reject Kant's theory of arithmetic as demonstrably false.

Just as Leibniz is closer to logical empiricism than his usual classification as a "rationalist" would lead one to believe, so Locke is further from logical empiricism than a "British empiricist" would commonly be expected to be. In the first place, he explicitly distinguished within the genus of certain universal propositions, the instructive from the trifling ones, a distinction which corresponds almost exactly to Kant's distinction between those a priori propositions whose predicate is not contained in the subject and those whose predicate is so contained. And had he used the Kantian terminology he would have said not only that the axioms and theorems of Euclidean geometry are synthetic a priori propositions, but even that the true laws of nature, if only we had better evidence than the inductive kind, would be seen to be synthetic propositions about necessary connections (this interpretation will be textually substantiated in Chap. 3). Underlying this view is a conception of necessary truth which makes sense only if it makes sense to speak of apprehension of universals and of immutable relations between them—which should be enough to make a modern "empiricist" reluctant to look up to Locke as a congenial forefather. Let us not repeat forever the usual vague statement that, after all, Locke believed, unlike the rationalists, that "all knowledge is derived from experience"; for unlike the modern empiricists he did not consider it a logical impossibility that a priori knowledge of syn-thetic propositions "about reality" be obtained. He held, indeed, that all ideas (to be distinguished from propositions) "come into the mind through the channels of sensation and reflection," but once this metaphorical statement is clarified by translation into the formal mode of speech, it turns out to be either false or tautologous: Locke did not want to maintain (no more than did Hume) that all descriptive predicates have meanings that can be grasped only by experience of instances to which they apply, but he wanted to maintain this with regard to simple descriptive predicates. Yet, he had no useful criterion of such simplicity except the causal/psy-chological one which makes his thesis analytic. This concept of simplicity is, however, of great importance for the theory of necessary truth, since one may be inclined to characterize as synthetic, neces-sary statements whose descriptive terms occur essentially yet cannot be eliminated through analysis.

In Hume we find the "psychologism" which is repudiated by the logical empiricists of the present who are in other respects more indebted to Hume than to any other big name in the history of philosophy: for his criterion of distinction between propositions "about matters of fact" and a priori propositions is in terms of what can or cannot be conceived to be otherwise. To be sure, he frequently speaks of "contradiction" when he raises the question (that powerful dialectic weapon against rationalistic pretenses of a priori demonstration) "Can p be supposed false without con-tradiction?" But since such questions can be decided only by "thought experiment," not by formal deduction, it is not clear that this formulation, preferred as it is by the modern analytic philos-ophers, is any less "psychologistic." Hume thus raised, by his own dialectic practice, a problem which verges into the problem of whether conceptual analysis can be so formalized as to dispense with the much decried appeal to the intuitive evidence of necessary connections—a question we examine and answer negatively at the end of this book.

CHAPTER 1. *Leibniz*

A. *Are All Necessary Truths Reducible to (Partial or Complete) Identities?*

FOR LEIBNIZ, necessary truths (also called by him "truths of reason") are propositions which are demonstrable by the principle of contradiction, or the principle of identity alone.[1] Leibniz' criterion of necessary truth accordingly coincides with Kant's criterion of analytic truth, and therefore it would be not inaccurate to represent Leibniz as the most prominent ancestor of the widely held contemporary doctrine that all necessary truths are analytic. Whether Leibniz intended the stated criterion as the very *definition* of "necessary truth" or only as a distinguishing property is a question upon which it is difficult to pronounce, since Leibniz himself probably failed to consider it. He certainly held that a necessary proposition is a proposition whose contradictory is impossible, but whether this gives an independent meaning to "necessary" is highly doubtful: either "p is impossible" is defined to mean "not-p is necessary," in which case we have a circle, or it is defined to mean "p is self-contradictory" (which is suggested by Leibniz when he says that a possible idea is an idea which is not self-contradictory); in either case, no meaning has been assigned to "necessary" by virtue of which "all necessary truths are analytic" would itself be a synthetic statement. However, what I wish to examine is whether Leibniz' generalization about necessary truths, whatever its own logical status may be, could have been consistently maintained by Leibniz himself.

Let us consider necessary propositions expressible by means of

---

[1] In the present discussion we shall not distinguish between these principles, although one might argue that if "if p, then p" and "not-$(p$ and not-$p)$," or "$A = A$" and "$A \neq$ non-A," be regarded as merely different formulations of one and the same principle, then with equal right one could hold that there is only one logical principle altogether. It would, indeed, be unplausible to regard logical equivalence generally as a sufficient condition for identity of propositions, but this question of the conditions of identity of propositions is not relevant to the present discussion (it will be dealt with especially in Chap. 10, below).

7

propositional logic, e. g. " if p, then $(p$ or $q)$." [2] If this proposition is necessary in Leibniz' sense, then a contradiction must be deducible from its denial. But in order to accomplish this deduction, we require the use of *logical equivalences*, viz.

(if p, then q) $\equiv$ not-$(p$ and not-q); not-$(p$ or q) $\equiv$ (not-p and not-q).

Unless these equivalences, which lead from the denial of the above proposition to the explicit contradiction " p and not-p and not-q," are themselves necessary truths, the proposition in question has not been shown to be necessary, since a contradiction is deducible even from the denial of a contingent proposition if we are allowed the use of contingent propositions as premises. But how could they be shown to be necessary in Leibniz' sense? It will perhaps be said that the first equivalence is a definitional identity, or would be such an identity if the logical system contained a definition of " if, then " in terms of " not " and " and " as primitive connectives. Although this view has its difficulties (especially if " if, then " is construed intensionally) ,[3] let us disregard them for the moment, and ask instead whether the second equivalence could likewise be interpreted as definitional. The relevant definition would be one of " or " in terms of " not " and " and," in the contextual form: p or q = not-(not-p and not-q). However, this definition helps to reduce the equivalence in question to an identity only if the law of double negation, $p \equiv$ not-(not-p), is presupposed; and surely this necessary truth cannot be said to be reducible to an identity on the basis of a definitional equivalence.

The point of this illustration from propositional logic is that in most cases the reduction of a necessary truth to an identity, total or partial, presupposes principles of deduction which are themselves necessary truths but cannot be held to be in turn thus reducible. Often such principles of deduction are equivalences legitimizing substitutions. Leibniz implicitly recognizes such equivalences when he speaks of the demonstration of syllogisms by the principle of contradiction:

I say, then, that the principle of contradiction alone suffices to

---

[2] Strictly speaking, this is a propositional form, not a proposition, since p and q are variables. But in referring to such forms as propositions, one tacitly binds the variables by universal quantifiers: for every p and q, if p, then $(p$ or $q)$.

[3] Cf. below, pp. 373-4.

demonstrate the second and the third figures of the syllogism
by means of the first. For example, we may conclude in the
first figure, in *Barbara*:

all *B* is *C*

all *A* is *B*

Then all *A* is *C*.

Suppose that the conclusion is false (or that it is true that
some *A* is not *C*), then one or the other of the premises will
be false also. Suppose that the second is true, the first must
then be false, which maintains that all *B* is *C*. Then its contradictory will be true, i. e. some *B* will not be *C*. And this will
be the conclusion of a new argument, drawn from the falsity
of the conclusion and the truth of one of the premises of the
preceding argument. Here is this new argument: some *A* is
not *C*. This is opposed to the preceding conclusion supposed
false. All *A* is *B*. This is the preceding premise supposed true.
Then some *B* is not *C*. This is the present true conclusion,
opposed to the preceding false premise. [*New Essays concerning
Human Understanding* (New York, Macmillan, 1896), Bk. IV,
chap. 2, § 1].

If we analyze this demonstration of the *OAO* syllogism in the third
figure from the first figure *AAA* syllogism carefully, we shall see that
Leibniz was guilty of considerable oversimplification in claiming
that the principle of contradiction *alone* suffices for that purpose.
Leibniz presupposes, in his demonstration, the principle of contra-
position according to which " if *p*, then *q* " is equivalent to " if
not-*q*, then not-*p* "; he uses it in arguing that one premise of the
syllogism must be false if the conclusion is false. But the only
way in which this equivalence could be reduced to an identical
truth would be by substituting, in the identity " (if *p*, then *q*)
$\equiv$ (if *p*, then *q*)," " if not-*q*, then not-*p* " for one side of the equivalence to be demonstrated. Similarly, in inferring from the falsehood
of " all *A* are *C* " the truth of " some *A* are not *C*," the equivalence
of " not-(all *A* are *C*) " to " some *A* are not *C* " is presupposed, and
by the same reasoning as the above it is unlikely that this equivalence could be reduced to an identity without circularity. Again,
in the same passage from which the above quotation is excerpted,
Leibniz complains against the habit of logicians to make use of

" conversion " (i. e. such equivalences as that of " no *A* are *B* " and " no *B* are *A* ") to reduce one figure to another, and thus to demonstrate derivative types of syllogism from a few fundamental types (perhaps just one type). He holds that, quite on the contrary, these equivalences ought to be demonstrated by means of syllogisms. But whichever of these methods of reducing logical axioms to a minimum be preferred, the demonstrations presuppose principles of demonstration, whether in the form of equivalences or of syllogistic principles, which are necessary truths yet are in no clear sense reducible to identities.

Leibniz' theory of demonstration as a reduction to identities with the help of explicit definitions, and the characterization of necessary truths as explicitly or implicitly identical propositions, *prima facie* overlooks the role of *axioms* in a demonstration. Leibniz, indeed, insisted that one should not rest satisfied with the self-evidence of such axioms as Euclid's axioms " the whole is greater than its part " and " equals added to equals yield equals," but should try to demonstrate them, i. e. reduce them to identities; and since he supposed such axioms to be themselves necessary truths, he was committed to the claim that they in turn are reducible to identities. This was by no means a merely dogmatic claim of Leibniz'. He actually demonstrated the mentioned Euclidean axioms, the latter by ingeniously using an identical proposition (but no definitions),[4] the former by means of a definition of " greater " (via its converse " smaller ") and the syllogism principle.[5] As reported by Couturat, Bernouilli objected in a letter to Leibniz against the demonstration of Euclid's axiom " the whole is greater than its part " that the syllogism principle, on which Leibniz' demonstration was based, is no more evident than the demonstrated axiom; to which Leibniz' retort was that the syllogism principle itself is not required as an independent axiom but admits likewise of demonstration by the principle of identity. Here is the demonstration as reported by Couturat (*La Logique*, p. 370) :

Si $A < B$ et $B < C$, il en resulte: $A < C$. En effet, dire que $A < B$, c'est dire que: $A + D = B$, et dire que $B < C$, c'est dire

---

[4] Hypothesis: $c = a$, and $d = b$; to be proved: $a + b = c + d$. Proof: in the identity $a + b = a + b$ substitute c for a and d for b on the right hand side. See L. Couturat, *La Logique de Leibniz d'après des documents inédits* (Paris, 1901), p. 206.

[5] *New Essays*, p. 204.

que: $B + E = C$. Dans cette dernière égalité remplaçons B par $A + D$, en vertu de la première; il vient: $A + D + E = C$, ce qui signifie que $A < C$.

Leibniz here succeeds in dispensing with the axiom of the transitivity of class inclusion by constructing an explicit definition of class inclusion in terms of class equality,[6] and thus apparently saves his theory that demonstrations require nothing more than the principle of identity (or identical propositions which are special cases of the principle of identity), explicit definitions, and the rule (regarded by Leibniz as the very definition of equality) that equals may be substituted for one another. However, the method of explicit definition which, as illustrated, makes it possible to use axioms economically, has its limits. Leibniz seems to have overlooked the fact that such operation symbols as " $+$ " do not admit of explicit definition at all, but are either " implicitly defined " by such axioms as the associative and commutative axioms for addition, or else are defined by what is known as "recursive definition." In either case such a symbol is not eliminable,[7] and therefore the mentioned axioms do not admit of demonstration in Leibniz' sense (reduction to identities) ; yet he would not have hesitated to acknowledge them as necessary truths. Indeed, the associative law for addition is tacitly assumed in the above demonstration of the syllogism principle, since "$A + D + E = C$" is recognizable as an instance of the definiens for "$A < C$" only if it is construed as "$A + (D + E) = C$," which equation cannot be deduced from "$(A + D) + E = C$" without the associative law.

But even if all axioms could be eliminated with the help of explicit definitions, as Leibniz seems to have assumed, the theory that all necessary truths (except the principle of identity itself) are demonstrable in Leibniz' sense faces an obvious difficulty, so obvious that it is surprising that it should have escaped the attention of a logician as acute as Leibniz. The relevant explicit definitions, as illustrated by the above definition of class inclusion, generally are not

[6] In terms of modern symbolic logic, Leibniz' definition would be expressed: $A < B =_{df} (\exists C) (A + C = B)$; here C may be null, in which case A would be equal to B. A more customary definition of class inclusion in terms of class equality, which has the advantage of not requiring quantification, is: $A < B =_{df} A \cdot B = A$.

[7] More accurately speaking, a recursively defined symbol is not eliminable from a sentence in which it occurs with variable arguments, like: $(x) (y) (x + y = y + x)$.

arbitrary stipulations but rather *analyses* of concepts preanalytically understood. If one wishes to construe a definitional equation like "$A < B = {}_{df} (\exists C) (A + C = B)$" as a syntactic rule of substitution, one must nonetheless admit that the *justification* for the rule lies in the *necessary truth* of the corresponding equivalence in the object language. In other words, the definition is seen, in terms of the antecedent meanings of the constants involved, to express a *correct analysis*. But to demonstrate the correctness of the analysis in the sense of reducing it to an identity would be a circular procedure, since the required substitution of equivalent expressions would have to be justified by appeal to the very correctness of the analysis; and similarly the question would be begged if it were maintained that the analysis is simply a special case of the principle of identity.[8]

One might conjecture that Leibniz, being primarily a mathematician, aimed his characterization of necessary truths as truths reducible to identities at the equations of arithmetic, whose demonstration is not syllogistic at all. Indeed, Leibniz illustrated what he meant by such reduction to identity by reducing "$2 + 2 = 4$," allegedly with the sole help of the definitions of 2, 3, and 4 in terms of the successor relation, to an identity. But, as Frege, who quoted Leibniz' demonstration in his *The Foundations of Arithmetic* (trans. Austin, New York, 1950), noticed, the demonstration presupposes tacitly the associative law of addition: $a + (b + c) = (a + b) + c$, and here again we have an equation which could not be reduced to an identity without circularity (that it is an " identical " equation means, of course, only that it is postulated to hold for all values of the variables). What these considerations suggest is that Leibniz' criterion of necessary truth is either circular or insufficiently general. To see this, we need only realize that the self-contradictoriness of the negation, if proposed as a general criterion of necessary truth, must be intended in the following broad sense: " not-p " is self-contradictory if it is reducible to an explicit contradiction, i. e. a conjunction at least two conjuncts of which are contradictories of each other, with the help of definitional identities and/or principles of deductive inference. But if " principle of deductive inference " means " necessary truth used as rule of inference," the criterion is circular. To illustrate: is the negation of " if (if p, then q) and

---

[8] The difficult topic of necessary truth and correct analysis will occupy us again at several junctures in the book. See especially Chaps. 5, 9, 10, 13.

(if q, then r) , then (if p, then r) " self-contradictory? Now, a contradiction is indeed deducible from " (if p, then q) and (if q, then r) and p and not-r " if we are permitted to use *modus ponens* or *modus tollens* as principles of inference. But to justify their use is to show that they themselves are necessary truths.[9] And if " principle of deductive inference " means " logical truth used as rule of inference," then the criterion is not significantly applicable to logical truths themselves, which surely constitute a respectable subclass of necessary truths.[10] That is, in order to apply the criterion, one would already have to know, independently of its application, which propositions are logical truths.

B. *The Problem of " Compossibility "*

But besides the mentioned weakness of Leibniz' criterion of necessary truth, there is another, connected with his view that necessary propositions, unlike contingent propositions, are nonexistential and conditional: "As for the *eternal truths*, it must be observed that at bottom they are all conditional and say in effect: such a thing posited, such another thing is. For example, in saying: *every figure which has three sides will also have three angles*, I say nothing else than that, supposing there is a figure with three sides, *this same* figure will have three angles " (*New Essays*, Bk. IV, chap. 11, § 13) . This view could be equivalently expressed by saying that all necessary propositions (" necessary truth " and " eternal truth " are synonyms for Leibniz) are entailment-propositions, propositions of the form " if p, then necessarily q," " having property P entails having property Q." However, Leibniz explicitly recognizes a class of " eternal " truths which are not reducible to this form at all: judgments of *possibility*, involved in what he called (in a sense quite different from the Aristotelian sense) *real definitions*. For example, he holds, against Locke, that the judgment " $3 = 2 + 1$ " is not an instance of intuitive knowledge but only a definition, yet adds that insofar as this is a real definition it involves

---

[9] Logicians may urge here the distinction between the rule of inference " S_2 is derivable from S_1 and (if S_1, then S_2) " which belongs to the meta-language, and the necessary proposition of the object-language " for any p and q, if p and (if p, then q) , then q." But this distinction does not invalidate my point: the justification of the rule is still the necessity of the corresponding proposition.

[10] We shall return to this point below, pp. 28-30, 106-8.

the judgment that the defined kind of entity is possible, i. e. not self-contradictory. If " p " stands for the proposition that there are instances of the defined concept, this judgment of possibility can be put in the form " it is possible that p." Judgments of compatibility would be special cases of such judgments, arising if the concept in question is defined by a conjunction of predicates, e. g. " regular polygon bounded by six sides." Strangely, Leibniz does not seem to have considered the question of whether his criterion of necessary truth was applicable to propositions of this kind—which on Leibniz' theory cannot be contingent since all contingent propositions assert, according to that theory, existence.[11] But even apart from Leibniz' theory, it seems undeniable that true propositions of the form " it is (logically) possible that p " are necessary. For it is the mark of a necessary proposition that it is capable of being known to be true by analysis and comparison of concepts (supplemented by formal deduction in the case of necessary propositions that are not intuitively evident) , without recourse to empirical evidence. But if such is the method appropriate for establishing a proposition of the form " p entails q," the same method is appropriate for establishing the negations of such propositions, i. e. propositions of the form " it is possible that p and not q." (It should be noted that the judgments of possibility which are allegedly implicit in real definitions are always judgments of " compossibility," since in order to be definable a concept must be complex and to judge that instances of the concept are possible is then to judge that the elements of the concept are mutually compatible.) To be sure, we sometimes argue for a logical possibility from empirical fact, by the principle that what is actual must be possible. For example, in order to show that " all A are C " does not follow from " all B are A and all B are C "—i. e. that a proposition of the form " all B are A and all B are C and some A are not C " is logically possible—we might produce an empirical model: all dogs are animals and all dogs are quadrupeds, but some animals are not quadrupeds. However, such empirical models do not strictly prove logical possibility since it is not logically certain

---

[11] That Leibniz should have identified contingent propositions with propositions asserting (empirical) existence in the face of the contrary-to-fact character of many physical laws, such as the first law of motion, must either be explained as an oversight or else it must be confessed that it is not clear what Leibniz meant by " asserting existence."

that a given empirical proposition is true. To make the proof of logical possibility pure, i. e. not resting on empirical assumptions, we should interpret the variables " *B*," " *A*," and " *C* " in such a way that the resulting propositions are necessary. For example, let *B* = even numbers, *A* = numbers, *C* = numbers greater than one.

What Leibniz overlooked, then, is that judgments of compossibility (e. g. " being a regular polygon is compatible with being bounded by six sides ") are negations of entailment-propositions and as such are not reducible to entailment-propositions, and hence do not conform to his criterion of necessary truth. Since according to Leibniz every derivative (demonstrable) necessary truth is based on a real definition (as illustrated by the demonstration of " 2 + 2 = 4 " from the real definitions of 2, 3, and 4) , it follows that there is for every derivative necessary truth which conforms to Leibniz' criterion at least one necessary truth which does not. And if, anticipating Kant's terminology, we call a necessary truth conforming to Leibniz' criterion " analytic," this could be expressed by saying that according to Leibniz' theory there must be at least as many *synthetic* necessary truths as there are *analytic* necessary truths. There is a further reason, however, why Leibniz' theory must be held to involve admission of synthetic necessary truths, as pointed out by Bertrand Russell in Chapter 2 of *A Critical Exposition of the Philosophy of Leibniz* (Cambridge, 1900) . Leibniz held that there are simple, unanalyzable concepts which can be reached by analysis in a finite number of steps. But an a priori proof of the possibility, i. e. self-consistency, of a defined complex concept requires its complete analysis into simple elements, for not until the simple conceptual elements have been reached can we be sure that further analysis will not reveal an incompatibility. We may have analyzed *A* into elements *B* and *C* which seem compatible, but possibly further analysis of *B* into *D* and *E* will reveal a contradiction, in that *D* will be seen to be incompatible with *C*. However, while one cannot be sure a priori of the possibility of *A* unless one has a complete analysis of *A*, it could hardly be maintained that *A* *is* possible if no explicit contradiction has emerged by the time the analysis has been completed. Consider, for example, the concept " irregular cube." To see that it is self-contradictory, we only require the incomplete analysis of " cube " into " regular solid bounded by squares ": a contradiction has emerged before the concepts "regular solid" and "square" are further analyzed. On the other hand, consider the concept "round square" and let it be analyzed into "round figure which is rectilinear, foursided, equilateral, and equiangular." The judgment that this is a self-contradictory concept can be supported only by the judgment that roundness and rectilinearity, as predicated of figures, are incompatible attributes; yet these attributes may well be simple if any attributes at all are simple. But if they are simple, then it is not possible to show by analysis of "round" that "x is round" entails "x is not rectilinear," in other words, they cannot be said to be *analytically* incompatible the way "x is a cube" is analytically incompatible with "x is an irregular solid" or the way "x is prime" is analytically incompatible with "x is divisible by more than two integers." Leibniz, then, in recognizing relations of incompatibility between simple concepts recognizes implicitly that there are entailments, like "being round entails being nonrectilinear," which are not reducible to analytic entailments of the form "if x is A and B, then necessarily x is A."

It may not be amiss to anticipate a development in modern logical theory which is strikingly reminiscent of this idea of synthetic compatibility or incompatibility of simple concepts, in terms of which Russell criticized Leibniz' criterion of necessary truth (*Critical Exposition*, chap. 2). I am referring to Carnap's concept (originally suggested by Wittgenstein) of a "state description," defined as a complete description of a possible world by means of a conjunction of atomic sentences and denials of atomic sentences. Since a state description is supposed to be a description of a *possible* world, safeguards are needed for the consistency of state descriptions. It is for this reason that Carnap finds himself forced to lay down a *requirement of simplicity* to be satisfied by the language used for describing possible worlds: "the qualities and relations designated by the primitive predicates must not be analyzable into simpler components." [12] For suppose we had two primitive predicates "P" and "Q," where P is analyzable into the conjunction $Q.R$ (to borrow Carnap's own illustration, let "P" be "raven" and "Q" "black"). Then we could construct state descriptions containing as a sub-conjunction "Pa and not-Qa"; yet such state descriptions would be

---

[12] "On the Application of Inductive Logic," *Philosophy and Phenomenological Research* (Sept. 1947), p. 136.

inconsistent. Carnap points out that we can never be sure that Q is not analytically entailed by P " until we drive the analysis down as far as possible "; in other words, certain knowledge of the *synthetic* character of the proposition " for any x, if x is P, then x is Q " presupposes knowledge of the *simplicity* of properties P and Q. (Strictly speaking, though, Carnap's claim about synthetic propositions holds only for propositions not known to be false: that Q is not analytically entailed by P can be established without assumptions of simplicity of properties in case an object with property P and without property Q has actually been found; but Carnap is right if he is referring to *a priori* knowledge of logical independence.)

But does this requirement of simplicity actually guarantee that whatever is described by a state description is a *possible* world? That it does not is easily seen if we imagine a language equipped with *several* primitive predicates designating colors, for example. Surely if " blue " is eligible as simple primitive predicate, so is " red," but if we elect both, then we get inconsistent state descriptions containing " a is blue and a is red." Here we have an incompatibility which there is no good reason for calling " logical," since, redness being by hypothesis unanalyzable, we cannot say that " x is not blue " is deducible from " x is red " by *logical analysis*. It had therefore best be called " synthetic " incompatibility, and the same holds for the entire class of similar incompatibilities, viz. those between simple determinate qualities under a common determinable.

C. *Singular Statements and " Perfect Concepts "*

Returning to Leibniz, it remains to examine his application of the necessary-contingent distinction to *singular* statements, such as " Caesar crossed the Rubicon." It is very difficult to extract a consistent, intelligible doctrine from what Leibniz says about the logical status of this type of statement, mainly because such theological pronouncements as that God, the omniscient creator, knew all future predicates of an individual substance when he created it, and that therefore predicates which inhere, for the finite human mind, contingently in an individual substance inhere in it necessarily under divine perspective, obscure the logical questions to be discussed. (Specifically, it seems that Leibniz shifted the meaning of " necessary " from " not capable of being denied without self-contradiction " to " pre-determined " when he said that " Caesar crosses the Rubicon at time *t* " is at bottom a necessary truth, since Caesar was created by God who, being omniscient, must know all of his attributes.) Since for Leibniz contingent propositions, and only contingent propositions, assert existence, consistency required him to hold that singular propositions are contingent, for they entail the existence of an individual substance. That they do entail such existence follows from the following premises: (1) a statement whose grammatical subject is a definite description cannot be true unless there exists an object denoted by the description; (2) any proper name is synonymous with a definite description. That Leibniz implicitly assumed (2) follows from his speaking of *concepts* of individual substances ("individual concepts," in the present terminology of Carnap) : for if it makes sense to speak, say, of the concept of Caesar, then it ought to make sense to speak of *defining* the proper name "Caesar," but this can only mean to produce a definite description with which the name is synonymous. But suppose, now, that the concept of Caesar were defined as "the Roman emperor who was stabbed by Brutus," and consider in the light of this definition the singular, historical statement "Caesar was stabbed by Brutus." Would Leibniz say that it is contingent or that it is necessary? It is easy to see that either answer is compatible with his theory: the statement is necessary insofar as its denial is equivalent to the self-contradiction that the individual who was stabbed by Brutus was not stabbed by Brutus; and the statement is contingent insofar as it entails the existence of an individual (in other words, it is not a purely hypothetical statement such as necessary statements were by Leibniz supposed to be). A theory of necessary truth which, as illustrated, justifies incompatible answers to a question is, of course, inadequate.

The root of this inadequacy is the conception of necessary truths as being nonexistential. Leibniz evidently was not aware of his inconsistency on this point. It is not only singular statements of the form "the *AB* is *A*" which would be both contingent and necessary on his theory, but likewise universal statements of the form "all *AB* are *A*." For he followed Aristotle's logic in accepting *conversion per accidens* (if all *A* are *B*, then some *B* are *A*),[13] in

---

[13] See *New Essays*, Bk. IV, chap. 2, § 1, where identities are used for the syllogistic demonstration of the three kinds of conversion, the third being conversion per accidens. The demonstration, incidentally, seems to be a *petitio*, in that "some *B* is *A* " is alleged

which case " all AB are A " entails " some A are AB " and thus the existence of A's. Modern logicians distinguish the hypothetical and the existential interpretation of universal propositions, and with the help of this distinction easily avoid the latter contradiction: in case " all lions are animals " is a hypothetical universal it does not entail the existence of lions, and in case it is an existential universal it is equivalent to the conjunction " if anything is a lion, then it is an animal, and there are lions," and only the first component of the conjunction expresses a necessary truth. However, as regards the existential implication of singular statements, modern logicians are still faced with the difficulty which Leibniz should have been troubled by had he been aware of his inconsistency. If any singular statement entails the existence of its subject and no necessary statement has existential consequences, then no singular statements can be necessary, not even " the king of England is a king." And likewise such statement as " a is P or non-P," " $a = a$ " would have to count as contingent truths. But they are commonly held to be logical consequences, by the rule of instantiation (" what is true of all is true of any "), of the universal laws of logic " for every x, x is P or non-P," " for every x, $x = x$." And how can logical truths have contingent consequences? [14]

In conclusion it may be pointed out that Leibniz' implied claim, echoed later by some idealistic logicians, that any singular proposition would be seen to be analytic if we had a *perfect concept* of its subject rests on a disastrous confusion of an individual with a concept of the individual. What seems to have led Leibniz to this assertion is the vague notion that an individual substance is somehow identical with the sum total of its states: if Caesar is a class of states one of which is the state of crossing the Rubicon at t, then to suppose that Caesar might not have been in that state at t would

to follow syllogistically from " all A is A " and " all A is B," which it does only if " some A is A " is deducible from " all A is A," and " some A is A " is of course equivalent to " there are A's." On the other hand, there is nothing wrong with Leibniz' argument if it merely aimed at proving that the validity of conversion *per accidens* follows from the (assumed) validity of subalternation.

[14] Some aspects of the difficulty here touched upon will be discussed below, Chap. 9, in connection with the positivist (empiricist) thesis " analytic statements say nothing about reality," which is there critically examined. I have discussed the question of logic, existence and singular statements in the article " Logic, Existence and the Theory of Descriptions," *Analysis*, April 1953.

be to suppose that Caesar might not have been Caesar; and if the supposition of the falsity of p entails a contradiction, then p is a necessary truth—so Leibniz seems to have argued. However, what is relevant to the question whether "Caesar has property P" expresses a necessary proposition is only what is *meant* by "Caesar" (what properties are connoted by the name), not what the actual properties of Caesar are. Now, if by a "perfect concept" of Caesar, Leibniz meant a definition of "Caesar" from which all properties of Caesar are deducible, then his claim that "a complete or perfect concept of an individual substance involves all its predicates, past, present, and future" is the merest truism. Yet, such a definition could only have the form of an enumeration of all properties of Caesar, since, as Leibniz himself saw, the connections between successive states of a given substance are contingent: if the definition, for example, included all the states of Caesar up to time t, then the statement that Caesar will do such and such after t would not be deducible from the definition (Leibniz here again confuses the logical issues by bringing in the irrelevant notion of divine foreknowledge). But then "perfect concept of x" would be so used that "I have a perfect concept of x" is equivalent to "I know all properties, past, present and future, of x." Now, does "I know that x will be in state P at t" entail "it is necessary that x is in state P at t"? Evidently Leibniz thought that it did, but was thus guilty of a subtle and serious confusion: from the former statement it follows necessarily that the statement "x will be in state P at t" is *true*, since knowledge of a false proposition is logically impossible ("I know that p" entails "p is true"), but it does not follow that the statement is necessarily true. I may have foreknowledge of the outcome of the impending Presidential election, yet whatever its outcome may be, a different outcome is logically possible. It is likely that Leibniz' doctrine of the necessity, *sub specie aeternitatis*, of propositions that are contingent relative to finite knowers is the offspring of just this confusion: from the fact that God's foreknowledge of a proposition about the future, call it "p," entails the truth of p (we can agree to this even though we may not know what "God" means, since this term occurs vacuously in the entailment), he fallaciously inferred that, given the assumption of such foreknowledge, p is a necessary truth. This is a fallacious argument of the form: p entails q; p; therefore q is necessary. Should Leibniz reply that his inference is valid because the premise to the effect that God has complete foreknowledge is itself a necessary proposition (viz. a proposition analytic of the meaning of " God ") , the following rejoinder would be in order: since " God foreknows that p " entails " p is true," and " p is true " entails " p," it could not be a necessary statement unless " p " itself were a necessary statement. Hence the premise which Leibniz requires for defending his argument presupposes that all true singular statements *are* necessary statements, which is just the question at issue. His imaginary reply, therefore, begs the question.[15]

---

[15] For a penetrating analysis of Leibniz' sketchy and obscure theory of singular judgments, see C. D. Broad's study " Leibniz' Predicate-in-Notion Principle and Some of Its Alleged Consequences," *Theoria*, *15* (Lund, Sweden, 1949) , 54-70.

A. *A Priori Knowledge and Necessity*

K A N T ' s explicit definition of a priori knowledge is a negative one: "knowledge that is independent of experience and even of all sense impressions " (*Critique of Pure Reason*, 2d ed., intro., I).[1] The kind of independence in question is not, of course, genetic, for Kant explicitly says that "undoubtedly all our knowledge begins with experience." What he had in mind is that a judgment is a priori if the *evidence* on which it is accepted is not empirical. This leaves us, of course, with "empirical" as an undefined term, but we must not deny to an epistemologist the privilege of taking some terms as undefined in order to be able to define others (the meaning of "empirical evidence" is, indeed, easily *illustrated*, by explaining, for example, that if the judgment "the straight line is the shortest distance between two points" were empirical, then it would be accepted on the evidence of repeated physical measurements of length). Kant proceeds to formulate a *criterion* in terms of which we can "infallibly distinguish pure (= a priori) knowledge from empirical knowledge":

> If we find, in the first place, a proposition which is conceived as *necessary*, then it is a judgment a priori; if, furthermore, it is not derived from any other proposition which is itself necessarily valid, then it is absolutely a priori. Secondly, experience never bestows on its judgments true or strict, but only supposed or comparative *universality* (through induction), so that we should properly say: as far as our observations go, there are no exceptions to this or that rule. If a judgment, then, is thought as strictly universal, i. e. in such a way that no exception at all is admitted even as a possibility, then it is not derived from experience, but is absolutely a priori [intro., II].

---

[1] All translations from the German in this chapter are mine.

Little analysis is needed to see that Kant's two criteria really coalesce into one, the criterion of necessity. For what does the contrast between "strict" and "only supposed" universality amount to? Kant surely does not mean that there are no universal empirical propositions that are true, i. e. that have no exceptions. All he means is that we never know with certainty that such a proposition is true, that there always remains the possibility of its being false. But then a "strictly" universal proposition is one which has no *conceivable* exceptions, which is another way of saying that it is necessary. We may confine our attention, therefore, to necessity as the touchstone of a priori knowledge.

If we call "subjective" a property of a proposition p which is such that to ascribe it to p is to say something about cognitive attitudes toward p, then there can be no doubt that necessity, and therewith a priori truth, in Kant's sense is a subjective property of propositions. To say that p is necessary is to say that p cannot be *conceived* to be false or is deducible from propositions that cannot be conceived to be false. Indeed, Kant explicitly says that in predicating a modality (such as necessity) of a judgment, one does not add anything to the "content" of the judgment but specifies the way in which the relation of the components of the judgment (subject and predicate, or antecedent and consequent) is conceived.[2] As we shall see, the attempts at explication of the concept of necessary truth which followed the Kantian era are characterized precisely by the ambition to de-psychologize, if I may coin a word, this concept, and one might say that to this extent their *Leitmotif* was "back to Leibniz!" It must be said, however, in all deference to the genius of Kant, that while "p cannot be conceived to be false, or is deducible from propositions which cannot be conceived to be false" seems to be the primary meaning he

---

[2] Kant's own formulation is somewhat obscure: "The modality of judgments is a very special function of theirs. whose distinguishing characteristic is that it adds nothing to the content of the judgment (for besides quantity, quality, and relation nothing is left as part of the content of the judgment), but concerns only the value of the copula in relation to thought" (*Critique of Pure Reason*, Transcendental Doctrine of Elements, Analytic of Conceptions, chap. 1, sec. 2). Especially is it not clear what he means by "content": "p is possible" and "p is necessary," which are forms of positive modal judgment, surely are not equivalent, and in that sense do not have the same content. I think, however, his intention was to say that a modal judgment is about cognitive attitudes.

attached to "*p* is necessary," it is impossible to make Kant out as *consistent* in his usage of this central term. When he says that it is a necessary (or a priori) truth that two straight lines cannot enclose a space, or that the straight line is the shortest distance between two points, he is clearly referring to the impossibility of imagining an exception. However, a serious deviation from the specified meaning can be spotted in Kant's discussion of causality. In the very introduction to the *Critique of Pure Reason* where the difference between empirical and a priori knowledge is explained, Kant cites the principle of causality, that every change has a cause, as an example of a necessary proposition. In support of his claim, made in criticism of Hume, that this is a *necessary* proposition he says: "indeed, in the latter (the proposition "every change has a cause") the very concept of cause contains so evidently the concept of a necessary connection with an effect and of strict universality of the rule, that it would become entirely unrecognizable if one wanted, following Hume, to derive it from a frequent conjunction of an event with a preceding event and the resulting habit (and thus merely subjective necessity) of association of ideas." What Kant maintains here is that the concept of necessary connection is indispensable for an adequate formulation of the principle of causality, thus: "for every change there is an antecedent event which is necessarily connected with it." (The serious ambiguity, insufficiently attended to by both Kant and Hume, that this might mean "for every event there is an antecedent which is necessarily followed by the event" or "for every event there is an antecedent which necessarily precedes the event" need not detain us in this context.) But the principle, thus formulated, does not entail that *it is necessary* that for every change there is an antecedent event which is necessarily connected with it; in other words, it is perfectly compatible with the proposition, maintained by Hume, that it is conceivable that there should occur a change which is uncaused in the sense that there is no antecedent necessarily connected with it. It is, indeed, unlikely that Kant intended to maintain the intuitive inconceivability of an uncaused change in the sense in which he maintained the intuitive inconceivability of a space that did not conform to the propositions of Euclidean geometry. As a matter of fact, the neo-Kantian interpreters of Kant have emphasized that Kant held the "principles of experience," of which the principle of causality is one, to be necessary in the sense of being *necessary presuppositions* of empirical science. This, however, is a complete shift of meaning of the term "necessary": from the fact that acceptance of proposition p is a *sine qua non* for the pursuit of inductive science, in the sense that from his very use of scientific method one can infer that the scientist believes p, it does not follow that p is a necessary proposition in the sense that it cannot be conceived to be false.

The poverty of the cited argument for the necessity of the principle of causality is clearly revealed if we consider that the same argument, if consistently employed, would have forced Kant into contradiction with his explicit admission that *specific causal laws*, unlike the principle of causality, are contingent propositions. For in line with his rejection of Hume's contention that the alleged necessary connection between cause and effect consists only in a "subjective necessity" (the pressure of the "gentle forces of association") he held that the concept of "objective necessity" is involved in a specific causal law like "the heat of solar radiation causes a block of ice to melt" just as it is involved in the general principle of causality. But then this specific causal law would have to be held to be a necessary proposition if the fact that the concept of necessary connection is a constituent of proposition p were a sufficient reason for holding p to be necessary. But quite apart from this consideration, the mentioned shift of meaning of the word "necessary" can be clearly traced in Kant's famous "proof" of the principle of causality in the section entitled "second analogy (of experience)." Kant observes that without the concept of causal order it would be impossible to distinguish objective and subjective temporal order of events. Mere perception, he says, is unable to determine the *objective order* of successive phenomena. For example, I might at this moment hear a voice and the next moment see the person whose lingual movements caused the sound; the effect, the sound, is perceived first, and the cause, the lingual movements, second. If I understand Kant (which is not easy), he is saying that in judging the lingual movements as the objectively earlier event I implicitly make the causal judgment that the lingual movements are the cause and the sound the effect. At any rate, Kant does maintain that if there were no causal order among a series of events $e_1, e_2 \cdots e_n$, then their *real* temporal relations would be indeterminate, it would be arbitrary whether we say e_1 is earlier than e_2 or e_2 earlier than e_1 or e_1 simultaneous with e_2. How he could maintain this in view of the (I should think) undeniable fact that we often agree that one event *really* preceded another event yet is causally unrelated to the latter, and that the proposition agreed upon is surely not self-contradictory (if it were, temporal sequence would be indistinguishable from causal sequence), I leave to the profounder Kant scholars to decide. For the sake of the argument, let us concede that the proposition that there is an objective temporal order of events entails the principle of causality. It is clear that this would amount only to a proof of the necessity of the proposition " if there is a real (objective) temporal order, then every event has a cause," but not to a proof of the necessity of the consequent of this conditional. In other words, what Kant would have proved at best is that the principle of causality is *necessarily presupposed* by the belief in an objective temporal order. He would not have established that a world devoid of objective temporal order—i. e. a world in which sometimes the impact of the stone is followed by the breaking of the window and sometimes follows the breaking of the window, in which a state of nonuniform density of a gas is sometimes followed by a state of uniform density and sometimes the reverse sequence occurs—is *intuitively inconceivable*. He is thus guilty of equivocation upon the term " necessity."

The central point to be kept in mind is that Kant's explicit distinction between the concepts of necessary and analytic truth made it impossible for him to adopt Leibniz' apparently nonpsychological criterion of necessary truth, the self-contradictoriness of the negation (in other words, the *logical* impossibility of exceptions). The alternative criterion which accommodates analytic truths as a subclass of necessary truths inevitably employs the wider concept of *inconceivability* (whether or not it be called " psychological "), for the word " possible " in Kant's statement " no exceptions (to an a priori truth) are admitted as possible " cannot mean what it meant for Leibniz: " consistent with the law of identity (or the law of contradiction)." However, if it were not for the tacit shift from " cannot be conceived to be false " to " necessarily presupposed by what is claimed as knowledge of objective reality," the extension of the term " necessary truth " would have been far smaller for Kant than he claimed it to be, and much of his verbal disagreement with Hume would never have arisen.

B. *The Definition of "Analytic"*

It has often been pointed out that Kant's definition of an analytic judgment as a judgment whose predicate is (implicitly) contained in the concept of the subject (see *Critique of Pure Reason*, intro., IV) is unsatisfactory, not only because the literal meaning of the metaphor " contained " is not clear, but also because ever so many judgments (or propositions, as we say nowadays) do not have subject-predicate form and yet the analytic-synthetic division was intended by Kant as exhaustive with respect to the class of true propositions.[3] Let us first give our attention to the latter limitation. That Kant should not have been aware of it is particularly surprising since the table of the twelve different forms of judgments (" logical functions of the understanding ") played such an important role in his doctrine of the categories. Take, for example, negative judgments, like " no triangle has four sides." Kant surely would have classified it as analytic, yet the predicate is so far from being contained in the subject that it contradicts the subject; the cited definition of " analytic," therefore, is restricted not only to judgments of subject-predicate form but even to affirmative judgments of that sort.[4] Again, existential judgments, like " there are cows," would no doubt have been classified as synthetic by Kant, yet the only way they could be construed as having subject-predicate form would be by treating existence as a predicate, which would be contrary to Kant's own famous thesis that existence is not a predicate. Again, consider hypothetical judgments, like " if somebody is somebody's teacher, then somebody is somebody's pupil " (which is reducible to a substitution-instance of a theorem of the logic of relations) : Kant himself, in discussing the table of logical forms of judgments, mentions the relation of antecedent to consequent as distinct from the relation of subject to predicate; indeed, if the antecedent were construed as the " subject," then the expresssion " concept of the subject " would become unintelligible.

[3] *Self-contradictory* propositions, of course, are neither analytic nor synthetic in the Kantian senses of these terms; for this reason I characterize the divided class as the class of *true* propositions.

[4] Cf. on this point, Marc Wogau's illuminating study " Kants Lehre vom Analytischen Urteil," *Theoria* 1951, Pts. I-III. Kant lifted, though, this particular restriction in the *Prolegomena*, § 2: " the predicate of an affirmative analytical judgment is already contained in the concept of the subject, . . . In the same way its opposite is necessarily denied of the subject in an analytical, but negative, judgment."

Fortunately, Kant also gave a criterion of analyticity (though he did not set it forth as a *definition*) which is at least potentially free from the restriction to subject-predicate propositions and which also has the virtue of being, at least *prima facie*, nonpsychological. The principle of contradiction ("Satz vom Widerspruch"), he says, while expressing a necessary condition of truth in general, expresses a sufficient condition of analytic truth: "If the judgment is *analytic*, be it negative or affirmative, then the principle of contradiction must always be a sufficient ground for ascertaining its truth" (*Critique of Pure Reason*, "On the Supreme Principle of All Analytical Judgments"). I deliberately said "potentially free" because the restriction to the subject-predicate form is apparent even in Kant's formulation of this principle: "no object has a predicate which contradicts it" ("Keinem Dinge kommt ein Prädikat zu, welches ihm widerspricht"). It is not obvious, for example, how the statement "all *a* are *b*, but some *a* are not-*b*" is a violation of this principle: where is "object," where "predicate"? One might try to render the principle applicable by taking the class *a* as subject and "being wholly included in *b*" and "being partially excluded from *b*" as contradictory predicates. But this would be a tour de force, since the notions of class inclusion and class exclusion correspond to what was traditionally called the "copula" of a subject-predicate judgment, and so could not be used to form "predicates" in the traditional sense. It would be better to admit that Kant did not succeed in formulating a perfectly general principle of contradiction, i. e. one that is applicable to any form of proposition, but that if such a general version of the principle is substituted for Kant's, we have at least a criterion of analyticity that is not worse than Leibniz'. This general formulation is simply: $(p) - (p. - p)$, i. e. no proposition is both true and false.[5] Kant's intention, no doubt, was to say that an analytic proposition is a proposition from whose negation a contradiction, i. e. a statement of the form "*p* and not-*p*" is deducible.

In our discussion of Leibniz we have already pointed out that this is not satisfactory as a criterion of necessary truth, since "deducible" is presumably meant as short for "deducible with the help of necessary truths alone." But even as a criterion of analytic truth in Kant's sense it faces a similar danger of circularity,

[5] This interpretation of the formula assumes the synonymy of "$- p$" and "*p* is false."

which will become evident if we remember that the analytic-synthetic division was intended to exhaust the class of true propositions.
For by implication, if not by explicit statement, Kant held the
propositions of formal logic themselves to be analytic. Now, the
principle of contradiction, as we have already seen, is by no means
sufficient to demonstrate all propositions which both Leibniz and
Kant would have classified as analytic. In order to obtain, therefore,
a sufficiently wide criterion of analyticity, the reference to the
principle of contradiction ought to give way to reference to the
whole class of *logical truths*: p is analytic if a contradiction is
derivable from not-p with the help of logical truths alone. Consider,
for example, the conditional statement corresponding to the *tollendo
tollens* form of argument: if p entails q, and not-q, then not-p.
It is not immediately obvious that the negation of this complex
statement violates the principle of contradiction in its generalized
form. Close analysis reveals that in order to deduce an explicit
contradiction (p and not-p) from it we require the law of double
negation and, in order to show that " p and not-q " contradicts " it
is impossible that p and not-q " (the negative version of " p entails
q "), the axiom " if p, then p is possible." But now it turns out
that it is not significant to characterize the truths of logic as being
themselves analytic, since this would mean that from the negation
of a logical truth one can deduce, with the help of logical truths,
a contradiction—which is trivial, since we may simply use the negated
logical truth along with its negation as a premise. And if, following
the line of some modern philosophers, we say that the principles
of logic are a priori *because* they are analytic, then we are talking
nonsense if we use " analytic " in the specified sense.

In view of the difficulty—to be discussed in greater detail in
Chapter 5—of defining a concept of analyticity which is at once
distinct from the concept of a priori (or necessary) truth and allows
us to say significantly that the principles of logic are analytic, the
best course may be to restrict the range of significant application of
the term " analytic " (and therewith of " synthetic ") to statements
which do not themselves belong to logic because they contain
descriptive terms, like Kant's example " all bodies are extended." [6]
If so, then we have in the proposed reformulation of Kant's criterion

---

[6] Cf. the terminological proposals at the end of Chap. 5.

of analytic truth a criterion which at least is not obscurer than the concept of logical truth itself.

Let us now turn our attention to the question of what exactly is the relation between subject and predicate in an analytic judgment according to Kant. In the *Prolegomena to Any Future Metaphysic* Kant improved on the cited definition from the *Critique* insofar as he dropped the metaphor " contained ": "Analytical judgments express nothing in the predicate but what has been already actually thought in the concept of the subject, though not so distinctly or with the same (full) consciousness." The psychological language here used has been the focus of much criticism. For example, it has been said that the connotations of a term vary from individual to individual, and that therefore Kant's concept of analyticity is psychological. (It makes sense to say that " *S* is *P* " is analytic for so and so, but not to say simply " ' *S* is *P* ' is analytic.") Consider, for example, Kant's claim that " all bodies are extended " is analytic while " all bodies have weight " is synthetic; just how would Kant prove, so the objection runs, that people are not thinking of weight when they think of a body? Kant would, of course, admit that, by virtue of what Hume called " habits of association," the thought of a body is *accompanied by* the thought of weight, just as the thought of a dog might be accompanied by the thought of barking. But he would deny that having weight is part of the *meaning* of " body." And he would, had he been reared in the language of contemporary analytic philosophers, support this claim by appeal to the fact that the concept of a weightless body (unlike that of a body devoid of inertia) is *not self-contradictory*; or that " *x* is a body " does not analytically *entail* (though it may factually imply, i. e. imply by virtue of an empirical law) " *x* has weight." If Kant's conception of analyticity, then, is to be condemned as " psychologistic," at least he will enjoy the company of many subtle contemporary analysts of reputation. When we argue nowadays " it does not seem self-contradictory to suppose that a body existed all alone in space, and since weight is a relation of a body to other bodies (consisting in its being attracted to other bodies), it follows that weight is not part of what is *meant* by ' body,' " we equally rely on " thought experiments."

The problem of philosophical semantics which is implicit in Kant's statement about the relation of subject and predicate in analytic judgments is simply the problem of what a suitable criterion of *identity* (total or partial) *of concepts* might be.[7] That Kant failed to solve this problem is surely a forgivable sin if one considers that the entire problem of the identity conditions of intensions (when are two properties identical, when are two propositions identical?) is still highly controversial nowadays in spite of the professed rejection of "psychologism" in philosophical semantics. In his study referred to above, Marc-Wogau concentrates on just this difficulty with Kant's doctrine of the analytic judgment. Consider the judgment "every triangle has three angles." It would not help to say that "having three angles" is a constituent of the concept "triangle" if and only if it occurs in the *definition* of "triangle," for thus the burden would merely be placed on the question "what is meant by *the* definition of a concept?" We might define "triangle" to mean "plane figure bounded by three straight lines and having three angles"; in that case the judgment would be analytic by the above criterion of partial identity of subject and predicate. But it would commonly be said that such a definition involves a redundancy: "plane figure bounded by three straight lines" is sufficient, one would say, since the other property is *deducible* from this definition. But in what sense is it "deducible?" The situation is not quite analogous to the redundancy in the definiens for "square": equilateral, four-sided rectangle; for here the redundant predicate "four-sided" can be extracted simply by defining "rectangle" ("four-sided rectilinear figure all of whose angles are right angles"), while "triangular" is not in the same straightforward sense contained in the definiens of "trilateral." Perhaps a formal deduction of "*x* is triangular" from "*x* is trilateral" requires the theorem "if a closed figure has *n* sides, then it has *n* angles," but if "*P* is contained in *S*" is used in the sense of "*P* is deducible from the definition of *S* together with axioms or theorems of the system in which *S* is defined," then we obtain of course a concept of analyticity which is far wider than the one Kant had in mind ("all triangles have as the sum of their angles 180 degrees" could be analytic in that sense!) and which, moreover, turns "analytic" into a term relative to a deductive system, which was definitely not Kant's intention. Kant, then, would be hard pressed were he asked whether the concept "triangle" is adequately

[7] See below, Chap. 10.

defined as "rectilinear figure with three sides and three angles" or as "rectilinear figure with three sides" or as "rectilinear figure with three angles." [8]

Since the interpretation of "*P* is contained in *S*" as meaning "*P* occurs either directly or indirectly—through expansion of definienda into definientia—in the definiens of *the definition* of *S*" comes nearest to giving an objective meaning to Kant's term "analytic," it is with considerable curiosity that we look to Kant's own statements about the nature of definitions.

In the *Critique* we read, in the section entitled "The discipline of Pure Reason in its Dogmatic Use" (Transcendental Doctrine of Method, chap. I, sect. I): "As the very term 'to define' indicates, to define means nothing more than to express the complete concept of an object within its limits and in underived manner." The explanations of the terms "complete" and "within limits," given in a footnote, make it clear that Kant meant to say that the definiens must express, in clear language, a necessary and sufficient condition for applicability of the concept, and must contain no redundancy; and by the requirement of "Ursprünglichkeit" is meant, as he explains in the same footnote, that the defining property should not stand in need of demonstration. It is obvious that Kant had the Aristotelian distinction between essence and property in mind, according to which "a plane figure with the sum of its angles equal to 180 degrees" could not serve as definiens for "triangle" because, even though it is convertibly predicable of triangles, it does not express the *essence* of triangularity but rather "flows" from the latter. And since to clarify Kant's concept of analyticity is the same as to clarify the expression "essence of a concept," this explanation gets us nowhere; in fact, the notion of essence is made no clearer by Kant than it was by Aristotle himself. In his *Logic* (*Vorlesungen zur Logik*) he makes the traditional distinction between *nominal* and *real* definitions (§ 106). But it is simply impossible to make any consistent sense of his disconnected remarks on the distinction.[9] A nominal definition, we are told, is an arbitrary stipulation of a meaning for a given name, while a real definition demonstrates

---

[8] Amusingly, as Marc-Wogau brings out, Kant was inconsistent in his claims as to what is to be regarded as the definition of "triangle." See *loc. cit.*, p. 151.

[9] And since Kant authorized the publication of these lecture notes, we cannot hold his students responsible for this blemish.

the possibility of the defined object from its " inner " marks (I have nowhere found as much as a hint of the meaning of " inner "). Real definitions, we are told, are to be found in mathematics, " for the definition of an arbitrary concept is always real." What Kant elsewhere says about mathematical concepts leaves no doubt that "arbitrary concept" here means "constructed concept." The mathematician, Kant held (following Locke, whose distinction between ideas of substances and ideas of modes must have influenced him more than he liked to admit),[10] does not abstract his concepts from empirical objects but *constructs* them prior to experience of instances. But consider, then, the definition of " ellipsoid " as meaning "solid generated by rotating an ellipse around either one of its axes," where " ellipse " is similarly given a genetic definition, viz. " closed curve all of whose points are such that the sum of their distances from two fixed points is constant " (this definition is usually called analytic but Kant would have called it " genetic " because we can derive from it a recipe as to how an ellipse might be constructed). This is undoubtedly the sort of thing Kant had in mind when speaking of the real definitions of constructed mathematical concepts which guarantee the possibility of the defined object since we can, following the recipe, construct on the blackboard or on white paper objects satisfying them. Yet if the definiendum " ellipsoid " has no antecedent usage and has just been invented as an abbreviation for the complex definiens, then the same definition is nominal according to the explanation given! The carelessness of Kant's thinking (or at least lecturing) on the nature of definitions is sufficiently illustrated by this point, and we must therefore conclude that to the extent to which the meaning of Kant's " analytic " depends on the meaning of " *the* definition of the subject-concept," it is obscure.

Before leaving the subject, I would like to call attention to a most interesting observation made by Marc-Wogau, connected with Kant's statement that, strictly speaking, concepts of natural kinds, like gold, cannot be defined at all:

> For, as an empirical concept consists only of a few marks of a certain kind of object of the senses, it is never certain whether one might not mean by a word denoting an identical object at

---

[10] Cf. the self-conscious confession of indebtedness to Locke in the *Prolegomena*, § 3.

one time more, at another time fewer marks of the object.
Thus one person's concept of gold might contain, besides the
weight, the color and the solidity, the property of being un-
capable of rusting, while another person may not know this
property. A fixed set of marks is used only as long as they
suffice for the purpose of distinguishing the kind from others;
through new discoveries, however, some marks get removed
and some get added, and consequently the concept is never
perfectly fixed [*Critique of Pure Reason, loc. cit.*].

Marc-Wogau comments that thus the sentence " gold does not get
rusty in water " is analytic for the first person, synthetic for the
second. Similarly, an identity sentence of the form " $a =$ the x with
property P " (where " a " is a proper name) might be said to be
analytic for a person in whose usage " a " is precisely an abbreviation
for that description, and synthetic for a person using the same
proper name as abbreviation for another description which, though
denoting the same object as the first, is based on a predicate Q
which is not synonymous with P. However, is all that Kant's aperçu
amounts to that the same class term may be given different definitions by different people, such that instead of saying " S is analytic "
we ought to say " S is analytic *as used* by X "? It rather seems that
Kant saw, though none too clearly, that statements about natural
kinds, like " gold is yellow," cannot be classified as analytic or
synthetic in the sense in which statements about mathematical
objects are so classifiable, for the reason that " analytic " was defined
in terms of " definition," and there can be no " definitions " of
natural kinds in the same sense of the word as there can be definitions of mathematical concepts. To be sure, Kant did not clearly
explain *why* concepts of natural kinds should not be " strictly
definable." But perhaps he could have made his point as follows.
Suppose that " gold " were defined as a yellow metal with a definite
atomic weight and a definite melting point. If this were a " definition " in the same sense in which " ' square ' means ' equilateral
rectangle ' " is a definition, then it would be self-contradictory to
classify an object which had all the defining characteristics except
the color as gold, just as it would be self-contradictory to classify, say,
a rhombus as a square. If a scientist observing such an anomalous
specimen insisted, " Still, this *is* gold, so we must recognize that not

all gold is yellow," he would have to be interpreted as recommending a redefinition of "gold," not as pronouncing an empirical generalization refuted. But if he said instead, " This is not a species of gold, it's a different species though closely similar to gold," this would likewise be an acceptable comment. Just which way the discovery of the goldlike, hitherto unknown, specimen will affect his classification of natural kinds will depend on pragmatic considerations. Now, Kant might hold that no analogous situation could occur in connection with geometrical and arithmetical concepts, that there could be no occasion for " redefining " such concepts in the light of new discoveries about their instances; and that this suggests that " definition " does not have the same meaning in " definition of ' gold ' " as in " definition of ' square.' " [11]

C. Synthetic A Priori Truth in Geometry

Of all the synthetic a priori propositions alleged as such by Kant, those that illustrate his conception of an a priori truth as a universal proposition exceptions to which are *inconceivable* most clearly are geometrical axioms, like the famous axiom " two straight lines cannot enclose a space." In fact, if one were pressed to explain the relevant meaning of the word " inconceivable," one might well do it denotatively by giving such examples as the inconceivability of a space enclosed by two straight lines. As to the *intuitive* nature of geometrical knowledge Kant made two claims: first, that our knowledge of the axioms is intuitive (" intuitive " being contrasted with both " empirical " and " analytic ") , and secondly, that even the deduction of theorems from the axioms requires spatial intuition. The latter claim was not any more far-fetched than the former, considering the role played by *constructions* in the proofs of Euclidean geometry such as the proof of the theorem about the sum of the angles of a triangle (see particularly the *Critique*, " Transcendental Doctrine of Method," chap. 1, sec. 1) . However, Kant here failed to make the distinction, often urged nowadays, between the context of *discovery* and the context of *justification*. If it were granted that constructions are indispensable for the discovery of proofs, it still would not follow that recourse to constructions is required for validating a proof once discovered. Hilbert has shown that if only

[11] We shall return to this problem later. See below, pp. 112-16.

all the axioms tacitly assumed by Euclid in his proofs are made fully explicit, then purely *formal* proofs of the theorems can be given. We shall concentrate, accordingly, on the former claim, of the inconceivability of the falsehood of the Euclidean axioms. It has been exposed to heavy fire since the publication of non-Euclidean systems of geometry discredited Kant's doctrine of the finality of Euclidean geometry. We shall begin with the question of whether the axioms are a priori, and then turn to the question whether they are synthetic.

A rather naive argument against the claim of self-evidence for an axiom like "two straight lines cannot enclose a space," which is nevertheless often advanced, is that this proposition has even been shown to be false, since it does not hold in Riemannian geometry; which geometry is actually suited for the description of physical space if only we consider sufficiently large areas. Now, it is clear that if a system of pure geometry contains the contradictory of the sentence "a straight line is uniquely determined by two points," the term "straight line" does not in that system mean what it means in the system containing the contradicted sentence. For to the extent that the primitives "point," "straight line," "plane" have any meanings at all as part of such an uninterpreted system of geometry, they mean whatever entities satisfy the axioms, and the same entities cannot satisfy mutually contradictory axiom sets. For example, Riemannian "straight lines" can be interpreted as great arcs on a spherical surface, and with this interpretation it becomes true to say that two straight lines may enclose a space. But it is not then the *proposition* expressed by the sentence "two straight lines cannot enclose a space" in the Euclidean system which has been contradicted. Those who are anxious to defend the thesis that all a priori truth is analytic may seize the opportunity to point out that what on this analysis is an a priori truth is the proposition that two *Euclidean* straight lines cannot enclose a space, which is analytic because "Euclidean" can be defined only in terms of satisfaction of just such axioms as the one in question. But discussion of the tricky question whether the axiom is analytic or synthetic had better be postponed until careful attention has been given to the question of whether any of the arguments against the *necessity* of the axiom are sound.

A well known objection—one, indeed, which people are apt to

echo in rather thoughtless manner just because it is "classic"—is
that inconceivability is altogether relative to experience and accepted
scientific theory. It is said again and again that the history of science
amply proves that what is self-evident to one generation is rejected
as false by the next generation on the authority of well-confirmed
scientific theory. And the classical example of this is the question
of the conceivability of antipodes. Thus John Stuart Mill, in the
context of arguing for the empirical character of geometrical truths,
writes:

> There are remarkable instances of this in the history of science;
> instances in which the most instructed men rejected as impos-
> sible, because inconceivable, things which their posterity, by
> earlier practice and longer perseverance in the attempt, found
> it quite easy to conceive, and which everybody now knows to
> be true. There was a time when men of the most cultivated
> intellects, and the most emancipated from the dominion of early
> prejudice, could not credit the existence of antipodes; were
> unable to conceive, in opposition to old association, the force
> of gravity acting upward instead of downward [*System of Logic*
> (1887), Bk. II, chap. 5, § 6].

But this argument, plausible as it sounds, is spoiled by an ambiguity
of the word "conceivable." That people on diametrically opposite
points of a sphere should both remain attached to the sphere without any tendency to "fall off" is inconceivable in the same sense
in which it is inconceivable that a person could walk on the surface
of a lake, or that a person could jump off a cliff and find himself
rising instead of falling. Here "inconceivable" means "unbelievable" but not "unimaginable." Experience has developed in us
an irresistible tendency to expect A to be followed by B, but if we
did not admit that an exception is in some sense imaginable, it
would be difficult to explain what we mean by saying that "A is
always followed by B" is a *contingent* (or *empirical*) truth. That
people ever found the existence of antipodes unimaginable in the
sense in which a space enclosed by two Euclidean straight lines, or
a space of four dimensions (in the ordinary, not the generalized,
sense of "space"), is unimaginable, is a wildly unplausible assumption; at any rate, the historical evidence that they declared this sort
of thing "impossible" or "inconceivable" is not relevant, since

we declare many things impossible or inconceivable which we find it impossible to *believe* but which we can *imagine*, or *think of*, without excessive difficulty. Who could believe that there is a man who will never die? But who has serious difficulty in forming the concept of an immortal man, or even of a man whose appearance remains unaltered during a thousand years? [12]

Curiously, Mill admits that once we have acquired through experience with straight lines the notion of straightness, mere reflection upon this notion suffices for revealing the truth of the axiom. He approvingly quotes Bain's statement (as going " to the very root of the controversy ") : " We cannot have the full meaning of Straightness, without going through a comparison of straight objects among themselves, and with their opposites, bent or crooked objects. The result of this comparison is, *inter alia*, that straightness in two lines is seen to be incompatible with inclosing a space; the inclosure of space involves crookedness in at least one of the lines " (*System of Logic*, § 5) . But if the fact that reflection on the meaning of a sentence *S* is sufficient to produce assent to *S* does not prove that *S* expresses an a priori truth, what could " a priori truth " mean? Mill may have been right in holding, following Locke and Hume, that such geometrical concepts as straightness are derived from sense impressions of straightness (and in that sense are empirical concepts) , but it surely is possible for a necessary proposition to contain empirical concepts. It appears, then, that it is rather obscure what Mill was denying when he denied that the axiom in question is a *necessary* truth. And similarly we must challenge anyone who, while admitting that enclosure of a space by two straight lines cannot be imagined in the sense in which dogs that can fly and speak French can be imagined, denies that the axiom is a necessary truth, to explain what he means by a " necessary truth."

There are those who hold that if the negation of a proposition is inconceivable in an absolute sense, i. e. not just in the sense

---

[12] Unfortunately Whewell, whose doctrine of the necessity of geometrical axioms Mill attacked, was himself guilty of this equivocation on the term " inconceivable " (as meaning sometimes " unimaginable " and sometimes " unbelievable ") , and for this reason Mill's criticism is much more persuasive than it would otherwise be. Thus Mill cites with considerable glee Whewell himself as reporting that such revolutionary theories as the Copernican, and Galileo's theory of uniform motion as not requiring to be sustained by force, were at the time rejected as inconceivable.

that habits of association produced by experience make it *psychologically* impossible to believe it, this can only be because the proposition is definitionally true, "analytic." Since "*p* is definitionally true" means presumably that *p* is deducible from logical principles (such as the principle of identity) with the help of adequate definitions, it would indeed be difficult to explain the absolute inconceivability of the negation of a logical principle in the same way.[13] But be this as it may, let us see whether Kant can be successfully refuted by proving that such a geometrical axiom is analytic. We may formulate the axiom as an axiom of plane geometry as follows: two straight lines have either no point in common or else exactly one. When Kant pronounced it as "synthetic" he could hardly have had in mind his definition of a synthetic judgment as one whose predicate is not contained in the subject, for if there are any propositions which do not have subject-predicate form, this is one. Let us, then, take "analytic" in the sense Kant must have intended when he said that the principle of contradiction is the sufficient ground of analytic judgments: the judgment cannot be denied without self-contradiction. The difficulty faced by the claim that our axiom is analytic in this sense is that the only explicit definition of "straight line" which would enable a proof of analyticity is one which Kant would have regarded as itself a synthetic axiom: a straight line is a line which is uniquely determined by two points (i. e. given two points, there is one and only one straight line containing both).[14] Given this definition, the axiom could indeed be formally demonstrated: if two straight lines did have two points in common, then there would be two distinct straight lines containing two given points, which contradicts the definition of "straight line." The fact that a definition which seems perfectly adequate could be rejected by a Kantian as question begging [15]—since on the same general grounds on which he regards the axiom to be demonstrated as synthetic he would hold the definition to express a synthetic judgment—is indeed a forceful

---

[13] On the question whether logical principles can significantly be said to be "analytic" in the above sense, see below, Chap. 5.

[14] Kant mentions somewhere that the proposition "three points uniquely determine a plane" is synthetic, hence one would expect him to hold the same view with respect to the analogous proposition about the straight line.

[15] The problem of definitions begging the question of analyticity, here touched upon, will be discussed in some detail below, Chap. 8.

reminder that, unless one can clarify the relevant sense of " adequate definition," the concept of analyticity is hopelessly obscure. But let us see whether there is some way in which a Kantian could be forced to surrender. One might argue that since " straight line " has different meanings in different systems of geometry, we have to fix the relevant concept by specifying a definite kind of plane, thus: " straight line in a Euclidean plane," " straight line in a Riemannian plane," etc. We would then be led to the question of what is meant by " Euclidean plane." Now, a type of plane, so we might argue, can be defined in no other way than as the type of plane for which the axioms of a given plane geometry hold. More precisely, the idea is this: we formulate the axioms " two straight lines in P have either no point or exactly one point in common," " given a point in P and a straight line in P not containing that point, there is exactly one straight line in P which contains that point and has no point in common with the given straight line," and others. So far the axioms are propositional functions, neither true nor false, since they contain the variable " P"; hence it would not make sense to ask whether they are analytic or synthetic. But the only way " P " could be given a meaning that guarantees the truth of the axioms would be by the definition " P is whatever satisfies these axioms." Now the axiom will read " two straight lines in a plane in which two straight lines have either no point in common or exactly one point in common have either no point in common or exactly one point in common," which is surely analytic. But the trouble with this trick is that it leads us into a circle. For a type of plane has been defined in terms of " straight line," but our starting consideration was that " straight line " is ambiguous until a definite type of plane is specified.

It is difficulties of this sort that presumably led such mathematicians as Hilbert to abandon the quest for *explicit* definitions of the terms " straight line," " point," " plane," and instead to define them implicitly as whatever entities satisfy the formal axioms formulated by means of them. The Kant critique since Hilbert accordingly took the form that the axioms of *pure* geometry are neither analytic nor synthetic, for they are propositional functions, not propositions. The question arises of whether this may be regarded as a refutation of Kant, and this is to ask whether Kant meant by *pure* geometry what is nowadays meant by it. The question answers itself: Kant, after all, lived *before* Hilbert. But is it possible to make the meaning of " pure geometry " intended by *Kant* intelligible?

It seems clear that the Kantian concept of " pure geometry " can be defined only in terms of the notion, going back to Plato, of *a priori concepts* ("innate ideas"). An a priori concept would have to be defined as a concept which, though it is not purely formal (like the logical constants, " not," " implication," etc.), is neither ostensively definable nor analytically definable in terms of ostensively definable concepts. That Kant thought of " straight line " as just such an a priori concept cannot be doubted by anyone who is aware of the impression which Plato's theory of innate ideas (whatever its cognitive content may be) must have made on Kant via Descartes. Kant would say that no instance of a perfect straight line could be given in sense perception ("empirical intuition"); hence ostensive definition is out of the question. But I think that he moreover held the concept to be unanalyzable, a *simple* concept. For his proof of the synthetic character of the axiom " the straight line is the shortest distance between two points " is that the subject-concept is purely qualitative while the predicate is quantitative. Yet any conceivable analysis of " straight line " would have to be in what Kant would call " quantitative " terms: " class of points which is uniquely determined by *two* points " is quantitative too! But by the same argument Kant should even have denied that the statement " the circle is a closed curve all of whose points are equidistant from a given point " is analytic: if we understand what Kant means by saying that straightness is a *quality*, we must surely confess that circularity is in the same sense a quality. Now, if Kant were asked why on earth he rejects such definitions as not really *analyzing* the subject-concept, he would, I think, make the reply that you could not teach someone the meaning of the terms " straight " and " circular " by means of such quantitative descriptions unless he had, stimulated by sense experience, already acquired these concepts. If so, then Kant implicitly used the expression " analysis of concept *C* " in such a way that a given definition could be said to express an analysis of *C* only if it is possible to make a person who had never experienced an instance of *C* think of *C* by producing that definition. Thus " color between yellow and blue " would not express an analysis of the concept *green* if it is impossible to make a person who has not seen green before think of green by means of that description.[16]

Supposing that "straight line" and "point," as used in pure geometry in Kant's sense of "pure," express such simple a priori concepts (dispositions, perhaps, to remember intellectual visions enjoyed in Plato's heaven of Forms), what follows with regard to the question of whether the axioms of such a pure geometry are analytic or synthetic? If "*S* is analytic" means "*S* is deducible from logical truths *with the help of adequate analyses* of the terms of *S*," and the relevant terms of *S* are not analyzable at all, does it then follow that *S* is synthetic? It seems to me that the question does not admit of a nonarbitrary answer, because philosophers have not taken the trouble to specify whether the statement "*S* is *not* deducible from logical truths with the help of adequate analyses" is to be taken as true in case no adequate analyses of the relevant terms can be produced at all. It is somewhat like the question of whether a man who never beat his wife has or has not stopped beating her. In fact, as we have seen, Kant himself raised the question of what sorts of concepts are definable at all—though he sadly neglected to clarify the relevant meaning of "definable"— and maintained that concepts of natural kinds, for example, are not definable. This did not prevent him from declaring elsewhere that "gold is yellow" is an analytic judgment. In the same way, his implicit view that "straight line" is not definable did not prevent him from declaring that "the straight line is the shortest distance between two points" is *not* analytic. What he did not consider was the possibility that the division analytic-synthetic is not significantly applicable to statements whose relevant terms are unanalyzable.[17]

[16] We shall return to this criterion of complex, or analyzable descriptive concepts in Chap. 9.

[17] Although a suitable restriction of the class of statements to which the analytic-synthetic dichotomy applies would, as we shall see again later, spare philosophers some embarrassment, no such restrictions are usually considered by philosophers operating with the dichotomy. In particular, the supposed unanalyzability of the relevant predicates in a given statement is usually regarded as a basis for classifying the statement as synthetic. Thus ethical intuitionists who hold ethical predicates like "right" and "good" to be unanalyzable pronounce statements connecting such predicates with naturalistic predicates for this very reason as synthetic.

D. Synthetic A Priori Truth in Arithmetic

If Kant's proof of the synthetic character of the axioms of pure geometry leaves much to be desired—mainly, as we have seen, because of the unclarity of his analytic-synthetic distinction—this holds to an even higher degree of his proof that judgments like "$7 + 5 = 12$" are synthetic. His statement in support of this conclusion, viz. that by merely thinking of the sum of 7 and 5 we cannot discover that it is equal to 12, can only mean that this truth is not *self-evident*. But had Kant given only a minimum of thought to the implied claim that all analytic truths are self-evident, he would have disavowed it. By a series of definitions of the form $n = m + 1$, any true equation of the form "$x + y = z$" (where the variables stand for integers) can be reduced to an identity; since the denial of such an equation would, therefore, be equivalent to a violation of the law of identity, Kant would surely have to admit that these equations are analytic by his own criterion of analytic truth; yet if all such equations were self-evident, there could be no need for *learning* addition.

However, when Kant stated that the principle of contradiction is the sufficient ground of all analytic truth, he overlooked like his predecessor Leibniz that without additional axioms which are not reducible to identical propositions formal demonstration could hardly take a step. Thus associative, distributive, and commutative laws of addition and multiplication are presupposed in the proofs of theorems of arithmetic and algebra; and in proofs by mathematical induction the principle of mathematical induction is presupposed. Now, a staunch and stubborn defender of Kant might argue that Kant was right after all, for this reason: if the axioms from which a theorem is formally deduced are synthetic, so is the theorem, and it would be a mistake to suppose that since the *implication* from axioms to theorem is analytic the theorem itself is analytic. And here he might quote Kant's own words:

> All mathematical judgments are synthetic. This proposition seems to have escaped the notice of the analysts of human reason up to date, indeed it seems to go against all of their opinions even though it is incontestably certain and of great consequence. For as they found that all the deductions made by mathematicians proceed in accordance with the principle of

contradiction (which is required by the nature of apodeictic certainty), they supposed that the axioms themselves are known on the basis of the principle of contradiction; which is an error: for it is indeed possible to prove a synthetic proposition by the principle of contradiction but only by presupposing another synthetic proposition from which the former is deducible, yet never in itself [*Critique*, intro., V].

This, however, is a poor defense of Kant. For as we have amply illustrated in the discussion of Leibniz, if the use of axioms other than the principle of identity in the demonstration of a proposition entails that the proposition is *not* analytic, then demonstration of an analytic proposition becomes almost a logical impossibility. Such a narrow definition of "analytic" would in fact entail that principles of formal deduction, like the principle of the hypothetical syllogism (if p implies q, and q implies r, then p implies r), are synthetic [18]; yet Kant characterized logic as a purely formal science in which pure intuition is not operative. Indeed, it is likely that Kant never reflected on the question of whether such an axiom of arithmetic as the associative law of addition is analytic or synthetic, and had he reflected on the question he might have become painfully aware of the inadequacy of the definitions of "analytic" which he offered.

When Frege, about a century after Kant, re-examined the question of the nature of arithmetical truth, he based his discussion on a far more careful and acceptable definition of analytic truth than Kant's: "If, in carrying out this process (viz. the proof of a given proposition), we come only on general logical laws and on definitions, then the truth is an analytic one, bearing in mind that we must take acount also of all propositions upon which the admissibility of any of the definitions depends" (*The Foundations of Arithmetic*, transl. Austin, p. 4e). Since the associative law of addition, which Frege showed to be tacitly assumed in Leibniz' famous proof of "$2 + 2 = 4$," would hardly have been counted by him as a "general logical law," one might wonder why he decided in favor of the view that arithmetical truths are analytic. The puzzle is solved, however, if we remember that Frege anticipated the reduction of arithmetic to logic which was carried out in detail in Russell and Whitehead's *Principia Mathematica*. That is, if all the axioms of

---

[18] Cf. above, pp. 12-13.

arithmetic should themselves be provable on the basis of " general logical laws," then Frege would be right in holding all the truths of arithmetic, axioms and theorems, to be analytic in the defined sense. Consider, for example, arithmetic as axiomatized by Peano. The primitive terms " zero," " number," and " successor " need not be interpreted for purposes of formal deduction of theorems from the axioms (supplemented with definitions, explicit or recursive). But the system thus constructed then does not contain any arithmetic *truths* at all, since the axioms as well as the theorems are propositional functions. Given, however, Russell's logicist interpretations of the primitive terms, the axioms become deducible from logical laws,[19] and hence may be said to be analytic in Frege's sense. Notice that Leibniz' proof of " $2 + 2 = 4$," which Frege cited and corrected, does not establish the analyticity of the equation, since the primitive terms used in the definientia, viz. *1* and *successor*, are given no interpretation and hence the derived formulae cannot be said to have a truth-value at all.[20]

Frege's definition of " analytic " explicates well what is meant by saying that the logicist (Russell's) philosophy of arithmetic has refuted Kant and established the analytic nature of arithmetic truths. There is, however, a subtle difficulty here which was touched upon in the discussion of Leibniz and which is generally overlooked. What did Frege mean by " all propositions upon which the admissibility of any of the definitions depends "? Primarily he must have been referring to propositions asserting unique existence, involved in definitions of the form " $y = (\imath x)\phi x$," e. g. the definition of a certain number as the limit of a converging sequence. But he may also have been thinking of the difference between *arbitrary* and *explicative* definitions. After all, any statement could be made to express an analytic truth in his sense if any definition whatever were admissible. Now, the proposition upon which, e. g., the admissibility of Russell's definition of the number one depends is none

[19] I disregard here the difficulty connected with the axiom of infinity—given Russell's definition of " number " and the theory of types, the infinity of the set of natural numbers cannot be proved without assuming the axiom of infinity, and the latter does not seem acceptable as a " logical law "—since it will be discussed later, in Chap. 6; see also Chap. 13, p. 387.

[20] In other words, " analytic " is a semantic, not a syntactic, concept. Compare the distinction made by Carnap in his *Introduction to Semantics* (Cambridge, 1942) between " *L*-true " and " *C*-true."

other than the proposition: $A \in 1 \equiv (\exists x)[(y)(y \in A \equiv y = x)]$, which is intended to express, in the form of a contextual definition, the *correct analysis* of the concept "one." Frege would presumably say that unless this proposition is true (or more accurately, unless the proposition constructed from the above propositional function by universal quantification over the free class-variable A is true), the corresponding definition would be inadmissible. But this proposition could be demonstrated as analytic in the specified sense only by using the corresponding definition as a rule of substitution (thus it would be turned into a substitution-instance of the law of identity), and such a proof would of course be grossly circular. It seems that we are thus confronted with the following choice: either we intend the division analytic-synthetic to *exhaust* the class of true proposition (every true proposition is either analytic or synthetic), in which case we have to admit that the sort of equivalence propositions, just illustrated, which are asserted as the result of logical analysis of a concept, are *synthetic a priori*; or else we shall have to rule that the analytic-synthetic distinction is not applicable to those propositions on whose validity, in Frege's words, the admissibility of the definitions used in a proof of analyticity depends. Since "synthetic" is defined by Kant as the contradictory of "analytic," [21] we must of course admit that anything of which these terms are significantly predicable is either analytic or synthetic. The question remains, however, of whether the range of significant predicability may not be narrower than the class of propositions. Frege's definition of "analytic" rather suggests that "analytic" is not significantly predicable of analyses (explicative statements) nor of logical laws, since this concept is defined with reference to analyses and logical laws.

[21] The most clear-cut inconsistency (to be distinguished from carelessness) in Kant's use of the terms "analytic" and "synthetic" consists in his so defining "analytic" that all analytic judgments are true, and at the same time defining "synthetic" as the contradictory of "analytic," and yet so using "synthetic" that no synthetic judgment could be self-contradictory. The inconsistency can be resolved by either denying the exhaustiveness of the disjunction "either analytic or synthetic" and replacing it by the disjunction "either analytic or synthetic or self-contradictory," or by substituting in the definition of "analytic" "truth-value" for "truth," such that analytic judgments may be analytically true or analytically false (self-contradictory). Most present-day uses of "analytic" correspond to the former terminology, which is also adopted in this book. ◉

CHAPTER 3. *Locke*

A. *The Ground of Necessary Truth: Immutable Relations between Ideas*

> If, then, the perception that the same ideas will eternally have the same habitudes and relations be not a sufficient ground of knowledge, there could be no knowledge of general propositions in mathematics; for no mathematical demonstration would be other than particular: and when a man had demonstrated any proposition concerning one triangle or circle his knowledge would not reach beyond that particular diagram.
>
> —*Essay Concerning Human Understanding*, Bk. IV, chap. 1, sec. 9.

As the above quotation shows, Locke held that the certainty of our knowledge of universal propositions is due to our (intellectual) "perception" of eternally fixed relations between the constituent concepts.[1] We can be sure that any particular which exemplifies C_1 also exemplifies C_2 because we know that $C_1 R C_2$, says Locke. What is this R? Presumably it is entailment, although Locke speaks vaguely of "agreement" between two ideas (which may be intuitively or discursively perceived) and so uses this vague word that compatibility is a kind of "agreement": for, if R above is the latter relation, then we could hardly infer that x exemplifies C_2 from the fact that x exemplifies C_1! But how can we perceive that C_1 will at all times have R to C_2? Locke must have meant that we feel certain of this invariance, but then the very way in which he accounted for the certainty of universal propositions such as those of mathematics could invite a Cartesian skeptic to ask: how do you know that relations between concepts are immutable? Is not this itself a universal proposition, that $C_1 R C_2$ *at all times*?

Actually the only way of answering such a piece of skepticism is

---

[1] Locke's usage of "idea" in the *Essay* is, of course, notoriously ambiguous. He verbally disagrees with the realists who hold that there are universals, extramental entities, *in rebus*, but it is clear that when he speaks of relations between ideas, such as incompatibility and "coexistence," he is speaking not of mental images but of universals or properties. I shall therefore employ the modern terminology of "properties" or "concepts" (in what Carnap calls the "objective" sense), which is less ambiguous.

47

to point out that a sentence of the form " C_1 has R to C_2 at time t,"
or " C_1 has R to C_2 at all times " does not make sense; logical
relations do not hold between temporal entities (particulars) , hence
it does not make sense to say that they hold at some time or at all
times between given terms (cf. below, pp. 121, 186-7, 413) . However,
a more serious shortcoming of Locke's explanation of the possibility
of certain knowledge of universal propositions is the following.
He attempts to deduce universal propositions about particulars,
specifically those of the form " all A are B," from propositions about
relations between universals, yet he never fully clarifies just what those
relations are. One of the types of " agreement " between universals
that he enumerates is " coexistence," illustrated by the proposition
" all gold is fixed." But the statement, verbally about universals,
" being gold coexists with being fixed " can only mean that anything which has the first property also has the second property, hence
it is obscure why coexistence should be counted as a relation
between universals. It is not a relation between universals in the
sense in which diversity, one of the forms of " disagreement " betwen
ideas, is a relation between universals: " squareness is distinct from
roundness " is not translatable into the statement about particulars
" whatever is square is not round," for the same rule of translation
would lead us from the truth " squareness is distinct from whiteness " to the falsehood " whatever is square is not white."

In fact, the only kinds of " agreement " between distinct ideas
mentioned by Locke which could be interpreted as relations between
universals are *entailment* and *compatibility*. The latter relation
may be disregarded in this context, because Locke refers to perceptions of relations between ideas as the source of knowledge of
universal propositions, and surely a proposition of the form " C_1
is compatible with C_2" cannot warrant a universal proposition about
particulars. His view, then, must have been that it is because we
perceive, e. g., that triangularity entails a sum of angles equal to
180 degrees, that we may predict with absolute certainty that any
existent triangle that might ever be found has the latter property
(Q). But, as he well knew, triangularity does not entail Q in the
sense in which, say, squareness entails foursidedness. We cannot by
mere analysis of the concept " triangle " discover Q but have to
presuppose geometrical axioms (of which we have, according to
Locke, intuitive knowledge) . And one of those axioms is a famous

assertion of *existence*, viz. that for any straight line S and a point P outside of S there exists exactly one straight line passing through P and parallel to S. How, then, could Locke maintain that the necessary connection between triangularity and Q is knowable by mere reflection upon "ideas" without concerning oneself with questions of existence? The obscurity of Locke's conception of "perception of agreement" between ideas as the source of a priori knowledge of universal propositions will be felt further if we try to apply it to Euclid's axiom "equals added to equals yield equals." This axiom asserts: for any magnitudes a, b, c, d, if $a = b$ and $c = d$, then $a + c = b + d$. Here the antecedent may be said to entail the consequent, but surely the terms of the relation of entailment are not universals or properties; they are rather propositional functions. Locke was apparently thinking of the subject and predicate of Aristotelian A-propositions when he wrote of "agreement between two ideas," and hence it is no surprise that his theory of a priori knowledge becomes unintelligible when it is applied to propositions, such as the above, which are obviously not of subject-predicate form.

Unlike Kant and Leibniz, Locke nowhere speaks of "necessary" truths (or propositions) in contrast to "contingent" ones, but instead contrasts *certainty* of knowledge with mere probability—and following tradition reserves the honorific term "knowledge" for certain knowledge. It is, of course, important to distinguish the propositions "it is known with certainty that p" and "p is a necessary truth." For example, if Fermat's theorem, that famous undecided proposition of algebra, is true, then it is a necessary truth; yet mathematicians so far can only conjecture that it is true, they do not know for certain. Again, "being known with certainty" is a time-dependent predicate, in the sense that a proposition may not be known with certainty at one time but known with certainty at another time, while it would not make sense to ask *at what time* a given proposition is a necessary truth.[2] However, it seems that Locke was aware, though none too clearly, of this distinction, for he allows that there may objectively exist an "agreement" between two ideas although we do not perceive it:

> it is fit to observe that certainty is twofold; certainty of truth, and certainty of knowledge. Certainty of truth is, when words

---

[2] See below, p. 121.

are so put together in propositions as exactly to express the
agreement or disagreement of the ideas they stand for, as really
it is. Certainty of knowledge is, to perceive the agreement or
disagreement of ideas, as expressed in any proposition [Bk. IV,
chap. 6, sec. 3].

Thus, with reference to Fermat's theorem, "$n > 2$" may *really
entail* "there is no solution for the equation: $x^n + y^n = z^n$," though
we do not perceive the entailment. By "certain truth," then, Locke
meant in this context nothing else than "necessary truth." And
his theory of necessary truth [3] might be reconstructed as follows:
a necessary truth is a true proposition of the form "xRy," where
x and y are universals ("concepts" in the objective sense) or propositional functions, and R is one of the following relations: entailment, incompatibility, compatibility, identity, difference; further
any proposition about particulars which follows from such a proposition (as "no squares are circles" follows from "squareness is
incompatible with circularity") is a necessary truth. By including
functions in the range of x and y [4] we make it possible to apply
Locke's vague concept of "agreement (or disagreement) of *ideas*"
to propositions which do not have subject-predicate form, like the
cited axiom of Euclid and Fermat's theorem. If R is identity or
difference, then, according to Locke, we have *intuitive* knowledge
of the truth of xRy—and this, he says, is the summit of certainty
(and, we might add, of triviality) ; but if R is entailment or incompatibility, xRy may be but indirectly known, by inference from
propositions that are intuitively known—this is *demonstrative* knowledge, which is less certain than intuitive knowledge.

What Locke called "intuitive knowledge of identity and diversity
(of ideas)" raises some interesting questions. Although the examples

[3] The theory (or "explanation") of a priori knowledge which Russell offered in
his lucid *The Problems of Philosophy* (London, 1912), ch. 10, seems to be essentially the same as Locke's theory, though Russell was not aware of it (indeed, the only
reference to Locke is a reference to him as one of those "empiricists" who held that
"all knowledge is derived from experience"!).

[4] The propositional functions to be substituted may be quite complex, e.g. they
may be conjunctions of propositional functions. Thus the parallel axiom, which Locke
must have regarded as intuitively evident, can be pressed into the form "x entails y"
only if for "x" we substitute "x is a straight line and y is a point outside of x" and
for "y" we substitute "there is exactly one straight line passing through y and
parallel to x."

of pairs of "diverse" ideas he gave were pairs of *incompatible* ideas (whiteness and blackness, triangularity and circularity), he could not have failed to distinguish mere difference from incompatibility: whiteness is distinct from roundness, yet the same particular may exemplify both universals. The difference between these two relations is reflected also by the fact that a statement of incompatibility of universals entails a universal proposition about particulars while a statement of mere difference does not: " whiteness is incompatible with blackness" entails " no surface is simultaneously both black and white all over," but " whiteness is different from roundness " surely does not entail " nothing is both white and round." Now, many contemporary empiricists would hold that a nominalistic language is in principle adequate for the expression of all genuine knowledge, though the translation of intensional statements into such a language may present practical difficulties.[5] By a nominalistic language I mean a language containing no other names than names of particulars and only individual variables (and accordingly corresponding to the language structure of the lower functional calculus enriched with names of particulars and predicates applicable to particulars) ; and by an intensional statement I mean a statement containing names of, or variables ranging over, such abstract entities as universals or propositions, like " roundness," " that the sun is larger than the moon " (the latter expression is not a sentence but a description of a state of affairs, occurring in such nonextensional contexts as " he believes that the sun is larger than the moon "). But let us see now whether intensional statements—" roundness is different from whiteness," " roundness is incompatible with squareness "—are even in principle translatable into such a language. For the latter statement one might propose the translation " the sentence ' for any x, if x is round then x is not square ' is necessary." If it should turn out, indeed, that a metalinguistic statement of the form " S is necessary" (where S is the name of a sentence) can only mean " the proposition expressed by S is necessary," then the success of the translation would be merely deception. But as reasons against the translatability of modal statements into an extensional metalanguage will be presented later,[6] the point will not be pressed now;

[5] See N. Goodman and W. V. Quine, " Steps towards a Constructive Nominalism," *Journal of Symbolic Logic, 12* (1947).
[6] Cf. below, pp. 121, 181. 195 f.

instead we ask how such a translation would fit into Locke's theory of necessary truth. It should be obvious that it just could not be fitted in. For Locke explains the necessary truth of the universal proposition " nothing which is round is square " with reference to the truth of the intensional statement " roundness is incompatible with squareness." The perception of the incompatibility of the attributes is, acording to him, the " ground " of our certain knowledge of the proposition expressed by the extensional statement.

But a " nominalist " will have even greater difficulty with the translation of " whiteness is different from roundness " into his favored language. Surely, neither " nothing which is white is round " nor " some things which are white are not round " would be adequate: some white things *are* round, and it is not self-contradictory to suppose that all white things are round even though whiteness and roundness are distinct attributes. Presumably he would again try a translation into the metalanguage: " white " is not synonymous with " round." But thus translated, the statement would express a *contingent* truth: it is clearly conceivable that these two predicates should be used synonymously, even though in fact they are not so used. Furthermore, on this interpretation the intensional statement in question would be specifically a statement about the English language whose correct translation into, say, German would be, not " das Weisse ist verschieden von dem Runden " but " ' white ' ist nicht gleichbedeutend mit ' round.' " [7] Again, the law of identity for universals, " every universal (attribute) is self-identical," would on this interpretation turn into the empirical generalization, which is surely false, that any two tokens of the same predicate have the same meaning. And consistency would compel a similar interpretation of the law of identity for individuals. Thus Leibniz' criterion *par excellence* of necessary truth would cease to be a necessary truth and turn into a contingent falsehood!

It should be evident, then, that if knowledge of necessary truths is considered " genuine knowledge," then Locke's theory of necessary truth is incompatible with the nominalists' claim that all genuine knowledge is in principle expressible in a nominalistic language. For the intensional statements which according to Locke are the ground of the necessity of extensional statements (specifically

---

[7] The whole problem of identity of attributes, or of synonymy, here touched upon, will receive detailed discussion in Chap. 10.

of universal statements about particulars) do not seem to be adequately translatable into such a language. And before rejecting Locke's theory for that very reason, a nominalist would do well to re-examine his faith in the adequacy of a nominalistic language. Consider, for example, the simple intensional statement "B_2 is darker than B_1," where "B_2" and "B_1" are names of distinct shades of blue and thus names of universals. We might translate this statement into a universal statement about particulars by constructing the relational predicate of the first level "being-darker-in-color-than": for any x and y, if x is an instance of B_2 and y an instance of B_1, then x is darker-in-color than y. But suppose we were asked why we are so sure that there are no exceptions to this generalization. Would it not be plausible to reply, with Locke, that we are so confident because we perceive that the *universals* B_2 and B_1 stand in the specified relation and *must* stand in that relation as long as they remain self-identical? [8] And are we not thus forced back into the intensional language?

B. The Contingent Universality of Laws of Nature

One of the main themes running through Locke's *Essay* is that our knowledge of nature is severely limited, since we do not see any necessary connections between different secondary qualities, or between secondary qualities and powers, or between the primary qualities of the "insensible particles" of substances and the secondary qualities and powers of the substances themselves. By "powers" Locke meant all dispositional properties (as we say nowadays) except those whose direct manifestation consists in the occurrence of sensations; thus he calls solubility in a given liquid a "power," but not so colors, although he calls colors (secondary) "qualities" and defines qualities as powers of objects to produce specific kinds of "ideas" (sensations). The well-known (and well-worn) confusions involved in the distinction between primary and secondary qualities will not be discussed in this context, since our analysis will be focused on Locke's conception of "necessary connection." For this purpose it will be sufficient to identify the three types of properties of substances and of the items of which they

---

[8] In the terminology of the British idealists, the relation is *internal*. For a critical comment on the concept of "internal relation," see below, pp. 73-5.

are composed by enumeration: primary qualities are such qualities as mass, size, shape, state of motion; secondary qualities are such qualities as colors, tastes, smells, temperatures; and powers are such properties as solubility, malleability, thermal and electrical conductivity. Locke's thesis might now be stated as follows: we do not know with certainty any proposition of the form "every instance of natural kind K has property P" unless P is contained in the nominal essence of K (in which case the proposition would be "trifling," uninformative); and by "nominal essence" of K Locke meant a complex idea composed of ideas of observable qualities of observable things, in contrast to the "real essence" which is the sum total of the primary qualities of the insensible particles of which instances of K are composed and which *determine* the observable qualities of the latter (for example, the color of a metal is part of its nominal essence, the atomic weight is part of its real essence).

But Locke does not say or imply that such propositions about natural kinds *are* contingent. In other words, he does not say that *there is no* necessary connection between the concept "being gold" and the concept "being soluble in aqua regia"; he only says that *we do not see* any such necessary connections, and that this is the reason why we cannot be certain of the truth of informative universal propositions about natural kinds. More than that, he held that if we knew the real essences of substances and saw necessary connections between the primary qualities of the particles and the observable qualities of the perceptual objects, then we would see a necessary connection between being gold and being soluble in aqua regia, just as we do see a necessary connection between being a Euclidean triangle and having an angle sum of 180 degrees.[9] If we use the Kantian terminology, this means nothing less than that according to Locke true generalizations about natural kinds are *synthetic a priori* propositions, though in most cases (exceptions will be considered presently) the finite human mind has, for lack of adequate ideas of natural kinds, only *a posteriori* knowledge of such propositions. In other words, Locke held that if the informative proposition "all gold is soluble in aqua regia" is true (which we cannot know), then it is just as much an a priori truth as the proposition about the sum of the angles of a triangle, although our

---

[9] This clearly nonempiricist aspect of Locke's epistemology is noted by W. Kneale, in *Probability and Induction* (Oxford, 1949), p. 71.

knowledge of this proposition is of the same imperfect kind as would be our knowledge of the proposition about the triangle if it were based on repeated measurements of the interior angles of particular triangles.

As it will be argued in the sequel that this very view convicts Locke of serious confusion about the notion of necessary truth, it is wise first to support the above interpretation by citations. After referring to Newton's " corpuscularian hypothesis " as " that which is thought to go farthest in an intelligible explication of the qualities of bodies," he says " whichever hypothesis be clearest and truest . . . our knowledge concerning corporeal substances will be very little advanced by any of them, till we are *made to see what qualities and powers of bodies have a necessary connexion or repugnance one with another*; which, *in the present state of philosophy*, I think, we know but to a very small degree: and I doubt whether, *with those faculties we have*, we shall ever be able to carry our general knowledge (I say not particular experience) in this part much farther " (Bk. IV, chap. 3, sec. 16, italics mine). And in section 25 of the same chapter: " I doubt not but if we could discover the figure, size, texture, and motion of the minute constituent parts of any bodies, we should know without trial several of their operations one upon another, as we do now the properties of a square or a triangle." Locke emphasizes, however, that even if we knew the real essences of substances, our knowledge of nature would still fall short of the ideal of mathematical certainty, since *we cannot discover* any " connexion " between primary qualities and the secondary qualities (or sensations—Locke notoriously confused qualities, originally defined as powers of producing " ideas," with the ideas which are their manifestations) " determined " by them. And a careful analysis of his language reveals that he did not deny the existence of such " connexions " but only the possibility, for the finite human mind, of discovering them:

> It is evident that the bulk, figure, and motion of several bodies about us, produce in us several sensations, as of colours, sounds, taste, smell, pleasure, and pain, etc. These mechanical affections of bodies having no affinity at all with those ideas they produce in us (there being no *conceivable connexion* between any impulse of any sort of body, and any perception of a colour or smell

which we find in our minds) , we can have no distinct knowledge of such operations beyond our experience . . . As the ideas of sensible secondary qualities which we have in our minds, can *by us be no way deduced* from bodily causes, nor any correspondence or connexion be found between them and those primary qualities which experience shows us produce them in us; so, on the other side, the operation of our minds upon our bodies is as unconceivable. [Bk. IV, chap. 3, sec. 28. Italics mine.]

The context leaves no doubt that by " conceivable," in the expression " no conceivable connexion," Locke meant " conceivable by us." It seems that for Locke the contingency of a proposition was not absolute but relative to cognitive powers. In this respect he falls in line with Leibniz, who, as we have seen, held that singular propositions about individual substances are only contingent relative to the finite human mind with its imperfect concepts of individual substances. But let us examine, now, the question of just *why* Locke should have thought that we would have demonstratively certain knowledge of generalizations about natural kinds if the two conditions he mentioned were satisfied, viz. (1) knowledge of the real essences of natural kinds, and (2) insight into necessary connections between primary and secondary qualities.

Consider Locke's example " gold is soluble in aqua regia." Let " Q_g " denote the set of primary qualities of gold ($=$ the qualities of the atoms of the substance, e. g. mass of the gold atom and shape and size of the gold atom) which Locke calls its " real essence "; and analogously " Q_a " is to denote the primary qualities of aqua regia. Then the above proposition would be deducible from the following premises:

(1) gold has Q_g, (2) aqua regia has Q_a, (3) if a solid characterized by Q_g is immersed in a liquid characterized by Q_a, there results a solution. The third premise states a connection between primary qualities and a secondary quality, for " being a solution " must be counted as a secondary quality of a liquid since secondary qualities are those qualities of observable substances which are not predicable of the insensible particles, and surely " being a solution " is not predicable of an atom.[10] Now, if the fact that a proposition is a necessary

[10] Besides, Locke *contrasts* primary qualities with powers—though in this he is

consequence of a set of premises is to warrant the judgment that it is itself necessary, it must first be shown that the premises are themselves necessary propositions. Yet how could (3) be anything but a contingent generalization? It is a proposition of the same kind as "whenever nitrogen and hydrogen combine in the volume proportion 1:3, there results a gas with the unpleasant odor of ammonia." What would it be like for superior intellects to perceive a necessary conection between antecedent and consequent? Locke might reply that just as a mathematically untrained human intellect might not see that "x is a triangle" entails "x has an angle sum of 180°" even though the entailment objectively holds, so here the antecedent may, for all we know, entail the consequent, though the human intellect is too weak to see this. However, what the mathematical demonstration enables us to see is that the proposition about triangles is entailed by the axioms of the geometry (specifically, the parallel axiom), which leaves it an open question whether "x is a triangle" entails "x has an angle sum of 180°." What the proof establishes is only that the conjunction of "x is a triangle" with the axioms of the geometrical system entails "x has an angle sum of 180°." Moreover, if a geometry in the sense of an empirical theory of physical space (not in the sense of a pure calculus) is conceived as a hypothetico-deductive system, then the very evidence on which the axioms are accepted consists in the truth of the theorems they imply; the parallel axiom, for example, would be accepted because it is found that the angle sum of a triangle *is* 180°. It follows that if the theorems are initially regarded as contingent truths, then the axioms must likewise be regarded as contingent: if *q* is contingent, then *p* can be a *reason* for *q* only if it is itself contingent (no contingent propositions are deducible from necessary propositions). But then we might say to Locke that just because such generalizations as "gold is soluble in aqua regia" are contingent, any premises that might explain this uniformity would themselves have to be contingent. Indeed, Locke's claim that we are ignorant of any necessary connection between being gold and being soluble in aqua regia was probably meant in the sense of ignorance of the *explanation* of the observed uniformity. And

inconsistent with (a) his definition of "quality" as a power of producing ideas, and (b) his inclusion of "mobility" in the list of primary qualities.

then Locke must have confused " q follows necessarily from p " with " q is necessary."

It might be added that even if premise (3) were a necessary proposition, this surely could not be said of (1) and (2), which describe the " real essences " of natural kinds. The atomic weight of gold, e. g., has to be empirically discovered unless " gold " is defined in terms of that primary quality. But if the names of natural kinds were defined in terms of such primary qualities, then it could not be said that we are, for the most part, ignorant of the real essences of natural kinds.

A famous doctrine of modern " empiricism " is that any proposition about physical reality, especially a universal proposition, is no more than probable. But it is clear that modern empiricists cannot count the " empiricist " Locke among their ancestors. For Locke seems to have held that the axioms of Newtonian mechanics have the same sort of self-evidence as the axioms of Euclidean geometry. The cause of our ignorance about nature (i. e. ignorance of the necessary truth of generalizations about natural kinds) is, according to him, our ignorance of primary qualities and of " connexions " between primary and secondary qualities in a given substance; but he did not think we are equally ignorant of " connexions " between changes of motion and changes of geometrical properties of bodies, as the following quotation brings out:

> That the size, figure, and motion of one body should cause a change in the size, figure, and motion of another body, is not beyond our conception. The separation of the parts of one body upon the intrusion of another, and the change from rest to motion upon impulse; these, and the like, seem to us to have some connexion one with another [Bk. IV, chap. 3, sec. 13].[11]

---

[11] There is, indeed, another passage in Bk. IV which is in apparent contradiction to the quoted one: " the coherence and continuity of the parts of matter, the production of sensation in us of colours and sounds, et cetera, by impulse and motion, *nay the original rules and communication of motion*, being such wherein we can discover no natural connexion with any ideas we have, we cannot but ascribe them to the arbitrary will and good pleasure of the wise Architect " (chap. 3, sec. 29, italics mine). However, Locke must on the whole have inclined towards the view that the laws of motion state " necessary connexions " which at least the minds of great physicists like Newton are not too feeble to perceive. This interpretation is further confirmed by the following passage: " The complex ideas that our names of the species of. substances properly stand for, are collections of such qualities as have been observed to coexist in an

Locke, to be sure, nowhere even attempts to analyze the notion of "necessary connexion." And it is hard to anticipate how he would have reacted to Hume's claim that the "necessary connexion" between impact of A on B and subsequent motion of B is nothing but our firm expectation of the second event when we witness the first event, the expectation itself being the result of observation of the "constant conjunction" of two kinds of events. But since he uses the same expression, "necessary connexion," when referring to the certainty of the propositions of mathematics, and there is no indication of deliberately ambiguous usage, it is natural to interpret Locke to have believed, just as Kant did, that the axioms of mechanics have a certainty which such inductive generalizations as "gold is soluble in aqua regia" lack. Presumably Locke thought that, if A is the event of a body impinging on a mobile body of equal or less mass, and B the event of the latter body subsequently moving, one could foresee *a priori* that B would happen if A happened. It is strange that he did not even try to give an argument supporting this claim of a priori predictability. For unless this claim is made good, there is no reason whatever to suppose that we would be able to predict a priori the powers of substances (such as the solubility in aqua regia of gold) if only we knew their real essences.

C. *Trifling Propositions and Genuine Knowledge*

Kant's conception of an analytic judgment as a judgment whose predicate is contained in the subject was clearly anticipated by Locke; he called them "trifling propositions." That all gold is malleable, "is a very certain proposition, if malleableness be a part of the complex idea the word 'gold' stands for. But then here is nothing affirmed of gold, but that that sound stands for an idea in which malleableness is contained; and such a sort of truth and certainty as this it is to say, 'a centaur is four-footed'" (Bk. IV, chap. 6, sec. 9). But if "analytic" is used in this sense, then it is equally clear that Locke anticipated Kant's claim that the propositions of mathematics are *synthetic a priori* truths:

---

unknown substratum which we call 'substance'; but what other qualities necessarily co-exist with such combinations, we cannot certainly know, unless we can discover their natural dependence; *which in their primary qualities we can go but a very little way in . . .*" (chap. 6, sec. 7, italics mine).

we can know the truth (of?), and so may be certain in propositions which affirm something of another, which is a necessary
consequence of its precise complex idea, but not contained in
it: as that "the external angle of all triangles is bigger than
either of the opposite internal angles"; which relation of the
outward angles to either of the opposite internal angles, making
no part of the complex idea signified by the name "triangle,"
this is a real truth, and conveys with it instructive real knowledge [Bk. IV, chap. 8, sec. 8].

That such a truth is not analytic in the Kantian sense seems indeed
undeniable. No contradiction is deducible from its negation without the use of extralogical (specifically geometrical) postulates.
Locke could have given even more striking examples of necessary
geometrical truths which are not formally demonstrable. Consider
the proposition: "Given a straight line S and a circle C such that
S has more than one point in common with C, then S has exactly
two points in common with C." If anyone claims that this proposition is demonstrable on the basis solely of definitions of the geometrical terms involved, let him produce the goods! And if he
should reply that it is nevertheless systematically analytic, i. e.
demonstrable within an adequately formalized Euclidean geometry,
he would throw himself open to a double retort: (1) What is
the criterion of "adequate formalization"? Presumably that enough
postulates should be explicitly listed to enable one to produce
a purely *formal* proof, independent of spatial intuition, of the
theorems of the system. But then the claim of the systematic analyticity of our proposition is trivial. (2) In the same sense of
"systematically analytic," empirical generalizations like the laws
of mechanics would become systematically analytic the moment the
empirical science in question were cast into the form of a deductive
system. But surely no law of mechanics has the sort of self-evidence
which the cited geometrical proposition has. Besides, even if a
formal demonstration on the basis of explicit definitions were
possible, it would be deception to suppose that for this reason
spatial intuition plays no part in geometrical knowledge. For such
definitions as "straight line = line uniquely determined by two
points," "circle = closed line all of whose points are equidistant
from a given point" are arrived at in no other way than by

analyzing spatial intuitions (and, as was noted in our discussion of Kant, it is for this reason that Kant could not be forced to concede by exhibiting a formal proof based on such definitions). A logical empiricist would no doubt reply that if our proposition belongs to formal geometry, then, the geometrical terms being uninterpreted, it is not a proposition at all but a propositional function, and if it is a proposition about physical space, " straight line " being interpreted to mean the path of a light ray, then it may well have exceptions in view of the " bending " of light rays in intense gravitational fields. But this objection is irrelevant if we take the proposition to make an assertion about visual space.[12]

At any rate it is clear that if the thesis of the analyticity of all a priori knowledge is part of what is meant by " empiricism," then Locke was no empiricist at all. " To the extent that knowledge is a priori it is not about reality " is a battle cry of modern logical empiricism. Does this mean that from an a priori truth nothing can be deduced as to the properties of empirically given objects? But surely the a priori knowledge that " ' x is a cube ' entails ' x has 12 edges ' " warrants the deduction that all the cubical pieces of sugar in that sugar bowl have 12 edges! Locke notes that in precisely this sense all mathematical knowledge is *real*: " Is it true of the idea of a triangle, that its three angles are equal to two right ones? It is true also of a triangle wherever it really exists. Whatever other figure exists that is not exactly answerable to that idea of a triangle in his mind, is not at all concerned in that proposition " (Bk. IV, chap. 4, sec. 6). Of course, no logical empiricist would deny that we have a priori knowledge of the cited proposition about the contents of the sugar bowl. But what, then, is he denying when he avers that this is not knowledge " about reality "? Anything more than that the proposition which is known a priori is contingent? But is it not trivial to insist that whatever is deducible from an a priori truth is itself an a priori truth? Perhaps the empiricist battle cry could be interpreted as the exhortation " let's not confuse a priori knowledge and empirical (factual) knowledge; they are quite distinct, and the methods for acquiring knowledge of mathematical truths are no more suitable for acquiring knowledge of empirical truths than the methods for catching lions are

[12] The logical empiricists' attempt to explain geometry without admitting synthetic a priori propositions will be discussed in more detail below, Chap. 8.

appropriate for catching fish." But then the dictum of the "factual emptiness" of a priori knowledge becomes redundant once the distinction between a priori and empirical (factual) knowledge is recognized, and it is none too clear just who the philosophers are that need the exhortation. Even "rationalists" like Leibniz, who attempted to deduce propositions of physics like the law of inertia from an a priori principle like the principle of insufficient reason, did not attempt the self-contradictory feat of deducing a contingent truth from an a priori truth: what they tried to show was that physical propositions commonly accepted on empirical evidence admitted of a priori deduction from a self-evident principle, just as Euclid performed an a priori deduction from (to him) self-evident axioms of such empirically confirmed propositions as the Pythagorean theorem. It is one thing to attempt a deduction from self-evident principles of propositions that *seem* to be contingent, another thing to attempt such a demonstration of propositions that *are* contingent. Unfortunately the modern philosophers who frequently sound this "empiricist" battle cry seem to think that to believe in synthetic a priori knowledge is *equivalent* to confusing a priori and empirical knowledge. But this equivalence would hold only—as will be argued in detail in Chapter 5—if "synthetic" were synonymous with "empirical" (and accordingly, if "analytic" and "a priori" were synonymous). And it is significant in this connection that Locke *both* distinguished genuine knowledge from pseudo-knowledge (knowledge of synthetic propositions and knowledge of "trifling" propositions) within the genus "a priori knowledge" *and* discussed at considerable length the difference between a priori knowledge and empirical knowledge.

D. Simplicity of Ideas

We have seen, while examining the doctrines of Leibniz and Kant, that the concept of *unanalyzable* (simple) ideas plays an important role in connection with the question of whether a given self-evident proposition is analytic. Locke has some highly significant things to say on the subject of simple ideas, and in fact it is impossible to state the precise sense in which he was an empiricist without speaking of simple ideas: what contrasts his epistemology with that of the rationalists Leibniz and Kant is not the denial of synthetic a priori knowledge—for Leibniz implicitly (though inconsistently) denied it, and Locke implicitly affirmed it—but the thesis that all simple ideas originate from sense perception and/or "reflection" (i. e. introspection). Locke, indeed, did not do as skillful a job as Hume in tracing the empirical origin of Kant's innate simple concept par excellence, the concept of causal necessity, but he nevertheless proclaimed this empiricist thesis with vigorous emphasis. But what did Locke mean by a "simple" idea? What was his criterion of distinction between simple and complex ideas? If to say of an idea (like the idea of redness) that it is simple is to say that perception of instances of redness is causally necessary for acquiring the idea—in other words, that the only way one could make someone understand the meaning of "red" is ostensive definition—then the empiricist thesis as stated is a mere tautology. But the thesis was not, of course, intended by Locke as a statement *analytic* of the meaning of "simple idea." It was definitely intended as an empirical law of genetic psychology. It is, indeed, not inconceivable (though perhaps *unbelievable*) that a congenitally blind man should have color images, or that—to anticipate Hume's famous exception to the thesis under discussion—one should be able to form an image of a missing shade of a given color in a series of equally spaced shades of that color. These are strictly factual questions of psychology. That Locke himself regarded them as factual questions is evident, for example, from his references to the lack of ideas of colors in the minds of blind people as proof of his thesis:

> A studious blind man, who had mightily beat his head about visible objects, and made use of the explication of his books and friends to understand those names of light and colors which often came in his way, bragged one day, that he now understood what "scarlet" signified. Upon which his friend demanding, what scarlet was? the blind man answered "It was like the sound of a trumpet." Just such an understanding of the name of any other simple idea will he have who hopes to get it only from a definition, or other words made use of to explain it [Bk. III, chap. 4, sec. 11].

But although Locke does offer a definition of "simple idea" relative to which his empiricist thesis is not a tautology, the definition offered raises a formidable difficulty for his claim that simple ideas are undefinable. The definition occurs implicitly in the following passage: " there is nothing can be plainer to a man than the clear and distinct perception he has of those simple ideas; which, being each in itself uncompounded, contains in it nothing but one uniform appearance or conception in the mind, and is not distinguishable into different ideas " (Bk. II, chap. 2, sec. 1). Surely, if the ideas of colors, and of the determinable " color " itself, are " in themselves uncompounded," so are such ideas of shape (Locke speaks of " figure ") as straightness and circularity. Now, Locke says that the names of simple ideas are " incapable of being defined," " the reason whereof is this, that the several terms of a definition signifying several ideas, they can all together by no means represent an idea which has no composition at all " (Bk. III, chap. 4, sec. 7). But what about such definitions as " the straight line is the shortest distance between two points," " the straight line is the line which is uniquely determined by two points," " a circle is a closed line all of whose points are equidistant from a given point "? Again, Locke lists the idea of number (the determinable, not ideas of determinate numbers) as simple, as, likewise, the idea of the number one. (Presumably he thought that all the natural numbers larger than one are definable, as the immediate successors of their immediate predecessors, but not unity itself.) What would he have said about the Frege-Russell definitions of number and of the number one in particular? Again, infinity as predicated of the series of natural numbers is considered a simple idea by Locke; what would he have said of the modern definition in terms of one-to-one correspondence? Again, in the section where he urges us to observe the limits of definability (" if all terms were definable, it would be a process in infinitum "), he ridicules scholastic as well as " modern " definitions of " motion." Since Locke's parody raises a vexing problem which is still with us nowadays as we ask what, after all, an *analysis* of a concept is, it is worth quoting in full:

> The atomists, who define motion to be " a passage from one place to another ": what do they more than put one synonymous word for another? For what is " passage " other than motion? And if they were asked what " passage " was, how would they better define it than by " motion "? For is it not at least as

proper and significant to say " Passage is a motion from one
place to another," as to say " Motion is a passage? " etc. *This is
to translate, and not to define,* when we change two words of
the same signification one for another [Bk. III, chap. 4, sec. 9,
italics mine].

Actually, if the criticized definition were rewritten by putting
" *change* of place " in place of " passage from one place to another,"
there would be nothing circular about it and it would be a perfectly
good example of traditional definition *per genus et differentiam*:
bodies change in many different respects—such as color, shape, temperature, degree of solidity—and change of place is one among
them; the notion of change is thus more general than the notion
of motion. Nevertheless, if we can attach any meaning to Locke's
definiens for " simple idea " at all, we will agree that the idea of
motion *is* simple, just like ideas of colors. Of course, if it should
be maintained that the more generic idea of change is " distinguishable " within the idea of motion, one could only reply that in the
same sense the generic idea of color is " distinguishable " within
the idea of redness, or the generic idea of taste within the idea of
sweetness—and one would just have to confess that Locke's definition of simplicity of ideas is too vague to be of any use at all. The
point of chief importance in the above quotation, however, is the
distinction between *translation* and *definition* there drawn. By
saying that the names of simple ideas are undefinable Locke evidently meant, not that no synonyms could be produced, or that no
other expression of equal extension with the defined expression
could be produced, but that no complex of words would have the
power to evoke the idea in question in a man who had not antecedently perceived instances of the idea. Thus he would presumably
have maintained that one who understood the meanings of " change "
and " place " still could not be made to understand the meaning of
" motion " by pronouncing the definiens " change of place " unless
he had witnessed instances of motion in the first place; and similarly
that one who had never seen a circle would not be enabled to
imagine a circle, or to identify visually a presented circle as a circle,
by being told that a circle is a closed line all of whose points are
equidistant from a given point. Now it turns out, however, that
there is no a priori guarantee whatever that all simple ideas (in
the vague sense of Locke's definition) should be undefinable or

that all definable ideas should be complex. It is entirely conceivable that a man who had never perceived an instance of orange,
yet had perceived instances of yellow and of red, and who was also
acquainted ostensively with the relation of betweenness (in the sense
in which a shade of a given color is between two neighboring shades),
could imagine an orange patch and/or identify an orange patch
if he were told " orange is the color between yellow and red."
And it is likewise conceivable that a person who was ostensively
acquainted with the meanings of " straight line," " right angle," and
" equal " but who had never seen squares, would *not* be able to
imagine a square if he were told " a square is a closed figure bounded
by equal straight lines in such a way that adjacent sides always form
right angles"; but surely the idea of squareness is *complex* in the
sense of being " distinguishable into different ideas."

Two important consequences follow. (1) In view of the vagueness of Locke's definition of " simple idea," the only tolerably clear
criterion of simplicity to be extracted from the *Essay* is the psychological-genetic criterion of undefinability (in the specified sense),
and therefore the *general* empiricist thesis " all simple ideas are
caused by perception (or introspection) of instances " does resolve
into a tautology. Only *applicative* statements of the form " this is a
simple idea (e. g. the idea of redness is simple) " would have factual
content. But any such statement is, whether true or false, a hypothesis of empirical psychology which it may, moreover, be practically
impossible to subject to controlled experimental test. No general
epistemological thesis seems to remain that would serve to identify
Locke as an empiricist. If the thesis is " *some* ideas are caused by
perception (or introspection) of instances, and could not have
originated otherwise " (though it may be doubtful *which* they are),
then it would be difficult to find a rationalist who would disagree.
But more important in connection with our topic is (2) that a
simple idea in Locke's psychological-genetic sense could hardly be
identified with an *unanalyzable* idea and, correspondingly, Locke's
notion of " definition " cannot be identified with the notion of
analysis. When a philosopher claims that such geometrical concepts
as circle, ellipse, and parabola are *analyzable*, he surely does not
commit himself to any such dubious causal laws of psychology as
the claim of definability in Locke's sense would amount to. When
Russell offers " class of similar classes " as the analysis of the concept

of number, he surely does not mean to imply that one who had not antecedently acquainted himself with particular numbers through usual counting procedures but who understood the meaning of "similar classes" would come to understand the meaning of "number" by just being told "that's a class of similar classes."

But what, then, do philosophers mean by the contrast simple-analyzable (concepts)? It seems fair to say that even contemporary analysts whose language and thought is immeasurably more precise than Locke's are no less uncertain than Locke on this point. A look at recent statements by Carnap about simplicity of predicates should suffice to substantiate this charge (or rehabilitation of Locke, depending on one's point of view). As was pointed out in the discussion of Leibniz, the desire to guarantee the consistency of any given state description that a given language allows to be constructed led Carnap to lay down a requirement of simplicity: only *simple* predicates are eligible as primitive predicates. Carnap confesses "that an exact explication of the concept of simplicity cannot easily be given" but thinks that "nevertheless, the concept seems clear enough for many practical purposes" ("On the Application of Inductive Logic," p. 137). As an example of a simple property he gives "a certain shade of blue," and answers the objection that an analysis of this property is possible as follows: "The spectral analysis of this blue into spectral colors as its components or the physical analysis of it in terms of electro-magnetic waves are, of course, not analyses in the present sense; *they do not show the experience to be composite but rather establish, by way of induction, certain correlations between this color blue and other experiences.*" (My italics) It seems that a criterion of the simplicity of P used by Carnap is that the *experience* consisting in the seeing of an instance of P should be unanalyzable, unified. But what if in observing a patch of a given shade of blue I discriminate the shade from the hue? Is the truly simple property, then, the shade in abstraction from any hue? But a shade can be perceived only as a shade *of* a given color! It is similar with perception of sounds: every sound has both a determinate pitch and a determinate loudness; if, let us say, middle C were a simple quality in Carnap's sense then a perception of an instance of middle C should not be analyzable into pitch and loudness components; yet there could be no perception of pitch abstracted from loudness. The difficulty comes out clearly also if we consider predicates designating shapes, like "circular" and "elliptical." If the sight of a given shade of blue is simple, so is the sight of, say, a circular disk. But even if we abstract from the color components of the visual sense datum, we can still discriminate between the shape and the size of the sense datum; and if it be replied that no particular size is *designated* by the predicate "circular," it must be said that nonetheless any observable instance of the designated shape also has size (necessarily) and that the perception of a determinate size, accordingly, is a component of the perception of the round disk. Now, what would Carnap say if it were maintained that the meaning of "circular" is analyzable by means of either the definition of synthetic geometry or the definition of analytic geometry? Would he not have to say, to be consistent, that "these are not *analyses* in the present sense; they do not show the experience (of seeing a circular shape) to be composite but rather establish, by way of induction, certain correlations between this shape of circularity and other experiences"? Would it be so unplausible to regard it as an *inductive* conclusion that a figure which looks, as viewed normally, circular turns out to satisfy an equation of the form "$x^2 + y^2 = k$" when embedded in a Cartesian coordinate system? It must be confessed, then, that Carnap has not elucidated the *relevant* sense of "analyzable" in which such properties as determinate shades of color or determinate shapes are not analyzable. Consequently the concept of simple descriptive predicates, which is part and parcel of the new foundations of deductive and inductive logic laid by Carnap at the present time, must be declared as no clearer than Locke's concept of simple ideas.

All the objects of human reason or enquiry may naturally be divided into two kinds, to wit, *Relations of Ideas*, and *Matters of Fact*. Of the first kind are the sciences of Geometry, Algebra, and Arithmetic: and in short, every affirmation which is either intuitively or demonstratively certain . . . Propositions of this kind are discoverable by the mere operation of thought, without dependence on what is anywhere existent in the universe . . . Matters of fact, which are the second objects of human reason, are not ascertained in the same manner; nor is our evidence of their truth, however great, of a like nature with the foregoing. The contrary of every matter of fact is still possible; because it can never imply a contradiction, and is conceived by the mind with the same facility and distinctness, as if ever so conformable to reality—*Enquiry into Human Understanding* (1748), Sec. IV, pt. 1.

A. *Hume and Logical Empiricism*

H u m e is commonly pointed to by contemporary logical empiricists as one of the great ancestors of their movement, and since one of the theses identifying this school is that there is no such thing as synthetic a priori knowledge, it is thereby implied that this thesis may be traced back to Hume. It is, indeed, natural to impute such a view to Hume, since Hume's epistemology was attacked by Kant, the great apostle of synthetic a priori knowledge. It is, however, my purpose to demonstrate that this interpretation of Hume is without foundation, for a very simple reason: while Hume clearly distinguished, as demonstrated by the above quotation, between *a priori* (necessary) and *empirical* (contingent) truths, he never as much as raised the question whether all a priori truths are analytic; and how can one impute to a writer an affirmative answer to a question which he never asked? This does not, of course, mean that Hume implicitly admitted synthetic a priori knowledge (which, as we saw, may be said of Locke), for he was not aware of the distinction that must be made if the question of synthetic a priori knowledge is to have a sense at all. Specifically, he wrote indiscriminately of the " possibility," " conceivability," " imaginability,"

" noncontradictoriness " of the negation of an empirical proposition as the criterion of its being empirical, not necessary; and unlike Kant he did not pay much attention to the distinction between intuitive inconceivability and logical inconsistency. There are passages, indeed, where Hume emphasizes the distinction between a *tautology* and a *synthetic judgment*, but then there is no evidence that he held the modern empiricist view that syntheticity is incompatible with necessity. Thus he writes in the *Treatise of Human Nature* (Bk. I, Pt. II, section 4) : " In common life 'tis established as a maxim, that the straightest way is always the shortest; which would be as absurd as to say, the shortest way is always the shortest, if our idea of a right line was not different from that of the shortest way betwixt two points." He rejects, that is, the definition of " straight line " as meaning " shortest distance between two points " on the ground that if definiendum and definiens were synonymous, then the axiom " the straight line is the shortest distance between two points " would be a tautology, which it is not.[1] But he does not go on to say that this " maxim " is no more than an empirical generalization.

It is, therefore, surprising that Kant himself interpreted Hume as having denied the possibility of synthetic a priori knowledge:

> Hume being prompted (a task worthy of a philosopher) to cast his eye over the whole field of *a priori* cognitions in which human understanding claims such mighty possessions, heedlessly severed from it a whole, and indeed its most valuable, province, viz. pure mathematics; for he thought its nature . . . depended on totally different principles, namely, on the law of contradiction alone; and although he did not divide judgments in this manner formally and universally as I have done here, what he said was equivalent to this: that mathematics contains only analytical, but metaphysics synthetical, *a priori* judgments [*Prolegomena*, trans. P. Carus, § 4].

What Kant means is that the only a priori (" pure ") science whose possibility and existence Hume conceded was mathematics—or arithmetic, more accurately—and that he held the propositions of mathematics to be analytic. Kant must have been misled by Hume's use

[1] Would it be overcrediting Hume to suggest that he here anticipated at one stroke Moore's exposition of the " naturalistic fallacy " and the paradox of analysis?

of the word "contradiction." From the fact that Hume says that
p cannot be denied without contradiction one cannot infer that
Hume holds *p* to be analytic in Kant's sense; for Hume used
"contradiction" in a wider—or perhaps we should say looser—sense
than "formal contradiction." Whatever is inconceivable is contradictory, in Hume's terminology. Surely Hume would have agreed
with Kant that it is inconceivable that the straight line should
anywhere fail to be the shortest distance between two points that
lie on it, though he emphasized that neither the word "straight"
nor the word "shortest" has an absolutely precise meaning. But
as our quotation brings out, he explicitly denied that the "maxim"
is an analytic statement.

In order to stimulate the reader's interest in the particular problem of interpretation of Hume just outlined, I shall examine a
recent (unsupported) empiricist claim that for Hume all knowledge is either analytic or empirical. Reichenbach writes in *The
Rise of Scientific Philosophy* (1951, p. 86): "He (Hume) arrives
at the result that all knowledge is either analytic or derived from
experience: mathematics and logic are analytic, all synthetic knowledge is derived from experience." Naturally, our curiosity as to
what Reichenbach means by "analytic" is immediately aroused.
The definition offered is simple enough: it means "self-explanatory" (p. 18), as illustrated by the famous example of analytic
truth: "all bachelors are unmarried." Presumably "self-explanatory" is itself synonymous with "self-evident." Reichenbach later
says (p. 38) that the principles of logic are analytic. And, of course,
all mathematics is held to be similarly analytic. But the view that
all the propositions of logic and mathematics are self-evident is
too absurd to warrant discussion, and if Reichenbach did not mean
by "self-explanatory" the same as "self-evident," i. e. "so obviously
true that no sort of proof is required to produce assent to the
proposition," then he has simply defined the technical term "analytic" *per obscurius.* Indeed, Reichenbach mentions later (p. 223)
that not all truths of logic are obvious, and gives the example " if
any two men either love each other or hate each other, then either
there is a man who loves all men or for every man there exists
some man whom he hates." This admission, however, does not
prevent him from adhering to the position that all logical truth
is analytic: "Logic proves that this combination (= sentence?) is

analytic; but the analytic character is by no means obvious." Is
Reichenbach, then, saying that, even though all logical and mathematical truths are self-evident, it may not be self-evident that they
are self-evident? But as it is obscure what this might mean, we must
conclude that it is not even clear what view Reichenbach is ascribing
to Hume, since he has not made clear his meaning of " analytic."
The confusion is multiplied as we turn to Reichenbach's handling
of the term " synthetic." On the same page on which he pronounces
that logical truths are analytic, he tells us that factual statements
are *synthetic* in the sense that " they add something to our knowledge." Now, since " analytic " and " synthetic " are incompatible
predicates of statements, one would infer that, according to Reichenbach, the statements of logic and mathematics add nothing to our
knowledge, which is surely equivalent to saying that there is no
such thing as logical and mathematical knowledge. As we shall
see below (Chap. 7), the most charitable interpretation of this
view is that it amounts to a terminological proposal regarding the
term " knowledge "—a proposal, indeed, which there is no good
reason to accept. But be this as it may, what becomes now of
Reichenbach's interpretation of Hume? Notice that Reichenbach
actually holds that the sentences of logic do not express knowledge,
for he writes " logic formulates rules of language—that is why logic
is analytic and empty " (p. 222) : a *rule*, obviously, is not a proposition, i. e. something that could significantly be said to be *known
to be true*. " Knowledge " of propositions of logic and mathematics
then becomes a contradiction in terms. But since Hume is claimed
to have held the view that logic and mathematics consist of *analytic*
statements, by implication the view is imputed to him that there is
knowledge (or, at least, *genuine* knowledge) only about matters
of fact. Yet, for Hume as well as for Locke, mathematics (at least
arithmetic) is precisely the science which best illustrates the very
ideal of *knowledge* (*genuine* knowledge, knowledge in the honorific
sense of the word) !

B. " Relations of Ideas " and " Matters of Fact "

The precise meaning of Hume's division of " the objects of human
enquiry " into " relations of ideas " and " matters of fact " comes
out most clearly in the discussion of " seven different kinds of phi-

losophical relation," at the beginning of Part III of Book I of the *Treatise*—though, as we shall see presently, it is only after a good deal of interpretation that a tolerably precise meaning emerges. *Resemblance, contrariety, degrees in quality,* and *proportions in quantity or number* are said to be relations " which depending solely upon ideas, can be the objects of knowledge and certainty"; they are contrasted with *identity, relations of time and place,* and *causation,* "which may be changed without any change in the ideas." Let us attempt to clarify this, for Hume, fundamental distinction by means of a comparison of a judgment of equality and a judgment of spatial relation: " $2 + 2 = 4$ " vs. " body A is one mile from body B." What Hume meant by saying that the relation of equality "depends solely upon ideas " is probably, in application to our sample judgment of equality, that the equality of 4 and $2 + 2$ *follows* from the meanings of the terms " 4 " and " $2 + 2$ " alone; while, on the other hand, the truth of the judgment of spatial distance cannot be established by merely reflecting on the meanings of " body A " and " body B." Suppose we call relations of the former kind, following a well known philosophical terminology, *internal,* and relations of the latter kind *external.* We may then construct a general definition of this distinction, without departing appreciably from the framework of Hume's terminology, as follows:

R is an *internal relation* = a proposition of the form xRy is, if true, *necessary,* and if false, *impossible*

R is an *external relation* = a proposition of the form xRy is *contingent,* i. e. if true it is nonetheless logically possible that it should be false, and if false it is nonetheless logically possible that it should be true.

To illustrate, the denial of " $2 + 2 = 4$ " can be shown to entail the contradiction" $4 \neq 4$," and hence one who denied this statement would attach an unusual meaning either to the term " 4 " or to the term " $2 + 2$." On the other hand, Hume would say that if a house A stands in fact at a distance of one mile from house B, we could nevertheless conceive that this spatial relation between the *same* objects were different, i. e. without " changing our ideas " of the terms we could suppose that their relation were different. But had Hume been accustomed to the formal, or metalinguistic mode of speech, he would surely have seen that the distinction of different kinds of relations is ill-defined, owing to the tacit, and demonstrably untenable, assumption that if one proposition of the form xRy (where "R" represents a specific relation) is necessary, then all true propositions of that form are necessary, and the analogous assumption for the contingent propositions about external relations. Take, for example, our statement about the spatial distance of houses A and B. Should we describe the house named A as "the house which is exactly one mile south of B," then we obviously obtain an analytically true statement, while if the same object is described in terms of its appearance, the statement is contingent. Hume might reply that when he spoke of our "ideas of the objects (judged to be related in a certain way)," he meant the meanings of descriptions in terms of *intrinsic* properties only. This interpretation would save not only the classification of spatial and temporal relations as external, but also the classification of resemblance as an internal relation: for if we were permitted to describe, e. g., two people A and B relationally, say A as "the only uncle of the best player on our team" and B as "the only brother of the president of our college," it would surely remain a question of fact whether A and B resembled one another. But this way we merely cover one hole in Hume's distinction by uncovering another: just what could Hume mean by "ideas" of *numbers* if descriptions in terms of relations were excluded? How could a number be described at all except by its relations to other numbers, such as successorship, square, double, etc.? The stipulation, therefore, that only *intrinsic* descriptions may be substituted for x and y in the form xRy would make it impossible to classify "proportions in quantity or number" as either external or internal relations. What is left of Hume's division after such critical scrutiny, then, is not a division of relations—even numerical equality might hold contingently between two terms, as in "the number of the planets is equal to the square of the number of points that is sufficient and necessary to determine a plane (viz. 3)"—but simply the division of propositions into necessary and contingent. He might have said rightaway, without detouring over the unsuccessful division of relations into internal and external, that the objects of knowledge are propositions of two radically different sorts, viz. necessary and contingent. It was probably Locke's influence that led Hume to speak of "relations of ideas" in the first place, and as in the case of Locke the clear and sound core of the contention that mathematically certain knowledge is "about ideas" or "nonexistential" is that the objects of such knowledge are propositions which, in Hume's own terminology (see opening citation), "are discoverable by the mere operation of thought."

C. *Logical Possibility and Imaginability*

We must now turn our attention to the main problem of this chapter: what exactly did Hume mean by *possibility* when he divided true propositions into those whose falsehood is possible and those whose falsehood is impossible? Our opening excerpt ends with a statement of *reasons* for the assertion that "the contrary of every matter of fact is still possible." They are (1) that not-p (where p is a factual proposition) is self-consistent, (2) that not-p is, even though it be false, as easily conceivable as it would be if it were true. Now, Hume notoriously identifies (unlike, for example, Leibniz) the *conceivable* with the *imaginable*; "idea" is in Hume's usage synonymous with "mental image." To give just one quotation in support of this interpretation (which is borne out particularly by a study of Part II of Book I, "Of the Ideas of Space and Time"): Hume refutes the rationalist thesis that "every event has a cause" is a *necessary* proposition by pointing out that it is "easy for us to *conceive* any object to be nonexistent this moment, and existent the next, without conjoining to it the distinct idea of a cause or productive principle. The separation, therefore, of the idea of a cause from that of a beginning of existence is plainly *possible for the imagination*; and consequently the actual separation of these objects is so far possible, that it implies no contradiction nor absurdity" (Pt. III, sec. 3). And since "imaginable" is less ambiguous than "conceivable," just because "conceivable" is sometimes used in the sense of "logically conceivable" (self-consistent) [2] and sometimes in the narrower sense of "intuitively conceivable," let us

---

[2] The statement "p is self-consistent" means that no contradiction (a statement of the form "p and not-p") is formally deducible from p. Notice that "p and not-p" is inconsistent *with itself*, not just with its negation. For "p is consistent with q" means "it is possible that (p and q)," and clearly it is not possible that [(p and not-p) and (p and not-p)].

operate with the term " imaginable " in this context. The question arises whether Hume meant to say that imaginability of not-*p* and self-consistency of not-*p* are two *independent* reasons for the contingency of *p*, and if so, whether he regarded them as severally sufficient, or only as severally necessary but jointly sufficient reasons. The word " consequently " in the above quotation suggests that the reasons are not independent since imaginability entails self-consistency. Hume's argument might then be reconstructed as follows: " not-*p* is imaginable " is not, indeed, synonymous with " not-*p* is (logically) possible," yet the former function entails the latter, and the latter *is* synonymous with " *p* is factual (contingent) ." That Hume, indeed, considers the imaginability of not-*p* as a sufficient *reason* for the (logical) possibility of not-*p*, which latter is equivalent to the denial of the necessity of *p*, is further substantiated by the passage in the *Treatise* in which it is argued that no sort of proof of the principle of the uniformity of nature is possible:

> Our foregoing method of reasoning will easily convince us, that there can be no *demonstrative* arguments to prove, *that those instances, of which we have had no experience, resemble those, of which we have had experience.* We can at least conceive a change in the course of nature; which sufficiently proves, that such a change is not absolutely impossible. To form a clear idea of any thing, is an undeniable argument for its possibility, and is alone a refutation of any pretended demonstration against it [Pt. III, sec. 6].

I propose to show, now, that Hume is caught in a dilemma. Either " possible " is meant in the wide sense of " not self-contradictory " or in the narrower sense of " imaginable." [3] If the former, then " not-*p* is possible " does not entail that *p* is contingent; and if the latter, then imaginability of not-*p*, being *synonymous* with the possibility of that state of affairs, cannot be a *reason* by which the latter could be proved; in other words, if the latter, then Hume's

---

[3] Since " *p* is imaginable " resolves into " it is possible to imagine *p*," there must indeed be a third sense of " possible ": for if " possible " in this context meant " imaginable," " *p* is imaginable " would resolve into an infinite stutter " it is imaginable that it is imaginable that . . ."; and if it meant " not self-contradictory " then it would be difficult to show that a proposition which is not self-contradictory is nonetheless unimaginable. But an enumeration of *all* the senses of " possible " is not required by the above argument.

" proof " of the contingency of *p* is a *petitio principii*. In order to explain why I deny that " not-*p* is not self-contradictory " entails " *p* is contingent," I shall consider a proposition which Kant held to be both necessary (a priori) and synthetic, i. e. not logically demonstrable: space has three dimensions. Indeed, the confusion of Hume's which I wish to expose is simply the failure to distinguish the pairs " necessary—contingent " (or " a priori—empirical ") and " analytic—synthetic," as evidenced by his tendency to identify *imaginability* and *logical consistency* of a proposition.

Kant pointed out, in the *Prolegomena*, that the tridimensionality of space follows from the proposition " that not more than three lines can intersect at right angles in one point," which latter proposition is synthetic, i. e. not logically demonstrable. Those who reject the synthetic a priori will say, of course, that if the proposition is not logically demonstrable, then it is contingent. But if it were an empirical generalization, then its probability would be, or at least might be, increased by multiplication of confirming instances. Yet a man who wandered from place to place equipped with three straight rods and an instrument for measuring angles, repeating the experiment designed to test the tridimensionality of space, would surely be laughed at just as much as a man who went about confirming the law of the excluded middle by examining object after object in order to make sure that, for every given property, it either has it or does not have it. Hume himself would surely have admitted that this proposition is necessary, since one cannot imagine an exception to it; but had he properly distinguished, like Kant, the unimaginable from the logically contradictory, he would have agreed with Kant that it is synthetic a priori. At this point an advocate of the principle of logical empiricism " either analytically true or contingently true " might urge a distinction between the possibility of *imagining* an exception to a generalization and the possibility of describing an *operational test* a negative outcome of which would disprove the generalization. In a recent, suggestive paper, " Could Space be Four-dimensional? " (*Mind*, July 1952), Honor Brotman argues, indeed, that such an operational test of the tridimensionality of space can be described. The author gives an ingenious non-metrical definition of " square angle " as an angle whose " base can form a straight line together with the base of another angle if the backs of the two angles are placed together, provided also that this other angle can be made to fit the first angle." The author then asserts it to be an *empirical fact* " that only three lines can be put mutually at right angles, for we can discover experimentally only, that if we have two square angles AOB and COD, then there is but one way in which they can be placed so that one arm of each angle touches the other, and the other two arms together contain a square angle in a plane perpendicular to the touching arms." Brotman then argues that the following experience would refute, or at least might be interpreted as refuting, the generalization in question. Imagine a corner of a cube and the three mutually perpendicular edges meeting in that corner. Suppose, now, that we lay one end of a straight rod on that same corner in such a way that the rod forms angles with the three edges of the cube, and suppose that by the superposition test of equality of angles these angles turn out to be equal to the angles formed by the intersecting edges of the cube; then this rod might be concluded to be perpendicular to each of the mutually perpendicular edges. The author admits, indeed, that this conclusion would not be inevitable; after all, any test of congruence by superposition of a pair of angles presupposes that the angles remained equal to themselves in being moved about, so we might say that " although we haven't noticed, in moving the angles up to be compared, they have opened out slightly." Yet Brotman's contention is that we would at any rate have a *choice*: " either we can declare that the rods have become distorted, or we can speak about four rods mutually at square angles."

Now, if by saying that we *might* speak of four mutually perpendicular straight lines is meant that such an expression is not self-contradictory—agreed. But when the author jumps from here to the conclusion that it is a *question of empirical fact* whether space is four-dimensional, she presupposes that only contingent propositions can be synthetic. A Kantian might reply as follows: " It is just because such four-dimensionality is unimaginable, although the operational conception of four-dimensionality just reproduced is not logically inconsistent, that the inference to an unnoticed opening out of the angles would be *necessary*. To present an analogy: suppose that two observers interested in testing the Euclidean proposition that two straight lines cannot enclose a space (cf. above, Chap. 2, sec. C) started off from a common point of departure on rectilinear divergent journeys, and to their amazement found themselves meeting again. Would they have a *choice* between declaring the Euclidean proposition refuted or questioning the assumption that they travelled in a straight line? Not at all; for just because they could not imagine two real straight lines having two points in common, they would be forced to question the assumption. To be sure, it will be retorted (see above, p. 40) that "real straight line" here can only mean "Euclidean straight line," and that the latter term is implicitly defined by a set of axioms including the proposition in question, and that therefore the proposition would be saved by the force of *definitions*, not by the force of intuitive evidence. But it must be admitted that the "definitions" here are nothing else than axioms which are the verbal expression of geometrical intuitions. The non-Euclidean sets of axioms, after all, arose not as formal expressions of geometrical intuitions different from those glorified by Kant, but as purely formal denials of uninterpreted postulates. And to the extent that the non-Euclidean alternatives, such as several straight lines passing through a given pair of points, can be *visualized*, the visualizable meaning of "straight line" is such that the *proposition* one is imagining (e. g. many great arcs on a spherical surface passing through pairs of polar opposites) is perfectly compatible with the Euclidean proposition.

The foregoing reflections do not, indeed, refute the—currently fashionable—position that a proposition should be classified as contingent if the only source of its certainty is our inability to *imagine* its falsehood (although, as was already indicated in Chapters 1 and 2, the identification of necessary propositions with analytic propositions in the Leibniz-Kant sense of "analytic" is untenable on other grounds). However, such examples of intuitively necessary statements as "space is three-dimensional" do show that Hume's imaginability criterion of necessity leaves it at least an open question whether a given proposition may not be both synthetic and necessary: Hume's criterion certainly committed him to classifying this proposition as necessary, yet *it does not follow* from its being necessary in Hume's sense that it is analytic.

Let us turn now to the question of the adequacy of Hume's imaginability criterion. There are a number of formidable *prima facie* objections. First, why could not a proposition which is wholly unimaginable for all human beings nevertheless be true? Consider, for example, the proposition "there are sounds whose pitch is higher than the highest pitch audible (and accordingly imaginable) by human beings, and those sounds are sometimes heard by dogs." There is in fact empirical evidence for the truth of this proposition: the response of dogs to whistles that produce air vibrations of such high frequency that the corresponding pitch is inaudible by the human ear. But the statement which is thus empirically confirmable describes a literally unimaginable state of affairs. Similarly, it would be impossible, on Hume's theory, that there should exist in the universe colors which nobody has ever seen; for one cannot imagine a color that one has not seen, hence such a universe is unimaginable, and for Hume unimaginability equals impossibility. But it surely is not self-contradictory to suppose that there exist objects which have not been seen by anybody and which have a color different from any color that has been seen.

That Hume accepted not only the entailment from " *p* is imagin-able " to " *p* is possible " (in the sense of " possible " which is used to define contingency), but also the converse entailment from " *p* is possible " to " *p* is imaginable," comes out clearly in his critique of the notion of infinitesimal quantities, such as infinitesimal lengths and durations: " if it be a contradiction to suppose, that a finite extension contains an infinite number of parts, no finite extension can be infinitely divisible. But that this latter supposition is absurd, I easily convince myself by the consideration of my clear ideas " (Pt. II, sec. 2). Hume then argues in effect that since the smallest imaginable length is still finite, an infinitely repeated juxtaposition of that length to itself would yield an infinite length, which contra-dicts the hypothesis. In the first place, his argument is based on inconsistent premises. For he infers, on the one hand, that we lack an *idea* of infinitesimal length from our inability to *imagine* one, but implicitly grants, on the other hand, that we have an idea of infinitely great length, which is equally unimaginable. But secondly, Hume made an unnecessary detour: without detouring over the infinitely great, he might as well have said directly that we cannot imagine infinitesimal length and that such things *there-fore* cannot exist. For even though what he refers to as " an establish'd maxim in metaphysics ": that " *whatever the mind clearly conceives includes the idea of possible existence,* or in other words (sic!), *that nothing we imagine is absolutely impossible,*" corres-ponds only to the first of the above entailments, his illustration shows

that he also maintained the converse entailment: " We can form
the idea of a golden mountain, and from thence conclude that such
a mountain may actually exist (first entailment). We can form no
idea of a mountain without a valley,[4] and therefore regard it as
impossible " (converse entailment).

How was Hume misled to this absurd identification of the logically
possible with the imaginable? I think the impasse may be traced
back to two errors: first, he tended to misread, in the heat of his
animated critique of abstractions, his own principle " all *simple*
ideas are derived from corresponding impressions" as "all ideas are
derived from corresponding impressions."[5] This led him to conclude fallaciously from the premise that a given designative expression does not denote anything that can be imagined that it has no
sense at all, in other words, that it does not stand for a genuine
idea; whereas his principle as originally stated justifies this inference
only with regard to designative expressions that are not composed
of designative expressions and that are not translatable into compound designative expressions. Take, for example, the expression
" pitch higher than the highest pitch audible by the human ear."
The terms " pitch," " higher pitch," " audible," " human ear " *are*
ostensively definable and thus capable of calling up mental images;
but the compound expression does not have this property, and had
Hume been faithful to his original intention he would not have
denied it a sense for this reason. The second error is the error of
supposing that " p is meaningless " entails " p is necessarily false.'
This is, of course, erroneous, since if a sentence is meaningless,
then neither falsehood nor truth is significantly predicable of it.
But Hume, like Berkeley, frequently confused meaninglessness and
self-contradiction. To take Hume's own example (borrowed from
Descartes) of the mountain without valley: for Hume the expression " mountain without valley " has no sense at all, just like the
expression " infinitesimal length " (here the first error is committed,
the extension of the condition of significance for simple designators

---

[4] This seems to be a slip of the pen, copied from Descartes, for " valley without a
mountain."

[5] " No discovery could have been made more happily for deciding all controversies
concerning ideas, than that above-mentioned, that impressions always take the prece-
dency of them, and that every idea, with which the imagination is furnished, first
makes its appearance in a correspondent impression " (Pt. II, sec. 3).

to analyzable designators) ; for, since Hume does not distinguish the conceivable from the imaginable, his assertion that a mountain without valley is unimaginable means just that. But then he infers that no such object *exists*, which inference presupposes that it is false, not meaningless, to say " there exist mountains without valleys." But if " *p* is necessarily false (or expresses an 'absolute impossibility')" is equated with " *p* is meaningless," then we are driven, by the principle that if a sentence is meaningless so is its negation,[6] to the conclusion that there are no necessary propositions, or more accurately, that sentences purporting to express necessary propositions do not express propositions at all. Since this entails that it is inappropriate to speak of " knowledge " of mathematical propositions, it thus appears that Hume's imaginability criterion of logical possibility combined with his uncritical use of the principle that genuine ideas are " copies " of impressions drives him into a position contradictory to the one he explicitly took: that there is such a thing as knowledge of necessary propositions, though of a radically different sort from empirical knowledge. At any rate Hume, unaware, committed himself to one or the other of equally indefensible positions: that some propositions for which there is empirical evidence are logically impossible (as illustrated by the example on p. 79), or that there are only contingent propositions, that statements purporting to express necessary propositions cannot be meaningfully denied and are therefore themselves meaningless.

If one considers that Hume did nothing less than assign to man's power of imagination the exalted role of the *measure of logical possibility*, one will understand that Kant's admiration for Hume must have been inspired by more than his " inimitable style." For Hume went far beyond Kant's view that physical space cannot have properties which go against our mode of spatial intuition: he held virtually that it is meaningless to speak of unimaginable universes. Let us return at this point to the problem of four-dimensional space. It cannot be reasonably doubted that Hume would have rejected this speculation as meaningless and, committing the subtle inconsistency exposed above, would have pronounced the existence of such

---

[6] If " *p* is meaningful " is defined as " *p* is either true or false," this principle is easily proved. For by the laws of excluded middle and contradiction, " *p* is true or false " is equivalent to " not-*p* is true or false," and by negating both sides of a valid equivalence another valid equivalence is obtained.

a universe as "absolutely impossible." *Is* the speculation meaningless? When Einstein and other relativistic cosmologists say that by the statement that space is "curved" they mean no more than that (indirect) measurement of large volumes yields values deviating from the Euclidean values (e. g. from the Euclidean value for the volume of a sphere), it may well be that they are motivated to this disclaimer by the fear of being accused of meaningless speculation. But consider Poincaré's fiction of the two-dimensional beings who live on a spherical surface and verify by measurements that the surface they inhabit is non-Euclidean, "curved," even though they cannot *imagine* a third dimension into which the surface they inhabit is curved. The expression "third dimension" is as meaningless for them as color terms are for blind people, and if a speculating cosmologist among them offered to explain the verified non-Euclideanism of their two-dimensional world by the hypothesis that their world is embedded in 3-dimensional space, he would presumably be derided for talking meaningless metaphysics, if those beings had been reared in a Humean epistemology which identifies the conceivable with the imaginable. As far as I can see, this analogy serves the speculating cosmologist who believes in a four-dimensional universe, manifesting itself in the intrinsic non-Euclideanism of three-dimensional space, as an unbreakable line of defense against the accusation of talking nonsense. Notice that if the expression "fourth spatial dimension" be held to be meaningless for X because what it designates is unimaginable for X, then "fifth sense" would have to be argued to be meaningless for a blind man who possesses all senses but the visual; and even "color never seen by anybody" would then be meaningless for visually normal people. But provided there have been impressions of *some* colors, the word "color" stands for a genuine *idea* (or is meaningful), by Hume's theory of meaning; and similarly, the word "sense" is meaningful for the blind man, since it is ostensively definable via touching, smelling, hearing etc. to him, and so "fifth sense" must be conceded to have a meaning for him. Substitute "dimension" for the words "color" and "sense" and it will become clear, *mutatis mutandis*, that a *consistent* adherence to his theory of meaning should have led Hume to grant the logical possibility of unimaginable states of affairs. Consequently the Humean inference of "p is necessary" from "not-p is unimaginable" is invalid on Hume's own theory of meaning, for the latter allows for complex ideas whose referents are unimaginable.

D. The Heritage of " Psychologism "

It should be noted, however, that if Hume ever fell into a sorrowful mood over the contemplation of the strange consequences of his " psychologistic " criterion (as it is nowadays derogatorily called) of necessity, he might have comforted himself by noting that his adversary Kant was in no better position. For, throwing off the pathos of obscurity that glorifies Kant's idiom, we might express his argument for the *necessity* of the Euclidean character of physical space simply as follows: we cannot *imagine* a space in which two straight lines meet again, in which more than one straight line passes through a pair of points etc.; therefore such a space *cannot exist* (or, if we *postulate* such a space, we postulate a " Ding an sich " which is not a possible object of empirical knowledge.). We might say that, as regards synthetic propositions, the necessary—contingent distinction was for both Hume and Kant relative to human powers of imagination, and inasmuch as it seems to be a contingent fact that human beings have the powers of imagination that they have (just as it is a contingent fact that the congenitally blind—in the physiological sense of " blind "—cannot imagine colors), the inference from " *p* is necessary " in their sense to " the state of affairs *p exists* (or *is true*) " seems precarious. In other words, the imaginability criterion of necessity seems to be inconsistent with the necessary proposition that whatever is necessarily the case, must be the case. Locke's position with regard to " psychologism " was a curious, intermediate one: he followed Leibniz in contemplating the possibility that a proposition which for us is contingent, insofar as the only ground on which we believe it is inductive generalization, may be seen to be necessary by superior minds; yet, on the other hand, it never occurred to him that a proposition which for us is necessary in the psychologistic sense (self-evident) may be found false by a superior intelligence (such as a four-dimensional being!). The serious problem, then, which all these philosophers bequeathed to their philosophical posterity is the problem of a nonpsychologistic explication of the necessary—contingent distinction. And it is because the concept of logical inconsistency, which Hume, unlike Kant, did not sharply distinguish from the concept of unimaginability, seems to be more "objective" than the latter concept (according to Leibniz even God does not have the power to violate the laws of logic), that we find in contemporary analytic philosophy a strong tendency to return to Leibniz' identification of necessary truth with analytic truth.

However, before embarking on a detailed scrutiny of the attempts of modern analytic philosophers to "depsychologize" the concept of necessary truth, one more word about a characteristic dialectic method of Hume's and its remarkable similarity to a contemporary method of analysis. In showing that there is no rational ground for believing in the uniformity of nature and in universal causation, Hume used, as we have seen, this method: If p were a necessary truth, then the supposition of p's falsehood would imply a contradiction; but not-p does not imply a contradiction; therefore p is not a necessary truth. The very same method is widely used by contemporary analysts to test proposed analyses of concepts. For example, pragmatist philosophers of science usually maintain that "T is true," where T is a scientific theory, means nothing else than "T is highly confirmed by observational/experimental data"; from which analysis it follows at once that truth as predicated of scientific theories is *relative* to a given time. But those who reject this analysis would do so on the ground that if the analysis were correct, then "if and only if T is true, then T is highly confirmed" would express a necessary proposition, and if so, it would be self-contradictory to suppose that there is a true theory which is not highly confirmed, or a false theory which is highly confirmed. And since the supposition is in their judgment evidently not self-contradictory, they reject the analysis. The problem raised by this method of testing analyses is what "self-contradictory" means in this context and how a disagreement as to whether a given supposition is self-contradictory could be objectively resolved. Obviously, if "p is self-contradictory" meant "a contradiction is deducible from p on the basis of an adequate analysis of the relevant concept," then the whole method would be circular. Some analysts would say that the term "self-contradictory statement" makes sense only relative to a given language, where "language" means a system of rules, including definitions of the definable terms. They would, naturally, disown the described method, since it is based on what might be called an *absolute* concept of self-contradiction.

Here, then, is another serious problem which contemporary analysts have inherited from Hume. It will occupy us again at several places in Part Two, especially in the two concluding chapters.

The Concept of Analytic Truth in Contemporary Analytic Philosophy

THAT all necessary (or " a priori ") propositions are analytic, and that accordingly all synthetic propositions must be validated empirically, is a tenet which, at least in part, defines modern empiricism, and thus characterizes this philosophical movement as a reaction against Kantian epistemology—though, on the other hand, it is also continuous with Kant insofar as it inherited from him (1) the distinctions which are necessary for the formulation of its own credo, (2) the general philosophical task of reflecting on " the conditions of the possibility of knowledge," or of " logical reconstruction of knowledge," as this enterprise is nowadays called. However, as the method of analysis has increased in subtlety or sophistication, it has become evident that such a formula, like so many philosophical formulae that are continually used to identify " schools," has a deceptive verbal simplicity which conceals a conceptual muddle.

In the first place, the term " analytic " is sometimes used in the strict sense of demonstrability on the basis of definitions and principles of logic, sometimes in a broader sense which is often expressed as " certifiable as true by reflection upon meanings alone." It is argued in Chapter 5, in connection with an examination of C. I. Lewis' painstaking attempt to prove that all a priori truth is analytic, that the broader sense of " analytic " is not distinguishable at all from the sense of " a priori," so that by this interpretation the empiricist thesis is true but trivial. If, on the other hand, the strict sense is intended, then the latter is confronted by insuperable difficulties: (1) the concept of " logical truth " itself can be clarified only by presupposing an understanding of " entailment," hence of " necessary truth " (this is argued in detail in Chapter 6, in the course of an examination of the standard definitions of " logical truth," especially Carnap's definition) ; therefore the clarification achieved by substituting " analytic " for " necessary " is illusory. (2) If " analytic " is to be a term of interest to epistemology (not just to formal logic) , then, as Lewis has emphasized, the definitions which are to enable such formal demonstration must be qualified *as explicative statements. But characterization of the latter as themselves strictly analytic leads not only to an infinite regress of validation but also to the paradox of analysis. This paradox comes in for detailed discussion in Chapter 10. (3) There are necessary statements, of the " no surface is both blue and red all over at the same time" variety, which could not possibly be shown to be strictly analytic because their predicates designate unanalyzable properties. Much as an empiricist may frown at such claims of absolute unanalyzability (especially if, as is argued in Chapter 9, this turns out to be a psychological concept—" psychologism " again!), he will have to live with them if he accepts the old logical atomism which still underlies Carnap's recent* Grundlegung *of both deductive and inductive logic in terms of " state descriptions."*

That the slogan " all necessary truths are analytic " cannot really serve to define, even in part, a unified philosophical school is further evident if we consider that it leaves the important question of " conventionalism " with regard to necessary propositions entirely open. Thus Lewis holds that analytic truth is in no intelligible sense grounded in linguistic conventions, whereas most empiricists would incline toward some form of a linguistic theory of necessary truth. This question is under discussion in Chapter 7. The central issue here is whether the statement that a given proposition is necessary is, if true, itself necessary (an issue occasionally discussed in connection with modal logic), or whether it is a contingent statement about linguistic usage. It is argued that conventionalism is closely allied with the latter position, which however arises from a confusion between " the sentence S, as presently used, expresses a necessary proposition " and " the proposition which happens to be expressed at present by S is necessary." Yet, once the question of conventionalism is dissolved by the exposition of this subtle confusion, there remains a sense of intellectual discomfort about the apparent postulation of propositions as abstract entities. Although the position is taken, in opposition to the thesis of extensionality, that statements about propositions are not translatable into statements about sentences, it is maintained that the conception of propositions as possible objects of belief (and other cognitive attitudes) need involve no mystical platonism.

For a logical empiricist, belief in synthetic a priori knowledge is tantamount to confusion of the a priori and the factual. This dualism, expressed by the dictum " necessary statements say nothing about reality," is found to be undermined by three central notions developed by empiricists themselves for the purpose of logical reconstruction of scientific knowledge: ostensive definition, implicit definition, and reduction sentence. How the thesis, which is unobjectionable enough, that all meaning derives from ostensive definition of primitive predicates plays havoc with the conception of analytic statements as devoid of existential import, is shown in Chaper 9. The notion of implicit definition, which stems from the axiomatization of formal sciences, has recently been dragged into the logical reconstruction of empirical science as well. Not only are the entities postulated by a physical theory, like electrons, said to be implicitly defined by the axioms of the theory, but necessary statements involving simple descriptive predicates are characterized as somehow " implicitly " definitional. As argued in Chapter 8, this stretching of the notion of definition (and thereby of the notion of analyticity) saves the exhaustiveness of the disjunction " either analytically true or contingently true " only at the cost of destroying its exclusiveness. In this respect the most critical of the three critical notions is perhaps that of reduction sentence; the special problems raised by it, especially the question of whether the analytic-synthetic distinction is best construed, at least in certain contexts, as a distinction of degree, are discussed in Chapter 11.

Chapter 10 contains a discussion of the related notions of analysis and synonymy. It is urged that analyses (the modern counterpart of " real definitions ") are about concepts and cannot be construed as empirical statements about synonymous usage of expressions. The notion of identity as applied to concepts (or attributes) leads, however, to the paradox of analysis. As this paradox arises from the requirement of universal substitutivity of names of identical entities, even in nonextensional contexts, a relaxation of this requirement is just the needed cure. But then philosophical analysis will have to operate with a notion of degrees of synonymy (or identity of concepts). This conclusion foreshadows a " gradualism " with respect to the necessary-contingent and analytic-synthetic distinctions as argued for in Chapter 11.

The controversy about phenomenalism seems to have reached in recent years an impasse: it has come to be realized that no sense-statements are analytically entailed by physical statements, but, on the other hand, there seems to be no other way of specifying what physical terms mean except by pointing to possible sense experience; analogous considerations apply to the language of theoretical "constructs" in relation to the "thing language" (as Carnap calls the prescientific language of everyday life), and the "mentalistic" language of introspective psychology in relation to the language of physiology and behavioristics. It is argued in Chapter 11 that the root of the trouble is the attempt to force statements involving "open" concepts into the analytic-synthetic dichotomy. Instead it should be recognized that an implication may serve to (partially) explicate a concept even though it has a probabilistic character. It is shown that this kind of "gradualism" is already implicit in Carnap's theory of reduction sentences. It is further argued that the concept of "reduction sentence," construed as a kind of interpretative probability implication, enables a better understanding of scientific procedures, especially the procedure of "operational definition" in physics and psychology, than does the contrast analytic-synthetic.

Since the concept of entailment (and the related concepts of self-contradiction and logical incompatibility) is the primary tool by means of which analytic philosophers undertake to analyse concepts— as is amply illustrated in Chapter 13—one might justly complain that analytic philosophy is an obscure enterprise as long as the meaning of "entailment" remains obscure. Chapter 12 addresses itself to the charge that the foregoing analysis is relevant only to the pragmatic meaning of this fundamental logical constant and leaves us in the dark about its semantic meaning. The answer is given that a semantic interpretation of (relative to a given calculus) primitive logical constants—like "(logically) possible" or "not"—, in the sense of analytic definitions in terms of vocabulary intelligible to one who does not already understand them, is impossible. On the other hand, while the related terms "possible," "necessary," "entailment" are conceded to have only pragmatic meaning in some contexts, the thesis of Chapter 7 that "necessary" sometimes stands for an intrinsic property of propositions is reaffirmed, with special reference to those formal entailments in accordance with which we draw deductive inferences.

In Chapters 13 and 14 the "absolute" use of the concepts of entailment and self-contradiction which is characteristic especially of English analytic philosophy is defended against the "formalist" position that these concepts can be significantly used only relative to a language system. It is chiefly by means of intuitive judgments of entailment that the "explicandum" of a given explication is identified. Such insights into meanings lead to formulation of criteria of adequacy, i.e. necessary statements involving the explicandum which must be formally demonstrable on the basis of an adequate explication. Clearly, explication could never get started at all if one withheld assent to the necessity of such statements until an adequate explication is produced. And since the necessary statements in question are of the intuitively evident kind, disagreement about them at the start of an explication is indicative of a difference of interpretation, i.e. that the disputants have different explicanda in mind. In the course of Chapter 13 there is also a resumption of central questions about analysis and necessity which came up in earlier chapters. (1) How can we know the truth-value of a proposition before we know its analysis? (2) What is wrong with the conception of analysis as empirical investigation of linguistic usages? (3) How can we justify a procedure implicitly followed by many "philosophers of ordinary usage," to lay down as criterion of adequacy of an explication of a concept that there should exist instances to which the concept applies? (4) What can we make of the view that a correct analysis must describe the usual method of coming to know that the analyzed concept applies in a given case (criterion of "epistemic adequacy")? Tentative answers to these tricky questions are given within the framework of a conception of philosophical analysis as a mixture of intuition, concept-construction, and formal deduction which should not be confused with empirical sociology or with formal logic or with introspectionist psychology.

The book closes with a critique of "logical relativism," viz. the view that "p entails q" makes sense only if it is elliptical for "p entails q in language-system L." The main point of this critique is that the very choice of an adequate language system as framework for explications presupposes judgments of entailment and incompatibility which cannot, on pain of infinite regress, in turn be relativized to a language system. In this connection the thesis is reaffirmed that modal statements are not translatable into an extensional metalanguage and that in this sense the logical modalities are intrinsic properties of propositions.

CHAPTER 5. *Analytic Truth and*
A Priori Knowledge

A. Is "All A Priori Truths Are Analytic" Synthetic?

ONE of the theses that seem to define the rather loosely used word "empiricism," and at any rate the less loosely used expression "logical empiricism," is that all a priori truth is analytic; which thesis is, of course, equivalent to denying that there are synthetic a priori truths. Since the advocates of this thesis assume that the analytic-synthetic distinction is clear, they will surely permit it as a clear and legitimate question whether the universal proposition they assert is itself analytic or synthetic. It is true that according to Russell's theory of types no proposition may make an assertion about itself. Thus, if we observe this ruling, we may not deduce from " all necessary [1] propositions are analytic " that this very proposition is analytic if it is necessary. But no logical empiricist would acquiesce in the admission that at least one necessary proposition of second order (i. e. a proposition about propositions which themselves do not refer to propositions) is synthetic. There are no doubt some members of the school who would advance the thesis as no more than an inductive generalization. Their attitude is that if anyone claims there are synthetic a priori truths, it is for him to produce examples; and they feel confident that no matter which candidate is proposed, they could show (given sufficient time and analytic skill) that it is either analytic or else not a necessary proposition. However, some have made the far stronger assertion that there *can* be no synthetic a priori truths, that to say there are such is as self-contradictory as to say that there are square circles. Schlick, the founder of the Vienna Circle, is unambiguous on this point: " The empiricism which I advocate believes it to be clear that all propositions are, in principle, either synthetic a posteriori or tautological; synthetic propositions a priori seem to it to

[1] "A priori " and " necessary " are here used synonymously.

94

constitute a *logical impossibility*" (*Gesammelte Aufsätze*, Vienna, 1938, p. 25, translation and italics mine).

Obviously, whether this strong thesis can be maintained depends on what meanings are assigned to the terms "analytic," "synthetic," "a priori," "empirical" (a more customary synonym for Kant's "a posteriori"). Since "analytic-synthetic" and "a priori-empirical" are commonly intended as pairs of contradictories,[2] it will be sufficient to give independent definitions for two out of this quartet of terms, say "analytic" and "a priori," or "synthetic" and "empirical." Some writers define "synthetic" independently of "analytic" in a way which turns it into a synonym for "empirical," and clearly such a usage entails the logical impossibility of synthetic a priori truths. But it is surely absurd to define a traditional term in such a way that, on the basis of the definition, a traditional question formulated by means of that term becomes nonsensical, and then to announce that analysis has revealed the nonsensicalness of the traditional question. It will, therefore, be more profitable to regard "synthetic" as a synonym for "not analytic and not self-contradictory," and to examine whether the independent definitions of "analytic" and "a priori" commonly given warrant Schlick's thesis of the logical impossibility of the synthetic a priori.

The following definition of "a priori," as predicable of propositions, seems to combine clarity with conformity to traditional usage: "A proposition is said to be true *a priori* if its truth can be ascertained by examination of the proposition alone or if it is deducible from propositions whose truth is so ascertained, and by examination of nothing else" (Ambrose and Lazerowitz, *Fundamentals of Symbolic Logic*, p. 17).[3] Now, it is important to note, in connection with the question at issue, that such a definition of "a priori" is silent about the *reason why* any propositions are accepted as true

[2] As pointed out above, p. 46, "synthetic" is the contradictory of "analytic" only if self-contradictory statements are classified as analytic. A good term to use for this inclusive sense of "analytic" is Carnap's "*L*-determinate."

[3] I prefer it to C. I. Lewis' definition "that knowledge whose correctness can be assured without reference to any particular experience of sense" (*An Analysis of Knowledge and Valuation*, p. 35) not just because "assuring the correctness of knowledge" sounds like "assuring the foursidedness of a square," but because "a priori" is here negatively defined in terms of "experience of sense," which term badly needs clarification: is introspection, for example, included in "experience of sense," or the occurrence of moral sentiments? The latter question is particularly pertinent in connection with the problem of a priori knowledge of ethical propositions.

without any appeal to empirical evidence; in ascribing the property " a priori " to a proposition we merely state that it is true regardless of what the empirical facts may be and so could not be refuted by any empirical facts, leaving it an open question what the source of our cognitive satisfaction is. The theory that all a priori truth is analytic must be understood as an answer to just this question— " what is the source of a priori knowledge? "—which claims to avoid the metaphysical mystery in which Kant's answer was wrapped. The reason why such sentences as " all bachelors are unmarried," " $2 + 2 = 4$ " must be accepted as true as soon as they are understood, says our theory, is that their denial would involve an *inconsistent use of words*. Since, e. g., " some bachelors are married " is synonymous with " some unmarried men are married," one who asserted this could not be using the term " married " consistently. But is there any contradiction in supposing that though a given statement is accepted as true by any rational animal who understands it, regardless of what experience shows to be the case, the reason for such universal acceptance is not the instinctive avoidance of verbal inconsistency? If there is, it still requires to be demonstrated; and if there is not, then the concept of " synthetic a priori truth " is by no means self-contradictory.

The source of the view that the synthetic a priori is a square circle, which is rather popular among contemporary analytic philosophers, is probably a shift of meaning of the term " analytic " from the original restricted sense which Kant gave it to the broader and looser sense " true by virtue of *meanings* alone." To say that S is true by virtue of the meanings of its constituent terms can only mean that an honest denial of S implies (given correct employment of rules of deduction) *misinterpretation* of S. But analyticity in this broad sense does not imply analyticity in the strict sense, viz. reducibility to logical truths. We have seen (Chap. 2, B) that Kant's definition of analytic truth as truth certifiable by the principle of contradiction alone is best clarified as follows: with the help of adequate definitions S can be transformed into a synonymous sentence S' of such a kind that " not-S' " logically entails a contradiction,[4] i. e. a sentence of the form " p and not-p." Now, there is no

---

[4] If the reader will keep in mind that the concept of analytic truth is here sharply distinguished from the concept of logical truth—contrary to frequent confusions of the two—he will not feel tempted to condemn this definition as circular.

obvious guarantee that if *S* expresses in a language *L* an a priori truth in the sense defined (i. e. it would not occur to anybody who understands *L* to either defend or refute *S* by an appeal to empirical evidence), then it is analytic in the defined restricted sense.

It is noteworthy that the most elaborate attempt to *prove* the thesis of the analyticity of all a priori truth, viz. C. I. Lewis' in *An Analysis of Knowledge and Valuation*, is vitiated by just such a shift from the wide to the strict sense of "analytic." [5] Let us take a close look at the way Lewis initially formulates the question whether all a priori truth is analytic (the affirmative answer to which question constitutes one of the main theses of his book):

> All analytic statements are, obviously, true *a priori*; whatever is determinable as true by reference exclusively to the meanings of expressions used, is independent of any empirical fact. That the converse relation also holds; that whatever is knowable *a priori*, including the principles of logic and all that logic can certify, is also analytic, is not so obvious. It has, of course, frequently been denied; most notably in the Kantian doctrine which makes *synthetic a priori* truth fundamental for mathematics and for principles of the knowledge of nature [p. 35].

It will strike the attentive reader at once that Lewis' implied definition of "analytic" here corresponds closely to the definition of "a priori" that was approvingly quoted above. Since at the same time he emphasizes that the proposition "all a priori truth is analytic" is, unlike its converse, not self-evident, he ought to provide us with a clearly *different* definition of "a priori." Now there is, indeed, a verbal difference in the definitions of "analytic" and "a priori": an a priori truth is defined as one that is "independent of any empirical fact." Yet, what precisely are we to understand by the statement that *p* is "independent of any empirical fact"? Does it mean that *p* could not conceivably be false? But how is this different from saying that analysis of *p*, supplemented if necessary by application of the apparatus of formal logic, is sufficient for determining *p* as true? Suppose that somebody who

[5] In spite of the critique of Lewis contained in the following pages, I am greatly indebted to him in another respect, viz. for his lucid attack on "conventionalism" with respect to necessary propositions.

did not understand the meaning of " empirical fact " asked: " Isn't it an empirical fact that all cats are animals? But surely the truth of the statement ' all cats are animals ' depends on that fact? " He would, of course, be answered by pointing out that " all cats are animals " does *not* express an empirical fact—which is equivalent to saying that this statement is not empirical. Thus it turns out that, unless the definiens already used for " analytic " is used again for " a priori," the latter term is negatively defined as " not empirical." There would, indeed, be no objection to such a negative definition if a satisfactory positive definition of " empirical " were at hand.

There are three positive definitions of " empirical " (or its synonyms " contingent," " factual ") [6] that are widely adopted: (1) a proposition which, if true, *might conceivably* be false, and if false, might conceivably be true; (2) a proposition which is not true (respectively false) in all *possible worlds*; (3) a proposition whose truth-value can be ascertained only by experience. The first definition is particularly reminiscent of Hume, the second of Leibniz (and, via its semanticized twin, of Carnap). Now, it will be remembered from our discussion of Hume that Hume does not use the term " conceivable " at all clearly and univocally, and the same is true to a large measure of those contemporary philosophers who explain their usage of " empirical " by means of the first definition. Specifically, it is not clear whether " the falsehood of p is conceivable " means " not-p is self-consistent " (i. e. no contradiction is logically deducible from not-p) or has a narrower meaning, say " not-p is imaginable." If the former sense is intended, then " empirical " has been defined as the contradictory of " analytic " in the strict sense, the sense which is defined in terms of " logical truth." But in that case " a priori," the contradictory of " empirical," is of course synonymous with " analytic "; it is then a tautology to say that all a priori truth is analytic. And if the second sense is intended, then we get Hume's " psychologistic " criterion of contingency in terms of *imaginability* of alternatives, which we have seen to be

[6] It should be noted that I so use " empirical proposition " that " p is empirical " does not follow from " some of the constituent *concepts* in p are empirical." Thus " all cats are animals " does not express an empirical proposition though the concepts " cat " and " animal " are of course empirical.

unsatisfactory—at least pending a more careful analysis of the relevant meaning of "imaginable" (cf. below, p. 218).

The second definition is equally unilluminating. What does "possible" mean in the expression "possible world"? And the ready answer is: a world described by self-consistent [7] statements. Thus "empirical" is once more defined as the contradictory of "analytic" in the strict sense, and not as the contradictory of "a priori," as it should. The Leibnizian conception of truths of reason that hold in all possible worlds has currently recovered prestige among empiricists, owing to Carnap's translation of this conception into the semantic mode of speech. Instead of speaking, ontologically, of truths holding in all possible worlds, one speaks, semantically, of truths holding in all state descriptions which the primitive names and predicates of the given language system allow to be constructed.[8] But, apart from the consideration that we are here investigating the meaning of "empirical," and cognate terms, as predicated of statements of a *natural language*, not as predicated of statements belonging to a language system, Carnap's semantic reconstruction of the Leibnizian concept likewise fails (one is tempted to say, deliberately fails) to provide a distinction between "empirically true" and "true but not logically demonstrable" (i. e. "non-analytic" in the strict sense of "analytic"); [9] hence it is not relevant to our present problem of explicating the "a priori—analytic" distinction, an explication we badly need in order to vindicate Lewis' claim that the thesis of the analyticity of all a priori truth is valid but not trivial.

The third definition of "empirical proposition" is perhaps the

[7] Some may object to the term "self-consistent" on the ground that every statement is consistent with itself. But it seems to be a suitable term to mark out those statements which do not by themselves, without additional premises, entail a contradiction. It is admitted that laws of logic are required as *rules of deduction* for any demonstration of self-inconsistency (cf. p. 75 n.).

[8] For a detailed discussion of Carnap's concept of "*L*-truth," see the following chapter.

[9] The gratuitous character of Carnap's identification of "empirical" truth and "truth which is not logically demonstrable" is noted by Kneale in his penetrating paper "Truths of Logic," *Proceedings of the Aristotelian Society*, new ser. (1946): "But his decision to use the word 'logical' as though it were synonymous with 'a priori'" does not "settle the old dispute about the existence of synthetic a priori truths. If we adopt his usage we merely decree that anyone who wishes to discuss the question with us in future should adopt a new terminology" (p. 230).

most promising, for it turns Lewis' thesis into the thesis that all propositions which *can* be known independently of experience (i. e. a priori propositions) are analytic, which seems to be an interesting, nontautological thing to say. However, when Lewis speaks of analytic " truths," he evidently means (extralinguistic) propositions, not statements, since he emphasizes that analytic truth is independent of linguistic conventions. But then " analytic truth " in the broad sense can only mean truth by virtue of time-independent properties of, and relations between, the concepts (or " meanings," in Lewis' terminology) that are constituent of the proposition. If so, is not " analytic truth " synonymous with " a priori proposition " as defined by Ambrose and Lazerowitz? And is not to say that *p* can be known independently of experience synonymous with saying that nothing else needs to be done in order to assure oneself of the truth of *p* except examining the proposition *p* itself? Thus even our third definition of " empirical " fails to bring out a difference between Lewis' broad concept of analyticity and the concept of a priori truth.

A close examination of Lewis' argument confirms our suspicion that his thesis is either a tautology or else false, and that the appearance of significance arises merely from a covert equivocation. When the ambiguous term is used in one sense, the thesis is a tautology, when in the other sense, it is false, and it is because we are unaware of the equivocation that we delude ourselves into supposing the thesis both true and interesting. Specifically, we have a tautology whenever the terms " analytic " and " a priori " are used synonymously and a falsehood whenever " analytic " assumes the strict sense of " certifiable by logic plus adequate definitions." The following will serve the purpose of exposing the confusion under discussion: " Every analytic statement is such as can be assured, finally, on grounds which include nothing beyond our accepted definitions and the principles of logic. And statements belonging to logic are themselves analytic; hence capable of being certified from the definitive meanings of the constant terms constituent in them and the syntactic relations of these which they express " (p. 96) .

Is capacity of being " assured, finally, on grounds which include nothing beyond our accepted definitions and the principles of logic " a *definition* of " analytic statement " or is it a demonstrable

property of analytic statements? Now, if the former,[10] then it has
not been demonstrated that all a priori truth must be analytic in
this sense; and if the latter, then " analytic " must be used in that
context in the sense of " a priori," and again we have a claim for
which proof is wanting. To get directly at one of the main difficulties: what if the descriptive terms by which a given a priori
truth is expressed have unanalyzable meanings, such as not to admit
of " explicative " definitions? To say that the truth of S can, with
the help of adequate definitions, be assured on the basis of principles
of logic alone can only mean that after elimination of definable
descriptive terms we are left with a substitution-instance (S') of a
principle of logic—which is to say that all primitive descriptive terms
occur *vacuously* in S'. It follows that if color predicates, for example,
are irreducibly primitive (the sort of predicates one expects to find
in Carnapian state descriptions), then such famous a priori truths
as " nothing is simultaneously blue and red all over " could not
possibly be analytic in the strict sense, for replacement of the descriptive predicates " wholly blue " and " wholly red " with predicate
variables does not leave us with a statement form that is true for
all admissible substitutions (in other words, the descriptive terms
occur *essentially* in the statement.)   It is tempting to think that the
qualification " all over " marks such truths as strictly analytic after
all. Does not " x is wholly blue " mean " x is blue and has no other
color, i. e. is not red, not green, etc. (where x is a surface) "? Not so.
For surely a man who had seen no color except blue and hence did
not understand the meaning of " red," " green," etc., could grasp the

[10] At the very end of his chapter 5 Lewis says, indeed, that such a definition of
" analytic " would be circular: " Thus, confronting the question, ' What is analytic
truth and how do we know it?,' any answer supposedly indicated by taking logical
deducibility from definitions as the criterion of the analytic, would be an answer which
is circular. Because the acceptability of a definition depends on its being an analytic
truth. And the validity of any inference from a definition depends upon the analytic
truth of the principles in accordance with which it is drawn " (p. 130). But this
quotation merely shows that Lewis himself is anything but clear as to what exactly
he means by " analytic." For, since analytic truths are at any rate said to have the
mentioned property (though it is not the defining property) , Lewis is committed to
saying that correct explicative definitions as well as principles of logic " can be assured,
finally, on grounds which include nothing beyond our accepted definitions and the
principles of logic." And is it not obvious that this method of validation leads into
infinite regress if it is applied to explicative definitions and principles of logic themselves? (We shall return to this point on p. 103, below.)

intended meaning of the statement " this entire surface is blue "
(we may assume that ostensive definition of " blue " is still possible
even though no instances of "non-blue " could be presented, since
any two objects might differ in other properties P such that we
could say " these two objects are both blue but they differ with
respect to P "). Indeed, the statement simply means " every (discriminable) part of this surface is blue." One could express the
a priori truth in question as "no minimal discriminable part of a
surface is simultaneously blue and red " and thus effectively destroy
the appearance of analyticity.[11]

Another way of putting the matter would be to say that a conjunction like " x is blue and red " is not *formally* contradictory or
transformable into a formal contradiction by substitution of intuitively adequate definientia; and that it therefore cannot possibly be
maintained that the necessary statement " there is no x such that
x is blue and red " (where " x " may be taken to range over space-
time regions) is a *tautology* in the sense in which the early logical
positivists maintained that all necessary truths are tautologies. They
did, indeed, notice the difficulty which statements of this kind
presented for their theory of necessary truth. In particular, the
illustrated incompatibilities between the simple determinates of a
common determinable seemed to refute the doctrine of "logical
atomism " (as Russell called it), according to which logical relations
of entailment and incompatibility are due to the truth-functional
complexity of propositions; from which it follows that atomic
propositions cannot possibly stand in such logical relations to each
other. As reported by Waismann (" Was ist logische Analyse?"
Journal of Unified Science, 1939-40, sec. 7), Wittgenstein saved his
theory by the following reasoning. Let $p = P(a)$, $q = Q(a)$, where
" P " and " Q " are incompatible simple predicates. Now the truth-
table for " $p.q$ " seems to yield the result that this conjunction is
not a contradiction, since it is true in one case, viz. if p and q are
both true. However, it is nevertheless the case that this conjunction
is false for all possible combinations of truth-values of the simple

[11] Reduction to an analytic truth might also be attempted as follows: " x is red "
entails " the color of x resembles red more than it resembles green," and " x is green "
entails " the color of x resembles green more than it resembles red," which consequences are incompatible. But this argument begs the question. Since the triadic
relation " resembling y more than z " is a *primitive* perceptually given relation, the
judgment that it is asymmetrical cannot be strictly analytic.

components, for the case TT just is not a *possible* case. If, accordingly, we strike out the first line of the truth-table, we find that the conjunction *is* a formal contradiction, and the entailment " if p, then not-q " *is* a tautology. Moreover, we then obtain the valid equivalence " $p \equiv (p.-q)$," and thus the principle is saved " that in fact the conclusion of a deduction is contained in the premise." But this is surely no successful defense of the theory that all necessary truths are tautologies and all entailments are formal. For the statement " TT is not a possible case " is precisely the modal statement in question, the statement that the atomic propositions p and q are incompatible. And to argue that recognition of this incompatibility is simply the recognition that " if p, then not-q " is a tautology in the sense of being true in all possible cases would be to commit a glaring *petitio*. Similar a priori truths involving what are *prima facie* unanalyzable descriptive terms are: " Whatever has some shape, has some size, and conversely," " whatever is colored, is extended," " if x is warmer than y, then y is not warmer than x," " if x is earlier than y, then y is not earlier than x." But since the problem of unanalyzable predicates will be specifically discussed in a later chapter,[12] we may address ourselves now to other difficulties involved in Lewis' claim.

B. Are Explicative Definitions and Principles of Logic Analytic?

In criticizing what he calls the " conventionalist " theory of analytic truth, Lewis emphasizes that the *definitions* which give rise to analytic truth in the epistemologically important sense are not arbitrary stipulations but explications of meanings. This " epistemologically important " sense might be indicated by saying that a statement is analytic in that sense if it is true by virtue of correct analyses of the ordinary meanings of its terms. "All men are mortal " could be turned into an analytic truth by arbitrarily defining "man " as " rational, featherless and mortal biped," but unlike " all cats are animals " it is not analytic in the above sense. Lewis distinguishes three senses of " definition ": syntactic statements, like " ' U.S.' abbreviates ' the United States of America,' " semantic statements which "relate a symbol to a meaning" (dictionary definitions),

---

[12] In Chap. 9. See also the remarks on this problem on pp. 153 f., 214 f., 224 f.

and explicative statements which " relate a meaning to a meaning "
and thus are not about symbols at all. It is definitions in the latter
sense that are the source of analytic truth in the sense in question,
and this is the reason why Lewis holds that analytic truth (unlike,
of course, its linguistic expression) is not relative to linguistic rules
at all. A change of linguistic rules entails a change in the sentence
by which an analytic truth is expressed, but it cannot affect the
analytic truth itself. Lewis' point is easily clarified (though such
clarification may reduce it to a truism). If we change our semantic
rules in such a way that " triangle " and " circle " interchange their
meanings, then the sentence " all triangles have three corners "
ceases to express the analytic truth it formerly expressed; the latter
will now be expressed by the sentence " all circles have three
corners." The statements whose truth-value is affected by such
changes of linguistic rules are empirical statements of the form " *S*
expresses, in present usage, an analytic truth." But when I assert
the analytic truth itself, " all triangles have three corners," my assertion is not *about* linguistic usage, though it *expresses* a current
linguistic usage. Hence no change of linguistic usage can change
the truth-value of the statement we intended to make when we said
" all triangles have three corners." It appears, then, that Lewis'
thesis of the nonlinguistic character of analytic truth is merely a
corollary of the truism that the truth-value of a statement *S* does
not depend on the existence or nonexistence of a state of affairs *p*
unless *S* asserts the existence or nonexistence of *p*.[13]

Now, explicative statements, according to Lewis, differ from the
other two kinds of " definitions " not only in not referring to
symbols, but also in being true, or false, *a priori*. Thus, if "a man
is a rational animal " is meant as an explicative statement, then its
proper formulation is " the concept *man* is identical with the concept
rational animal," not " the symbol ' man ' is, as a matter of empirical
fact, used synonymously with the symbol ' rational animal,' " or
" no English speaking person would apply ' man ' to an object which
he does not believe to be a rational animal." If all a priori truth
is strictly analytic, then such true explicative statements will have

---

[13] This *reductio ad trivialitatem* should be regarded as a critique of the "conventionalists " (be they strawmen or real) rather than a critique of Lewis. For it is
useful to assert a truism while trying to show that a given philosophical thesis, often
verbally endorsed, is either meaningless or else trivially obvious.

to be strictly analytic. But does it as much as make sense to say of the statement "the concept *man* is identical with the concept *rational animal*" that it "can be assured on grounds which include nothing beyond our accepted definitions and the principles of logic?" The only way this statement could be validated by logic would be by exhibiting it as a substitution-instance of the law of identity; and in order to do so, one would require as premise a statement which legitimizes the mutual substitution of "the concept *man*" and "the concept *rational animal*." But no other statement could provide a justification of the substitution except the very explicative statement to be validated! Lewis indiscriminately calls the extensional statement "all, and only, men are rational animals" and the intensional statement "the concept *man* is identical with the concept *rational animal*" analytic. The difference might be expressed by saying that the second statement contains the names of the intensions (senses) of the predicates occurring in the first statement.[14] In calling the first statement strictly analytic one just points to the second statement as a sufficient ground of its validity.[15] Hence the latter cannot be characterized as "analytic" in the same sense, and it is only the subtle shift from "a priori" to "analytic" and back again that permits Lewis to characterize explicative statements as likewise analytic. In fact, the attempt to stretch the extension of "analytic" as indicated leads straight to what is known as the *paradox of analysis*. Just as in order to demonstrate the analyticity of "all and only *A*'s are *BC*'s" we need the premise "the intension of '*A*' is identical with the intension of '*BC*,'" so to demonstrate the analyticity of "the concept *being an A* is identical with the concept *being a BC*" we would need "the intension of 'the concept being an *A*' is identical with the intension of 'the concept being a *BC*.'" But if the latter statement were true, then "the concept *being an A* is identical with the concept *being a BC*" would be synonymous with "the concept *being an A* is

---

[14] The difference between the semantic functions of "men" and "the concept *man*" is like the difference between the semantic functions of "round" and "roundness": as Lewis elsewhere points out, the abstract noun is a name of the intension—"signification," in his own terminology—of its root adjective.

[15] On the relation between intensional statements and necessary extensional statements, cf. above, Chap. 3, A.

identical with the concept *being an A*," hence the explicative statement would, if true, be trivial.[16]

In closely similar manner, the claim that the principles of logic
themselves are analytic in the same sense as statements containing
descriptive terms essentially (like " all cats are animals ") may be
disposed of. Since the nature of " logical truth " will receive detailed
examination in the next chapter, we may confine ourselves here to
a statement of the chief difficulties. One could, of course, so define
" analytic " that there could be no doubt of the analytic character
of logical principles: *S* is analytic if it is either itself a logical principle or is deducible from logical principles with the help of
adequate definitions. But on the basis of such a definition, to say
that logical principles are analytic would be no more informative
than to say that logical principles are logical principles, and Lewis
just like the other philosophers who maintained that logical truths
are analytic surely intended to make a significant statement, a statement clarifying the nature of logical truth. To illustrate, consider
the law of the excluded middle, as formulated in the propositional
calculus: $(p) (p \vee -p)$.[17] How are we to validate this proposition by
reference to logical principles? Indeed, making substitutions in
accordance with the definition " $p \vee q =_{df} - (-p.-q)$," we may prove
it to be equivalent to " $(p) - (-p.--p)$," which, via the laws of double
negation and commutativity of conjunction, is in turn equivalent
to the law of contradiction: $(p) - (p.-p)$.[18] Hence we might say that
the law of excluded middle has been validated by reference to the

---

[16] Alonzo Church has correctly pointed out, using Frege's terminology, that all that is
required by the truth (not the analytic truth) of the explicative statement (analysis)
is the identity of the *denotations* of " the concept *being A* " and " the concept *being
BC*," not the identity of their *senses*; hence it is not the case that the truth of an
explicative statement entails its triviality (review of M. G. White vs. M. Black, " The
Paradox of Analysis," *Journal of Symbolic Logic*, Dec. 1946). A critical comment on
this solution of Moore's paradox will be found below, p. 276. The question of whether
and how explicative statements admit of an interpretation that would clearly distinguish them from generalizations about linguistic usage is postponed to Chap. 10.

[17] Some logicians formulate the law of the excluded middle in the metalanguage:
for every meaningful statement *S*, either *S* or not-*S* is true. But since " it is true that
p " expresses the same proposition as " *p*," the *proposition* expressed by the metalinguistic formulation seems to me to be identical with the proposition expressed by
the object-linguistic formula (not " $p \vee -p$," which is a mere schema, but its universal
closure) .

[18] For typographical reasons, hyphens are used as negation signs instead of the curl
of *Principia Mathematica*.

law of contradiction (the supreme postulate of consistency) analogously to the validation of a statement like " all wives are women ": we have shown that the proposition cannot be consistently denied, the only difference being that the definitions required for the demonstration are definitions of logical constants, not of descriptive terms. But, in the first place, in order to show that a denial of the law of excluded middle would be inconsistent with the law of contradiction, we require, in addition to the definition of " v," another logical principle, the law of double negation: $(p)(p \equiv --p)$. Assuming our primitive notation to contain the connectives " not " $(-)$ and " and " $(.)$, this law is translatable into: $(p)(-(p.-(--p)))$. $-(--p.-p))$, but no further definitional transformation is now possible that would show equivalence to the law of contradiction.[19] What, then, would be the precise meaning of the claim that the falsehood of this law is not " consistently thinkable "? No doubt we can construct an axiomatic system of propositional logic in which the law of double negation occurs as a theorem, and we might then say that its denial is *systematically inconsistent*, i. e. inconsistent with the axioms of the system. But this is, of course, the kind of inconsistency which the denials of *contingent* statements may likewise suffer from. And what about the axioms of the logical system? It could not be argued, clearly, that they are necessarily true because they cannot be denied without systematic inconsistency, for this would simply mean that their denials are inconsistent with them, which is true of any proposition! And as illustrated above, definitional transformations alone will not in general suffice for revealing self-inconsistency of the denial, but require for that purpose to be supplemented with further axioms of the system; [20] these axioms, accordingly, would still have to be validated in some other way. To add an illustration, translation into the primitive notation of "$-$" and " $.$ " will transform the axiom of *Principia Mathematica*, $p \lor q \supset q \lor p$, into $-(-(-p.-q).-q.-p)$, and it is not obvious without further axioms (such as commutativity of conjunction) that the latter is an instance of the law of contradiction.

Secondly, if the law of contradiction is the ultimate ground of validity of logical principles themselves, what is its own ground of

[19] It would not be relevant to invoke the *truth-table* test here, since this is no *generally effective* test of logical truth. See the following chapter.

[20] Cf. the critique of Leibniz' criterion of necessary truth, above p. 8.

validity? If it were valid for the same reason as the less "obvious" logical principles which are allegedly "reducible" to it (though, as illustrated, it would be exceedingly difficult to construct a system of logic with the law of contradiction as the only axiom!), then it would be valid because it cannot be denied without being denied; and, surely, even false propositions have that property.

I conclude, then, that it is only the tacit shift to the wide meaning of "analytic," the meaning which coincides with the meaning of "a priori," that permits Lewis to say that statements belonging to logic are likewise analytic. Indeed, reflection upon the meanings of the logical constants occurring in a statement like "if all the members of class K have property P, then any given member of K has P" is sufficient to produce assent to it. But this is to say no more than that it expresses an *a priori* truth. In the same sense a statement in which descriptive terms occur essentially, like "whatever is red, is colored," may be *a priori*, though it is doubtful whether it is strictly analytic.

C. The Question of Irrefutability

Our result so far is that the thesis which defines, in part, the school of "logical empiricism" is either untenable or trivial *if* by an "a priori" truth is meant a truth that can be ascertained by analysis of meanings, supplemented by deductive reasoning if necessary, alone. But it may be replied that what is here taken as the meaning of "a priori" is really intended, by those philosophers, as the definition of "analytic," and that the fundamental meaning of "a priori" is something else: *irrefutability by experience*. That the *reason* for the empirical irrefutability of a statement, it might be countered, is that to deny it is to change the meanings of some of its constituent terms, is by no means trivially obvious. If it were, Kant would have found it obvious, too, and would not have contrived his metaphysics of Reason as an explanation of such a priori truth. The character of the Kantian sort of explanation, which may be historically contrasted with the positivist sort of explanation, might be brought out by a simile. Suppose we found, as a "brute fact," that whatever we, or any other human being, saw looked blue. One obvious explanation of this fact of experience might be that everything that is visible to any being *is* blue (and the explanation is not tautological either, since "x appears blue" is not synonymous with "x is blue"). On the other hand, we might discover that our eyes and nervous system are so constituted that only light waves whose wavelength corresponds to this color can produce a color sensation. This sounds like the Kantian story: discover the limits of "possible experience" by discovering the "subjective conditions" of experience. Now, the point here is that the statement "everything that is visible is blue" which, *ex hypothesi*, no experience could refute, is surely not true by virtue of its *meaning*. In just this way, Kant thought that no experience could refute the axiom "the straight line is the shortest distance between two points," but that this could not be inferred from the meanings of subject and predicate, but only from the nature of our spatial intuition. That his explanation, once divested of the metaphorical elements that lend pseudo-intelligibility to metaphysical theories—the "forms" of Reason which the "stuff" of experience must conform to—reduces to a tautology, since "our mode of spatial intuition" can hardly mean anything but "finding such propositions as the Euclidean axioms evident," need not detain us in this context.

Yet it is idle to compare alternative explanations of the empirical irrefutability of such propositions as the propositions of arithmetic or the propositions of logic, if we are not clear about the meaning of "empirically irrefutable." It is *impossible* to make observations that would disconfirm "$2 + 2 = 4$" (assuming that this is meant as a statement of pure arithmetic, involving the notion of addition which Russell has explicated in terms of the notion of logical addition of classes, not as a statement about results of physical operations of addition). Yes, but what kind of impossibility is meant? Since many empirical statements are such that it is *practically* impossible to disconfirm them—the "there are mountains on the other side of the moon" variety—it is evidently *theoretical* impossibility of disconfirmation that is in question. Does "p is an a priori truth," then, mean "it is logically impossible (i. e. self-contradictory) to suppose that some experience showed p to be false"? This condition will no doubt be satisfied if "not-p" is itself self-contradictory. But if it is not at least logically possible that it should be satisfied if "not-p" is self-consistent, then the suggested definition will, contrary to its claim, have failed to distinguish the meaning of "a priori" from the meaning of "analytic"

—in which case it will be absurd to speak of an "explanation" of apriority in terms of analyticity.

Now, *prima facie* there are propositions of such a kind that the supposition of their empirical disconfirmation seems self-contradictory though they themselves can be denied without self-contradiction. But it will turn out that (a) it is at best the supposition of their complete (conclusive) disconfirmation which is self-contradictory, not the supposition of their *partial* disconfirmation; (b) that such propositions can easily be imagined to be false, and hence could not count as a priori truths anyway. The point can easily be established in terms of two, formally similar, illustrative propositions: the principle of causality in the unsophisticated formulation "every event has a cause," which Kant and his followers held to be both synthetic and a priori, and "every class of empirical objects which has at least one member has at least two members." To refute the proposition that every event has a cause would be to establish the proposition that at least one event has no cause. This latter proposition has the form: $(\exists x)(y)(-yRx)$, where the variables "x" and "y" range over events. Clearly, if the range of these variables is unlimited, then complete verification of this proposition (and thus complete disconfirmation of its negation) would involve exhaustion of an infinite class, which most philosophers (with the notable exception of Russell) would regard as logically impossible. *Mutatis mutandis*, the same may be said of the second of our illustrative propositions. To refute this proposition would mean to establish that there is a class K which has exactly one member.[21] Here again, an unlimited class of elements would have to be exhausted before the proposition could be pronounced as definitely refuted. Thus it appears that the claim of irrefutability here is equivalent to the claim that unrestrictedly universal propositions are unverifiable. But few philosophers would deny that such universal propositions are at least confirmable; hence consistency requires them to concede that evidence is conceivable which would partially disconfirm such propositions as the above in the sense of diminishing their probability. And as for (b): it surely is conceivable that there is not, never has been, and never

---

[21] It is assumed that the K's are defined by predicates that leave it a *logically open* question whether the class has more than one member. Such classes as the class of tallest men born in 1915 are therefore excluded from the range of "K."

will be, another individual that exactly resembles, in appearance, Winston Churchill; so the fact that it cannot be strictly disproved that the universe contains such a double of Churchill's is no proof at all that the existence of such a double is an a priori truth. Nor do we need to repeat Hume's arguments against the logical necessity of the principle of causality.

It is, indeed, impossible to find a meaning of the expression " theoretically irrefutable by experience " which at once differs from the meaning of "not capable of being self-consistently denied" (i. e. strictly analytic) and effectively serves to distinguish a priori from empirical truth. It is sometimes held that the mark of an a priori truth is that we adjust our linguistic rules in such a way that it could be maintained no matter what facts may turn up. Take, for example, the a priori truth that every tone is characterized by exactly one pitch. Suppose we try to refute it by sounding a chord. Then the defender of the proposition will, of course, say that a chord is not properly describable as a tone. Or suppose we try to refute the proposition " no particle can occupy more than one place at a time " by pointing out that this tennis ball, after all, occupies a spherical volume which is an aggregate of many " places." Then we would be told either that " place " was meant in the sense of " the total space occupied by the particle," or that " particle " was meant in the sense of " what occupies no more than one place at a time " (" point-particle," i. e. its instantaneous position can be described by a *unique* set of coordinates). This linguistic theory of the nature of a priori truth is nicely argued by Ernest Nagel among others. In the article " Logic without Ontology " [22] he applies the theory to the Aristotelian version of the principle of contradiction as an " ontological " truth: no subject can both have and not have an attribute at the same time and in the same respect. Suppose someone claimed as an exception to the principle the fact that the same penny may at the same time be both circular and ellipitical (and thus noncircular) relative to different angles of vision.[23] He would, of course, be told that the difference of per-

---

[22] In *Naturalism and the Human Spirit*, ed. H. Krikorian; reprinted in Feigl and Sellars, *Readings in Philosophical Analysis*.

[23] If a phenomenalist analysis of physical properties as dispositions to produce sense-data of definite kinds under definite conditions of perception is accepted, then the distinction between " attribute " and " respect " is unnecessary. If " x is round " means

spectives just constitutes a violation of the requirement of " sameness
of respect." But what should we tell him if he asked why the sameness of the degree of illumination of the penny's surface is not, in
this context, identified as sameness of respect? As Nagel points out,
the proper reply would be that the nature of the " attribute " in
question determines our definition of " same respect," i. e. once an
attribute (like shape, or color) has been selected, the " respect "
(normal perspective, or standard illumination) must be so chosen
that the principle remains valid.

But, unfortunately for the linguistic theory, this method of
" saving " propositions in the face of apparent exceptions by suitable linguistic conventions is equally applicable to propositions
ordinarily regarded as empirical. Consider once again the example
used by Poincaré to illustrate the transformation of generalizations
from experiment into " conventions ": under standard pressure, all
phosphorus melts at 44° C. The orthodox theory, which may be
called the " either-or " theory of philosophical semantics (not to be
confused with the two-valued Aristotelian logic which Korzybski
and his followers decry because they do not understand it!), is simple
enough: either " phosphorus " is defined in terms of this melting-
point, in which case we have an a priori truth which " says nothing
about reality "; or else " phosphorus " is not so defined, in which
case we have an empirical generalization which is clearly refutable
by contrary instances. This theory overlooks two points, the first
of which will occupy us at length in Chapter 11 of this book.
(1) Such concepts of natural kinds as " phosphorus " are *open*
concepts in the sense that no fixed rules of application have been
laid down that would cover all possible situations in which the
question whether the concept applies might arise, and that would
allow us to make a sharp distinction between defining and accidental
properties of members of the kind. (2) Such generalizations are
usually *incompletely* stated, as is evident from the accompanying
safety clause " other things being equal," and it therefore is not clear
what would count as a " contrary instance."

(1) It is conceivable, indeed, that a scientist would announce,

---

" x would appear round if viewed from a normal angle," then it does not make sense
to ask whether x *is* also round relatively to non-normal perspectives. But this matter
is irrelevant to the point Nagel wished to illustrate by the Aristotelian principle of
" ontology."

after having discovered that each element capable of existing in different states of aggregation is characterized by a unique melting-point, that such elements are *defined* by their melting-points—in just the way in which many modern chemists would say that the elements are defined by their atomic weight, or perhaps by their atomic number. But it can be shown that he does not mean "definition," in such contexts, in the sense which underlies the dichotomy "true by definition–true by empirical fact." For suppose that specimens turned up frequently which resembled phosphorus in all respects that were used to identify substances as "phosphorus" before the melting-point was discovered, but which melted at a different temperature. Would the scientist refuse to classify these substances as "phosphorus" on the authority of his "definition"? Clearly not. Since his selection of property P_1 out of a group of normally correlated properties $P_1 \cdots P_n$ as "definitory" purports mainly to identify a reliable sign of the other members of the group (such that to classify on the basis of P_1 is to make implicitly a number of predictions), such a procedure would defeat the very purpose of "definition" of natural kinds. Indeed, what he would be more likely to do is to *change the definition in the light of experience*, and thus save the hypothesis that the specimens are phosphorus. The advocates of the either-or theory will say, somewhat cynically, that this is well known but has no tendency to show that the distinction between definitional and empirical truth cannot be maintained in such contexts. If to say that the definition of "phosphorus" in terms of P_1 is *useful* is to say that P_1 is a reliable sign of $P_2 \cdots P_n$, then this statement is empirical; and the fact that after finding it to be false we abandon the definition merely illustrates that the advisability of adopting a given linguistic rule may depend on empirical facts. Yet, what is the criterion for deciding whether a given statement which is part of a scientific theory is a definition or a synthetic statement? What is the criterion for deciding whether a modification of a scientific theory which was occasioned by new observations is a change of definition or an abandonment of an empirical hypothesis? Certainly, the scientists themselves speak of redefinition in the light of new experience, but the question is what they mean by "definition." When it is said that a definition is a statement to the effect that two expressions are synonymous (and thus clearly a metalinguistic statement, to be distinguished from object-linguistic statements in which the defined expression is *used*, not *mentioned*), one must have one or the other of the following meanings of " definition " in mind: (a) definition as introduction of an abbreviating synonym, (b) definition as explicit statement of what is meant by an antecedently used term (generalization about actual usage, though in stating the generalization as a " definition " one may also *prescribe* future conformity to the described usage, especially if actual usage is to a degree vague) . But surely the scientist's statement " phosphorus is defined as the element with melting point M " cannot be adequately translated into " ' phosphorus ' shall henceforth be used as an abbreviation for ' element with melting-point M ' " (the way a mathematician might rule " ' x^3 ' is to be used as abbreviation for ' $x.x.x$ ' ") , nor can it be adequately translated into " ' phosphorus ' as used by us scientists has always meant ' element with melting-point M ' ": if it had always meant that, why bother to discover the melting-point by experiment? It remains the case, therefore, that this usage of " definition " does not fit into the conception of definition as a metalinguistic statement (whether declarative or not) which is about symbols in a sense in which this is incompatible with being about the objects symbolized. No chemist would admit that in " defining " oxygen as the element with atomic weight 16 he has made the claim that the existence of a sample of oxygen with a different atomic weight (isotopes!) is as logically impossible as the existence of a square circle. What he intended to do in laying down the " definition," whether or not he was able to formulate his intention clearly, was to indicate which member of a group of normally correlated properties is the most reliable indicator of the other members.

The concept of " correlation " which is intended when one says that a name of a natural kind stands for a correlation of properties requires, of course, analysis. To say that the set $P_1 \cdots P_n$ are thus correlated does not mean that any instance exhibiting one will exhibit all nor that it will exhibit a subclass of them; nor does it even mean that any instance exhibiting n-1 members of the set will exhibit the nth member, for in that case there could not be distinct natural kinds that differ in just one property. The relations between the members of a correlation are only probability implications, and the name of a natural kind crystallizes, as it were, a network of probability implications. In arguing " x has P_1, therefore x is a member of K " we are telescoping a whole set of probable inferences to the presence of the other members of the correlation which " K " stands for. If so, it cannot be supposed that some member of the correlation, no matter how complex, could serve as a property which is *logically equivalent* to the property of being a member of K: the inference to class membership is a probable inference to *other* members of the correlation which " K " names. This is the reason why " definition " of a natural kind is not " definition " in a sense usually recognized by conventional logicians.

In his early book, *Mind and the World Order*, C. I. Lewis developed what he himself called a " pragmatic " conception of a priori truth, according to which it is the mark of an a priori proposition " all A are B " that if we find, empirically, that the concept B does not apply to x, then we are determined to retract A as likewise inapplicable to x. What Lewis unfortunately over-looked is that this pragmatic criterion does not allow us to distin-guish strictly analytic from empirical truths. It is obvious that high confidence in the truth of " all A are B " will manifest itself in just such behavior regardless of whether the source of this confidence is empirical or logical evidence.[24] What is here sug-gested is that when a scientist announces a *definition*, suggested by empirical discoveries, of a natural kind, such as " oxygen is defined as the element whose atomic weight is 16," he simply expresses the sort of confidence which Lewis took to be the touchstone of a special kind of truth; that he is not making a terminological pro-posal of the kind " let us use the term ' oxygen ' to refer to the element whose atomic weight equals 16 " but rather announces " atomic weight 16 is the most reliable indicator of the members of the correlation of macroscopic and microscopic, qualitative and quantitative properties which constitutes the natural kind called ' oxygen '; in general, classification of chemical elements on the basis of their atomic weights has, as demonstrated by Mendelejeff's periodic law, more predictive fertility than classification on the basis of other members of such correlations." The temptation is, indeed, great to ask: just how are we to *delimit* the correlation of properties which, as you say, a common noun like " oxygen " stands

---

[24] Cf. on this point my *The A Priori in Physical Theory* (New York, King's Crown Press, 1946), Pt. I.

for? Surely, if today chemists discovered a new property, P_{n+1}, of oxygen, you would not say that "oxygen" connoted that property, along with $P_1 \cdots P_n$, before the discovery was made? But the question is inappropriate because it rests on the traditional conception of *connotation* of class terms as giving rise to a sharp division of properties into essential and accidental; it presupposes, that is, that a name of a natural kind has at any given time a fixed definition, though one fixed definition gives way to another under the pressure of empirical discoveries. The fact is, however, that scientists operate with *open* concepts of natural kinds. If "oxygen" were stipulated to be synonymous with the correlation $P_1 \cdots P_n$, then the scientist would be committed to classify an instance of the subcorrelation $P_1 \cdots P_{n-1}$ which lacked P_n as non-oxygen, while actually he may find it more convenient to classify such a specimen as a new species of oxygen in view of its strong similarity to instances of the correlation $P_1 \cdots P_n$. It is only blindness to the openness of such class concepts that can lead a philosopher of science to assimilate a statement like "this sample of oxygen does not have atomic weight 16" to a statement like "this square does not have four sides." [25]

Now to point (2), that commonly laws are incompletely expressed, through insertion of the "caeteris paribus" clause, and therefore are not strictly refutable.[26] The scientist, knowing that he does not know for certain that the conditions $C_1 \cdots C_n$ are *all* the conditions necessary for an occurrence of effect E (i. e. constitute a strictly sufficient condition for E), even though E has so far been observed to occur whenever this set of conditions was present, cautiously says "provided all the other necessary conditions are present, then, if . . . , then E." Thus a physicist experimenting with wires in order to find out how the length of a wire varies with the stress it is subjected to discovers direct proportionality of stress to strain. What he has strictly discovered, of course, is only that such a functional dependence holds within the experimentally explored range of the variables. So he says cautiously "under similar relevant

[25] The subtle problem of the "openness" of scientific concepts will be discussed in detail in Chap. 11.

[26] On this point, as well as on the just discussed openness of inductive concepts, see the penetrating remarks by G. H. von Wright, *Treatise on Induction and Probability*, chap. 6, secs. 2, 3.

circumstances this dependence always holds," and he may not know at the time exactly what all the relevant circumstances are. The subsequent discovery that above a certain limit of stress (which varies from material to material and which is called " the elastic limit ") the law does not hold, does not, then, compel him to abandon the proposition he asserted. In a case like this, one commonly speaks of " modifying " or " restricting " the law to special conditions. But if by the " law " is meant the definite proposition devoid of safety clause, then this would be properly described as refutation, not modification, and if what is meant is the indefinite proposition provided with the safety clause, then " precisification " would be a more suitable term: it is specified just which the " relevant " circumstances are.

The trouble with the claim that refutability is the mark of empirical laws is, then, this: if by the " law " we understand the proposition which the scientist usually means to assert (whether or not he says exactly what he means), we find that the law has a characteristic indefiniteness by virtue of which it is safe from strict refutation; and if by the " law " we mean a strictly refutable proposition, we might find people, laymen as well as scientists, denying that they ever intend to assert laws in that sense. The indefinite formulation, of course, corresponds to the assertion of a probability implication: uncertainty as to what circumstances are relevant reflects itself in uncertainty of the inference from the specified conditions to the effect. It is often said nowadays that we must abandon the " quest for certainty " in science and be content with the assertion of just such probability implications. But if what is called " law " is a probability implication, then either of two things must be meant by a " law ": (a) a statistical generalization, i. e. a statement of the form " in x per cent of the cases, condition C is attended by effect E," [27] or (b) a statement of the form " relative to the total available evidence, the degree of confirmation of the statement ' whenever C, then E ' is p." The difference between these two interpretations should be obvious: according to (a), there are known cases of C which are not attended by E, while according to (b) it just is not known for certain that there are not any excep-

---

[27] This type of formulation is aimed at one particular form of law, viz. causal laws, or laws of succession. For classificatory laws (" laws of coexistence ") the formulation would be " x per cent of the A's are B's."

tional cases. Now, notoriously, we have no definite rules telling us just what evidence would clearly refute a statistical generalization which refers to an infinite class (this is one of the reasons why some people reject the frequency theory of probability: it makes, they say, probability statements undecidable). And according to interpretation (b), a law is itself a statement of " inductive probability " (probability attributed to hypotheses relative to inductive evidence) and as such is analytic if true.[28]

Suffice it to conclude that the term " law " is not sufficiently unambiguous (even within the context of usage indicated by the appendix ". . . of nature ") to allow us to pronounce with confidence that laws, unlike a priori truths, are *refutable* propositions. However, even if the difficulty created by the " caeteris paribus " clause could be taken care of, there would remain the unanswerable argument of the " conventionalists " (and some of the analytically minded " pragmatists ") concerning the illusoriness of " crucial experiments," i. e. the view that experiments can always, theoretically, be designed that would bring to light brute facts clearly deciding against one or the other of two incompatible theories. That in order to deduce directly testable consequences from a theory to be tested we need to supplement it with other theories used as premises—e. g. the Einstein Red-Shift, which is one of the important empirical consequences of the general theory of relativity, cannot be deduced from the latter without the supplementary assumption of a law of the gravitational field, the law correlating wave length of light with color etc.—and that therefore the theory in question could always be saved in case of a negative result by suitably modifying those supplementary theories, has often been pointed out and has now the status of a truism of scientific methodology. But it seems to me to be a truism which is absolutely fatal to the claim that a priori truths are sharply distinguishable from empirical truths by the criterion of empirical irrefutability.[29]

[28] It is here assumed without argument that a satisfactory frequency interpretation of inductive probability is impossible.

[29] The above discussion of the conventionalist claim that experience by itself, isolated from a framework of conventions, could never strictly refute a law has been kept—perhaps unduly—brief, because the matter has been dealt with extensively by several writers, including myself in *The A Priori in Physical Theory*.

D. *Are Necessary Propositions Necessarily Necessary?*

If all of this is correct, then we come to the conclusion that there is no way of improving on the definition of " a priori truth " which constituted our starting point, viz. a true statement whose truth is ascertainable by reflecting on its meaning alone, or by logical deduction from statements of this sort. In which case, as pointed out, it will be difficult to escape from the conclusion that the thesis " all a priori truth is analytic " is either a tautology or else false. But let us make one more effort to see clearly what, on the above definition, we are saying about a statement in calling it " true a priori." Do we mean that any rational person could be brought to assent to the statement by just carefully explaining to him what the statement means (by definition of " rational," of course, a rational person would be able to follow a formal demonstration)? If so, then " *p* is a priori " would be a prediction [30] of psychological reactions, and we would only be warranted in saying, with regard to any given *p*, " the evidence makes it probable that *p* is a priori." Now, that " *p* is a priori " should itself be an empirical statement would be an innocent consequence if it were meant in the sense of " this sentence is presently used to express an a priori proposition." But this very statement about usage suggests that " a priori " is directly predicable of *propositions*, though derivatively of sentences that express a priori propositions. And would any philosopher be willing to admit that once we know which proposition *p* is expressed by a given sentence, it is still a *question of empirical fact* whether *p* is a priori? Should we not say, rather, that necessity is an *intrinsic* property of a proposition in the sense that it would make no sense to suppose that a necessary proposition *might not have been* necessary?

The question whether " it is necessary that *p* " is, if true, itself a necessary proposition is of fundamental importance for the problem of explicating the concept of necessary truth, since it is likely that any philosopher who answers it affirmatively will adopt the necessity of the necessity of *p* as a *criterion of adequacy* for proposed explications of necessary truth. He will, in other words, reject any explica-

---

[30] We could hardly define " *S* expresses a necessary truth " to mean " understanding the meaning of *S* *entails* believing *S* to be true," which would be grossly circular. Thus we are justified in speaking of a prediction of belief on the basis of understanding.

tion which entails the contingency of such modal propositions as failing to explicate the explicandum he has in mind. The same holds, of course, for the concept of logical truth: since all logical truths are necessary truths (whether or not the converse of this proposition be true also), any criterion of adequacy for explications of "necessary truth" is at the same time a criterion of adequacy for explications of "logical truth." This question cannot be decided by formal reasoning within an uninterpreted system of modal logic,[31] containing the usual explicit definition of "necessary" in terms of "possible": p is necessary = not-p is not possible. Indeed, an uninterpreted system of modal logic can be constructed without even raising the question of the necessity of the necessity of p; thus there is no postulate or theorem in Lewis' system S_2 that bears on the question, nor is the question informally discussed in the meta-language. In Appendix II to Lewis and Langford's *Symbolic Logic* (New York and London, 1932) it is pointed out that Lewis' system of strict implication "leaves undetermined certain properties of the modal functions, $\Diamond p$, $\sim \Diamond p$, $\Diamond \sim p$, and $\sim \Diamond \sim p$." Accordingly "$Np \rightarrow NNp$," as well as "$Np \supset NNp$" ($N \cdots =$ it is necessary that $\cdots$), is both independent of and consistent with the axioms of the system, and whether an axiom of modal iteration, e. g. "what is possibly possible, is possible" (which can be shown to be equivalent to "what is necessary, is necessarily necessary") should be adopted must be decided by extrasystematic considerations based on *interpretation* of the modal functions. Now, let us refer to the thesis that necessary propositions are necessarily necessary henceforth as the "*NN* thesis." What appears to be the strongest argument in favor of the *NN* thesis is based on the semantic assumption that "necessary" as predicated of propositions is a *time-independent* predicate,[32] where a "time-independent" predicate is defined as a predicate P such that sentences of the form "x is P at time t" are meaningless. The argument runs as follows.

Anybody who maintained that the proposition "it is necessary that every father have at least one child" is itself contingent, could

[31] By calling the system "uninterpreted" I mean that its metalanguage contains no semantic rules for the modal operators, not that it contains no semantic rules at all.

[32] The term "time-independent predicate" is borrowed from Carnap, who uses it in "Truth and Confirmation" (Feigl and Sellars, *Readings in Philosophical Analysis*) in order to show the difference between the concepts of truth and confirmation.

only mean that the *sentence* " every father has at least one child," which is in fact used to express a necessary proposition, might have been used to express a contingent proposition (e. g. " father " might have been used in the sense in which " man " is used). Indeed, a statement of the form " S expresses a necessary proposition " is incomplete, requiring expansion into " S expresses, in present usage, a necessary proposition," and once so expanded shows itself as a contingent, indeed historical, statement about verbal usage. But while the predicate " expresses a necessary proposition " is clearly time-dependent, " necessary " as predicated of propositions is just as clearly time-independent. This can be shown convincingly if we consider statements of the form " p entails q," which are reducible to the form " p is necessary " where p is a conditional proposition [33] (thus " that somebody is a father entails that somebody has at least one child " is reducible to " it is necessary that if somebody is a father, then somebody has at least one child "). Suppose a logic teacher—engaged in the demonstration that premises of the forms " all A are B " and " some A are not C " entail that some B are not C, while the entailment does not hold if the universal premise is replaced by its converse " all B are A "—were asked by a befuddled yet critical student: " You have shown that the conclusion is entailed by the first pair of premises but not by the second pair *at the present time*. How do you propose to prove that these logical relations will *always* hold? " Surely this student will have to be told that he has not understood what is meant by " entailment," that in terms of the intended meaning of " entailment " his question does not make sense; that he might just as well have asked how we know that the square root of 9 was equal

---

[33] It should be noted that the variables " p " and " q " are here meant as propositional, not sentential variables. This is to say that the admissible substituends for " p " and " q " in " p entails q " are names of propositions, which can be formed in two ways: either by prefixing " that " to the sentence expressing the proposition (sentences, be it noted, are not *names* of propositions any more than predicates of their intensions), or by constructing participial expressions corresponding to statements (" somebody *being* a father " corresponding to " somebody is a father "). The claim, which may be traced back to Carnap's *Logical Syntax of Language*, that entailment statements are metalinguistic statements containing names of sentences, is as untenable, and for similar reasons, as the claim that predications of truth, in ordinary language, are metalinguistic statements about sentences; cf. my " Note on the Semantic and the Absolute Concept of Truth," *Philosophical Studies* (Jan. 1952), and " Propositions, Sentences and the Semantic Definition of Truth," *Theoria, 20* (1954).

to 3 before the symbols " 3 " and " 9 " were invented by mankind. Thus it must be concluded that it is inconceivable that an entailment which in fact holds from p to q should fail to hold between the same propositions at some other time, simply because it does not make sense to say that an entailment holds *at some time*.

But this argument for the *NN* thesis assumes that the only ground on which the *NN* thesis could be rejected is the interpretation of " p is necessary," like " S expresses a necessary proposition," as a *historical* statement; once this assumption is granted, the *NN* thesis is easily established, since it is easy to show that modal statements are not historical statements. If this assumption is challenged, then some other argument is needed. Such an independent argument might be constructed on the following premise: if and only if S expresses a *contingent* proposition p, then it is possible that two people who both take S to express p nevertheless disagree about the truth-value of S. Let " p " be of the form " p entails q " (i. e. " it is necessary that if p, then q "). The question before us then reduces to the question whether two people who are in disagreement as to whether proposition p entails proposition q may nevertheless be interpreting the sentence " p entails q " in the same way. And since it is clearly possible that they should agree in their interpretation of " entails " and yet disagree as to whether p entails q, this is to ask whether the disputants could put the identical interpretation on the sentences " p " and " q." Some analysts would deny this possibility and hence conclude that true entailment statements are themselves necessary; thus Schlick said that correct interpretation and verification coincide in the case of analytic statements. But it seems to me obvious that they are wrong. Consider an entailment between fairly complex propositions, e. g. propositions of the forms " if p, then (if q, then r or not-s) " and " if q, then (if s and not-r, then not-p) ." They in fact entail one another, but a person not trained in formal logic may have difficulty seeing this and hence might conceivably dispute the entailment. Yet, if he explicitly agrees to the truth-table definitions of the connectives and moreover shows himself familiar with the relevant syntactic rules, it could hardly be denied that the two sentences express for him the same propositions as for the logician who recognizes their logical equivalence.

But then the only possible source of the disagreement is that one of the disputants is either unaware of some relevant rule of deduction or else employs an invalid rule of deduction or else makes a mistake in applying the relevant rules of deduction; for short, let us say that he commits a deductive error. Should we conclude, now, that the *NN* thesis is false, since the criterion of necessary propositions—viz. that if the proposition *p* expressed by *S* is necessary, then anybody who honestly denied *S* would not interpret *S* to mean *p*—does not seem to be satisfied by entailment propositions? Such a conclusion would be most unwise, since the same argument would prove that not even *first-order* propositions (i. e. propositions which are not about propositions) of appreciable complexity are necessary. Deductive mistakes might lead one, for example, to deny an arithmetical equation which expresses a necessary proposition.[34] And if the best reason one can adduce against *NNp* (where *Np* is equivalent to an entailment proposition) is at the same time an argument against *Np*, then the thesis that *if Np, then NNp*, has in fact been supported rather than undermined.

On the other hand, a seductive argument *against* the *NN* thesis is that to establish a proposition as necessary we must, in many cases, perform calculatory or deductive operations which are subject to error just like the processes of interpreting sense data that enter into the verification of empirical propositions about the physical world. Consider, e. g., the truth-table test for determining whether a given formula expresses a tautology. If after performing the test we say confidently that the proposition expressed by the formula is a tautology, it is because we confidently assume that no mistake was made in the calculations of truth-values. Since there is a finite probability of error in the calculation (proportional, roughly, to the complexity of the formula), we ought to say critically " on the evidence of the calculation test, it is highly probable that the proposition expressed by the formula is a tautology "; and since it does not make sense to ascribe probability to a necessary proposi-

---

[34] If by " understanding " an equation one means " knowing what the constituent symbols mean and understanding the meaning of their arrangement *and having a perfect grasp of the relevant rules of calculation*," then it would presumably follow from this very definition of " understanding " that it is impossible to understand an equation and still be uncertain about its validity. But such a definition would be an excellent example of a question-begging definition.

tion,[35] so the argument might conclude, " p is a tautology " is not itself a necessary proposition.

Before exposing the subtle error of this argument, I wish to reduce it to absurdity by showing that if it were valid it would prove that there are no tautologies at all, not even in the realm of first-order propositions. Let us ask ourselves by what sort of evidence we could establish the *truth* (not necessity) of a proposition of the form " p or not-p " (to take the simplest case of a tautology) , say " p_1 or not-p_1," where p_1 is an empirical proposition. The naive method would consist in verifying either p_1, or not-p_1, and then inferring, with the help of the principle " p entails $(p$ or $q)$," the truth of " either p_1 or not-p_1." Clearly, in using this method we establish the disjunction as an *empirical* truth only. But if we are not naive, i. e. if we recognize that the truth of this compound proposition is independent of the truth-value of its atomic component, then we shall adduce evidence for the truth of " p_1 or not-p_1 " which is at the same time evidence for the *necessary* truth of this proposition: the evidence of the truth-table. That is, we assert the truth of " p_1 or not-p_1 " on the ground that any proposition of the same form is true, i. e. on the ground that it is *necessarily* true. It follows that if the evidence of the truth-table be regarded as empirical evidence which only lends probability to the propositions it is evidence for, then not only " ' p_1 or not-p_1 ' is a tautology " but likewise " p_1 or not-p_1 " itself is an empirical proposition. (Note that the truth-table verdict is the only evidence on which " p_1 or not-p_1 " can be asserted in case the truth-value of " p_1 " is unknown.) Analogous considerations apply if the test by which a formula is established as a tautology is the deduction test.[36]

[35] Perhaps this premise is needlessly strong. One might hold that the propositions of inductive logic, of the form " $c(h/e) = p$," hold for necessary as well as for contingent values of " h." But the inductive irrelevance of empirical facts to necessary propositions might be expressed by the axiom that for any e, $c(h/e) = 1$ if h is a necessary proposition. And this premise would serve the above argument just as well.

[36] The argument against the *NN* thesis which has just been criticized may be found in Reichenbach's *Elements of Symbolic Logic*, § 34. Reichenbach's brief discussion of the question whether " p is a tautology " is itself a tautology (if true) is, moreover, confused, since no distinction is made between the statement that a given formula expresses a tautology and the statement that the proposition expressed by a given formula is a tautology. The former type of statement is obviously empirical, but this has no tendency to prove that the latter type of statement is empirical. In general, the failure to distinguish between " S expresses a necessary proposition " and " the

But just in case some nihilist or ultra-empiricist among analytic philosophers should boldly accept the consequence that there are no necessary propositions at all, it is advisable to refute the argument against the *NN* thesis unconditionally. The subtle error of the argument consists in a confusion of *necessity* as a *logical* property of propositions, and *certainty* as a *psychological* state. It is tacitly assumed that " p is necessary " is equivalent to, or at least entails, " p can be known with absolute certainty." Yet, it is easy to see that on this assumption the proposition of arithmetic " $63 \times 45 = 2835$ " would be no more necessary than the empirical proposition that day always follows and is followed by night (in fact, for a man with a poor training in arithmetic, the latter proposition would be necessary to a higher degree). The evidence on which one asserts such an equation is that calculations performed by oneself led to this result each time, and that calculations performed by other people competent at multiplication confirmed the result. Nevertheless, it remains logically possible that such a finite series of repetitions of the same calculation should have been infected with errors, and that future calculations should lead to a different result. We may feel confident that no mistake was involved in any of the steps of the calculation, yet it is logically possible that a mistake was made. Remember that the only certainty which Descartes' demon was powerless to undermine was the certainty of " I am uncertain "; the propositions of arithmetic fell a prey to the demon just like the propositions of physics. Some philosophers hold that it is the distinctive mark of empirical propositions that no matter how much confirming evidence may have been accumulated at a given time, it always remains possible that in the future disconfirming evidence will turn up. But this is surely an unsuccessful way of distinguishing empirical propositions from necessary propositions. The more complex a deduction, the greater the probability of a deductive error, and hence the greater the probability

proposition p (which happens to be expressed by S) is necessary " is widespread, especially among advocates of the linguistic theory of logical necessity (cf. Chap. 7). It is responsible, for example, for Strawson's, in my opinion invalid, thesis against Körner that entailment-statements are contingent statements about expressions (P. F. Strawson, " Necessary Propositions and Entailment-Statements," *Mind*, April 1948). The distinction is carefully observed, on the other hand, by C. Lewy, in the essay " Entailment and Necessary Propositions," in Max Black, ed., *Philosophical Analysis* (Ithaca, N.Y., 1950).

that a future repetition of the deduction should lead to a different result. Yet we know that the proposition which we judge in terms of deductive evidence is either necessarily true or necessarily false.

What marks a proposition as a priori is not that it is capable of being known, either as true or as false, with *absolute certainty*. It is rather that the only kind of cognitive activity which we admit as appropriate to its validation is conceptual analysis [37] and deduction—the " mere operation of thought." In this sense of " a priori," " p is a priori " is itself a priori whether or not it be true, for it is by " the mere operation of thought " that we determine whether a proposition is a priori. For example, if by analysis of truth possibilities I establish the truth of the proposition " if New York is overcrowded, and if it is unpleasant to live in New York if New York is overcrowded, then it is unpleasant to live in New York," without investigating empirically whether the atomic components of this compound proposition are true or false, then I have *by the same analysis* established the *necessary truth* of this proposition. For the analysis establishes that *all* propositions expressed by sentences of the form " if $(p$ and $($ if $p,$ then $q))$, then q " are *true*. And if the nonempirical evidence in terms of which p is established as true coincides with the evidence in terms of which p is established as necessarily true, then " p is necessary " is necessary in the same sense in which " p " is necessary. What is decisive is that if a necessary proposition is not mistakenly believed to be contingent, then its truth is known simply as a corollary of its necessity, by the principle " if Np, then p " (whatever is necessarily the case, is the case). To add a simple illustration: by reflecting on the meanings of " square " and " equilateral " we come to know that " x is square " entails " x is equilateral." The entailment, however, can be expressed in the form " it is necessary that there be no square which is not equilateral," and by " if Np, then p " this entails " there is no square which is not equilateral."

What led us into this discussion, ending in final acceptance, of the *NN* thesis [38] was the doubt whether the definition of " a priori "

[37] " Conceptual analysis " is here used broadly so as to cover also intuitive apprehension of relations between concepts, e.g. that " x is later than y " is incompatible with " y is later than x." In this way the above definition of " necessary truth " allows for intuitively necessary propositions as a subclass of necessary propositions.

[38] It should be noted that the *NN* thesis is compatible with the view that, where p

in terms of the psychological concept "assent" did not entail that in classifying a proposition as a priori we assert a generalization of psychology. But it now appears that the definition "capable of being known by conceptual analysis and deduction alone," whether or not it be considered "psychologistic," is quite consistent with the view that we are making in no sense an *empirical* statement about a proposition when we classify it as a priori. For, to repeat, the same intellectual operations by which we would normally establish such a proposition as true also establish it as *necessarily* true.

E. *Epistemological and Terminological Questions*

The main lesson to be learned from the preceding discussion, however, is that the question whether there are *synthetic a priori* truths, which is answered negatively by the logical positivists but which has been resuscitated in recent years as semantic analysis has become more sophisticated, is not a clear question as long as the term "analytic" (and its contrary "synthetic") is used as loosely and ambiguously as it is used in some quarters. I shall, therefore, make some terminological recommendations which I at least, even if nobody else, intend to accept (at least for the remainder of this book). In the first place, it would be desirable not to use "analytic" in the broad sense of "true by virtue of meanings," since this sense is indistinguishable from the sense of "a priori," and the thesis of the analyticity of all a priori truth thus becomes trivial. (Should the reader be tempted to object that an *explication* need not be trivial, and that the thesis "all a priori truth is analytic" may be intended as just that, he is urged to suspend judgment until he has read the next chapter, in which it will be argued that we have to fall back on the "explicandum," the concept of necessary truth, in order to explain the concept of logical truth which enters into the definition of the alleged "explicatum," the concept of strictly analytic truth.) But if, because of some mis-

---

is a necessary but *nonmodal* proposition, p does not entail Np. "Np entails NNp" must be distinguished from "Np entails that p entails Np." Should one suppose that the latter entailment holds, one would probably do so through fallacious identification of this entailment with the valid entailment "$(Np$ and $p)$ entails Np"; but the principle of exportation which holds for material implication does not hold for entailment. In the essay already cited, Lewy argues against "Np entails that p entails Np," but he does not reject the NN thesis.

leading traditional connotations of "a priori" (or "necessary"),
philosophers insist on labeling this broad sense "analytic," let
them use the more discriminating term *broadly analytic*. There is
no reference to logical truths as the ground of analyticity in the
definition of "broadly analytic," and hence we need not fear an
infinite regress if we classify logical truths (which are characterized
by absence of descriptive constants) themselves as broadly analytic,
together with such a priori truths as are neither logical truths nor
deducible from logical truths with the help of adequate eliminative
definitions (i. e. definitions enabling elimination of the defined
term). The latter subclass of broadly analytic truths correspond
to what are frequently called "statements true by *implicit* definition," which will receive detailed attention in a later chapter.
Broadly analytic truths are distinguished from *strictly analytic*
truths, which are defined as truths which, though not themselves
logical principles, are deducible from logical principles. They are
so deducible either *directly*, by substitution of descriptive constants
for the bound variables of a logical principle, or indirectly with
the help of adequate eliminative definitions. In the former case
they might be called *logically true*, in the latter case *definitionally
true*.[39] These categories may be illustrated by the following statements: (a) logical principles—for any property *f*, there is no *x*
such that *fx* and not-*fx*; (b) strictly analytic statements which are
logically true—nothing is both a cat and not a cat; (c) strictly
analytic statements which are definitionally true—all bachelors are

---

[39] At the end of a recent study ("Bolzano's Definition of Analytic Propositions,"
Methodos, 2, 1950) J. Bar-Hillel recommends a terminology which is substantially
"in accord with Carnap's terminology," and I do not wish simply to ignore his proposal, without indicating my reasons for departing from it. Bar-Hillel in effect proposes
that "logically true" be used in the sense of "necessarily true (true a priori)," as is
evident from his proposal "let us use 'factually true' for 'true but not logically
true.'" According to this terminology, however, it would be an open question whether
all logically true statements are deducible from logical truths, and for this reason the
terminology is misleading. Bar-Hillel further proposes the term "analytically true"
for what I would call "trivially analytic": "Let us call sentences of the form '*A-B*
is *B*' and '*A-B* is not non-*B*' 'analytically true.'" If we adopt this proposal, we have
to say that there are many logical truths which are not analytic, and since "synthetic"
is widely used as an abbreviation for "nonanalytic and noncontradictory," we would
be saying that many logical truths are synthetic. Bar-Hillel would of course say that
"synthetic" should be used in the sense of "factually true or factually false," not in
the sense of "nonanalytic and noncontradictory." But this proposal likewise expresses
simply the resolution to get rid of the synthetic a priori by terminological fiat.

unmarried; (d) broadly analytic statements which are not strictly analytic—no surface is blue and red at the same time.

It should be kept in mind that in establishing a statement as strictly analytic one presupposes broadly analytic statements, viz. logical truths and—in the case of strictly analytic statements that are not logically true, like "all bachelors are unmarried"—analyses. Now, it is often believed that a philosopher who believes in synthetic a priori knowledge is thereby committed to the postulation of a cognitive faculty, call it the faculty of intuitive apprehension of necessary connections, which an empiricist epistemology must repudiate. An empiricist epistemology holds, I suppose, that the only propositions that we can know to be necessary are those I call "strictly analytic." But there emerges now a gross incongruity: if a synthetic a priori proposition is one that is broadly but not strictly analytic, and broadly analytic propositions constitute the ground of validity of strictly analytic propositions, must not the same faculty be involved in knowledge of strictly analytic propositions as is alleged to be involved in knowledge of synthetic a priori propositions? To be sure, if logical truths could be established by some purely formal procedure, and if similarly analyses of concepts could be formally validated, then the situation would be far different. But I hope to show, gradually, that such a "formalistic" attitude is untenable, and that accordingly we must put up with "intuitive apprehensions of necessary connections" as long as we grant that there are necessary propositions at all. Whether there are necessary propositions that cannot be established as such by recourse to that subclass of necessary propositions called "logical truths" will then appear as a question of far less epistemological interest than has attached to it since the empiricist revolt against the "synthetic a priori."

CHAPTER 6. *The Concept of Logical Truth*

A. *Quine's Definition of Logical Truth*

As we have seen, a definition of analytic truth which is at once sufficiently exact and such as to redeem the thesis of the analyticity of ·all a priori truth of triviality inevitably uses the concept of logical truth. There is unfortunately a widespread habit (commendably resisted by Quine, however) of using " analytic " synonymously with " logically true," or to use " true by definition " as one cover-all term of contrast to " empirically true." Such indiscriminate usage may lead to unsuspected trouble. Suppose, for example, that we say of a principle of logic, like " if p and (if p, then q), then q," that it is *true by definition*, hoping secretly that this declaration will discourage proclamation of the myth of the inner eye of reason. What exactly is meant here by the phrase " true by definition "? It turns out that if a statement is said to be true by definition, it is said to be a definitional transcription (i. e. transcription with the help of definitions serving as rules of substitution) of a statement which is either itself a logical principle or a substitution instance of a logical principle.[1] Now, if we make use of the contextual definition of " if, then " in terms of " or " and " not," we may indeed transform the above logical principle into the equivalent logical principle: either not-p or not- (either not-p or q) or q. But if " not " and " or " have been elected as *primitive* logical constants, we can hardly continue to say that this logical principle is true by definition.

It is perhaps some such consideration as this which motivated Quine to make a sharp distinction between analytic and logical truth, and I think it is wise to follow him here. The concept of synonymy enters into the definition of analytic truth, but not into the definition of logical truth. A logical truth is defined by Quine as a true statement containing only logical constants essentially.[2]

[1] Cf. W. V. Quine, " Truth by Convention," reprinted in Feigl and Sellars, *Readings in Philosophical Analysis*.

[2] The qualification " essentially " serves the purpose to bring such statements as " all white men are white," in which descriptive constants occur inessentially, within the

Let us formulate immediately without ceremony the main questions raised by this definition: (1) is the definition *effective* in the sense of describing a method for deciding whether a given statement is logically true? (2) Does the definition satisfy the criterion of adequacy that all logical truths (though perhaps not *only* logical truths) are *necessary* truths? (3) Do we have a *general* definition of "logical constant" which would lend generality to the defined concept of logical truth, or must the latter be relativized to a language system?

The answer to the first question is clearly negative. If we could first determine in some way that S is true, then, provided we have antecedently enumerated a list of terms to be counted as "logical constants," it would be easy enough to determine thereafter whether S is logically true. But the definition is silent about a relevant decision procedure. In other words, the definition can at best be used to determine a statement already known to be true as logically true, but not to determine whether a statement whose truth-value is initially unknown is logically true; in this respect it is inferior to Wittgenstein's definition of the same concept, to be discussed in the sequel. Now to the second question. It is widely held that necessary truths are nonexistential, purely conditional propositions; this is precisely the way Leibniz characterized the "truths of reason." But on Quine's definition it is clearly possible for existential statements to be logically true. Consider, for example, the axiom of infinity which is required by the logicist reduction of arithmetic (provided the simple theory of types is adopted and numbers are defined as special kinds of classes) in order to insure the existence of an infinity of distinct natural numbers. This axiom can be formulated in purely logical notation. One of several possible formulations which brings out this feature is: the universal class of individuals (defined as the class of self-identical individuals) is similar to a proper subclass of itself. The relation of similarity (or one-one correspondence) is easily definable in terms of the familiar basic logical constants (terms such as "not," "all," "or"). It follows that if the axiom of infinity were true, it would be a logical truth; yet it

---

extension of the defined term. Nothing of much importance would hinge on the alternative convention adopted in the preceding chapter to restrict the term "logical truth" to abstract statements devoid of descriptive constants altogether, like "anything which is both A and B is A."

seems undeniable that finite universes are logically possible. But we can go even further. According to the logicist analysis of number concepts, a statement like "there exist 10^6 individuals" is theoretically no less reducible to a statement in purely logical notation than the statement "there exists an infinity of individuals," although the latter is even practically so reducible while the former is not. Therefore the contingent proposition "there exist 10^6 individuals" would be logically true if it happened to be true. But according to ordinary usage of "logically true" (a usage ordinary among philosophers only, as goes without saying), what is logically true does not just happen to be true; rather it is necessarily true.

Quine might well defend his definition by pointing out that the foregoing criticism is based on the assumption that a sharp distinction can be made between necessary and contingent truths, which assumption he does not share. In fact, Quine has publicly advocated a pragmatic gradualism, as it might be called, according to which there are degrees of necessity (or "apriority") of propositions, measured by degrees of reluctance to abandon them in the face of apparently contrary evidence; and he has suggested that logical truths are simply those with the highest degree of *pragmatic apriority* so defined:

> There are statements which we choose to surrender last if at all, in the course of revamping our sciences in the face of new discoveries; and among these there are some which we will not surrender at all, so basic are they to our whole conceptual scheme. Among the latter are to be counted the so-called truths of logic and mathematics, regardless of what further we may have to say of their status in the course of a subsequent sophisticated philosophy [Feigl and Sellars, p. 270; see also "Two Dogmas of Empiricism," reprinted in Quine, *From a Logical Point of View*].

However, while there may be strong grounds for accepting such a pragmatic theory of necessary truth, the above objection to Quine's definition of logical truth would still stand even if such a theory were accepted. For the more likely it is that a mistake was made in the course of the procedures of verification that led to acceptance of a proposition p, the greater our readiness ought to be to surrender p when confronted with apparently contrary evidence. Now, the likelihood of a mistake, in counting, increases in general with the number of objects to be counted. And if the number is as high as 10^6, the probability of an error in counting is appreciable. It follows that even if the statement "there exist 10^6 objects" were true, it would not be a necessary truth in the pragmatic sense. Yet it would be a logical truth in Quine's sense. It would be an irrelevant reply to say "but the only logical truths in Quine's sense that have so far been discovered *are* necessary truths in the pragmatic sense." For in judging the adequacy of a definition we must ask which *possibilities* are excluded, and which permitted, by it. To give an analogy: suppose we lived in a universe in which people are so well informed and rational that they never believe false propositions. Could we then defend the definition "X knows that $p = X$ believes that p, and p is highly probable on the total evidence available to X" on the ground that *as a matter of fact* it does not lead to the unacceptable conclusion that some false propositions are known, since, even though there are false propositions which are highly probable on the total evidence available at a given time, nobody *as a matter of fact* believes false propositions? Whoever argued that way would betray serious misunderstanding of what it means to say of a given term that it means such and such in ordinary usage. As long as the above definition leaves it a logical possibility that false propositions should be known—as it does—it is inadequate. Similarly, the debated definition of "logical truth" does not exclude the logical possibility that contingent propositions might be logically true, and must therefore be rejected.

B. *What Is a Logical Constant?*

However, even if it should be held that the distinction between necessary and contingent propositions is too obscure to deserve consideration in a discussion of so exact a concept as "logical truth," Quine's definition would still leave us with the troublesome question: by what criterion are we to distinguish logical constants from nonlogical constants? [3]

The customary procedure of logicians who define their meta-

[3] The following up to p. 138, as well as pp. 142-3, is reprinted with slight alterations from my article "Logic and the Concept of Entailment," *Journal of Philosophy* (June 1950). Acknowledgment is made to the editors of the *Journal of Philosophy* for permission to reprint.

logical concepts with respect to a specified deductive system is to define "logical constant" simply by *enumeration*. But while such definitions serve the function of criteria of application, they clearly cannot be regarded as analyses of intended meanings. To give an analogy, suppose we defined "colored" by enumerating n known colors, i. e. colored $= C_1$ or $C_2 \cdots$ or C_n. And suppose we subsequently became acquainted with a new color which we name "C_{n+1}." On the basis of our definition it would be self-contradictory to say that C_{n+1} is a color, or at any rate we could not say that it is a color in the same sense as the initially enumerated ones. Thus so-called definitions by enumeration do not tell us anything about the meaning of the defined predicate, and the same is true of many recursive definitions. In fact, recursive definitions of "logical constant" given by logicians usually amount to an enumeration of logical signs with the additional stipulation that any sign definable in terms of these alone is also a logical sign. The problem of defining this basic metalogical concept *explicitly*, however, cannot be said to have been solved.[4]

Frequently the explanation is given that logical signs are purely *formal* (or syntactic) constituents of sentences, as though it were perfectly clear what was meant by that. But in classifying a sentence as having such and such a form we presumably point out what it has in common with other sentences. Why, then, could not the sentences "the sky is blue" and "all examination booklets are blue" be said to be formally similar on account of sharing the constituent "blue," if it is all right to call the sentences "the sky is blue" and "the weather is nasty" formally similar because they contain the "is" of predication as a common element? If all we can reply is that the latter is a formal sign while "blue" is a descriptive sign, the above explanation leaves us no wiser than we were before.

Logical terms are, as usually understood, contrasted with descriptive terms, and if, therefore, an independent definition of "descriptive term" were at hand, a logical term could simply be defined as a non-descriptive term. It will appear, however, that such an independent definition presents grave difficulties. To begin with, it would not be clarifying to define a descriptive term as one that refers

[4] A critical comment on the proposed solution by Reichenbach, in his *Elements of Symbolic Logic*, will be found later in this chapter.

to an *observable* feature of the world as long as we have no clear criterion of observability. Are numbers, for example, observable features of the world? This could not plausibly be denied since numbers are observable properties of collections,[5] although of a higher type than the properties which could be ascribed to the elements of the collection singly; and yet number predicates would by most logicians be classified as logical terms, in view of the logicist reduction of arithmetic. Again, it would not be illuminating to define descriptive terms as those terms that may function as substituends for variables, where variables are divided, say, into individual, predicate, and propositional variables. For if the logician were asked why, for example, no connective variables, i. e., variables taking connectives as values, occur in his system, he would presumably reply that connectives are not descriptive terms. Perhaps we shall fare better if, instead of looking for an explicit definition, we try a contextual definition, like the following: T occurs as a descriptive term in argument A, if A would remain valid, respectively invalid, if any other syntactically admissible term were substituted for T in all its occurrences. But this definition is open to objections from two angles: (1) if it is our aim to define " logical term " negatively, as " non-descriptive term," then this definition makes it impossible to define a valid argument as one such that the implication from premise to conclusion is true just by virtue of the meanings of the logical constants involved. At least this is an objection from the point of view of those who are not satisfied with accepting " valid " as a meta-logical primitive. (2) While the mentioned condition is no doubt necessary, in line with the idea that the logical validity of an argument does not depend upon the subject-matter which the argument is about (briefly, the idea that logic is a *formal* science), it is not sufficient. For example, the identity-sign occurs inessentially in arguments of the form " if $x = y$ and $y = z$, then $x = z$; $x = y$ and $y = z$; therefore $x = z$": any other relation could be substituted for identity here and the argument would remain valid since it is in fact just a special case of " if p, then q; p; therefore q." If we now say that identity is a descriptive constant, we must surrender the thesis

[5] One might take exception to this statement on the ground that the logicist thesis defines numbers as properties (or classes) of *classes*, and that classes, unlike collections, are abstract entities. But then the question would arise in what sense the logicist definitions provide a justification of the *empirical application* of number concepts. The question transcends, however, the scope of this discussion.

of the reducibility of mathematics to logic, since numbers are not definable in terms of logical constants without identity; and if we say that identity is a logical constant, then we must admit that logical constants are capable of vacuous occurrence in valid arguments (or in tautologies). The point is that a term may occur inessentially in valid arguments without being descriptive. But let us not give up before having explored the possibility of a *positive* definition of " logical constant."

The process by which terms used in deductive arguments are actually identified as logical and as determining the logical form of the argument is to replace constants with variables until only those constants are left over on whose meanings the validity of the argument depends. But the definition thus suggested, in terms of *essential occurrence* in deductive arguments, has already been seen to be unsatisfactory, since one and the same term may occur essentially in one argument and inessentially in another. This is particularly obvious if our arguments contain defined terms: in " x is a triangle, therefore x has three sides," " triangle " occurs essentially, but in " x is a triangle, all triangles have property P, therefore x has P," " triangle " occurs vacuously. The explicit definition of " logical term " proposed by Reichenbach [6] seems to me, indeed, to break down because of this circumstance, viz. that the concepts " logical term " and " term occurring essentially in every necessary implication in which it occurs " do not have the same extension. Reichenbach attempts to clarify the distinction between logical and descriptive terms by means of the distinction between expressive and denotative terms. Denotative terms are substituends for individual, predicate, or propositional variables, and expressive terms are those which do not denote. A logical term is then defined as an indispensable expressive term, or one definable in terms of such. This definition leads, however, to such embarrassing consequences as that the connectives " or," " and," etc., are not logical terms. For while " or," for example, may be used, and mostly is used, as an expressive term, it could be used as value of a dyadic predicate variable. Instead of writing " p or not-p " one would then write " or $(p$, not-$p)$." To be sure, as such a denotative term it is definable by means of the corresponding expressive term, but *ipso facto* the latter is not indispensable: definitional eliminability works both

---

[6] See *Elements of Symbolic Logic*, § 55.

ways. If I understand Reichenbach correctly, he hoped to overcome this difficulty by defining " logical term " with respect to a language in which the following notational convention is observed: in a tautologous formula only such denotative terms may occur as have a vacuous occurrence. Thus we should not express universality by a second level predicate " Un " and write, for example, $Un(fx \vee -fx)$ (instead of the more usual formula $(x)(f)(fx \vee -fx)$), since " Un " here would occur essentially, i. e. the function obtainable from this proposition by substituting an appropriate variable for the second level predicate would not be universally assertable. But this convention will not do the job of saving the initial definition, since it presupposes that the concepts " logical term " and " term having an essential occurrence in tautologies " have the same extension, which they do not. To add an illustration to the one already offered, in the tautology " $(p \vee q) \supset (p \vee q)$ " the logical term " $\vee$ " occurs inessentially. And any tautology that contains defined predicates illustrates the possibility of essential occurence, in tautologies, of nonlogical terms.[7]

But even if these anomalous cases of vacuous occurrence of logical constants could be discounted for some reason, the general definition of " logical constant " in terms of " essential occurrence in valid deductive arguments " would be open to further objections. In the first place, since terms that would not normally be classified as " logical " may occur essentially in arguments containing defined terms, one would have to specify either that the arguments referred to are to be formally valid or that they are to contain no definable

[7] One may reply that while logical terms may, indeed, occur vacuously in some tautologies they do not occur vacuously in all tautologies and that this is the reason why they cannot be treated as values of variables. The suggested definition of " logical term " as " term occurring essentially in *some* tautologies " leads, however, into the following dilemma. Either " tautology " is so used that only sentences in primitive notation could be tautologies, or more broadly (and more in accordance with ordinary usage) so that sentences containing defined terms could also be tautologies. In the former case, there could be no defined logical terms at all, since obviously a defined logical term cannot occur (and *a fortiori* cannot occur essentially) in sentences which contain no defined terms. In the second case, however, terms that are ordinarily regarded as descriptive, like " bachelor," would turn out to be logical, since they occur essentially in such tautologies as " all bachelors are unmarried men." If, to avoid the latter consequence, the definition of " logical term " is restricted to non-descriptive languages, it becomes circular again, since a nondescriptive language is presumably a language containing besides variables only logical constants.

predicates. This, however, is a real dilemma. Relatively to the first specification, the definition is circular, since an argument is said to be formally valid if it is valid by virtue of the meanings of the logical terms alone; and relatively to the second specification we get a concept which is applicable only to fictitious *completely analyzed* languages.

The criterion of essential occurrence in valid inferences furthermore faces the difficulty that constants which are ordinarily regarded as nonlogical may occur essentially even in inferences that involve no *defined* descriptive terms. " x is extended " follows from " x is colored," " x is colored " follows from " x is red," " x is not blue " follows from " x is red." If these predicates should be unanalyzable—and there is surely as much reason to suppose them unanalyzable as to suppose that *any* predicates are unanalyzable—then the above statements are either statements of irreducibly *material* (synthetic) entailments, or else their predicates would have to be accepted as logical constants by the above criterion. It is easy to prove that the first alternative is inevitable if those predicates are classified as nonlogical constants. If a nonlogical constant occurs essentially in an inference, then the only way in which the inference can be shown to be *formally* valid is by replacing that constant with its definiens; thus the inference from " x is a father " to " x has at least one child," in which " father " occurs essentially, can be translated into the formal inference from " x is a man who has at least one child " to " x has at least one child." Since the assumption of unanalyzability of the predicates " blue " and " red " makes it impossible to exhibit the inference from " x is red " to " x is not blue " as formally valid, we have to recognize this inference as irreducibly material, unless we adopt " blue " and " red " as logical constants just because they occur essentially in some valid inferences. But we have not yet come to the end of the absurdities facing a philosopher who adopts the debated criterion of " logical constant " in order to arrive at a neat definition of logical truth. Consider Kant's famous " ought implies can," interpreted to mean " ' act A is obligatory ' entails ' A is capable of being performed.' " If obligatoriness should be an unanalyzable ethical concept, then this entailment would be either material or else " obligatory " becomes a strange addition to our stock of logical constants. Since presumably the latter alternative could not be taken seriously, we would have to recognize this as a material entailment, and the thesis that all logical necessity depends on the forms of statements alone would have to be surrendered just because of the way the extension of the term " logical constant," and therewith of the term " logical truth," has been restricted.

As just suggested, some philosophers, notably " empiricists," feel strongly that entailment is essentially a *formal* relation between statements. If an entailment seems to depend on the *meanings* of descriptive terms, like " ' x is a father ' entails ' x has a child,' " this appearance, it is maintained, can be effectively destroyed by elimination of defined terms. The animus behind this formalistic theory of entailment is presumably the dread of *intuition* as the final judge of entailment relations. If we reflect, however, on the fact that whether an entailment be formal or material depends altogether on what terms are designated as " logical constants " (a formal entailment being defined as one that holds by virtue of the meanings of logical constants alone) , and on the further fact that such designation is to some degree arbitrary, we shall find it difficult to appreciate this issue as a genuine one. The ideal of getting along with a minimum of primitives leads the logician to select a small set of primitive logical constants (e. g. the notion of " not both "—i. e. Sheffer's stroke function—and the notion of " all ") , and whether a term is eligible to the title " logical constant " depends on the frequency with which it occurs essentially in deductively valid inferences. But at the same time the ideal of economy with independently valid forms of argument induces him to expand the stock of logical constants by introducing *defined* logical constants. A close analysis of this procedure of extending the boundary of logical truth by definitional introduction of new logical constants will reveal that the extension of " logical truth," as defined by Quine, cannot be delimited without conventional decisions, and that consequently the formalistic theory of entailment cannot even be evaluated as true or false. I would like to illustrate the point in terms of a " logical constant " that has been singularly effective as a tool of expansion of the domain of logical truth: *identity*.

The only way in which identity is explicitly definable on the basis of such primitive logical constants as " not both " and " all " is the Leibnizian way, which involves universal quantification over a predicate variable: $x = y =_{df} (P) (Px \equiv Py)$. To this definition, however, several objections have been raised. According to some philosophers, it is "evidently" a logical possibility that distinct objects should agree in all properties.[8] According to others, quantification over predicate variables is the formal reflection of an ontological commitment (recognition of universals as existing) which no tough-minded empiricist could incur; they are the nominalists whose own commitment, whether it is called "ontological" or "methodological," to Occam's razor plagues them with the formidable task of reducing the higher functional calculus to the lower functional calculus. Again, there is the, somewhat outdated, objection that Leibniz' definition involves the vicious-circle fallacy; and in order to make the definition both conform to the vicious-circle prohibition and adequate, Russell argued, the axiom of reducibility must be assumed; but Russell himself recognized the latter as a "logical truth" only with great compunction. Finally, however, there is the view that identity is not only not definable in terms of the less problematic logical constants, but is not even a genuine concept; putting it in the formal mode of speech, this is Wittgenstein's view that identity is something that is *shown by* the symbolism employed but should not be symbolized at all, since if it is, then nonsense results. If a logical system conforming to this view were constructed, it would contain no sign of identity, but the function of this sign would be taken over by the metalinguistic rule that only *different* constants may be substituted for different variables.[9]

As this brief survey of philosophers' opinions about identity shows, it cannot be maintained without further ado that the concept of identity may be definitionally introduced into the functional calculus. Indeed, most logicians speak simply of "addition" of the identity sign to the primitive logical constants of the lower functional calculus, realizing that a definitional introduction would

[8] See, e. g., F. P. Ramsay, "The Foundations of Mathematics," in F. P. Ramsay, *The Foundations of Mathematics and Other Logical Essays* (New York, 1931), p. 31.

[9] See the criticisms raised by Carnap against this convention, in *Logical Syntax of Language*, § 16a. I would add to Carnap's objections that even in formulating such a rule of substitution, which is to enable elimination of the identity sign from the object language, the term "identical" must be employed in the metalanguage when one speaks of identical and different variables or constants. Wittgenstein, though, would not accept this as a valid criticism, since according to the mystical philosophy of language he sketched in the *Tractatus*, anything one attempts to say *about* language is nonsense anyway.

involve transgression into the "higher" regions of functional logic. But how, then, is designation of this concept as a "logical" constant to be justified? As already demonstrated, it could not be maintained that whenever the sign of identity occurs in an argument it occurs essentially. As a matter of fact, in any argument which results from the substitution of identity for the relation-variable in a theorem of relational logic (such as "if R is asymmetrical, then R is irreflexive"), identity occurs but vacuously.[10] Now, if identity should be excluded from the stock of logical constants, then the whole reduction of the concepts of arithmetic, algebra and analysis to logical concepts would be impossible, since identity enters into the definition of the number one: $1 =_{df} \hat{\alpha}[(\exists x)\ (y)\ (x \in \alpha \equiv y = x)]$. But in that case no entailment between statements of those disciplines which contain extralogical primitives essentially (e. g. "x is greater than y" entails "y is not greater than x," where "x" and "y" are number variables) could be regarded as *formal*.

As already mentioned, it would not be a helpful alternative to the criterion of essential occurrence to say that logical constants are those terms which we need to characterize the *logical forms* of statements. For one thing, it is not obvious that one could define "logical form" in any other way than as "what is left over of a statement if, after elimination of defined terms, all terms are replaced by variables except the logical constants." Secondly, it depends on arbitrary notational conventions whether a given symbol is needed for an enumeration of possible forms of statements. For example, we might introduce "non-empty" as a second-level predicate, so that "$(\exists x)\ Px$" could be written "non-empty (P)," in which case existential statements would turn into a subclass of predications and cease to be counted as a separate form of statements. Similarly, if identity were treated as an ordinary value of a dyadic relation-variable, it would be redundant to mention "$x = y$" as a separate form of statement after "xRy" has already been mentioned.

But even if a good argument could be given in support of the claim, presupposed by the logicist thesis of reducibility, that identity

---

[10] Some logicians would forbid manipulation of the identity sign as a substituend for variables, but this prohibition is nothing but the counterpart of the *decision* to treat identity as a logical constant, and hence irrelevant to the question of justification of such decisions.

is a logical constant, the formalist theory of entailment would have to be regarded as a curious claim. A simple example will serve the purpose of exposing its unsoundness.

Since the relational predicate of arithmetic, " being greater than " $[G(x, y)]$, does not belong to the vocabulary of logic, the sentence " if $G(x, y)$, then not-$G(y, x)$ " could not, offhand, be said to express a formal entailment. This postulate of arithmetic, however, can be reduced to pure logic by defining numbers as properties (or classes) of classes and defining the mentioned arithmetical relation in terms of the logical concepts " similarity " ($=$ one-one correspondence) and " proper subclass." But the definition which enables such a reduction is obviously not an arbitrary stipulation; rather it expresses an analysis of a primitive concept of arithmetic. And what else does one judge, in judging this analysis to be correct, but that the propositional function " the number of A is greater than the number of B " entails and is entailed by the propositional function " B is similar to a proper subclass of A " (where A and B are finite classes) ? But since the nonlogical term " greater " occurs essentially in the corresponding conditional statement,[11] this is definitely not a formal entailment. We have succeeded in formalizing the entailment from " $G(x, y)$ " to " not-$G(y, x)$ " only by accepting the material entailment just mentioned. I anticipate the objection that analysis of a term belonging to an interpreted language must not be confused with *interpretation* of the primitives of a postulational system; that there is no sense in speaking here of an entailment holding between a proposition of arithmetic and a proposition of logic, since a postulate of uninterpreted arithmetic is no proposition. I submit, however, that if the logicist thesis is to be redeemed from the charge of triviality, it must be taken to assert that the terms of *interpreted* arithmetic are definable in terms of logical constants. For the thesis that uninterpreted arithmetic, as erected upon Peano's postulates, is logic could only mean one or the other of equally trivial propositions: (a) assertions of the form " if the postulates are true, for a given interpretation, then the theorems are true, for that interpretation " belong to logic; (b) Peano's postulates are satisfied by a logical interpretation. (a) is trivial, since in this sense

---

[11] By the conditional statement *corresponding* to the entailment-statement "'p' entails 'q'" I mean the statement " if p, then q," which occurs in the object language and does not contain names of statements.

any uninterpreted postulational system is logic; (b) is trivial, since the logical interpretation is by no means the only one which satisfies Peano's postulates. Any class of objects which is the field of an asymmetrical one-one relation R and which contains an object (a " first " element) which does not stand in the converse relation to any member of the field of R, and whose members are such that any property of the first element which is hereditary with respect to R belongs to all of them, would be a model for Peano's postulates (cf. B. Russell, *Introduction to Mathematical Philosophy*, chap. 1). If the model is geometrical, for example, one could then with equal plausibility say that arithmetic is reducible to geometry.

If I were to permit myself the use of inexact metaphorical language in the midst of an austerely exact discussion, I would say that as logic expands by naturalizing more and more alien concepts in its economic household, one material entailment is used to kill off another, and *ipso facto* material entailments are there to stay. Furthermore, that we can reduce an apparently nonformal entailment to a formal entailment by supplying a correct analysis for the troublesome nonlogical terms is no surprise. For is not such reducibility a tacit *criterion* of a correct analysis? Would Russell and Whitehead, for example, have proposed those definitions of the primitives of arithmetic in terms of logical concepts which they did propose, if these definitions had not enabled them to reduce, say, Peano's postulates to pure logic? Or, to take a simpler example, how could one controvert the claim that the admittedly necessary connection between the attributes " colored " and " extended " is at bottom a formal one, which would no doubt become evident if we knew the correct analysis of the attribute " colored "? It could not be controverted simply because no such analysis would be judged correct unless it enabled the purely formal deduction of the attribute " extended." (I shall return to this point in Chapter 8.)

C. The Concept of Tautology

After having seen how the difficulty, if not impossibility, of producing a general criterion for the distinction between logical and descriptive constants [12] undermines the formalist theory of entail-

[12] It should not be supposed that the mentioned difficulties can easily be overcome by defining logical constants as those terms which are indispensable for logical discourse about *any* subject matter. For surely it is not necessary, for example, to use

ment,[13] let us take a fresh look at the problem of analyzing the concept of logical truth. One of the undisputable contributions which Wittgenstein made to analytic philosophy is that he produced an explicatum for the concept of logical truth which, if it were adequate, would have the virtue of making all questions of logical truth in principle *decidable*: the concept of the *tautologous truth-function*. A compound (or "molecular") statement like " if Smith is a professor, then he is either intelligent or not " is a tautology in the sense that any statement of the same form, depicted as " if *p*, then either *q* or not-*q*," is true regardless of the truth-values of the component statements. This definition raises no problem as long as we confine ourselves to the ground floor of logic, called the " propositional calculus," since here the only statements that are to be determined as logically true, logically false, or "indeterminate" (i. e. neither logically true nor logically false) are just molecular statements. And the familiar truth-tables constitute a mechanical device for deciding into which of these three groups a given molecular statement falls. What is controversial, however, is just how this concept of tautology could be generalized so as to apply to functional logic, containing such statement forms as " $(x) [Px \supset Qx] \cdot (\exists x) Px \supset (\exists x) Qx$ " as well. When propositional logic is axiomatized and accordingly the truth-table test of logical truth is superseded by the deduction test, we can still use this mechanical decision procedure for determining whether the selected axioms are tautologies. But this test would clearly fail if applied

---

" or ": " *p* or *q* " can be replaced by " not neither *p* nor *q*." And if it should be replied that at least the primitive logical constants satisfy the above definition, one would overlook that no logical constant is intrinsically primitive; it is only *chosen* as primitive.

[13] Carnap recognizes, in his *Introduction to Semantics*, that a suitable general definition of " logical sign " is not yet known. On the other hand, an attempt to produce such a definition has been made by Karl Popper, in " Logic without Assumptions," *Proceedings of the Aristotelian Society*, new ser. 47 (1947); see also " New Foundations for Logic," *Mind*, July 1947. Popper constructs the definition on the basis of the term " absolutely valid inference," which is defined in such a way that it turns out to be synonymous with " inference of the form ' if *p* and *q*, then *p* ' " (this is ordinarily called " circular reasoning "). For an apparently fatal criticism of Popper's definition, see the review by J. C. C. McKinsey, in the *Journal of Symbolic Logic*, June 1948. But whether or not McKinsey's criticism is valid, I do not see that Popper's definitions of the logical constants in terms of " deducible " make the idea of logical truth any clearer than the idea of necessary truth, for what does " *q* is deducible from *p* " mean if not " if *p* is true, then *q* must be true "?

to the axioms or theorems of functional logic, such as: $(x) Px \equiv -(\exists x) - Px$.

Now, Wittgenstein thought that his concept of "tautology" was a *generally* adequate explicatum for the concept of logical truth because he believed in the thesis of extensionality, according to which all propositions are truth-functions of atomic propositions. If it should turn out that the concept of "atomic proposition" has fatal defects, the thesis of extensionality would be suspect for this reason alone. But since this concept will be critically examined later (pp. 251-5) we may as well concentrate here on difficulties that would persist even if the concept of atomic proposition were unobjectionable. The obvious way in which Wittgenstein's thesis would be used to make the concept of the tautologous truth-function applicable to statements involving quantifiers is as follows. The *universal* assertion of a function is construed as the assertion of the conjunction of its values, and the existential assertion as the assertion of the disjunction of its values: $(x) Px =_{df} Pa \cdot Pb \cdot \cdot \cdot Pn$; $(\exists x) Px =_{df} Pa \vee Pb \vee \cdot \cdot \cdot \vee Pn$. If we take n as sufficiently small, say 2, we can show by means of not too cumbersome a truth-table that such axioms or theorems of functional logic as above listed are tautologies. Moreover, since it depends only on the *form* of a molecular statement, and not on the number of atomic components, whether the statement is a tautology, we have thus a method for showing that a statement form is a tautology *in any finite world* (meaning by a "finite world" a world with a finite number of individuals named by a finite number of individual constants).[14]

---

[14] The so-called "finitists" hold that unrestrictedly universal statements are meaningless on account of being unverifiable: verification would involve testing an infinite number of substitution instances. Against this finitism it has been argued, e.g. by Carnap (*Logical Syntax of Language*, § 43) , that a universal statement may in some cases be established by a finite proof procedure without even considering a single substitution instance (the argument is used by Carnap in the context of rejecting the claim that sentences containing "impredicative" terms—terms introduced by definitions sinning against Russell's vicious-circle prohibition—are undecidable). However, it would be a weak argument against Wittgenstein to say that his atomistic thesis entails the undecidability of those truths of functional logic that are universal statements. For Wittgenstein could validly reply that each substitution instance of such a universal statement is finitely decidable by the truth-table method and that, as all substitution instances have the same form, decision of one substitution instance would be equivalent to decision of all substitution instances. It cannot, therefore, be argued against the atomistic thesis that it entails the undecidability of the universal truths of functional logic.

However, even if we disregarded entirely such *prima facie* non-extensional compound propositions as modal propositions and propositions about beliefs (and other " propositional attitudes "), there are two grave objections to the indicated reduction of functional logic to propositional logic.

The first of these may be called the argument *from the meaning of allness*. Let us take a close look at the alleged logical equivalence by means of which the reduction of functional logic to propositional logic is to be accomplished: $(x) Px = Pa \cdot Pb \cdots \cdot Pn$.[15] The entailment from left to right is easily justified in terms of the principle " what is true of all is true of any "—although one might argue that this very principle, which is as good a logical truth as any, could hardly be shown to be a tautology in the sense of propositional logic without presupposing the above equivalence, and so without begging the question at issue.[16]

But how are we to justify the converse entailment? The difficulty lurking here is implicitly recognized by Russell and Whitehead in a significant statement that occurs in the introduction to the second edition of *Principia Mathematica* (the most important innovation of which is the adoption of Wittgenstein's thesis of extensionality, enabling the authors to drop the undesirable axiom of reducibility):

> Given all true atomic propositions, together with the fact that they are all, every other true proposition can theoretically be deduced by logical methods. That is to say, the apparatus of crude fact required in proofs can all be condensed into the true atomic propositions together with the fact that every true atomic proposition is one of the following: (here the list should follow) [2d ed., p. xv].

We cannot deduce " $(x)Px$ " from the conjunction " $Pa \cdot Pb \cdots Pn$ " alone, but require the further premise that $a, b \cdots n$ are *all the individuals there are*. Can this proposition be formulated as a truth-function of atomic propositions?[17] Let us try. Its immediate for-

---

[15] We may confine ourselves to the case of allness, for the existential quantifier can be definitionally introduced on the basis of " all " and " not," and hence its reduction to the logical constants of propositional logic raises no new problem.

[16] This point is made by P. F. Strawson, in his penetrating review of G. H. von Wright's *Form and Content in Logic* (*Philosophy*, October 1951) .

[17] Russell recognized later that it cannot. See *An Inquiry into Meaning and Truth*, p. 255.

malization would be $(x)[(x = x) \equiv (x = a) \vee (x = b) \vee \cdots \vee (x = n)]$.
In order to reduce this universal statement to a truth-function of
atomic statements, we make use of the reductive definition of "all"
(waiving the question whether this procedure is not, after all,
circular), and obtain a conjunction of n truth-functions of the form:
$(a = a) \equiv (a = a) \vee (a = b) \vee \cdots \vee (a = n)$. But, lo and behold, each
conjunct of this conjunction is a tautology,[18] and hence the conjunction itself is a tautology. Something must have gone wrong,
for we set out to formalize a synthetic premise which is needed
for the deduction of "$(x) Px$" from atomic premises. Indeed, on
second thought, this result is not so surprising, for in ending the
series of substitutions of individual constants for the bound variable
after the n'th substitution, we just assumed that there are n, and
no more, individuals; so that all we have asserted is "if there are
just n individuals, then there are just n individuals." The moral
to be drawn is obvious: the synthetic premise in question, involving
the notion of allness, must always be presupposed whenever the
reductive definition under discussion is applied to a universal
statement, and hence the attempt to eliminate "(x)" from it by
means of that definition is comparable to the attempt to catch one's
own shadow.

But even if this difficulty could be circumvented, the question
would remain whether the analysis of a universal statement into
the conjunction of its substitution instances adequately renders
the meaning of "all." And it is easy to show that it does not. To
see this clearly, we need to keep in mind only that the very *significance* of an atomic statement "Pa" presupposes the *existence* of
the individual a. For, as Russell has emphasized, the individual
constants occurring in atomic statements are *logically proper* names,
which is to say that they have no connotation and hence would
mean nothing if they did not denote. Since the significance of a
molecular statement depends on the significance of its atomic constituents, it follows that if n individual constants occur in a given
molecular statement, then the significance of the latter presupposes the existence of at least n individuals. But consider, now, a
logical truth of functional logic like: $(x) (fx \supset gx) \cdot (\exists x) (fx \cdot hx)$

---

[18] Proof: the left-hand side is always a tautology, and the right-hand side is always
a tautology since it always contains one tautologous disjunct. Therefore the equivalence cannot fail to hold.

$\supset (\exists x) \ (gx \cdot hx)$.[19] Is it not strange to suppose that its significance varies with the number of existing individuals, such that it could not have the same meaning in different finite universes? But this *is* a consequence of the discussed atomistic reduction; for if the significance of S_1 presupposes the truth of p, and the significance of S_2 the truth of q, and p is not equivalent to q, then S_1 is not synonymous with S_2 (let e. g. $p =$ there are n individuals, and $q =$ there are m individuals, where $n \neq m$). One should think that the unique significance of such a statement could be grasped by simply grasping the meanings of the logical constants involved, without even raising the question of "what there is."

If, however, there should be a fatal flaw in the presented argument from the meaning of "all" a serious objection to the Wittgensteinian theory of logical truth would still remain. We have seen that, granted the validity of the atomistic thesis, the truths of functional logic can be shown to be tautologies in *any finite world of individuals*. But it would be fallacious to suppose that if a proposition is true in any finite world then it is also true in an infinite world. Thus, according to the logicist philosophy of mathematics, the existence of an infinity of individuals (entities of lowest type) is a necessary and sufficient condition for the existence of an infinity of distinct natural numbers. It follows that the proposition of arithmetic "there is no greatest integer" is, in logicist interpretation, true if *and only if* the world of individuals is infinite. This illustrates that a propositon which is demonstrably true in an infinite universe may fail to be a tautology, in fact may be false, in any finite universe; and that a proposition which is true in any finite universe, may be demonstrably false in an infinite universe.[20]

Further, the question remains at least debatable whether the thesis of extensionality holds for all types of propositions within which logical truths might be found, most notably the types of propositions that are usually mentioned as problematic in discussions of the question: modal propositions and propositions about propositional attitudes. A comprehensive discussion of this old

[19] To be quite accurate, what expresses a logical truth is the universal closure "$(f) \ (g) \ (h) \ (\cdot \ \cdot \ \cdot)$" of the above open sentence. If, on the other hand, "f," "g," "h" are what Quine calls "schematic letters," not bindable variables, then one would have to speak here of the common form of an infinite class of logical truths.

[20] This difficulty with the generalized concept of tautology is emphasized by von Wright in "Form and Content in Logic."

problem would be out of place here. Nevertheless a word about the way the extensionalists originally tried to take this hurdle may be appropriate. It was simply denied that such propositions as " I believe that John is a native Englishman " and " it is necessary that there be no father who does not have at least one child " contain a propositional component; indeed if this denial were valid, then these propositions would be atomic and so could not fail to be truth-functional. The denial was based on the assumption that these *prima facie* object-linguistic statements are adequately translatable into a metalanguage, as statements about sentences, and thus containing within themselves names of sentences, not sentences: " I believe ' John is a native Englishman ' "; " ' all fathers have at least one child ' is necessary." [21] If, however, these translations are inadequate—and it is not difficult to show that they are [22]—and the predicates of these statements (" is believed by so and so," " is necessary ") should irreducibly apply to propositions, not sentences, then the thesis of extensionality would be untenable. Here an advocate of the criticized theory of logical truth might reply that such a breakdown of the thesis of extensionality would affect his theory only if logical truths could be found among such nonextensional compound propositions. Conceivably no propositions of the forms " X believes that p " and " it is necessary that p " are logically true, and if so, their nonextensionality would not invadidate the theory of logical truth under discussion. Granted. But if, on the contrary, it could be shown that if p is necessary, then it is necessary that p be necessary (as I have attempted to show in the preceding chapter), then it would have to be conceded that some propositions of the form " it is necessary that p " are themselves necessary if there are any necessary propositions at all. And since, on any adequate theory of logical truth, logical truths are necessary truths, and whatever proposition is strictly implied by a logical truth is itself a logical truth, it would follow that there are logical truths of the form " it is necessary that p " if there are any logical truths at all. For this reason our later examination of the linguistic theory of logical necessity—which entails, as will be shown, that there are no necessary propositions at all—will have a definite bearing on the Wittgensteinian theory of logical truth.

[21] Cf. Carnap, *Logical Syntax of Language*, §§ 68, 69.
[22] See below, pp. 199-201.

D. *Carnap's Explication*: *L-truth*

I turn now to the Carnapian variant of Wittgenstein's theory of logical truth. It may, without detracting from Carnap's originality, be called a "variant" since it is an elaboration of Wittgenstein's idea that a logically true statement *exhausts the range of possibilities* and that this is evident from the very form of the statement. As truth-table analysis reveals, every formula of propositional logic can be written as a disjunction of truth-conditions, e. g. "$p \supset q$" as "$p.q \lor -p.q \lor -p.-q$." If the formula is a tautology, then the range of conditions that would make it true coincides with the total range of possible conditions. For example, "$(p.(p \supset q)) \supset q$" turns into "$p.q \lor p.-q \lor -p.q \lor -p.-q$." The test of whether the "disjunctive normal form" to which the formula has been reduced expresses a tautology is simply whether the disjunction of $n-1$ disjuncts is equivalent to the negation of the n'th disjunct, such that the whole disjunction may be regarded as an instance of "$p \lor -p$." Thus, the disjunction "$-p.q \lor -p.-q$" is not equivalent to "$-(p.q)$," hence "$p \supset q$" is not equivalent to an instance of "$p \lor -p$"; but "$p.-q \lor -p.q \lor -p.-q$" is equivalent to "$-(p.q)$," hence the *modus ponens* formula is equivalent to an instance of "$p \lor -p$." Carnap in effect extends this idea of the range of truth-conditions for a statement to languages that are more differentiated than the language of propositional logic in that elementary statements are not symbolized as units but as complexes of subject and predicate (or subjects and predicate in the case of relational predicates): the p's and q's are replaced by the *atomic statements* (another heritage from Wittgenstein) "Pa," "Qb," "Ra, b," where "a," "b" are names of individuals, "P," "Q" predicates designating simple qualities, "R" a relational predicate designating a simple relation. The disjunction of truth-conditions now takes the form of a disjunction of *state descriptions*, where a state description is a conjunction of atomic statements and negations of atomic statements which contains, for every atomic statement of the language, either it or its negation but not both (cf. above, p. 16). The "range" of a statement being defined as the class of state descriptions in which the statement is true, an *L-true* statement is defined as a statement with universal range, i. e. with a range comprising all state descriptions.

Before turning to the notorious difficulties besetting the notion of logical atomicity which is, in Carnap's scheme, presupposed by the notion of *L*-truth, I wish to examine whether this definition is useful as a *general* definition, i. e. a definition which is not relative to a particular language system. The conspicuous absence, in the definiens, of the concept of " logical constant " which, as we saw, stubbornly resists attempts at a general definition, seems to hold out hope in this direction. We shall be sadly disappointed, however, once we ask what exactly is meant by a " state description." The only general definition that can be given is " description of a possible world." But then little has been gained by Carnap's disguise in semantic terminology of the Leibnizian conception of " truths of reason " as truths holding in all possible worlds. The definition is still as circular as it ever was: a possible world can be nothing else than a world conforming to the laws of logic. In particular it must conform to the laws of contradiction and excluded middle, which requirement Carnap expresses formally by stipulating that a description of a possible world (state description) must contain, for any atomic statement, either it or its negation but not both.[23] Carnap, I am sure, would be the first one to admit that, if construed as a general definition in the indicated manner, his definition of *L*-truth would be circular. But while the definition ceases to be circular if the term " *L*-true " is, via the term " state description," relativized to a language system, it becomes on this alternative questionable whether logical truth has been " defined " in a sense in which a

[23] Modern logicians have often pointed out that there is no justification for the habit of traditional logicians to accord the privileged status of " laws of thought " to the laws of contradiction, excluded middle, and identity rather than to any other tautology. And as a *reductio ad absurdum*, as it were, of the view that these are the most fundamental postulates of logical thinking it is sometimes pointed out that in the system of *Principia Mathematica* they occur as rather remote theorems. It seems to me, however, that a defense of the traditional view within the framework of modern logic is still possible if only we observe the distinction between an uninterpreted axiomatic system of logic and its (normal) interpretation. If we wish to justify those axioms of *Principia Mathematica* that belong to propositional logic as being logical truths (not just as being deductively fertile " postulates " in the sense in which a postulate is neither true nor false), we must have recourse to the truth-tables, and the fundamental convention underlying truth-table calculations, that every proposition has at least and at most one of the truth-values " true " and " false," is nothing else but a metalinguistic formulation of the laws of contradiction and excluded middle. And the rule that the same truth-values must be assigned to the same propositional variables corresponds to the law of identity.

" definition " can be said to clarify the meaning of a term in use. This may be shown as follows.

The concept of state description, as used by Carnap, is a semantic concept which is defined relative to a semantic system in such a way that in the precise language of explicata only the expression " state description *in L* " has meaning; although a nonrelative term " state description " is informally used in the language of explicanda in the sense of " description of a possible world " (as Carnap explicitly states, circular definitions are quite in order in the presystematic clarification of the explicanda). It follows that " *L*-true " has an exact meaning only if the language system in which state descriptions are constructed is given. The complete specification of such a language system involves definitions of " simple descriptive predicate " and " individual constant " (the building blocks for the atomic statements) in the form of enumerations of such symbols. That what Carnap means by a " language " is not quite what is ordinarily understood by this word is evident from the fact that a language in Carnap's sense is partly defined by the stock of primitive descriptive terms, such that it is a contradiction in terms to speak of the *same* language as undergoing, say, an increase of primitive vocabulary.[24] Now, it would seem to follow from Carnap's definition of " *L*-true " as a language-relative term that a statement containing an added individual constant, say *m*, could not be called " logically true " in the same sense as a statement in a language whose stock of individual constants does not contain *m*. This is paradoxical.

Carnap might reply that he has, as a matter of fact, provided a *general* definition of " *L*-true " if this means a definition which refers to no language *in particular*: " *L*-true in *S* " (where " *S* " is a *variable* ranging over semantic systems) is defined in terms of " state description in *S*," and the latter term means " conjunction containing for every atomic statement of *S* either it or its negation

---

[24] The following remark may be regarded as a generalization of Max Black's criticism of Tarski's semantic definition of truth; see Max Black, " The Semantic Definition of Truth," *Analysis* (March 1948), especially sec. 6; this article is reprinted in Black's *Language and Philosophy.* The one defect, as it seems to me, of Black's criticism of this celebrated systematic clarification of the concept of truth as being " philosophically irrelevant " is that Tarski's definition of truth has but a vacuous occurrence in it; that is, *mutatis mutandis*, Black could have raised the same objections to *any* systematic clarification, in Carnapian style, of a concept in use. The whole problem of analytic mehod, here touched upon, is discussed in greater detail below, Chaps. 13 and 14.

but not both." Moreover, if a definition is desired that does not refer to language at all, Carnap is able to satisfy this desire by producing an *absolute* concept of *L*-truth that is predicable of propositions, conceived as extralinguistic designata of declarative sentences (see *Introduction to Semantics,* § 17) .[25]

For these reasons it is better to attack Carnap's definition from a different angle. The charge I wish to make good is simply that Carnap's concept of *L*-truth is not applicable to natural languages and hence in no sense clarifies the meaning of "logically true" as predicated of statements of natural languages. Carnap and his followers might concede the charge of inapplicability but nonetheless insist that they have accomplished the task of clarification. They might invoke the analogy of the idealizing concepts of physics which, though in a sense inapplicable to physical reality, are useful tools for predicting the course of physical events. In this analogy prediction of physical events, conceived as a prime objective of physics, corresponds presumably to the clarification of concepts in use, conceived as a prime objective of analytic philosophy, and the construction of such systematic concepts as "*L*-true" to the construction of ideal, theoretical concepts like "simple pendulum," "frictionless engine," "ideal gas," etc. But if the analogy is to hold, then it ought to be possible to resolve, with the help of such a systematic concept as "*L*-true," a disagreement among philosophers as to whether a given statement of a natural language is logically true or not. And I propose to show that this is not, at least not in general, possible; for which purpose I shall select a statement frequently used in discussions about the nature of a priori truth: "whatever is red is colored." The statement is, of course, "trivial" in the sense that it is so obvious that no ordinary person would even bother to assert it; but if this were a good reason for condemning a philosophical discussion about it as trivial, then much of logic would share this fate, since the fundamental principles of inference likewise are so "obvious" that ordinary mortals do not

---

[25] Discussion of the question whether the semantic formulation "'*p*' is true (or *L*-true)" is logically equivalent to the absolute formulation "it is true that *p* (or, it is logically true that *p*)" is omitted here, since I have discussed it, and answered negatively, elsewhere—see "Note on the Semantic and the Absolute Concept of Truth," *Philosophical Studies* (Jan. 1952) ; also "Propositions, Sentences and the Semantic Definition of Truth," *Theoria* (1954). On the relation between the semantic and the absolute concept of *L*-truth, see also below, Chap. 14.

bother to state them explicitly. It might be added that this statement happened to be picked by whatever philosopher first became
puzzled about it merely as illustrative of a class of statements of
which " whatever is round has shape," " whatever is hard has degree
of solidity," and " whatever is large has size " would be equally good
illustrative examples.

What led some philosophers to doubt that this statement is
analytic in the Kantian sense is that " colored " cannot be said to
be a predicate contained in " red " the way, say, " equilateral " is
contained in " square." We say that redness is a *species* of color just
as we say that squares are a species of equilateral figures, but the
relation between the species and the genus cannot be analyzed in
the same way: we can supply a differentia which, added to the
genus " equilateral " (E) (viz. " rectangular parallelogram " (R)),
yields the species " square " (S); in other words, we can equate
the class S with the product of classes E and R. But we cannot
similarly specify a differentia which, added to the genus " colored,"
yields the species " red." Briefly, the inference from " x is red "
to " x is colored " does not have the form " p and q, therefore p." [26]
But the only other analysis that might throw this inference into a
form accredited as formally valid would be a disjunctive analysis
of " colored " as meaning " red or green or blue or . . ."; the
inference would then have the form " p, therefore p or q." Yet, the
defect of this analysis lies in the " etc." symbolized by the dots.
It is not the difficulty of exhausting all named colors which frus-
trates the attempt at explicit definition. It is rather that " colored "
is capable of conveying the *same meaning* to two people who are
acquainted with different ranges of colors, while on the proposed
definition this would be impossible. It is clear that, where " P_1,
$P_2 \cdots P_n$ " are names of colors, " P_i " cannot be synonymous with
" P_i or P_r " ($i \neq r$), since a person acquainted with the color named
by " P_i " might not be acquainted with the color named by " P_r." [27]

[26] This is correctly pointed out by B. Blanshard, in *The Nature of Thought*, 2, 406.
See also the penetrating study by A. N. Prior, " Determinables, Determinates and
Determinants (I.) ," *Mind*, January 1949.

[27] It is assumed here that color predicates are only ostensively definable, but the
argument could easily be reconstructed if we assumed that some color predicates are
verbally definable on the basis of a set of ostensively defined color predicates. The
problem of ostensive definition in relation to necessary truth is discussed in detail
below, Chap. 9.

On the proposed disjunctive definition, " colored " is, for the person acquainted with both P_1 and P_2 (setting $i = 1$, $r = 2$), synonymous with " P_1 or P_2 or $\cdots P_n$," while for the person with less extensive color acquaintance it would be synonymous with " P_1 or P_3 or $\cdots P_n$"; hence " colored " would have different meanings for those two persons. But actually such a supposition is no more plausible than the supposition that two people could attach the same meaning to " red " only if they had seen exactly the same red objects. Awareness of a common quality of a set of qualities is the same sort of abstraction as awareness of a common quality of a set of particulars; hence, if it were true that two people must have acquainted themselves with the same set of denotata of the predicate if they are to attach the same meaning to the predicate, this would be true in one case as well as in the other.

It seems to me to follow that if " $P_1, P_2, \cdots P_n$ " stands for a set of unanalyzable determinate qualities under a common determinable Q, then " Q " itself is an unanalyzable, or only ostensively definable, term. If this is correct, then " red " and " colored " must be logically independent predicates; [28] and it follows that in a language which contains both the determinate predicate " red " and the determinable predicate " colored " among its primitive predicates, some state descriptions will contain such conjunctions as " Red (a) and not-Colored (a)." But in such a language " whatever is red, is colored " would not be logically true, on Carnap's definition. Should Carnap try to avoid this difficulty by ruling that if a family of determinate predicates are contained in the set of primitive predicates, then that set must not also contain the corresponding determinable predicate, he would thereby admit that the controversy as to whether there are entailments that are not analytic, or necessary truths that are not logical truths, cannot be solved in terms of his explication of " logically true." [29] For it would

---

[28] On the connection between simplicity and logical independence of predicates, see above, p. 16.

[29] As will be pointed out in a later chapter, Carnap provides against the difficulty created for his concept of state description by the incompatibility of codeterminate predicates, like " blue " and " red " (if " blue " and " red " are both simple, primitive predicates, why could not the conjunction " blue (a) and red (a) " be contained in a state description?), by laying down a suitable convention governing the choice of primitive predicates. But he does not seem to be aware of the above-mentioned difficulty connected with the determinables we use to define a family of codeterminate predicates.—The method of incorporating " meaning postulates " into semantic systems,

follow that natural languages admit the expression of necessary truths which either cannot be expressed at all in a Carnapian language system or else are not logical truths.

E. *The Question of Epistemic Adequacy*

There is one further feature of Carnap's theory of logical truth which some might judge to be, from the point of view of philosophical analysis, a defect, although this is a defect it shares with other theories of logical truth as well as with analyses of other concepts that have been offered. The defect may be termed a violation of the *criterion of epistemic adequacy* of analyses. The criterion says that the analysis must be given in terms pointing to the usual method of coming to know (or verifying) that the analysandum applies in a given case.[30] To take a simple example which has become famous through H. Langford [31]: the analysis of " cube " as meaning " regular solid bounded by square faces, and square faces only " is epistemically adequate but not so an analysis into " regular solid with 12 edges," for one would not normally determine whether x is a cube by proceeding to count its edges, and one could know that x is a cube without knowing how many edges x has. Whether the criterion of epistemic adequacy should be adopted at all, is not in question now. Possibly its adoption reflects a commitment to the much debated view that to explicate the meaning of a statement is to describe its method of verification, and one might legitimately ask how one could, without begging the question, presuppose this criterion of meaning for the analysis of " meaning " itself.[32] But *if* it is adopted, then the Carnap-Wittgenstein analysis of the concept of logical truth in terms of the concept of range cannot be accepted without a serious restriction. The test of whether the range of a statement is universal is constructed on the assumption of the logical truth of the laws of contradiction and excluded middle.

which has recently led Carnap to a modification of the explication of " logically true," is critically discussed below, Chap. 14.

[30] This is actually one of the general criteria of adequacy for analyses which G. E. Moore formulated in replying to his critics' question " what is your analysis of the concept of a correct analysis? " See " Reply to My Critics," in P. A. Schilpp, ed., *The Philosophy of G. E. Moore*, Evanston, Ill., 1942. It will be discussed in more detail below, Chap. 10.

[31] See his " Moore's Notion of Analysis," in Schilpp.

[32] On this point, see my article " The Philosophical Analysis of Natural Language," *Methodos, 1* (1949). See also below, pp. 400 f.

This assumption is formally reflected by the "convention" to assign either T or F, but not both, to each elementary proposition, and the "convention" to include in every state description a given atomic statement or its negation but not both. It follows that at least the logical validity of these two simple and fundamental laws is not *known* as a result of such a formal test. Incidentally, this simple consideration shows that the claim that our knowledge of the laws of logic is purely *formal*, not *intuitive* as claimed by many traditional logicians, must be taken with a grain of salt.

A clear case of violation of the criterion of epistemic adequacy is the analysis of the concept of logical validity [33] in terms of the concept of " truth-frequency " of a form of inference. An inference from premises $p_1 p_2 \cdots p_n$ to conclusion q is said to be logically valid (or, simply, valid) under the following condition: if, first, all the defined nonlogical terms are replaced by their definientia, and next all the primitive nonlogical terms in the premises and the conclusion are replaced by variables, using the same variable for different occurrences of the same term, then any interpretation which satisfies the statement forms thus obtained from the premises also satisfies the statement form corresponding to the conclusion. This definition of the concept of logical consequence in terms of the concept of interpretation (or " model," as the term is used in connection with abstract axiom sets) is due to Tarski,[34] but the idea, if not the technical details, of the definition may be traced to Peirce who characterized necessary inferences as inferences leading invariably to true conclusions from true premises (the " truth-frequency," in other words, associated with such a method of inference is unity). Unquestionably this is a *property* of logically, or deduc-

---

[33] The concepts of logical truth, as predicated of statements, and of logical validity, as predicated of inferences, are closely connected, since to say that the inference from p to q is logically valid is synonymous with saying that the conditional statement " if p, then q " is logically true. Nevertheless, it cannot be inferred that a definition of logical validity would at the same time solve the problem of defining logical truth. For as was noted in the very first chapter, in connection with the critique of Leibniz, not all logical truths have conditional form. This would remain undisputable even if existential statements, like $(\exists x)\,(fx \vee -fx)$, were eliminated from the domain of logical truth; for statements of *compatibility* (e.g., ' $p \vee q$ ' is compatible with ' $p.-q$ '), and such statements as " $(x)\,(\exists y)\,(x = y)$ " (which follows from the law of identity) cannot be translated into conditionals.

[34] " Ueber den Begriff der logischen Folgerung," *Actes du Congrès International de Philosophie Scientifique*, Paris, 1936. An English translation by J. H. Woodger is contained in A. Tarski, *Logic, Metamathematics, Semantics*, London, 1956.

tively, valid inferences in the old sense of (a) a distinguishing mark, (b) a property (in the broad sense of "property," to be distinguished from the specific Aristotelian sense) which ought to be entailed by any adequate definition. Yet it should be obvious that this definition does not describe a method by which we actually establish an inference as logically valid, for if we did use the method of trying interpretation after interpretation, then all we would ever be justified in saying would be " on the evidence of a finite number of trials, it is *probable* that this inference is valid." In fact, the usual claim that an argument can be known to be logically valid without knowing the truth values of its premises and conclusion would then be untenable, but we have an effective decision procedure at least for forms of inference containing only propositional variables, such as "if p and (if p, then q), then q." [35]

To criticize Tarski's explication of the concept of logical consequence in terms of the concept of *model* (of a propositional function) on the ground of its epistemic inadequacy would be irrelevant because (a) Tarski did not claim that it is epistemically adequate, (b) there is no reason to contest that an epistemically inadequate definition may be clarifying nonetheless. However, I do think it is relevant to point out that it suffers from the defect of implicit circularity if it is meant as a perfectly general definition rather than as a definition relative to a language system. I reproduce (in English translation) his definition together with his explanation of the key term of the definiens "model":

> Let us assume that there correspond, in the language under consideration, to every extralogical constant certain variables, and in such a way that any given sentence is transformed into a sentential function if the constants occurring in it are replaced by corresponding variables. Let L be an arbitrary class of sentences. We replace all extralogical constants which occur in the sentences of the class L with corresponding variables, using the same variables for the same constants and different variables for different constants; in this manner we obtain a class L' of sentential functions. Let us call an arbitrary sequence of entities which satisfy each sentential function of the class L' a *model* or realization of sentential class L (it is in just this sense that

[35] We shall see below, Chap. 10, that the criterion of epistemic adequacy is intimately connected with some puzzling questions about the nature of philosophical analysis.

one usually speaks of the models of the axiomatic system of a deductive theory). In the special case in which the class *L* consists of a single sentence *X*, we shall call a model of class *L* also *model* of sentence *X*.

On the basis of these concepts the concept of logical consequence may be defined as follows:

Sentence *X* is a *logical consequence* of sentential class *K* if and only if every model of class *K* is at the same time a model of sentence *X*. [" Ueber den Begriff der logischen Folgerung," loc. cit.].

According to this definition, to say that " Socrates is mortal " is a logical consequence of " all men are mortal and Socrates is a man " is to say that the function " $[(x) (fx \supset gx) \cdot fy] \supset gy$ " is true for all values of the predicate variables f and g and of the free individual variable y—on the assumption that " (x) ," " $\supset$ " and " $\cdot$ " have previously been identified as logical constants. However, as I pointed out previously, it is through a process of preformal (or intuitive) determination of arguments as valid or invalid that a given constant is identified as logical, and therefore one will have to recognize that some statements logically follow from others independently of Tarski's definition before one could ever use the latter for the purpose of determining what follows from what. Perhaps Tarski would admit all this, but then the question might legitimately be raised why the above necessary equivalence should be set forth as an *analysis* of the concept " logical consequence " any more than " x is a cube if and only if x is a cube with 12 edges " would normally be proposed as an analysis of the concept " cube."

But furthermore, unless Tarski's definition is restricted to formal entailments, i. e. entailments that do not depend on the meanings of descriptive constants, it is based on a presupposition which again convicts it of implicit circularity. The presupposition I refer to is the prior elimination of defined extralogical constants. The inference from " x is a male parent " to " x is male " is logically valid on Tarski's definition, but not so the inference from " x is a father " to " x is a male." Tarski notes parenthetically the necessity of eliminating defined terms before formalizing an inference:

(for purposes of simplification certain inessential [*sic!*] complications will—here and in the following—be disregarded which are connected, on the one hand, with the theory of logical types, and on the other hand with the necessity of eliminating any defined signs that might occur in the sentences under consideration, i. e. of replacing them with the undefined signs).

In order to see that the process of "eliminating defined signs" presupposes again recognitions of entailments that are wholly independent of any application of Tarski's definition, consider the arithmetical inference: class A has two members; class B has two members; the product $A \cdot B$ is empty; class C is the logical sum of A and B; *therefore* C has 4 members. Suppose that it had been attempted sometime before the era of logicism, i. e. before the reduction of arithmetic to logic was undertaken by Frege and Russell, to determine the validity of this inference in terms of Tarski's definition. Since *ex hypothesi* the number signs " 2 " and " 4 " would be regarded as extralogical constants (specifically, descriptive predicates of the second level), one would obtain the argument form: $F(\alpha), F(\beta), \alpha \cap \beta = 0, \gamma = \alpha \cup \beta$: therefore $G(\gamma)$. And it is easy to see that by no means every model of the class of premises is also a model of the conclusion. How, then, is the obvious validity of the inference to be reconciled with Tarski's definition? Only by showing that the number signs can be so defined that the inference resulting from replacement of these signs with their definientia (though the relevant definitions, being contextual, do not allow *simple* replacement) *is* valid according to Tarski's definition. Indeed, the Frege-Russell contextual definitions, which allow the inference to be rewritten in purely logical notation, accomplish just that.

But is it not obvious that these definitions are acceptable *just because* they transform such inferences as the above into logically valid ones? In other words, it is a criterion of adequacy for definitions of arithmetical concepts in terms of logical concepts that valid arithmetical inferences, like the above example, should remain valid if definientia are substituted for definienda. And in that case logical validity must be recognizable *before* Tarski's formalization test is correctly applicable. Analogously, if a philosopher should one day produce definitions of " red " or " colored " which would show the inference of " x is colored " from " x is red " to be analytic (i. e. logically valid according to Tarski's definition), one of the essential criteria of adequacy which the definitions would have to satisfy [36] would be precisely that they enable transformation of the inference into an analytic one. Tarski's tacit assumption, therefore, that acceptable definitions of the definable terms occurring in an inference could be constructed *prior* to recognition of the inference as valid is not justified in all cases. That decision of the question whether one sentence logically entails another essentially presupposes analysis of the concepts involved, has recently been pointed out by Carnap, who recognizes [37] that we cannot positively know that two sentences are logically independent until we have driven the analysis down to unanalyzables. What Carnap does not explicitly say, however, is that an essential criterion of adequacy of such an analysis is that specified inferences involving the analyzed concept should remain logically valid when the definiendum is replaced by the definiens.

I cannot help concluding from this critical survey of the standard theories of logical truth that the concept of logical truth is no clearer than the concept of necessary truth which leading analysts have claimed to be able to *clarify* by means of the former concept. Some philosophers may feel that the expression " proposition capable of being known by conceptual analysis and deduction alone " is too vague to serve the purpose of sharply dividing true propositions into necessary and contingent ones, and may accordingly advocate a pragmatic gradualism, permitting us to say that one proposition is *more necessary* than another but not that one proposition is necessary and another is not. But if so, they ought to be equally " pragmatist " with respect to the concept of logical truth: what holds for necessary truth in this respect, holds for logical truth likewise. I can think of no better definition of logical truth combining generality and applicability to natural languages than " necessary truth formulated by means of *logical constants* and variables only." This definition shows that (a) the concept " logical truth " is less precise than is widely supposed, since we can give no better general, explicit definition of " logical constant " than " constant occurring essentially in *most* of the necessary inferences in which it occurs," and that (b) the concept of logical truth is so far from being a suitable explicatum for the concept of necessary truth that we need the latter concept for its explication.

[36] On the problem, here touched upon, of criteria of adequacy of definitions, see below, especially Chaps. 8, 13.

[37] *Loc. cit.*, see above, p. 16.

CHAPTER 7. *The Linguistic Theory of Logical Necessity*

SEVERAL able analytic philosophers have in recent years launched criticisms against a theory of necessary truth that seems to be motivated, whatever its merits may be, mainly by the desire to discredit the rationalistic myth of " intellectual intuition," or " the inner eye of reason," as the source of a priori knowledge. The advocates of this theory, the linguistic theory of necessary truth, should not be misunderstood as denying the existence of a priori knowledge. Perhaps they deny the existence of a priori knowledge in one sense of " a priori," but what they are trying to do is rather to accept as a fact that there is a priori knowledge in some sense (viz. in logic and mathematics) and then to discover just what that sense is. Berkeley did not deny that there are material objects, nor did Hume deny that there are causal connections; the objects of their criticisms were rather philosophical theories of the nature of material objects and of causal connection. Similarly, logical positivists and Wittgensteinians do not deny that there is a priori knowledge —at least not explictly—but they repudiate rationalistic *conceptions* of a priori knowledge.

Those criticisms of the linguistic theory, which need not be repeated here, seem to be in the main conclusive.[1] Nevertheless, the feeling persists in wide circles of analytic philosophers that a tough-minded empiricist is committed to some kind of linguistic theory, and that the valid criticisms that have been raised hit only objectionable formulations of a linguistic theory. It is my purpose to

[1] See esp. the following discussions: W. Kneale, "Are Necessary Truths True by Convention?" *Proceedings of the Aristotelian Society, 21* (1947); and "Truths of Logic," *ibid.*, new ser. *46* (1946); S. Körner, "On Entailment," *ibid.*, esp. pp. 161-2; C. D. Broad, "Are There Synthetic A Priori Truths?" *ibid.*, Supplementary Volume *15* (1936); S. Körner, "Are Philosophical Questions, Questions of Language?" *ibid.*, Supplementary Volume *22* (1948), esp. sec. II, 2; A. C. Ewing, "The Linguistic Theory of A Priori Propositions," *ibid.*, new ser. *40* (1940); W. V. Quine, "Truth by Convention"; C. I. Lewis, *An Analysis of Knowledge and Valuation*, chap. 5; B. Blanshard, *The Nature of Thought, 2*, chap. 30.

clarify this confused situation by showing that to the extent to which a radical linguistic theory is true it is mostly trivial, and to the extent that it is not trivial it is mostly either false or meaningless; but further, that abandonment of such a theory does not plunge a philosopher into any sort of mysticism or metaphysics that might make him disreputable in the eyes of those who admire above all a clear, sober head. The specific questions to be discussed in connection with the stated objective, if possible with a minimum of repetition of arguments already well presented by others, are the following:

(1) What exactly could be meant by saying that the truth, or necessary truth, of a proposition is *produced* by linguistic conventions?

(2) What if the result of careful analysis should be that propositions commonly called " necessary " are really a species of empirical propositions? Is such a result intrinsically absurd?

(3) What is wrong with the theory that necessary propositions are not really " propositions," and hence not objects of knowledge, but a special kind of *rules*—say, rules of inference or rules of substitution of symbols?

(4) Is not the view that logical necessity is an intrinsic property of propositions which in no intelligible sense " depends " on linguistic conventions inevitably tied up with Platonism? Does not its intelligibility depend upon the acceptance of propositions as abstract, subsistent entities?

A. Are Necessary Propositions a Species of Empirical Propositions?

When the linguistic theory was first expressed, by such ardent " positivists " as Ayer, it easily lent itself to the *reductio ad absurdum* that necessary propositions are really a special kind of empirical propositions, viz. generalizations about linguistic usage. But in the meantime it has been formulated more subtly, by Ayer himself in the introduction to the second edition of his positivist manifesto, and by such Wittgensteinians as N. Malcolm.[2] Let us examine a version of it which brings out what I take to be its central idea,

[2] See particularly " Are Necessary Propositions Really Verbal? " *Mind* (1940).

viz. that necessary truth is in some sense the product of linguistic conventions: "The existence of certain linguistic habits relevant to the use of a sentence *S* is a necessary and sufficient condition for the necessity of the proposition meant by *S.*" It is not too difficult to show, however, that linguistic habits can be neither sufficient nor necessary conditions for the necessity of a proposition. The persuasiveness of this theory is probably due to some such reasoning as this: If there exists a linguistic habit of applying the word "yard" to distances of three feet and only to such distances, then the proposition expressed by "every yard contains three feet" is identical with the proposition that every yard is a yard; hence, given that linguistic convention and no further facts at all, the truth of the proposition follows. But suppose we ask, "follows *from what?*" Evidently the answer is "from the law of identity." It has been tacitly assumed, then, that the law of identity ("every-thing is what it is," in informal language), of which the proposition that every yard is a yard is a substitution instance, is a necessary truth. If it were not, then no amount of linguistic conventions would suffice to make any proposition necessary. The verbalist (as we may call an advocate of the linguistic theory) might reply that such a law of logic itself derives its necessity from linguistic habits as to the usage of such logical constants as "if-then": "if *p*, then *p*" is a familiar version of the law of identity. But if all that is the result of linguistic habits is the *synonymy* of the sentences "every yard contains three feet" and "every yard is a yard" (their expressing the same proposition), then likewise linguistic habits will account only for the *synonymy* of such abstract tautologies as "if *p*, then *p*" and "it is not the case that *p* and not-*p*." We should not, indeed, *deny* that it is linguistic conventions which "give rise" to the necessity of the proposition thus expressible by different sentences; the question is rather what this assertion *means*. But first let us convince ourselves that the existence of a linguistic habit is not a necessary condition, any more than it is a sufficient condition, for the necessary truth of a proposition. If linguistic habits were to change in such a way that, say, a length of two feet came to be called a "yard," then, of course, the proposition *thereafter* expressed by the sentence "every yard contains three feet" would be false, and hence not necessary. But this has no tendency to prove that the proposition which was formerly expressed by this sentence has ceased to be a necessary truth and turned into a necessary falsehood. Indeed, this consequence of the view that necessary truth "depends" on linguistic habits in the sense in which, say, good health depends on the presence of fresh air, does not even have the virtue of being a meaningful statement: as pointed out above, Chapter 5, "necessary" is (in the relevant sense) a time-independent predicate, which means that a sentence of the form "p is necessary at time t—and perhaps not necessary at some other time" makes no more sense than, say, "p is a true proposition in New York, but possibly not in London." [3]

The linguistic theory, as formulated, lends itself, moreover, to deduction of a neat paradox. Our theory, while admitting that necessary statements of a natural language [4] are not statements *about* contingent linguistic habits, holds that what characterizes them as necessary is that the existence of such a habit is sufficient to guarantee their truth; one who denied such a statement—who said, e. g., " there are married bachelors "—would thereby break an established linguistic habit. Thus in pointing out that the expressions " bachelor " and " unmarried man " are used synonymously in English, one states a sufficient reason for accepting " all bachelors are unmarried " as true, and therefore the latter statement, according to our theory, is necessary (that actually the synonymy of these expresssions is only a sufficient reason for accepting the statement as a logical consequence of a logical truth— $(x)\ (f)\ (g)\ (fx.gx \supset fx)$ —is an important argument against the linguistic theory, but will be disregarded in this context). But if an empirical statement p describes evidence

[3] There is a venerable tradition of calling necessary truths " *eternal* verities " (the word " verities " is no doubt used to reinforce the emotive tone of " eternal "). It may well be that what some of the philosophers who use this expression mean by " eternal " is just that " necessarily true " is a time-independent predicate. But the terminology is unfortunate for two reasons: first, the most natural interpretation of a statement of the form " x has P eternally " is " x has P at all times," but if it does not make sense to say that x has P at some particular time, then it does not make sense either to say that x has P at all times; secondly, " true " is just as time-independent a predicate (though perhaps less obviously so) as " necessarily true " (see Carnap, " Truth and Confirmation " in Feigl and Sellars, *Readings in Philosophical Analysis*, and my correction of Carnap in " Propositions, Sentences and the Semantic Definition of Truth," *loc. cit.*, and in *Analytische Erkenntnistheorie*, chap. III, A.), hence eternality in the only acceptable sense could not serve to differentiate necessary truths from contingent truths.

[4] The relativization of necessary truth to *language systems* will concern us in Chap. 14.

for another statement q—in other words, if in stating p one gives an empirical reason for accepting q—then q is itself empirical. This contradicts the assumption that q is necessary. The solution of this little paradox is easy enough if, as urged in Chapter 5, we properly distinguish between " S expresses a necessary proposition " and " the proposition that p—which happens to be expressed by S— is necessary": in pointing to a certain language habit, we may indeed give a reason for accepting the former statement, which is clearly empirical. But since the advocate of the linguistic theory is likely to scoff at the suggestion that necessity is an intrinsic property of extralinguistic propositions (cf. above, pp. 119 f.) , he will probably have no use for this solution.

We thus find that even a formulation of the linguistic theory which does not at the surface entail that necessary propositions are empirical—and that therefore there are not any—entails this paradox if closely analyzed. Let us carefully note, however, that it is one thing to accuse the linguistic theory of denying the existence of necessary propositions, and quite another thing to accuse it of denying the necessity of true propositions of the form " p is necessary." It is not obvious that it is inconsistent to hold, on the one hand, that p is necessary, and on the other hand, that the proposition expressed by " p is necessary " is contingent. In Chapter 5 it was, indeed, argued that such modal propositions are, if true, themselves necessary. And if that argument is valid, then it is a sufficient refutation of the linguistic theory, since even if this theory could be so formulated as to be compatible with the existence of necessary propositions, it clearly entails the contingency of modal propositions. For if in order to determine whether " p " is necessary, one has to examine the present usage of the expressions constituting " p," [5] then the truth-value of " ' p ' is necessary " is *empirically* ascertained. But this is at any rate a separate question entirely, since the reasons for holding that there are necessary propositions—to be presented shortly—are independent of the reasons for holding that true modal propositions are themselves necessary propositions.

Let us note also that the same sort of criticism of the linguistic

---

[5] Of course, it is the sentences represented by the letter p, not the letter itself, that contain expressions. Hence it would be more accurate to use what Quine calls " quasi-quotes " in such contexts. But I deliberately sacrifice accuracy here to typographical convenience.

theory would be applicable if " linguistic rule (or convention) " were used in the more restricted sense of " explicitly formulated definition," and the thesis accordingly were that the logical necessity of a proposition is the result of conventional definitions. It is inaccurate to say that a logically true proposition is a proposition which *follows from definitions*. Definitions are, from the formal point of view, rules of substitution *by* which truth, as well as necessary truth, is transmitted from one statement to another. Thus through the definition " father = male parent " necessary truth is transmitted from the statement (p) " all male parents are male " to the statement (q) " all fathers are male." p would be necessary even if the abbreviation " father " had never been introduced into our language. And since q expresses the same proposition as p, the same holds for it. p itself is necessary because of derivability by substitution from a principle of logic: $(x) (f) (g) (fx.gx \supset fx)$. To simplify matters, let us consider this principle as a case of " if p and q, then p." In which sense is the necessity of this principle *created* by definitions? All we can say is that, by virtue of the truth-table definitions of the connectives involved, this principle must be true *if* every proposition is either true or false and no proposition is both true and false (this assumption being implicit in the " convention " of assigning just one of the truth-values " true " and " false " to each proposition). If you wish you may say that this assumption is itself logically necessary by virtue of the definition of " proposition ": we call " proposition " anything which satisfies the laws of contradiction and of excluded middle.[6] But this still does not end the regress: the definition again does not " create " logical necessity, but merely transmits it from the necessary proposition " every proposition is a proposition." [7]

It may be appropriate to comment in this connection on a recent

[6] It is sometimes said that these laws do not apply to natural languages because of the presence, in such languages, of vague and ambiguous terms. According to this view propositions, conceived as the sort of entities that strictly satisfy these laws, are indeed ideal entities like the perfectly elastic particles and frictionless planes of physics, viz. unambiguous statements with ideally precise meanings. (Cf. Ernest Nagel, " Logic without Ontology," in Feigl and Sellars, *Readings in Philosophical Analysis*, p. 196.)

[7] For a similar analysis of the dictum that the necessary truth of the statements of logic and mathematics flows from linguistic conventions, see Quine's excellent essay " Truth by Convention."

attempt by an able member of the Wittgenstein school of linguistic analysis to formulate a linguistic theory of necessity in such a way that it is not open to the charge of reducing necessary propositions to empirical propositions about language. Morris Lazerowitz writes (*The Structure of Metaphysics*, p. 271) :

> What makes a non-verbal sentence " A flea is an insect " express a logically necessary truth is the fact that the corresponding verbal sentence expresses a true proposition. The fact that " A flea is an insect " expresses a logically necessary proposition entails and is entailed by the fact that " As a matter of usage ' insect ' applies to whatever ' flea ' applies to " expresses a true empirical proposition.

But it is not clear what " As a matter of usage, ' *A* ' applies to whatever ' *B* ' applies to " means. If it is so meant that " As a matter of usage, ' black ' applies to whatever ' crow ' applies to " is true, although " all crows are black " expresses an empirical proposition, then clearly the mutual entailment asserted by Lazerowitz does not hold. Of course, the fact that " crow " and " black " are used the way they are in English is not a sufficient reason for the truth of " all crows are black." The latter statement is true because (a) " crow " means the property *crow*, (b) " black " means the property *black,* and (c) whatever has the first property also has the second. Lazerowitz, then, must mean that in case the extension of " *B* " is part of the extension of " *A* " by virtue of logical necessity, a rule of usage concerning " *B* " and " *A* " is the *sufficient reason* for the truth of " all *B* are *A*." Yet he emphasizes that it is an empirical fact that this rather than that rule of usage exists. That people who speak English do not apply the predicate " flea but not insect " to anything, regardless of any extralinguistic facts, is itself an empirical proposition. But then he is saying either that the truth of an empirical proposition about usage is a sufficient reason for the truth of a necessary proposition (which is a contradiction, since by definition of " necessary proposition " no empirical fact can entail a necessary proposition except in the vacuous sense in which a necessary proposition is entailed by every proposition) or else that the truth of an empirical proposition about usage is a sufficient reason for the truth of an empirical proposition to the effect that a given sentence expresses a necessary proposition. On the latter interpretation he avoids the paradox that the very concept " necessary proposition " is self-contradictory. But then Lazerowitz has given us at best a criterion for " the sentence ' p ' expresses a necessary proposition," not for " it is necessary that p," which latter statement does not mention " p," the *sentence*. He has failed, that is, to provide a reasonably complete definition in use of " necessary proposition." In order for a definition in use of " necessary proposition " to be reasonably complete it must contain not only a part elucidating the phrase " ' p ' expresses a necessary proposition " but also a part elucidating the phrase " the proposition *that p* is necessary." To present an analogy from the philosophy of mathematics: the logicist thesis of the definability of number concepts by means of logical constants is not sufficiently substantiated by rules for translating sentences of the form " class A has n members " into the language of *Principia Mathematica*. Both Frege and Russell supplied further rules of translation for what might be called " substantival " uses of numerical expressions, like " Two is the successor of One." A complete definition in use of " logically necessary " in linguistic terms, then, Lazerowitz has not provided.

The view is sometimes expressed that the conventional nature of logical principles is demonstrated by the fact that in proposing alternatives to the usual, two-valued, logic, one really does nothing else than propose different rules for the usage of logical constants. For example, if a three-valued logic is proposed in which the law of the excluded middle is replaced by the trichotomy " every proposition is either true or false or indeterminate," then, whatever " indeterminate " may mean, " true " and " false " must have different meanings from those they have in the two-valued logic; for, in the two-valued logic, " p is not true " entails " p is false," and as this entailment is constitutive of the meanings of " true " and " false," its not being valid in the three-valued logic indicates that " true " and " false " have changed their meanings. But I confess that this, undoubtedly correct, observation seems to me to prove nothing else than that the principles of two-valued logic are *necessary* propositions. For if from the fact that so-and-so denies S *it follows* that so-and-so has changed the usual meaning of S, then it follows that the proposition usually expressed by S is necessary. What is in an intelligible sense " conventional " is that a given sentence is used to express one rather than another proposition;

but what could be meant by saying that a proposition is necessary "by virtue of linguistic conventions" is simply obscure. To be sure, one could specify the meanings of logical constants "implicitly" by ruling that specified sentences containing them are to be true. For example: let "if, then" be so used that "if (if p, then q), then (if not-q, then not-p)" is true (presupposing a prior assignment of meaning to "not").[8] Is it not clear, then, that the logical law thus functioning as implicit definition is "true by convention"? But if the method of specifying the meaning of a term T by saying that T is meant in such a way that statement S containing T is true justified the assertion that the truth expressed by S is conventional, then any true statement could be made out as a conventional truth. Thus suppose that all the terms in the statement "the city busses running on Broadway are red" except "red" have been assigned meanings, and we now explain the meaning of "red" by saying "'red' means that color C for which 'the city busses running on Broadway are C' is true." Is the fact that the city busses running on Broadway are red, then, a result of linguistic convention?

B. *Necessity and Linguistic Rules*

Perhaps, however, the arguments advanced against the linguistic theory so far have missed its real point, which may be that *there are no necessary propositions*, that there are only contingent propositions plus certain kinds of linguistic rules; that sentences ordinarily said to express necessary propositions do not, indeed, express empirical propositions, but rather express no propositions at all. Thus a sentence like "if John is taller than Bill, then Bill is shorter than John" (*S*) might be said to *express a linguistic rule*, not a proposition in the sense in which a proposition is something that may be true or false, believed or disbelieved, verified or refuted. Perhaps the advocates of this theory would say that the illusion of there being necessary propositions has an origin similar to that of the illusion, in the opinion of the emotivists, that there are ethical propositions. We frequently use *declarative* sentences in expressing desires and aversions, instead of using openly expressive (or imperative) forms of speech; we say to the naughty child "stealing apples is wrong," instead of "don't steal apples," and

---

[8] Cf. Quine, "Truth by Convention," II.

this leads us to suppose that "stealing apples is wrong" expresses a proposition which calls for verification or refutation, belief or disbelief. Similarly, if instead of uttering a declarative conditional sentence we said (to the person whom we wish to instruct in the correct use of the words "taller" and "shorter") "instead of saying 'John is taller than Bill' you may, if you wish, say 'Bill is shorter than John' (it means the same thing), but don't ever say both 'x is shorter than y' and 'y is shorter than x'; that would be contradicting yourself," the directive, noncognitive function of the language used would be obvious. If we "inform" the person of the speech habits in the community, we do so in the same indirect manner in which we inform the naughty child of the moral attitudes of his elders. There is here, indeed, a striking analogy between the reasons for which emotivists deny that ethical sentences are descriptive (as contrasted with expressive) of emotions and the reasons for which advocates of the linguistic theory, like Ayer, deny that sentences commonly held to express necessary propositions are *descriptive* of linguistic habits.[9]

That a sentence like S is directive in function even though its grammatical form suggests that its primary function is cognitive (or assertive) is a plausible view. It is sometimes held against the linguistic theory that necessary propositions cannot be characterized as linguistic rules, since, after all, truth is predicable of necessary propositions while it is not of rules; a rule can be good or useful, but it is nonsense to call it "true." If this argument is used against the characterization of such sentences as S as linguistic rules,[10] it is absurd. For the same argument could be used to maintain that "stealing is wrong" expresses a proposition and cannot be regarded as equivalent in function to the imperative "don't steal": it is

---

[9] Cf. the intro. to the 2d ed. of *Language, Truth and Logic.*

[10] Strangely, Ayer himself, in the course of reaffirming the linguistic theory while repudiating the charge that according to it necessary propositions are a species of empirical propositions, uses this weak argument:" Just as it is a mistake to identify *a priori* propositions with empirical propositions about language, so I now think that it is a mistake to say that they are themselves linguistic rules. For apart from the fact that they can properly be said to be true, which linguistic rules cannot, they are distinguished also by being necessary, whereas linguistic rules are arbitrary " (*ibid.*, p. 17). The latter reason is particularly opaque, since if from "R is arbitrary" we are to infer that R is not necessary, "necessary" must in that context be a term of contrast to "arbitrary," and clearly "necessary" as predicated of propositions is contrasted not with "arbitrary" but with "contingent."

syntactically correct to say "it is true that stealing is wrong," while it is syntactically incorrect to say "it is true that don't steal." And that in fact philosophers do not in general regard the declarative form of a sentence as sufficient proof that the sentence expresses a proposition, or that its primary function is cognitive, should require no argument (*vide* the view that there are no ethical propositions). The only argument that is commonly given for denying the propriety of labeling such sentences as S "linguistic rules" is that truth is properly predicable of them; yet if the reason for this latter claim is that S expresses a proposition, the question has been begged, and if the reason is that S is a declarative sentence, the conclusion does not follow.

It would be futile to debate the question of whether S expresses a proposition or is just a linguistic rule unless we can agree on a *general* criterion of propositional significance. The confirmability criterion offered by the logical empiricists is not helpful in this context, for the following reason: in order to escape from the consequence that only empirical statements are cognitively meaningful (in other words, that a sentence either expresses no proposition or else expresses an empirical proposition), the more recent advocates of the criterion have benevolently recognized analytic and even self-contradictory propositions, by ruling that a sentence expresses a proposition if and only if it is either confirmable (in which case it expresses an empirical proposition) *or* analytic or self-contradictory.[11] Obviously, then, nobody who accepts this tolerant form of the confirmability criterion could advocate the version of the linguistic theory under discussion. The very debatability of this theory presupposes a criterion of propositional significance other than the confirmability criterion in the above form. What alternatives are there? That a sentence have declarative form is surely no sufficient condition of propositional significance, for not only "the sum of 2 and 3 is an odd number" but even "the sum of 2 and 3 is a communist" satisfies that condition. Shall we say, then,

[11] Thus Hempel reports, in "Problems and Changes in the Empiricist Criterion of Meaning" (reprinted in L. Linsky, ed., *Semantics and the Philosophy of Language*, Urbana, Ill., 1952), that "contemporary logical empiricism has added (to the fundamental tenet of modern empiricism that all non-analytic knowledge is based on experience) the maxim that a sentence makes a cognitively meaningful assertion, and thus can be said to be either true or false, only if it is either (1) analytic or self-contradictory or (2) capable, at least in principle, of experiential test."

that a sentence expresses a proposition if truth is significantly (though perhaps not truly) predicable of it? This criterion will readily be perceived to be circular: the range of significant predication of " true," as a predicate applicable to linguistic expressions, can be defined only as the class of sentences that express propositions.

C. Propositions and Belief

Let us try a new approach to the problem of propositional significance. Propositions are sometimes defined, nonsemantically, as objects of propositional attitudes, i. e. as anything that might be believed, disbelieved, doubted, supposed, etc. There are philosophers who passionately object to the postulation of propositions defined as such " objects," since this seems to them to amount to a postulation of Platonic, abstract entities. A fuller discussion of the " ontological status" of propositions is reserved for the final section of this chapter. At present I am concerned to show that on this nonsemantic definition of " proposition " some declarative sentences which, for whatever reasons, are commonly assigned truth-values by logicians express no propositions at all. Thus explicitly self-contradictory sentences do not express anything that could possibly be believed: that there are round squares, for example, is not something that could possibly be believed, and the impossibility in question is not just *psychological*. That somebody should believe both (and at the same time) p and not-p is itself a self-contradictory supposition. The frequent claim that people, alas, are capable of holding self-contradictory beliefs notwithstanding, the statement " X believes at t that p and not-p " is itself self-contradictory. It entails " X believes at t that p and X believes at t that not-p," and hence " X believes at t that not-p." But if someone reports that he believes that not-p, we all deduce *analytically* from the report that he does not believe that p; no psychological assumption about the workings of his mind is needed to justify the inference. In other words, part of what is meant by " X believes that not-p " is " X does not believe that p," just as " X does not now speak to a white man " is part of the meaning of " X now speaks to a man who is not white " (in either case the implicate leaves more possibilities open, has a greater range than, the implicans). And if so, the conjunction " X believes at t that p and X believes at t that not-p " is self-contradictory, though not *formally* so. It is, indeed, convenient to make the sentence-proposition distinction for self-contradictory sentences as well, since one might wish to talk about a self-contradictory state of affairs rather than a self-contradictory sentence belonging to a particular language such as English. Since the definition of a proposition as a class of synonymous sentences would allow an extension of the sentence-proposition distinction to such degenerate cases as self-contradictory sentences, it might be preferred by some to the one in terms of propositional attitudes. But the latter definition is clearly more relevant to the philosophical question here under discussion, whether there are necessary propositions or whether what looks like a special kind of proposition is really a linguistic rule. For, those who deny that there are necessary propositions would readily admit that the class of sentences synonymous with S can be distinguished from S, just as the emotivist in ethics will admit that the class of sentences synonymous with " it is wrong to kill " can be distinguished from the just quoted English sentence. It ought to be kept in mind, however, that these alternative definitions of " proposition," the semantic and the non-semantic one, are by no means coextensive.

If we conceive of a proposition as something that might be believed or disbelieved, we shall find that the claim that a sentence like S expresses no proposition at all can be rigorously established. The only premises we require in addition to the premise argued for above, *viz.* that it is logically impossible to believe an explicit self-contradiction, is that significant belief-sentences, i. e. significant sentences of the form " X believes that p " (where the values of " p " are propositions) , always express *contingent* propositions, and that a sentence " p " expresses a proposition only if corresponding belief-sentences " X believes that p " express propositions. Unless we deny from the start that there are necessary propositions—which is the question here at issue—we must admit that from the truth-value of the belief-sentence neither the truth-value nor the modality of its subordinate sentence can be inferred. But the belief-sentence itself expresses, whether true or false, a contingent proposition no matter whether the subordinate " p " express a contingent or a necessary proposition. Now, if " p " has the form " p and not-p," then " X believes that p " is self-contradictory and so does not express a contingent proposition, and so is not a significant belief-sentence; therefore " p " itself is devoid of propositional significance.

But it also follows that "not-p," the explicit tautology "if p, then p," is devoid of propositional significance, by the principle that if a sentence expresses no proposition, then neither does its negation.[12]

If all this is correct, then it has been established that there is no such thing as a *proposition* of the form "if p, then p" (of which S is a substitution instance, since the proposition expressed by "John is taller than Bill" is identical with the proposition expressed by "Bill is shorter than John"); although it is convenient in formal logic to classify the "law of identity" not as a prescriptive rule of consistent discourse but as a tautology, and hence necessarily true proposition in the same sense in which more complicated formulae which, as we shall see presently, express propositions in the specified sense are tautologies.

Our argument leads, however, to what looks at first sight like an embarrassing consequence. Consider a more complicated formula in propositional variables, such as: $(F) [p \supset [(- q \supset - p) \supset (- q \supset r)]]$. To understand what proposition is expressed by this formula it is necessary and sufficient that the meanings of the logical constants (including parentheses) and the rules of sentence formation of the propositional calculus be known.[13] All but the specialists in formal logic, who can size up tautologies of even the most complicated kind at a glance, will first have to interpret F and then, by some formal decision procedure, try to discover whether the proposition expressed is a tautology. But then it surely does happen that people actually doubt whether the proposition expressed by F is true; and through deductive (or calculational) error they may even come to disbelieve this proposition. A fortiori, it is significant to suppose that F be disbelieved, and hence significant to suppose that F be believed. Yet, F is logically equivalent to "$p \supset p$," since both are tautologies. And how can a sentence which expresses a proposition be logically equivalent to a sentence which does not? This contra-

[12] Cf. above, p. 82 n.

[13] To stipulate that, in addition to the mentioned conditions, it is necessary that the formula be correctly classified as either tautologous or contradictory or indeterminate would have the absurd consequence that it would be logically impossible to know what proposition is expressed by a given formula and yet to be ignorant, prior to the carrying out of analytical procedures, of whether this proposition is a tautology or not. It is surely significant to ask whether the proposition expressed by F is a tautology, and the question presupposes that F is understood to express a definite proposition *before* the latter is recognized as a tautology.

diction, however, is only apparent, arising through a shift from the nonsemantic to the semantic meaning of "proposition." It would be a contradiction only if "proposition expressed by S" were defined as "class of sentences L-equivalent to S," since on that definition all L-equivalent sentences express the *same* proposition. But on the nonsemantic definition, there is nothing contradictory or even unplausible in the view that F expresses a proposition while "$p \supset p$" does not. For the premises "p is believed" and "p is logically equivalent to q" do not entail that q is believed. And if this entailment does not hold, and one grants, as one must on the nonsemantic definition, that there are logically equivalent *yet distinct* propositions, it is hard to see how one could prove that "p may be believed" together with "p is logically equivalent to q" entails "q may be believed."

Let us dispose of one more apparent difficulty, closely related to the spurious one just discussed, with the proposed conception of propositions as possible objects of (cognitive)[14] belief. Since F expresses a tautology, the denial of F entails a contradiction. But, so it may be asked, how can it be logically possible to believe not-F if it is logically impossible to believe a contradiction? The answer is simply that for all intelligent beings but the omniscient being—who, as has been remarked, could not have any need for making deductions and hence must lack at least one possible perfection, that of being a perfect mathematician—belief is not hereditary with respect to the entailment relation. No doubt the assumption that X believes that (p entails q) would warrant the deduction of "X believes q" from "X believes p," but surely the premise that p entails q does not warrant it. In fact, it is just because one may inspect a proposition without seeing all that it entails that it is possible to believe propositions which, upon analysis, turn out to entail contradictions. For example, if a man believes each of the

[14] Some such qualification as "cognitive" is needed, since the verb "to believe" is used not only in the context "X believes that . . ." but also in the context "X believes in . . . (e.g. world government)," in which latter usage the phrase "X is for . . ." or "X favors . . ." might be substituted. Perhaps an explicit definition of "cognitive belief" could be given only in terms of "proposition," but we do not need to give an explicit definition in order to clarify the relevant sense of "belief"; we can clarify it denotatively. It is not difficult to see that the mental state (or disposition) designated by "believes" in a sentence like "I believe that it will rain here shortly" is different from the mental state (or disposition) designated by the word in a sentence like "I believe in the outlawing of atomic weapons."

following propositions (more accurately, corresponding instances of the following propositional forms) : if p, then q; if r, then s; p or r; not-q; not-s, does it follow that he believes both p and not-p? It would follow only if we could assert as a necessary truth that any man believes all propositions that are entailed by the propositions he believes; which, so far from being necessarily true, is not even true. On the proposed theory, then, it is consistent to hold that S_1 expresses a proposition and S_2 does not, even though S_1 and S_2 are logically equivalent in the sense of having necessarily the same truth-value.

An interesting consequence of our theory is that if p is what Locke called a trifling proposition, i. e. the meaning of a sentence of the form " if p and q, then p," then it is logically impossible to disbelieve p, and therefore p is not a genuine proposition. This may be elucidated in terms of such an analytic sentence as (B) " all bachelors are unmarried." To disbelieve that all bachelors are unmarried would be to believe something of the form " x is P and x is Q and x is not-Q," or simply " p and q and not-q." But if a man interprets B correctly, then he interprets it as equivalent to the negation of a statement of the form " p and q and not-q." It seems to follow that disbelieving the proposition supposedly expressed by B could not be due to deductive error, unlike disbelieving the proposition expressed by F; for no rules of inference, no logical principles, are needed to show that the negation of B is self-contradictory; the definition " bachelor = unmarried man " suffices for that purpose. But then to disbelieve the proposition expresed by B is to fail to interpret B correctly, i. e. to fail to grasp the proposition expressed by B; and in that case to disbelieve the proposition supposedly expressed by B would be at once to interpret B correctly and interpret B incorrectly. Since this is logically impossible, it is logically impossible to disbelieve the proposition supposedly expressed by B. It follows that B expresses no proposition at all. Indeed, it is hard to imagine that a man would ever say " I believe that all bachelors are unmarried " and mean by this anything else than " I believe that the *word* ' bachelor ' is applied to unmarried people only."

The above may be considered as an attempt to prove an ingenious *apperçu* of Broad's [15] to the effect that there are no analytic proposi-

---

[15] The *apperçu* is thrown out *en passant* in Broad's contribution to the symposium

tions at all if " analytic " is used in the narrow (but clear!) sense of a proposition of the form " if p and q, then p " or " all AB are A " (let us call this sense " analytic$_k$ "). The point is that if a sentence has the form of an implication whose consequent is contained in the antecedent as a conjunctive component, or can be brought into this form by definitional substitution, then disbelieving the proposition supposedly expressed by it would involve believing an *explicit* contradiction, not just believing an *implicit* contradiction, i. e. a proposition which can be shown, by correct application of rules of deduction, to entail a contradiction.[16] Since it is logically impossible to believe an explicit contradiction and a proposition is, by our definition, something with regard to which it makes sense to suppose that it is disbelieved, it follows that sentences which are analytic$_k$ express no propositions. Notice that conditional statements corresponding to syllogisms, whether valid or invalid, do express propositions by the stated criterion. To believe, for example, that all A are B and no B are C but some C are A, which proposition is the contradictory of the conditional proposition corresponding to a valid syllogism in the EAE mood, is logically possible, since no two components of the conjunction directly contradict each other; the conjunction, in other words, is not explicitly contradictory but only implicitly contradictory in that an explicit contradiction is deducible from it (with the help of valid syllogisms in other moods). Even though " some C are A " entails " not-[(all A are B) and (no B are C)] " we are not permitted to deduce from " X believes that some C are A " the conclusion " X believes that not-[(all A are B) and (no B are C)]," because, as I put it above, belief is not hereditary with respect to entailment. Our theory, therefore, is consistent with the possibility of disbelieving strictly analytic or logically true (but not analytic$_k$) propositions, owing to deductive error. Further, it is consistent with the existence of necessary propositions which are

" Are There Synthetic A Priori Truths?," *Proceedings of the Aristotelian Society*, Supplementary Volume (1936), pp. 104-5. Broad says cautiously that he " very much doubts " whether the sentence " all equilateral triangles are equilateral " stands for a proposition, where a " proposition " is defined as " something that can be true or false, that can be known or believed or entertained and so on."

[16] On the contrast explicit-implicit contradiction, cf. Chaps. 1 and 2, B. The view that sentences of the form " all AB are A " do not express propositions is also taken by Blanshard, in *The Nature of Thought* (New York, 1940), *2*, 405.

not strictly analytic, such as propositions asserting the asymmetry or transitivity of perceptually given, simple relations, like " if A is earlier than B, then B is not earlier than A " (irreversibility of time; see next chapter). For, if " earlier " is unanalyzable, then it cannot be shown that after elimination of defined terms we are left with a conditional statement whose consequent is a conjunctive component of its antecedent. And in that case we have no basis for asserting the *logical* impossibility of disbelieving this proposition (though this need not prevent one from suspecting very strongly that a man who verbally denies the statement " the relation of temporal succession is asymmetrical " is misinterpreting it).

It would, of course, be semantically naive to announce a " theory " of propositions as objects of beliefs (and of other " intentional acts," cognitive as well as volitional), and on the ground of that " theory " to make the " discovery " that some declarative sentences which are commonly held to express propositions, in a sense in which non-declarative sentences don't express propositions, really don't express propositions. The point is simply that the word " proposition " has several proper uses, whereof " possible object of beliefs " (or, if one prefer, " object of possible beliefs ") is only one. An equally proper use for it is " meaning of a declarative sentence." It is difficult to deny that analytic$_k$ sentences composed of meaningful terms are themselves meaningful and in that sense " express propositions " —indeed, I shall myself continue to use the word " proposition " in this sense. But it is not enough to be aware of this duplicity of meanings of " proposition." One further ought to see their relationship, which is this: anything which it is possible to believe (and to disbelieve) is something which it is possible to mean by a declarative sentence, *but not conversely*. As the word " proposition " is frequently used in both of these senses, it easily happens that the converse of the above universal statement is taken for granted. The assertion that declarative sentences of the trivially tautologous kind do not express propositions may be interpreted as an emphatic warning against this fallacious conversion.

I conclude that there is a kernel of truth in the theory that sentences commonly taken by philosophers to express necessary propositions really express no propositions at all but are properly characterized as linguistic rules. For example, if the sentence " all bachelors are unmarried " is used to make an *assertion*, this can be nothing else than the *empirical* assertion that the word " bachelor " is conventionally used to refer to an unmarried person. If the sentence is not used to convey this information, then it is not used assertively at all, but persuasively (or imperatively) in the sense of " please, apply the word ' bachelor ' only to unmarried persons." But it is no more than a kernel of truth. The linguistic theory sadly fails to appreciate what should be obvious to any philosophically unbiased mind: that with regard to theorems and axioms of logic and mathematics that are not analytic$_k$ (what Locke called " trifling " propositions!), it is proper to speak of knowledge, belief, and dis-belief of the propositions expressed by them, in just the same sense of those " intentional " words in which they are used to characterize cognitive attitudes toward empirical propositions that are objects of inquiry. The only sense in which rules can be said to be " known " is the sense of " knowing *how*," not the sense of " knowing *that*." But it is surely one thing to know *how* to use a rule of deductive inference, such as " from S_1 and (if S_1, then S_2), S_2 is derivable," and quite another thing to know *that* the proposition corresponding to this rule (the proposition expressed by the object-linguistic formula " $[p.(p \supset q)] \supset q$ ") [17] is necessarily true, as a result of either a truth-table or a deduction test. And it is one thing to know *how* to use the binomial theorem as a rule of calculation, another thing to know *that* it is a necessary proposition, this knowl-edge being the outcome of a complicated proof. In the critical sense of " knowledge," " *A* knows that *p* " means " *p*, *A* believes that *p*, and *A* has good reasons for believing that *p*." Now, deductive reasons and inductive reasons differ in kind, to be sure, just as entailment and probability-implication are different logical rela-tions. Accordingly, it may be useful to distinguish the sense of " know " which is defined in terms of standards of cognitive justifi-cation appropriate to inductive reasoning from the sense defined in terms of standards appropriate to deductive reasoning. But the similarity between these concepts of knowledge justifies our speaking of knowledge generically simply as the disjunction of the distin-guished knowledge-concepts. And in this generic sense of " knowl-edge " we know both contingent and necessary propositions.

[17] Whenever I speak, for the sake of brevity, of " the proposition " expressed by a statement form, I mean, of course, the propositions expressed by substitution instances of the statement form.

While it must be admitted that in a statement like "I know that being a father entails being male," the word "know" refers to nothing more mysterious than familiarity with linguistic usage, the theory that to assert an entailment is always to assert a contingent proposition about verbal usage (cf. above, p. 166) is easily reduced to absurdity. Since its proponents cannot but admit that the *same* entailment may be asserted in different languages, the contingent propositions in question must refer to synonymous sentences of different languages. Thus " the proposition that p entails the proposition that q " cannot be analyzed as a statement exclusively about the sentences " p " and " q "; it must somehow refer to all sentences synonymous with " p " and " q." Since synonymous sentences express the same proposition, the following criterion of adequacy for a "linguistic" analysis of entailment propositions is inescapable: the truth-value of an entailment proposition does not change if the sentences by which it is expressed are replaced by synonymous sentences; in other words, if p entails q, and " r " is synonymous with " p " and " s " is synonymous with " q," then r entails s. This criterion is at once satisfied if the entailment proposition is analyzed as a statement about classes of synonymous sentences, thus: every member of the class of sentences synonymous with " p " has relation R to every member of the class of sentences synonymous with " q "—where R is some suitable relation between expressions corresponding to the entailment relation. But if this metalinguistic statement is a contingent generalization that *says more* than " ' p ' has R to ' q,' " then it must be logically possible that although " p " has R to " q," some sentence synonymous with " p " does not have R to some sentence synonymous with " q." And this is evidently logically impossible. If, e. g., some Chinese sentence " r " were found not to entail, in Chinese, the Chinese sentence " s," it would follow at once that " r " and " s " are not synonymous respectively with " there are fathers" and "there are parents." Indeed, if we can be a priori certain that a relation R which is found to hold between sentences " p " and " q " will also hold between any synonym of " p " and any synonym of " q," the reason must be that R is not a formal relation but holds between two sentences only by virtue of their *meanings*. (We shall return to this point against the linguistic theory on p. 199; cf. p. 413) .

D. *Necessary Propositions and Rules of Inference*

Let us examine, now, the more specific claim made by one variety of linguistic theory, that there are no necessary propositions, since what seem to be necessary propositions are really *rules of inference*. In order to dispel at once the suspicion that fire is being opened here on a strawman, a statement of this view may be quoted:

> In arguing for a conventionalist interpretation of necessary truths, it is important for me to say that I am not prepared to equate such propositions with empirical generalizations about the way in which people actually use words and make transitions from one statement to another. I shall argue that a necessary proposition always lays down a rule and that a rule is never to be equated with an empirical proposition [Karl Britton, " Are Necessary Truths True by Convention? " *Proceedings of the Aristotelian Society*, Supplementary Volume *21* (1947)].

It is clear from the context of the quoted passage that "rule" there means " rule of inference." This view is reminiscent of the teachings of the early logical positivists, like Schlick, that the " eternal " truths of logic and mathematics are really " transformation rules " which we apply to the only genuine propositions there are, viz. empirical propositions. Thus Schlick said that " $7 + 5 = 12$," Kant's celebrated example of synthetic a priori truth, expresses no proposition at all but is simply a rule of substitution of synonymous symbols. Had Schlick been allowed to live through the recent years of progress in semantics, he would no doubt have been the first one to repudiate such a statement: if this equation expresses synonymy, then any other equation expressing the number 12 as a function of other numbers (e. g. $12 = \sqrt{144}$) could be interpreted similarly, and the question would arise how one who understands the meanings of arithmetic symbols could fail to know any true equations connecting them, and indeed could have any need for proofs. After Frege, we say nowadays that the symbols " $7 + 5$ " and " 12 " have no more the same *sense* than " the evening star " and " the morning star," although the identity of the entities denoted by them admits of a priori proof, while the identity of the objects denoted by the latter descriptions admits only of empirical proof. The really fatal defect, however, of the view that the allegedly necessary statements of logic and mathematics are transformation rules is that such sentences exercise different functions in different contexts. Specifically, while it must be admitted that in the context of empirical inquiries (such as counting empirical classes) the equations of arithmetic are used as rules of inference, it is equally clear that in the context of arithmetical inquiry the same equations are used to express propositions to be proved. As a matter of fact, there is no other way of *justifying* the use of such equations as rules of inference except to show that they express propositions which are necessarily true.[18] The same holds for *logical* rules of inference. Any rule of inference which is, in the metalanguage, formulated by means of variable names of propositions, such as the *ponendo ponens* rule " from S_1 and $S_1 \supset S_2$, S_2 is derivable," is to be justified by proving that the corresponding object-linguistic formula built up by means of propositional variables, such as " $(p . (p \supset q)) \supset q$," is a tautology, and thus expresses a necessary proposition. There is a danger of circularity in such " justification " if the rule of inference refers to formulae of functional logic, since there the only available technique for proving theorems is the deductive technique, which involves the use of rules of deduction. But the justification is not circular if the rule refers to the propositional calculus only, since here the truth-table test is possible. That in everyday deductive reasoning—as well as deductive reasoning occurring in empirical sciences—the laws of logic function as transformation rules has no tendency at all to prove that they are not propositions in the context of systematic logic in which their regulative use is, without circularity, justified.

Indeed, if the fact that a sentence may in some contexts function as a rule of inference were a good reason for denying that it is used to assert a proposition in any context, it would follow that even most empirical propositions are not really propositions at all.

---

[18] The equations which are used to infer one empirical proposition from other empirical propositions are, of course, semantically interpreted, they are not formulae of an uninterpreted calculus. If I am to infer, with the help of " $7 + 5 = 12$," that there are 12 coins in my purse from the premises that there are 7 dimes and 5 nickels and no other coins in my purse, then " 7," " 5," and " 12 " as they occur in the equation must mean what they mean in the empirical statements, and if they meant nothing at all (in the sense in which the formalists hold arithmetic symbols to be " meaningless "), then there would be no *statements* to make inferences from.

Whenever a statement of an assumed law of nature is used for purposes of prediction, it is used as a rule of inference (what Carnap called, in the *Logical Syntax of Language,* a " *P*-rule "). And if I speak confidently of " *most* empirical propositions," it is because a careful analysis of singular statements usually brings universal quantifiers to daylight. Even a modest singular statement like " this thing is red " can be analyzed into a universal conditional, viz. if any visually normal observer looked at this thing under standard optical conditions, it would appear red to him. Is utterance of this sentence, then, issuance of an " inference ticket," and not assertion of a proposition?

It remains to state what is perhaps the most decisive objection against the theory that the laws of logic are not propositions but *rules of symbolism*. Briefly, the objection is that whatever rules one may have initially stipulated, and however arbitrary such stipulations may be, one will thereafter have to *find out* what these rules entail, and the statement that such and such is entailed by the rules could hardly be characterized as itself a rule. Consider again the *ponendo ponens* principle, formulated as a rule of deduction in a metalanguage, and let us for the sake of the argument agree that there is no sense in predicating validity or necessary truth of such a rule since it simply constitutes, together with other rules of deduction such as a rule of substitution, a definition of what is to be understood by " logical consequence " in the respective system. When we derive, by applying the rule to the axioms of a logical system, a new theorem, we surely make a discovery. Even if the deductions are performed upon uninterpreted formulae, such that truth is not predicable of the theorems any more than of the axioms, it will be perfectly proper to say after a successful deduction " now I *know* that this is a theorem in the system, i. e. that this formula is entailed by the axioms." But that formula F_1 entails formula F_2, that any interpretation of the free variables in F_1 which turns F_1 into a true proposition also turns F_2 into a true proposition, is itself a logical truth, and it would be simply nonsense to characterize it as a *rule*. The same point may be illustrated in terms of the method of truth-tables, that automatic decision procedure applicable to the ground floor of logic. It is not unplausible to interpret the law of contradiction " no proposition is both true and false " as the *imperative* " don't contradict yourself! "—and the rule to assign to each elementary proposition no more than one of the truth-values " true " and " false " could accordingly be regarded as the formal expression of compliance with that imperative. To object to such an interpretation of the law of contradiction on the ground that it is, after all, significant to predicate truth (and even necessary truth) of this law, while an imperative is neither true nor false, would be just as question-begging as to object to the emotivist interpretation of " it is wrong to kill a child " as an imperative, that it is, after all, significant to say " it is true that killing children is wrong " but not to say " it is true that don't kill a child." Nevertheless, it remains a *cognitive* problem to decide whether this supreme requirement of consistency is satisfied by such-and-such assertions. For example, it is something that may or may not be *known* (in just the same sense of " knowledge " that is intended when we speak of knowledge of empirical propositions) that if one were to deny a proposition of the form " if (if p, then q) and (if not-s then not-r) and (p or r), then (if not-q, then s) " one would contradict oneself and thus violate the requirement of consistency. It is therefore a complete *non sequitur* to infer from the fact that a given formula can be established as a tautology without presupposing the truth of any propositions, simply by following *rules* of symbolism, that the formula itself is a rule and does not express a proposition. That decision is not cognition, that it does not make sense to predicate truth or falsehood of a decision, is a trivial observation; that it *is* a cognitive question what behavior is consistent with or necessitated by a given decision is perhaps an equally trivial observation, yet one that is worth repeating in view of such superficial statements as that logical truths are merely rules of symbolic transformation (and so not really " truths " at all) ; as though there were any sense in the characterization of a statement like " inferences drawn in accordance with the *ponendo ponens* rule invariably lead to true conclusions from true premises " as itself a rule of symbolic transformation!

E. Propositions and the Charge of Platonism

Let us turn, now, to the final and perhaps crucial question of this chapter: Does the abandonment of the linguistic theory, in any form, involve one in Platonic postulation of those weird abstract

entities called " propositions"? We seem to have arrived at the
conclusion that some propositions, whose existence is no more
problematic than that of any propositions, have an *intrinsic* property
called " necessity," to be distinguished from the *extrinsic* property
of *sentences* to express necessary propositions, and that it does not
even make sense to say that the possession of this property by a
given proposition " depends on," or " is produced by" linguistic
conventions or habits. Necessity is an *intrinsic* property of propositions in the sense that " *p* is necessary and *q* is not necessary " entails
" *p* and *q* are different propositions." Actually, this is equivalent
to saying that " is necessary " is a complete, time-independent predicate, unlike " expresses a necessary proposition "; for the sentences
" *p* is necessary " and " *p* is not necessary " could fail to be contradictory only if they expressed no definite propositions, and required
to be supplemented with a temporal reference to contingently
existing linguistic rules. In his subtle paper " Entailment and
Necessary Propositions " (in *Philosophical Analysis,* ed. Black) , C.
Lewy observes the distinction between " *p* is necessary " and " *S*
expresses a necessary proposition," arguing that while the latter
proposition is obviously contingent (" it is obviously possible that
the *sentence* ' there is nobody who is a brother and is not male '
should have been used to express a contingent proposition and not
a necessary one "), the former proposition is itself necessary, since
to suppose it contingent would be to suppose the contradiction
that the same proposition which is necessary might have been contingent. As suggested above, this view that logical modalities are
intrinsic properties of propositions is equivalent to the view that
propositions are *nontemporal* entities, entities of which change is
not significantly predicable. For consider this analogy. Is it self-
contradictory to suppose that the same man who in fact is tall
might not have been tall? If, to be sure, we take the Leibnizian
view that the concept of a particular man contains all the predicates—
past, present, and future—which are truly predicable of that particular man, then the supposition would be self-contradictory, since
on that view any true predication upon an individual is analytic.
But just *because* the view has this consequence, it need not be
taken seriously; it clearly does make sense to suppose that one
empirically discovers hitherto unknown properties of an individual.
The fact is that the supposition that John, who is tall, might not

have been tall makes sense, for height is a property with respect to which individuals may be significantly supposed to *change*. If and only if it makes sense to suppose that *x*, described in a certain unique way (e. g. as the human being born at place *P* and time *t*), had a property *P* at one time and did not have *P* at some other time, then it makes sense to suppose that *x*, while actually having *P* at *t*, *might not* have had *P* at *t*. It would not make sense, for example, to suppose that *x*, which in fact has the property of being a tree, might not have been a tree. If the miracle should happen that a place so far occupied by a tree suddenly gets occupied by a giraffe, one might describe this phenomenon by saying that a particular object *x* suddenly disappeared and was simultaneously replaced by a different object *y* in a perfectly inexplicable way, but one would hardly describe it by saying that the *same* object *x* which a moment ago had the property of being a tree now had the property of being a giraffe.[19]

Lewy's view, then, that it is self-contradictory to suppose that the same proposition which in fact is necessary might have been contingent, comes to this: " *p* is necessary *at t_1* (but perhaps not at t_2)" does not make sense, just as " *x* is a tree *at t_1* " does not make sense. But further, while the predicability of time-dependent properties upon *x* is a necessary condition for the predicability of *change* upon *x*, it is not a sufficient condition. For such time-dependent properties as " being believed by *X* " or " being expressed by sentence *S* " are clearly predicable of propositions, yet it would not make sense to say that a proposition had *changed*. Propositions have no histories, they are " timeless " entities. When philosophers speak as though propositions did have histories, by saying, e. g., that the proposition " John hitting Peter " acquired at t_2 the property of being exemplified by the actual world, a property which it did not have at t_1, they provoke the just accusation of Platonic reification: John is the sort of entity that has a history, and we can easily describe the change that occurred by focusing on John as subject

---

[19] Perhaps the distinction between predicates determining a *class*, in the usual sense of logic, and predicates determining a *natural kind* could be explicated in terms of this concept of "significant predicability of change with respect to *P*." As with most distinctions, one is nevertheless likely to encounter borderline cases: what about metamorphosis, or sudden mutation? Here an identical individual is said to move from one natural kind to another, and the concept of *individual identity* involved in such language cries out for analysis.

of change (at t_2 John has a property, viz. hitting Peter, which he does not have at t_1) , without producing metaphysical mystification.

Nevertheless, even after a philosopher has carefully rebutted the charge of literal reification, by explaining that " proposition " is meant to refer to timeless entities (in the specified sense) , just like " number," there are those " tough-minded " souls that can be brought to shiver simply by referring to propositions as " entities." Our view that logical necessity is an intrinsic property of propositions leaves us, therefore, with the task of explaining just what these propositions are. Before leaving the critical discussion of the linguistic theory, therefore, I shall attempt to contribute to the solution of this time-honored puzzle. I shall try to accomplish the impossible by emphasizing the similarities between the statement " there are propositions " and the statement " there are sense-data." It is a common property of such languages as English, German, and French that they allow the formation of adjectives and adjectival nouns by which one may refer collectively to the type of object appropriate to a given transitive verb. Thus " edible " coresponds to " to eat," " visible " to " to see," " audible " to " to hear," etc. Many of these verbs designate activities whose objects exist in their own right, i. e. their existence is, from the point of view of common sense at any rate, independent of the activities in which they are occasionally involved. That there are edibles which have not been eaten and never will be eaten, that there are visible objects which never have been seen and never will be seen—such assumptions make good sense. Now, in the case of the verbs " to perceive " and " to believe," ordinary language does not contain adjectives or adjectival nouns corresponding to them in quite the way in which " edible " corresponds to its verb. Perhaps this is due to the implicit realization that there are no objective entities here whose existence is presupposed by the significance of statements of the form " I believe x," " I perceive x." In other words, there are no ordinary words that designate the classes of possible values [20] of " x " in the contexts " I believe x " and

[20] When Russell speaks of *possible* values of the argument of a function he means, of course, *logical* possibility, in the sense of " what may be significantly supposed." Thus sounds are not possible values of x in the context " x is happy," in the sense that it is insignificant to predicate happiness of sounds. The English ending " -ible," in " visible " and " edible," is actually ambiguous as between logical possibility (in the specified sense) and empirical possibility. For example, a certain star might be said

" I perceive *x*." We have, to be sure, the nouns " belief " and " perception," but it is clear that these are related to their verbs the way " walk " is related to " to walk," and " dance " to " to dance," not the way " edible " is related to " to eat." It might be suggested that " perceptible," which is not too artificial a word, serves the described function. This proposal, however, overlooks that there are purely *phenomenological* uses of " to perceive," and of the determinate verbs falling under it (" to see," " to hear," etc.), i. e. uses in which " I perceive a *K* at place-time *P* " does not entail that there is a *K* at *P*. If I say " I see a snake over there," whereupon someone assures me that there are no snakes in this neighborhood, and I reply " perhaps so, but just the same I saw a snake," then I am using " to see " phenomenologically (contrast this linguistic situation with a situation just like the described one except that the reply is worded " perhaps so, but just the same *I thought* I saw a snake ").

As an artificial noun which could be used as grammatical object to the verb " to perceive " (and to its determinate forms) even where the verb is used phenomenologically and the mental state designated by it is one of delusive perception, philosophers invented the famous word " sense datum." In the technical sense-datum language, the circumlocution " I thought I saw a snake " can be avoided and replaced by the straightforward statement " I saw a snakelike sense-datum " (that we have to borrow words from the thing language in order to characterize the sense data, is an unfortunate accident, whatever its philosophical implications may be). But several philosophers, apparently forgetful of the original motivation for the invention of the sense-datum language, and of the fact that " I perceive a sense-datum of kind *K* " can always be translated into " I *seem to* perceive a physical object (or event) of kind *K*," have raised the question of the *ontological status* of these sense data. " Do sense data exist? And if so, what kind of existence do they have, mind-dependent or mind-independent? " they ask. But it is clear that if there is no other rule of usage for the term " sense

to be invisible at a given moment, yet it is not meant that it would be nonsense to suppose that it were seen at this moment; and yet the same word " invisible " would be used in a sentence like " numbers are invisible." But in saying that ordinary language contains terms denoting the semantically appropriate kind of objects of such verbs as " to see " and " to eat," I do not mean to imply that these terms are always used in what may be called their categorial sense.

datum " than the one laid down above, then to assert the existence of sense data can mean no more than to assert the occurrence of perceptions, of both the veridical and the delusive kind. I suggest that *mutatis mutandis* the same may be said about the question whether propositions exist, and if so in what sense. It is true that the word " proposition," unlike the word " sense datum," does occur in ordinary language, but it does not occur there in the technical sense assigned to it by philosophers (though there is, of course, some continuity between the technical sense and the ordinary usage). If Mr. Smith asserts " it is wrong to kill a baby," and an emotivist who did not hear distinctly what he said asked him to repeat his assertion, whereupon Smith repeats with emphasis " I asserted the proposition that it is wrong to kill a baby," the emotivist would make himself utterly unintelligible if he snapped back " how could you assert such a proposition, there is no such proposition! " This technical sense stipulated for the word is " anything which is a possible value of ' x ' in the context ' A believes (cognitively) x.' " But to assert the existence of propositions in this sense is, then, to assert merely that the function " someone believes x " is sometimes true. And as far as I can see, this is in no way different from the entirely uncontroversial claim that beliefs occur, whatever the correct analysis of the concept " belief " may be.

Perhaps philosophers who cannot bear to countenance propositions any more than they can bear to countenance ghosts, are unconsciously under the influence of Hume's strange, and strangely mistaken, doctrine that " whatever is distinguishable, is separable." The point is simply that it is quite legitimate to make up words in order to talk about distinguishable aspects of an event without being guilty of postulating a separate existence of those aspects. Thus, consider the following sentences: (1) I see *clearly* what looks like a *snake*; (2) I see, *not very clearly*, what looks like a snake; (3) I see clearly what looks like a *tiger*. All three of them describe perceptual sitautions. If it were said that the situations described by (1) and (2) differ with respect to their subjective constituent but agree with respect to their objective constituent, and that (1) and (3) agree with respect to the subjective constituent while they differ with respect to the objective constituent, everybody would understand what is meant by the " subjective " and the " objective " constituent of a perceptual situation. And if one then, following philosophical tradition, named the objective constituent of a perceptual situation a " sense datum," he would have made the meaning of " sense datum " as clear as it needs to be. The assertion of the existence of sense data in this sense would commit one to nothing more disturbing than the existence of perceptual situations; for it is clear that it would not make sense to speak of the existence of a sense-datum outside the event of sensing a sense-datum (in this respect sense data are profoundly unlike edibles and kickables), no more than it makes sense to speak of the existence of the cheshire cat's grin divorced from the grinning cat.

The same distinction between subjective and objective constituents applies to the kind of cognitive situation called " belief " (and, of course, the cognate situations called " disbelief," " doubt," etc.). Here we might use as illustrative sentences: (1) I believe *firmly* that Eisenhower will be our next president; (2) you believe just as firmly *that Eisenhower will not be our next president*; (3) he believes, though not quite so firmly as I do, that Eisenhower will be our next president. What ontological commitment do I incur in naming the objective constituent shared by (1) and (3), a " proposition "? That there are propositions which are either believed or disbelieved? This is the innocent assumption, well known to be true, that beliefs and disbeliefs occur. " But can you say, with equal innocence, that there are propositions which are neither believed nor disbelieved nor even thought of? " Well, can I say without being guilty of uttering nonsense that there are unsensed sense-data? The answer is affirmative, if this means that not all perceptions which *may* occur *do* occur. And similarly there is nothing obscure in the statement that not all beliefs or disbeliefs which *may* be held, *are* held, nor that some suppositions which might be made are not made. Thus the proposition that the planets revolve around the sun in elliptical orbits was not believed or disbelieved or even thought of 2000 years ago. In technical philosophical language, this may be expressed by saying that 2000 years ago it did not enter as objective constituent into any cognitive situation. If the latter mode of speaking causes anybody intellectual discomfort, it is surely because he visualizes the proposition as a *thing*, ready to become object of consciousness. But then it is *he* who is guilty of " reification," not the philosopher who " accepts " propositions.

Some English critics of Carnap's conception of (abstract) *designata* of meaningful expressions—such as propositions and properties [21]— have pointed out that "to mean," unlike "to name," is not a transitive verb, and that accordingly it is fallacious to infer from the fact that an expression has meaning that *there is a meaning* which it means, e. g. from the fact that a declarative sentence is meaningful that *there is a proposition* which is meant by the sentence. But why the use of the passive form "is meant by" in conjunction with "there is" should convict one of Platonistic sin is not clear. Consider a semantic statement like "predicate '*P*' is ambiguous." Suppose an explication of the relevant concept of ambiguity were·given in terms of the type-token distinction and a semantic relational predicate "*x* means *y*" whose domain consists of tokens, as follows:

$$(\exists x)(\exists z)(\exists y)(\exists u)(x \in {}^{\iota} P {}^{\prime} \cdot z \in {}^{\iota} P {}^{\prime} \cdot x \neq z \cdot y \neq u \cdot x \text{ means } y \cdot z \text{ means } u).$$

It will now be convenient to have a term for referring to the range of the variables "*y*" and "*u*," just as we have the term "token" to characterize the values of "*x*" and "*z*," and the term "property" serves this function excellently. Yet, according to Ryle and Ayer the very adoption of the passive mode of speech "property *y* is meant by token *x*" convicts one of Platonism! Analogously, a statement like "there are propositions which are not designated by any sentence of language *L*," or "there are propositions which are not believed by anybody at this time," will provoke these critics of Carnapian semantics. Yet, these existential statements are proved to be ontologically innocent by simply pointing out that they formulate part of the content of such uncontroversial statements (forming bases of existential generalization) as "there are no sentences of language *L* which express the proposition expressed by sentence *S* (which itself belongs to language *L'*) ," "the proposition that Hitler is still alive is not believed by anybody at this time." To assert the existence of a proposition *p* which is not the objective constituent of any belief or any other cognitive state of mind, is simply to deny the existence of beliefs or other cognitive states of mind with *p* as objective constituent. And once the synonymy of these two existential statements, the one positive and the other

---

[21] See G. Ryle, "Meaning and Necessity," *Philosophy* (1949) ; also A. J. Ayer, "Thinking and Meaning" (inaugural lecture) , London, 1947.

negative, is realized, no offense ought to be taken at either mode of speech. It may, indeed, lead to Platonic mystification to speak of a *time* at which a given proposition existed without being thought of, either affirmingly or rejectingly or doubtingly, since thus propositions are somehow assimilated to those *temporal* entities which common sense calls "things"; a noncognized proposition is thus assimilated to an unobserved thing. But here again it might be explaind that the statement "there is a p such that p is not thought of at time t" is meant simply as an indefinite formulation (or as formulation of part of the content) of the ontologically innocent statement "at time t nobody supposes or believes or doubts or disbelieves, etc., that p_1."

The enemies of propositions will be quick to point to the fallacy in the foregoing argument: the step from "$\cdots p_1 \cdots$" to "$(\exists p) \cdots p \cdots$" (existential generalization) begs the question. It presupposes that "p_1" is a genuine name, which it can be only if there are propositions. It is like the inference from "roundness is a property shared by all nickels" to "there is a property which is shared by all nickels." But since the apparent name "roundness" is contextually eliminable by translation of the above sentence into "all nickels are round," the apparent basis for existential generalization disappears.[22] Indeed, if the nominalist can actually provide rules for contextual elimination of propositional names and variables, then he will be justified in saying to the realistic logician and semanticist, "Sire, je n'ai pas besoin de cette hypothèse." But I have serious doubts about the possibility of such contextual elimination, which I shall substantiate presently. In the meantime I would like to inquire what it means anyway to believe that "there are propositions." Quine has offered a much debated *criterion* of a man's "commitment" to a special kind of ontology: look at the variables of quantification in his language; if they belong to the primitive notation, then the user of that language is committed to the belief that the entities over which they range exist. But he has not, to my knowledge, discussed the question what it means to say that such entities exist. Now, within a realistic language we encounter only qualified existence assertions, not what may be called "categorial" existence assertions: "there are attributes (or

[22] Cf. Quine, "Designation and Existence," in Feigl and Sellars, *Readings in Philosophical Analysis*.

propositions) satisfying the function $f(\phi)$ (or $f(p)$) "—e. g. " there are propositions which nobody believes," " there are attributes which are possessed by only one individual "—not " there are attributes (or propositions)." In Carnap's terminology, categorial existence assertions are *external* to a given language.[23] We may not like Carnap's claim that the corresponding questions like " are there propositions? " are devoid of cognitive meaning (unlike the questions concerning qualified existence which are formulated *within* a given language), but whosoever claims the contrary should offer an interpretation of such questions. I suggest that we take Quine's criterion of ontological commitment as the very *definition* of ontological commitment and thereby assign a cognitive meaning to categorial existence assertions. That is, to say " there are propositions " is to say that the propositional names and variables which we employ in order to say what we want to say are *not* contextually eliminable, that they belong to the " ultimate furniture " of our language. Thus nebulous questions about the ultimate furniture of the (extralinguistic) universe are reduced to less nebulous questions about the ultimate furniture of cognitive language. The question whether propositions and other abstract entities exist is not, indeed, decidable empirically, not even in the indirect empirical way in which scientists decide whether atoms and electrons exist, but it is nonetheless a cognitive question: it is decidable the way questions of semantic analysis are decidable, by examining whether proposed translations into a language with a specified primitive vocabulary preserve the meanings of the translated statements.

F. *Are Propositions Logical Constructions?*

Let us now examine the definition of propositions as classes of (synonymous or *L*-equivalent) declarative sentences, which appeals to philosophers intent on deflating the realm of assumed abstract entities. Carnap, in *Meaning and Necessity*, uses the relation of *L*-equivalence to construct those classes of sentences (" *L*-equivalence classes ") which he advises philosophers who do not like abstract entities, even if they are named " designata," to substitute for propositions. But, as Carnap notes, this construction leads

[23] Cf. " Semantics, Empiricism and Ontology," in *Semantics and the Philosophy of Language,* ed. Linsky.

to the consequence that there is only one necessary proposition. This is awkward, especially since it makes good sense to say that A believes that p yet does not believe that q, where " p " and " q " are L-equivalent sentences in the language spoken by A (e. g. let $p = (2 + 2 = 4)$ and $q =$ there are infinitely many solutions for the equation: $x^2 + y^2 = z^2$). To avoid the contradiction that a man may believe and at the same time not believe one and the same proposition, a stronger relation, some relation of *synonymy*, is required for the logical construction of propositions: a proposition is a class of synonymous declarative sentences. But now we face the objection that since classes are themselves abstract entities, no gain in concreteness has really been made by substituting classes of sentences for propositions. This objection, however, could be answered by saying with Russell (some of the time) that classes are merely logical fictions in the sense that statements about classes can be translated into a language devoid of class names and class variables. Presumably some such rules of translation for statements about propositions into a language containing sentential variables but no propositional variables would look as follows:

$$f(p) =_{df} (S_1) \ (Syn \ (S_1, \ ' \ p \ ') \supset f(S_1))$$

$$f(p, q) =_{df} (S_1) \ (S_2) \ (Syn \ (S_1, \ ' \ p \ ') \cdot Syn \ (S_2, \ ' \ q \ ') \supset f(S_1, S_2)) \ [24]$$

and similar rules for functions of n propositional variables. These contextual definitions, however, have disturbing consequences. A formal implication, in Russell's sense, is vacuously true if there are no values satisfying its antecedent. The above definientia, therefore, would be vacuously true if there were no sentences expressing propositions p and q. Such a supposition is not *prima facie* self-contradictory: for significant sentences do not usually assert their

[24] I am aware that these contextual definitions do not conform, as they stand, to the principle emphasized by logical-constructionists (see e. g., J. Wisdom, " Logical Constructions," *Mind*, 1931-33) that to say something about a logical construction is to say something, but *not necessarily the same thing*, about familiar entities. This is already evident in the case of the contextual definition of class symbols which is given in *Principia*: $f\{\hat{x}\phi_x\} = (\exists \psi)[(\psi!_x \equiv_x \phi_x) \cdot f(\psi!\hat{x})]$, for this definition leads, e. g., from the sentence " $a \in \hat{x}\phi_x$ " to the nonsentence " $a \in \psi!\hat{x}$," and in order to save the definition, the special definition " $a \in \psi!\hat{x} =_{df} \psi!a$ " had to be added. Similarly the above contextual definition would have to be supplemented with suitable grammatical conventions in order to preclude such ungrammatical sentences as, e. g., " it is true that ' the moon circles around the earth.' "

own existence; the sentence "it is true that there are 9 planets," for example, does not entail the existence of the sentence "there are 9 planets" (after all, the planets existed, presumably, before the English language came into existence). We must not confuse what is entailed by the *occurrence* of a sentence S with what is entailed by the *meaning* of S. Let us take, now, as a value of "$f(p, q)$" the statement "p entails q."[25] If there are no sentences expressing p and q, this entailment will hold by virtue of the above definitional equivalence. But for the same reason the following entailments would also hold: p entails not-q, not-p entails q, and not-p entails not-q (if there is no sentence designating p, then there is no sentence designating the negation of p—at least in a logistic language). It is easily deduced that p and q must be self-contradictory propositions. And as the same deduction could be made if we assumed just one of the propositions p and q to be verbally unexpressed, we arrive at the strange theorem that verbally unexpressed propositions are self-contradictory (not to be confused with the entirely different assertion that it is self-contradictory to assume the existence of a verbally unexpressed proposition!).

This argument against the logical-construction theory rests on two premises which an advocate of the theory might well challenge: (1) that the proposed definiens is adequately expressible by means of material implication, and (2) that the assumption of the existence of verbally unexpressed propositions makes sense. Against (1) he might contend that an *intensional* "if, then" must be used in the definiens ("any sentence S_1 which meant the same as 'p' *would* entail any sentence S_2 which meant the same as 'q'"). But notice that this reply would force him into the uncomfortable position of having to admit that sentences about propositions, which he interprets in the footsteps of Carnap's *Logical Syntax of Language* as "pseudo-object-sentences," cannot be adequately translated into an *extensional* metalanguage. Against (2) he might hold that ordinary usage of the word "proposition" only warrants the meaningfulness of the assumption that a given proposition is verbally unexpressed in a *given* language (e.g. if the science of electrochemistry is un-

---

[25] It is true that if we substitute for "p" and "q" statements—as we should—the result is not a correct sentence of ordinary English. However, "p entails q" is here written, for typographical convenience, as short for "the proposition that p entails the proposition that q" or simply "that p entails that q."

known to some African tribe, then the propositions of that science are not expressed by any sentences of the language of that tribe); but that to speak of propositions unexpressed in *any* language is to relapse into that Platonism which the logical-construction theory is designed to redeem us from.

The stated argument against (2) would perhaps be endorsed by Carnap, since he takes designation as a three-termed relation involving not only a sentence and a proposition but also a language: " S designates p in L " we must write in the Carnapian language of pure semantics if we wish to make sense. And this suggests perhaps that the only meaningful supposition that can be made is that there is no sentence *in a given language* designating a given proposition, not that there is no sentence in *any* language designating a given proposition. But actually " $- (\exists S) (\exists L) (S$ designates p_1 in L) " is just as well-formed a sentence as " $- (\exists S) (S$ designates p_1 in L_1)," so I don't think the fact that designation is a three-termed relation involving a language can be used as a valid argument against (2). That it is the semantical rules governing the constituent terms of S—and thus the semantic system to which S belongs—which determine what p is designated by S, is true enough but has no tendency to prove that for every p there must be some S belonging to some semantic system which designates p. No principle of pure semantics is violated by the argument that " it is true that there are 9 planets " entails the existence of the *proposition* that there are 9 planets (by the rule of existential generalization applied to a singular statement whose subject is a proposition) but not the existence of any *sentence* expressing that proposition (if it did entail the latter, then the logical equivalence of " it is true that p " and " p " would be violated, since clearly the proposition that there are 9 planets does not entail that sentences exist). Therefore it is logically possible for a proposition to exist without being designated by any sentence. It would be naively irrelevant to point out that it is self-contradictory to suppose that such an unexpressed proposition were ever identified. It is similarly self-contradictory to suppose that an unnamed thing is named, yet who would infer that " there exist unnamed things " is self-contradictory?

Further, it is noteworthy that the identification of propositions with classes of sentences in the sense of the suggested contextual definition does not in the least guarantee that every proposition must be verbally expressed. In the first place, the truth of a universal implication (see the above definientia) does not entail the existence of values satisfying its antecedent. Secondly, does the existence of a class guarantee that the class has members? It would, naturally, if " existence " of classes *meant* their non-emptiness, and in *Principia Mathematica* this is the explicit definition actually given: $E!\alpha =_{df} (\exists x)\, x \in \alpha$. But in the very same work a clearly different notion of class existence is also used, symbolized by existential quantification over class variables: $(\exists \alpha)\, f(\alpha)$. That this notion, coresponding to Quine's dictum " to be is to be the value of a variable," is clearly distinct from the one that is explicitly defined is evident from the way it is proved that at least two distinct classes exist: the universal class is one of them, indeed it demonstrably exists in the explicitly defined sense of class existence (the existence of at least one individual is provable in *Principia Mathematica*) , the other class, however, is none other than the null class! Clearly, the null class could not without contradiction be said to exist in the sense explicitly defined in *Principia Mathematica*. What is directly proved from the non-emptiness of V is that V is distinct from Λ. Thereupon it is informally concluded by the authors that there exist at least two classes, which informal deduction would be formalized as the deduction of: $(\exists \alpha)\,(\exists \beta)\,(\alpha \neq \beta)$, from: $\Lambda \neq V$. And this deduction is a legitimate instance of existential generalization if and only if class names are construed, not as " incomplete symbols," but as names of values of quantifiable class variables; [26] which proves that existence is here meant in Quine's sense.

The point of this digression into the meaning of class existence is that it is by no means obvious that the logical-construction theory of propositions reduces the notion of verbally unexpressed propositions to nonsense or at least to self-contradiction; since the very logicians who repudiate intensions speak of the existence of classes in such a way that even the null class can be said to exist. However, it is possible to construct an argument against the logical-construction theory which is independent of the controversial premises (1) and (2) . Let us ask whether the universal implication in sentential

---

[26] This formalization of Russell's and Whitehead's informal deduction is, indeed, inconsistent with their " no-class theory," i. e. the theory that class names are incomplete symbols and thus may not be used as substituends for variables. This goes to show that it is difficult to extract a consistent theory of class existence from *Principia Mathematica*.

variables which is offered as a reductive translation of " p entails q " (which is a possible value of " $f(p, q)$ ") [27] is supposed to be a *contingent* or a *necessary* proposition. Suppose the former. Then " p entails q " is itself a contingent proposition. This consequence contradicts the thesis that true entailment propositions are themselves necessary, which was defended in Chapter 5. But apart from the argument there given, the consequence seems absurd, since it entails that the hypothesis " p entails q " might be confirmed by examination of the syntactic relations of some pairs of sentences synonymous with " p " and " q " respectively, but subsequently might be disconfirmed by examination of further such sentence pairs (cf. p. 181). In other words, if we seize the first horn of the dilemma about to be constructed, we are committed to the view that a statement of the form " p entails q " is an inductive generalization of the form " (x) (y) $(fx \cdot gy \supset xRy)$," and thus the same logical kind of statement as, say, " every cat fears every dog"! Suppose, on the other hand, that it is a necessary proposition. In that case it is itself an entailment proposition which may be expressed as follows: " that S_1 is synonymous with ' p ' and that S_2 is synonymous with ' q ' entails that S_1 entails S_2." That is, it is the *proposition* that S_1 entails S_2, which is said to be entailed by the stated assumptions. But thus propositions have raised their ugly heads again and a further reductive translation will be no more successful in killing propositions than was Hercules in decapitating the many-headed Hydra.

Even if this dilemma could be answered, I would reject such reductive translations on the ground that sentences are simply the wrong kind of values (or names of sentences the wrong kind of substituends) for the variables " x " and " y " in the context " x entails y," in just the same way as sentences are the wrong kind of values for " x " in the contexts " I believe x " or " x is possible." The appropriate substituends in these contexts are the names of the *intensions* of sentences, which in English are formed by prefixing " that " to the sentence. It is a property of a sentence that it belongs to the English language, that it is composed of so many words, that it is of the declarative type, that it is often uttered by so-and-so with passion. But entailing such and such consequences is, like the property of being true, not a property of sentences as such but only

[27] In the intro. to the 2d ed. of *Language, Truth and Logic* Ayer suggests just this translation, on pp. 6-7.

of sentences as meaning such and such propositions (thus " ' *p* ' is true " is elliptical for " the proposition expressed by ' *p* ' is true "). This point is easily established by considering what one would accept as correct translations of entailment statements or of predications of truth into another language. If, for example, the English sentence " it is true that there are 9 planets " were synonymous with the metalinguistic sentence " ' there are 9 planets ' is true," then, since the name of a sentence formed by quoting the sentence does not belong specifically to the language to which the named sentence belongs but is rather a metalinguistic name common to all languages that use the quoting device, it would be correct to translate the English sentence into the following German sentence: " there are 9 planets " ist wahr. But while " the sentence ' there are 9 planets ' contains one noun " is correctly translated into " der Satz ' there are 9 planets ' enthaelt ein Hauptwort," it is clear that a correct translation of " it is true that there are 9 planets " into German would be the *object-linguistic* sentence " es ist wahr, dass es 9 Planeten gibt." *Mutatis mutandis*, the same holds for entailment statements.

The above argument amounts, incidentally, to a rejection of Carnap's early thesis (which is a consequence of Wittgenstein's thesis of extensionality) that apparently nonextensional statements such as modal statements about propositions and statements about propositional attitudes (as well as, presumably, indirect quotations) are *pseudo-object statements*, to be translated into metalinguistic statements which mention but do not use subordinate sentences (See *Logical Syntax of Language*, §§ 67-9). In *Meaning and Necessity*, Carnap has abandoned the attempt at translation of modal sentences into an extensional metalanguage that is purely *syntactic*. But his more recent translation of " $N(p)$ " into the *semantic* statement " ' *p* ' is *L*-true in *S* " is equally open to the above objection.[28] Carnap's criterion of pseudo-object statements was that a " parallel " syntactic statement could be constructed which is logically equivalent to the

---

[28] In this connection, see also A. Church's critique of Carnap's more sophisticated attempt at extensionalization of belief sentences in *Meaning and Necessity*: " On Carnap's Analysis of Statements of Assertion and Belief," *Analysis* (April 1950), which is frequently referred to in the relevant literature. I have myself discussed this problem in some detail in " Necessary Propositions and Linguistic Rules," *Semantica* (*Archivio di Filosofia*, Rome, 1955). For further discussion of Carnap's semantic explication of " necessity," see below, Chap. 14.

object statement: thus " ' rose ' is a thing word " has the same logical content, according to Carnap, as " roses are things." But actually this claim of logical equivalence has never been established, and it is in fact false. The conjunction " ' rose ' is a thing word, but there are no thing words " is self-contradictory, but the conjunction " roses are things, but there are no thing words " is not self-contradictory. If it were, then " roses are flowers, but there are no flower words " should likewise be self-contradictory, and it clearly is not, since the first conjunct is analytic and the second factual, and no factual statement can contradict an analytic statement. Since the translation into the formal mode of speech thus is not logically equivalent to the translated statement in the material mode of speech, it requires to be clarified in what sense the former statement " clarifies " the meaning of the latter.

It must be concluded that there is no obvious interpretation of the dictum " a proposition is a class of sentences " that would make it consistent with ordinary usage of the word " proposition." And I suggest that no disquieting postulation of " entities " is involved in the definition of a proposition as anything that may significantly be said to be believed or disbelieved (or " intended "—in the Brentano sense—in some other mode). One who speaks of propositions as of objects of beliefs need not be guilty of Platonic hypostasis any more than one who speaks of values as of objects of preferences (interests), or one who speaks of sounds as of objects of hearing.

If the foregoing argument is correct, then we can abandon the linguistic theory of necessary truth—allowing, of course, that *some* necessary statements do not, in the specified sense, express propositions at all—and recognize logical necessity as an intrinsic property of propositions, without any fear of committing ourselves to a mystical Platonism.

CHAPTER 8. *Analytic Truth and Implicit Definitions*

A. *Implicit Definition, Formal Systems, and Descriptive Predicates*

ONE reason why the characterization of analytic truth as "truth certifiable by reference to definitions (or linguistic meanings) alone" is not satisfactory is that it is not clear which meaning of the highly ambiguous term "definition" is intended. Such indecision about the meaning of "definition" may easily lead to verbal disagreement among philosophers about the existence of synthetic a priori propositions. Thus H. Langford once published a brief paper, carrying the alarming title "A Proof that Synthetic a Priori Propositions Exist," [1] in which he argued that the necessary (a priori) proposition "all cubes have 12 edges" is synthetic, on the ground that it is not formally demonstrable on the basis of an explicit definition of "cube" alone, but only if extralogical *postulates* are added. His argument could be strengthened by formulating the proposition in question without using the definable word "cube," thus: every solid that is bounded by congruent square faces has twelve edges. For then the usual counterargument that a cube, after all, could be defined as a twelve-edged solid, which forces the advocate of the synthetic a priori into the uncomfortable position of having to defend the notion of "essential" ("real") definition, could not arise. Langford could have said the same, *mutatis mutandis*, about the theorem "all triangles have an angle sum equal to 180°" which cannot be demonstrated without the use of such an extralogical postulate as the parallel postulate. But philosophers who repudiate the synthetic a priori would presumably reply that Langford argued in terms of too narrow a conception of analytic truth. If the only kind of definition we allow, they would presumably say, are explicit definitions, then not even "2 + 2 = 4" could count

[1] *Journal of Philosophy* (Jan. 1949).

as analytic, since its demonstration requires the associative law for addition $[a + (b + c) = (a + b) + c]$ or a recursive definition of addition $[a + (b + 1) = (a + b) + 1; \ a + 0 = a]$. But such postulates, they might say, amount to implicit definitions of the explicitly undefined (primitive) terms of a deductive system, and if such implicit definitions are permissible means of proving analyticity, then the exhaustiveness of the disjunction "either analytically true or contingently true" can be maintained.

But let us take a closer look at the concept of implicit definition. When the term "implicit definition" is used in connection with formal postulational systems, it refers to a set of formal postulates, i. e. postulates whose extralogical terms, the "primitives" of the system, are not interpreted. Such a set is said to implicitly define the primitive extralogical terms it contains. Thus a postulate like "for any two distinct points on a plane there is exactly one straight line containing both points," as occurring in, say, a formal reconstruction of Euclidean plane geometry, is said to constitute together with the other postulates an implicit definition of the primitive terms "point," "straight line," "plane," "containing." But if the postulational system is fully formalized with the help of symbolic logic, then these primitive terms turn out to be free *variables*, specifically predicate variables. Thus the above postulate, as part of a formal geometry, looks as follows:

$$(x)(y)(z)[Px \cdot Py \cdot x \neq y \cdot Qz \cdot Rzx \cdot Rzy \supset (\exists u)(Su \cdot Rzu \cdot Rux \cdot Ruy \cdot$$
$$(v)(Sv \cdot Rzv \cdot Rvx \cdot Rvy \supset v = u))].$$

The free predicate-variables "P," "Q," "S," "R" are the primitive terms. What is meant by saying that these free variables are implicitly *defined* (a manner of speaking which may understandably offend some logicians) by the postulates is that the latter determine by their structure a class of properties and relations, viz. interpretations satisfying them, and that the free variables may be regarded as "ambiguously denoting" (to borrow Russell's early phrase) such interpretations. But it is clear, then, that the postulates are propositional functions, not propositions, and that the same holds for the theorems deducible from the postulates. And since "true" is not predicable of propositional functions (though "provable," the syntactic concept, is), it looks as though it made no sense to speak of "truth by implicit definition."

Indeed, if by an "implicit definition" is meant a set of uninterpreted postulates in the specified sense, then it *is* nonsense to speak of "truth by implicit definition." But in that case it becomes a puzzle what could be meant by saying, as happens so frequently in the context of criticisms of Kant's theory of geometry, that geometry considered as a branch of pure mathematics is a body of analytic truths. The adovcates of the thesis of the reducibility of pure mathematics to logic are, of course, well aware of the fact that geometrical axioms, unlike arithmetical axioms, cannot be translated into purely logical notation so as to appear as logical truths. Thus Peano's postulates of arithmetic, intended not as propositional functions but as propositions involving the concepts ordinarily associated with the terms "0," "number," "successor," can be turned into logical truths on the basis of intuitively acceptable definitions of these arithmetical primitives in terms of logical constants. But we cannot similarly define the concepts ordinarily associated with the geometrical primitives "point," "straight line," "between," etc. in terms of logical concepts. In which sense, then, could it be maintained that the propositions of a formal geometry are analytic, deducible from logic? There are two possible lines of argument in support of this view: (1) the axioms of a formal geometry, containing uninterpreted extralogical primitives, are not *asserted*, nor are the theorems. If "*T*" stands for a theorem and "*A*" for the axiom set from which *T* is deduced, then "*T*" is to be construed as elliptical for "if *A*, then *T*." This conditional statement (meaning: any interpretation satisfying the axioms also satisfies the theorem) is analytic, indeed a logical truth;[2] (2) the axioms of a formal geometry contain free predicate variables, and are thus propositional functions. But arithmetic constitutes a possible model for such an uninterpreted axiomatic system. That is, the uninterpreted primitives "point," "straight line," etc. can be arithmetically interpreted in such a fashion that the axioms turn into theorems of arithmetic. And since arithmetic is reducible to logic, geometry is thus indirectly reducible to logic.

The first argument has been disposed of by Quine, in his excellent article "Truth by Convention," where he points out that if geometry is reducible to logic in this sense, then *any* science capable of

[2] For an explicit statement of this view, see Hempel, "Geometry and Empirical Science," in Feigl and Sellars, *Readings in Philosophical Analysis*.

axiomatization, like mechanics, biology, or psychology, is reducible to logic in the same sense. And the second argument may be answered in similar fashion. Any synthetic statement, be it necessary or contingent, can be formalized, i. e. all descriptive terms may be replaced with variables until only *logical* constants remain, and the resulting statement form (propositional function) may be turned into a logical truth by substituting suitable predicates for the predicate variables. Take, for example, the law of inertia in the form " for every *x*, if *x* is a body isolated from external forces, then *x* is either in uniform motion or at rest." Using " *B*," " *I*," " *U*," and " *R* " as predicate variables, we obtain the statement form " for every *x*, if *Bx* and *Ix*, then *Ux* or *Rx*." Now, assign to " *B* " the meaning " integer," to " *I* " the meaning " prime," to " *U* " the meaning " indivisible by two," and to " *R* " the meaning " equal to two," and you obtain a logical truth. Surely, this is a queer sense of " reducing " mechanics to logic!

All this, indeed, is no argument against the orthodox view of logical empiricism, that if the axioms of a system of geometry are not propositional functions or arithmetical tautologies, then they belong to what is called " physical geometry," which is an empirical science of physical space though, like mechanics and other physical sciences, it may be cast into deductive form; and that pure (formal) geometry is a part of pure mathematics in no other sense, indeed, than pure mechanics (or, for that matter, " pure " deductive theology) is a part of pure mathematics. However, the empiricist critics of Kant maintain that if by a " proposition of geometry " one understands a proposition formulated by means of specifically geometrical terms (occurring essentially), which cannot be defined by means of logical constants (unlike arithmetical terms), then such a proposition is nothing more than a physical hypothesis which is in principle disconfirmable. But this view I find unacceptable, as I have already indicated in Chapters 2 and 3. In the attempt to refute it, the phrase " true by implicit definition " will be encountered again, but with an entirely different significance.

In the already cited paper " Geometry and Empirical Science " (a clear statement of the empiricist, anti-Kantian conception of geometry), Hempel emphasizes that it is always an *empirical* question whether a given set of " coordinative " definitions (i. e. interpretations of the primitives of an axiom set by means of descrip-

tive terms) satisfies a given axiom set. I would like to challenge
this claim by considering one of Hilbert's " axioms of order " which,
as reported by Hempel, had to be added to the explicitly stated
postulates of Euclidean geometry in order to make a strictly formal
deduction of the theorems possible: " if A, B, C are points on a
straight line, and if B lies between A and C, then B also lies between
C and A." Formalized, this postulate would read:

$$(x)(y)(z)(u)[Px \cdot Py \cdot Pz \cdot Su \cdot Cuy \cdot Cux \cdot Cuz \supset (By, x, z \supset By, z, x)]$$

The specifically geometrical (or topological) term " between " has
been replaced by the relation-variable " B " which does not refer
to any *particular* three-termed relation. Consider now a statement
to the effect that such and such an interpretation satisfies the postulate—which is equivalent to saying that the proposition obtained
from the above propositional function by substituting such and such
definite predicates with specific meanings for the free predicate
variables is true. We can easily think of interpretations such that
it is a *question of empirical fact* whether the resulting proposition
is true. For example, if " P " is interpreted as " person," " S " as
" family," " Cxy " as " x contains y," and " By, x, z " as " y is
jealous of x on account of z," there results the proposition " for
any persons x, y, z who belong to the same family, if y is jealous
of x on account of z, then y is jealous of z on account of x," which
is false as a matter of psychological fact. Again, suppose the class
of elements " P " were interpreted as " man " and " S " as some
particular class of men, and the three-termed relation as " x is able
to defend y against z." It would then clearly be a question of fact
whether the resulting proposition is true.

But surely, nobody would wish to maintain that the truth of
the proposition about spatial order, which is a possible interpretation
of the postulate and which suggested the abstract postulate in the
first place, is similarly a question of empirical fact? Could one
conceive of any observations that would disconfirm the proposition
" for any three collinear particles, if the first lies between the second
and the third, then it lies between the third and the second "?
The antecedent " a body cannot move rectilinearly from place A to
place C without passing through place B " (taking this as an interpretation of " B lies between A and C ") surely *entails* the consequent " that body cannot move rectilinearly from C to A without

passing through *B*." Thus the customary spatial interpretation surely yields an *a priori* truth. It is easy to show, however, that in any clear sense of "definitional truth" this cannot be a definitional truth. For, as "between" occurs as a primitive in Hilbert's axiomatization of Euclidean geometry, it is not, in this system, explicitly definable. What can be explicitly defined is only a corresponding abstract term referring to the entire class of 3-termed relations having the same symmetrical property as spatial betweenness, thus:

$$Bx, y, z =_{df} (\exists R) [Rx, y, z \cdot (Rx, y, z \supset Rx, z, y)].$$

This is a definition of abstract betweenness, or of the betweenness-family of three-termed relations, on the basis of which statements of the form "*R* is symmetrical if it is a member of the betweenness-family" are analytic, indeed. But the categorical statement "*this R* (with which we have ostensive acquaintance) belongs to the betweenness-family" is synthetic.

Philosophers who adhere to the principle "every significant self-consistent statement is either analytic or contingent" here take recourse to saying that the statement is nonetheless *implicitly definitional*, which seems to mean that although it is not possible to deduce the statement from logical truths with the help of explicit definitions, anybody who denied the statement would *contravene established usage*. Now, in the context of examining this concept of "truth by implicit definition," I shall argue for two theses: (1) the fact that anybody who denies sentence *S* is using some constituent expression of *S* in an unconventional sense is evidence for the assertion that *S* expresses a necessary proposition, but not for the assertion that *S* is analytic in the strict sense; (2) while the above mentioned fact is perhaps a *necessary* condition for the truth of the statement "*S* expresses a necessary proposition," [3] it certainly is not a sufficient condition; for a sentence could satisfy this condition if it expressed a contingent but universally believed proposition.

But before arguing for these propositions, I would like to illustrate the concept of "truth by implicit definition" by one more example, which may be more convincing than the above geometrical "postulate." After all, one might argue with some persuasiveness that "*x*

---

[3] Strictly speaking, this holds only on the assumption that no errors of deduction (or calculation) are committed; cf. above, p. 122.

lies between y and z" is *synonymous* with "x lies between z and y," such that, putting synonyms for synonyms, we can reduce Hilbert's "postulate" to an explicit tautology of the form "if p, then (if q, then q)." We had, therefore, better turn our attention to an example of "truth by implicit definition" which demonstrably cannot be reduced to a logical truth by the device of putting synonyms for synonyms.

Consider the proposition that the relation of temporal succession is asymmetrical. Formalized: for any events x, y, (if Sx, y, then not-Sy, x). A definition of "event" as any value of the individual variables which *satisfies* this universally asserted function would obviously beg the question. Rather, the class of events should be defined as the field of the relation S, i. e.

$$\hat{x}(x \in \text{event}) =_{df} \hat{x}((\exists y)(Sxy \vee Syx)).$$

Here again, the relation is meant as the *specific* relation, having the predicated formal property, with which we are ostensively acquainted, not the class of relations formally similar to the given one, like the arithmetic relation "x is greater than y." Now, there is an obvious definition of "after" in terms of the converse "before," which would turn our proposition into a logical truth: $Sx, y =_{df} -\breve{S}x, y$ (read: x does not precede y) $\cdot -SMx, y$ (read: x is not simultaneous with y). By virtue of this definition,

$$"(x)(y)(Sx, y \supset -Sy, x)"$$

is equivalent to

$$"(x)(y)(Sx, y \supset -(-\breve{S}y, x \cdot -SMy, x))."$$

If we now replace "$\breve{S}x, y$" by its synonym "Sy, x," we obtain:

$$(x)(y)(Sx, y \supset -(-Sx, y \cdot -SMy, x)),$$

which is equivalent to : $(x)(y)(-Sx, y \cdot -SMy, x \supset -Sx, y)$, which is a logical truth (the descriptive relational predicates occur vacuously in it). But this demonstration is illegitimate because it is based on circular definition: "succession" has been defined in terms of "precedence," and then "precedence" in terms of "succession." It might be replied that the replacement of a *single* expression with a single expression, like "Sxy" with "$\breve{S}yx$," should not be called "definition"; and that, since it is not the case that any constituent of the definiens of "Sxy" was defined in terms of the definiendum, the definition is not circular after all. But this reply is weak for two reasons: (1) The explanation of the meaning of a relational predicate in terms of the converse relational predicate (like "parent" in terms of "child") is, indeed, not a case of *analysis*, since no concept is explicitly mentioned in the definiens which is not explicitly mentioned in the definiendum. Nevertheless it is a perfectly good instance of definition if "definition" is used in the broad sense of "explaining the meaning of one term by means of other terms whose meanings are already understood." Since "R" and "$\breve{R}$" are but different symbolic expressions for the same concept, anybody, indeed, who has the concept of $\breve{R}$ has the concept of R at the same time; but this is irrelevant to the question of whether somebody might understand what "$\breve{R}$" means without understanding what "R" means. (2) In order to prove that the corresponding proposition about the converse relation, precedence, is logically true, one would have to use a similar definition of "$\breve{S}xy$" in terms of "Sxy." But even if the above liberalization of the prohibition of circular definition were granted, we would now have a case of circular definition, since we are defining R in terms of its converse, and the converse of R in terms of R. The circle can be broken only by taking either R or its converse as primitive. But then we would get into the paradox that the asymmetry of R (or $\breve{R}$) is logically demonstrable while the asymmetry of $\breve{R}$ (or R) is not, in spite of the theorem of logic that if a given relation has a given formal property, then its converse must have it too!

That there are statements which can be demonstrated to be logically true if circular definitions are admitted and not otherwise is perhaps surprising (at least it should come as a shock to those who think all is well with the concept of analytic truth). Philosophers with a sense of humor might ask why on earth we should not accept "truth by circular definition" as a new species of analytic truth. In case they are serious with this question, they ought to be reminded that the concept here under scrutiny is not the concept "true by *stipulated* synonymy," but the concept "true by explication of the meanings of terms in actual usage." Obviously one does not clarify the meaning of a term by using a complex expression which can be clarified only by using that very term.

It should be noted also that " true by circular definition " is by no means the same as "true by question-begging definition." If I prove the analyticity of " all *A* are *B* " by defining " *A* " to mean the same as " *B*," then the definition is question-begging (i. e. it begs the question of analyticity) if there is no evidence for the adequacy of the definition except the fact that it turns the debated statement into an analytic one. To decide whether or not a definition begs the question of analyticity is not an easy matter, because an important criterion of adequacy of a proposed definition is just whether it turns specified statements involving the definiendum into analytic truths (cf. below, pp. 222-4). It is far easier to decide whether a definition is circular in the explained sense. It could no doubt be argued that the alleged circular definition of temporal succession is also question-begging, but that is another question entirely.

Let us consider one more attempt to prove that the necessary proposition expressed by " $(x)(y)(Sx, y \supset -Sy, x)$ " is a logical truth. " The entire question of circular definition," it might be countered, " need not be raised if we agree that ' *p* ' expresses a logical truth provided it can be transformed into a logically true sentence by *putting synonyms for synonyms*. Now, though

$$\text{`` } Sx, y \equiv -Sy, x \cdot -SMx, y \text{ ''}$$

is not acceptable as a definition, it is true because the left-hand expression is synonymous with the right-hand expression." This argument, I am afraid, begs the question and could not convince anyone who doubts whether " $(x)(y)(Sx, y \supset -Sy, x)$ " is analytic. It is like proving that " whatever is red is colored " is analytic by saying that " red " is synonymous with " red and colored." Just because " ' $p \supset q$ ' is analytic " says the same as " ' *p* ' is synonymous with ' $p \cdot q$,' " such a proof would beg the question.

B. *The Logical Empiricist's Dilemma*

Now, to the promised argument for the two theses stated above. The following principle surely follows from the meaning of " intuitively necessary proposition ": if *S* expresses, for some interpreter, an intuitively necessary proposition p, then anybody who believes that S is false interprets S to express some other proposition than p. As suggested by the qualification " intuitively," this principle holds only for necessary propositions that can be known without elaborate deduction, since somebody might interpret S to mean p and still believe it to be false owing to a mistake in deduction. But since this discussion restricts itself to necessary propositions that are " intuitively evident " (as one used to say, once upon a time, without blushing), the mentioned complication of the problem may well be disregarded. The principle, intended as a formulation of a necessary condition (but not sufficient condition) for the truth of " S expresses, for some interpreter, a necessary proposition," may be illustrated as follows. Suppose an anthropologist visited a tribe whose language he did not understand, and not being accompanied by an interpreter had to learn the language by observing the linguistic behavior of the natives. Suppose that various observations of situations in which a sentence of the form " xRy " is used (" x " and " y " here symbolize proper names or descriptions, and " R " a relational predicate, of the tribe language) suggest to the anthropologist the hypothesis that " xRy " means " x happened after y." Suppose, furthermore, that by that time he had sufficiently familiarized himself with their language to be able to test semantic hypotheses about it by means of the technique of interrogation. He thus asks the natives " could it ever be the case that xRy and also yRx? " and to his surprise gets an affirmative answer. He surely would not conclude that this tribe does not share the belief, universally held by civilized man, in the irreversibility of time, but rather he would abandon his hypothesis about the meaning of " R."

No doubt this is the sort of thing philosophers have in mind when they say that such " intuitively evident " propositions as the one under discussion are simply propositions true *by virtue of implicit linguistic rules*. The rules are said to be " implicit " if, like the rule governing usage of " follows after," they cannot be formulated as explicit (or contextual) definitions. My criticism of this fashionable " linguistic " theory of necessary truth is twofold: (1) it is confusing to widen the extension (or dilute the intension) of the term " analytic " to such an extent that necessary propositions which clearly are not formally deducible from logical truths alone come to be called " analytic "; such a usage merely leads to *verbal* disagreements with

the advocates of the synthetic a priori; (2) if the expression " contravening usage " is employed in the *vague* sense of " violating explicit
or implicit linguistic rules," then the boundary between " contravening customary usage of some constituent expression of *S* " and
" disbelieving the proposition customarily expressed by *S* " is anything but clear. This would mean that the distinction " analytically
true–factually true " is vague—a consequence unacceptable to most
" empiricists."

The cogency of the second criticism will readily be felt if we
repeat the story of the visiting anthropologist, changing only the
particular linguistic experiment involved. We assume again that the
meaning of a relational predicate " *R* " is to be discovered, but that
observations of the contexts in which the predicate is used suggest
to the anthropologist the hypothesis that it means " warmer." He
might then test the hypothesis in terms of the following question:
" suppose body *x* is at a distance from body *y* at time t_o and has
relation *R* to *y* at t_o; and suppose that then *x* and *y* are brought
into contact and left in contact for a while, say till t_1; could
it be that *x* at t_1 has *R* to *x* at t_o? " What our anthropologist
is actually doing here is to take the second law of thermo-
dynamics, in the qualitative formulation " heat always flows from
warmer to colder bodies," as an implicit definition of " warmer," or
its converse " colder." Assuming that the natives are sufficiently
educated to understand this somewhat sophisticated question, would
an affirmative answer disprove the semantic hypothesis? Evidently
considerations of probability must enter here. Since it is highly
improbable that the physical experiences of these people should
differ in the mentioned respect from the physical experiences of
the rest of mankind, the anthropologist would do well to consider
his hypothesis refuted; just as he did well to abandon his previous
hypothesis, concerning the synonymy of " *R* " and " follows after,"
considering that a state of affairs intuitively inconceivable for civilized man is probably just as inconceivable for these natives. However, the statement which was thus employed by the anthropologist
as an " implicit definition " of " warmer" *expresses an empirical
proposition*. The fact, consequently, that anybody who denied *S*
would be taken to assign to *S* a meaning other than the intended
one does not warrant the conclusion that *S* expresses a necessary

proposition; it may just be that S expresses a contingent proposition which on the strength of empirical evidence is firmly believed.

One might reply that the indicated difficulty with the concept "true by implicit definition" could be circumvented if the ambiguous expression "could it be that . . ." in the linguist's questionnaire were replaced with the unambiguous expression "is it logically possible that. . . ." Waiving the obvious reflection that a questionnaire containing such a technical term would be intelligible to philosophically educated people only, the trouble with the amendment is this. "*p* is logically possible" means "*p* is not self-contradictory," and this means that from *p* alone no contradiction can be deduced. But then to ask whether *p* is logically possible is the same as asking whether the contradictory of *p* is analytic in the strict sense of "deducible from logical truths." And thus no criterion has been provided for "truth by implicit definition" in contradistinction to strictly analytic truth.

It must be emphasized that when the axioms of an *empirically interpreted* deductive system (whether the interpretation be complete or only partial) [4] are said to implicitly define the primitive descriptive terms of the system, "implicit definition" cannot be used the way it is used in the discussion of *uninterpreted* axiomatic systems. Thus it is said by some that the axioms of Newtonian mechanics implicitly define the term "particle" as used in Newtonian mechanics, that the postulates of Maxwell's field theory implicitly define "*E*" and "*H*," and that the equations of quantum mechanics, including the uncertainty relation, implicitly define the entities, as well as their measurable traits, to which the equations refer,[5] and here the sentences characterized as implicit definitions are

---

[4] A deductive system is said to be partially interpreted if it is not the primitives but some of the defined terms of the system which are interpreted in terms of observables (cf. R. Carnap, *Foundations of Logic and Mathematics*, p. 65, and C. G. Hempel, *Fundamentals of Concept Formation in Empirical Science*, II, 7). It is easy to see why such a method provides but a partial interpretation of the primitives. Suppose, for example, that a term "*A*" of the system is explicitly defined as the conjunction "*B* and *C*," where "*B*" and "*C*" are primitives. If "*A*" is interpreted to mean, say, "dog," then the meanings of "*B*" and "*C*" are limited to properties of dogs, but it has not been specified which properties of dogs they mean. Concerning the bearing of the method of partial interpretation on the analytic-synthetic distinction, see below, pp. 318-21.

[5] Cf. H. Feigl, "Notes on Causality," and E. Nagel, "The Causal Character of Modern Physical Theory," both in Feigl and Brodbeck, *Readings in the Philosophy of Science*; also A. Pap, *The A Priori in Physical Theory*.

at the same time said to express physical propositions. It would also be said by some philosophers that a purely phenomenological language, like the language of sound experience, could be axiomatized in such a way that the axioms would " implicitly define " the primitive descriptive terms of the language, like " higher-in-pitch-than " in the axioms characterizing the designated relation as transitive and asymmetrical. The philosophical task before us is not so much to find evidence pro or con the claim that an empirically interpreted language contains statements that " implicitly define " explicitly undefined descriptive terms of the language,[6] but to clarify the meaning of the claim. In a way our enterprise may be characterized as " metaphilosophy," for it is philosophers who have brought the expression " true by implicit linguistic rules " into usage, without ever satisfactorily explicating its meaning. The thesis I wish to argue is that a clarification of this widely used semantic concept will throw the " empiricist " into a dilemma: either he will have to admit that the disjunction " either analytic or contingent " is *not exclusive*, since many contingent propositions are analytic in his widened sense of " analytic," or else he will have to admit that it is *not exhaustive*, since the only way in which he can avoid the first alternative is by restricting the meaning of " analytic " and therewith acknowledging propositions that cannot be conceived to be false and yet are not analytic.

In the first place, what exactly is meant by " contravening usage "? If somebody used the expression " that happily married bachelor . . . ," it would be clear enough what is meant by saying that he contravened the conventional usage of " bachelor ": even though the convention to use " bachelor " in the sense of " unmarried adult man " may not be laid down anywhere in the form of an explicit definition, we could easily get people to agree that such a definition more or less exactly expresses what they meant all

---

[6] This notion of " implicit definition " has recently been made formally precise by Carnap, though he prefers the term " meaning postulate " (" Meaning Postulates," *Philosophical Studies*, Oct. 1952). Thus the statements that the relation " warmer " is asymmetrical and transitive are characterized as meaning postulates by Carnap. Since the terms which are " introduced " by the meaning postulates are descriptive constants, they are not " postulates " of the same sort as the postulates of an uninterpreted axiomatic system. (Accordingly Carnap predicates " *L*-true " of statements entailed by meaning postulates; whereas the theorems of an uninterpreted system can be characterized, syntactically, as provable, but not, semantically, as *L*-true). The concept of " meaning postulates " will be discussed further in Chap. 14, below.

along by " bachelor." Would it be equally clear what is meant by "contravening usage" if a person were accused of contravening usage because he said: "I heard a tone, then a second tone of higher pitch than the first, then a third tone of higher pitch than the second but of lower pitch than the first"? Philosophers who are sensitive to the limits of verbal definability and who accordingly realize that the expression "higher pitch," unlike the expression "bachelor," is understood by ostensive definition only, would probably hesitate to call this statement "self-contradictory." Yet they would say that a person talking that way violated the "logical grammar" of sound-predicates.[7] Actually, it would be possible to reject the above statement as self-contradictory on the basis of an explicit grammatical ruling: by appending the comparative ending " -er " to an adjective, one intends to form an expression designating an *ordering* relation, i. e. a relation which is asymmetrical, transitive, and connex. Hence the above statement would be self-contradictory for similar reasons as the statement " there are two (or more) highest mountains in Africa." But suppose our language were less economical than it is (and for all I know there may be languages of the sort to be described), such that we could not use one indivisible relational predicate designating an ordering relation of specific kind, but instead had to use a relational predicate which was purely descriptive, without syntactic properties indicating the formal properties of the designated relation; those formal properties would then have to be pointed out in a separate statement about the relation. Thus instead of saying " x has a higher pitch than y " we might say, at two strokes, " x pitches y, and (x) (y) (z) (if x pitches y and y pitches z, then x pitches z), and (x) (y) (if x pitches y, then not-$(y$ pitches $x))$." The purely descriptive statement " x pitches y " would then leave it a *logically* open question whether the asserted relation between x and y is transitive; just as the statement " x can defeat y " does not logically entail that if y can defeat z, then x can defeat z.

If the primitive language just sketched contained the statement that the relation of " pitching " is transitive, that statement would be synthetic. Yet I suspect that anybody who said that pitching is not transitive would still be accused, by the adherents to the

[7] On rules of " logical grammar " see M. Schlick, " Meaning and Verification," in Feigl and Sellars.

linguistic theory of necessary truth, of " contravening usage." And what interests me above all is the meaning of " contravening usage " in this context. I can think of no other analysis of " anybody who denied *S* would contravene ordinary usage " than " anybody who denied *S* would, if he meant anything at all, interpret *S* to express some other proposition than the proposition it ordinarily expresses." But is it not obvious that the statement just made would be neces- arily true of any sentence which expresses a proposition that is universally believed? And since a highly confirmed empirical proposition may well be universally believed, we come to the con- clusion that the proposed criterion of necessary truth " true by virtue of explicit *or implicit* linguistic rules " does not effectively differentiate necessary from empirical truth. Suppose we found a child who had been taught the meanings of " cold " and " hot " by ostensive definition, and that extensive verbal agreement between him and ourselves as to what objects are cold and what objects are hot leads us to assume that the conventional meanings of these terms had been communicated to the child. How would we react if we subsequently found him affirming that snow is hot? Would we not suspect that the child had not grasped the conventional meaning of " hot " after all? We surely would, for the reason that the proposi- tion " snow produces sensations of cold " is, *on empirical grounds*, so certain that we refuse to countenance the possibility of its disconfirmation.

When the advocates of the linguistic theory are pressed that way, they usually reply: " But we know perfectly well *what it would be like* for snow to feel hot; that's why this proposition is empirical and meaningful (though false, in all probability). Do you know what it would be like for one event to both precede and follow the same event, or for a thing to be both red and blue all over, etc.? " Yet I have never been able to discover the difference between the question " do you know what it would be like for *p* to be false " and the question " can you *conceive* (or *imagine*) *p* to be false? " And if the questions are synonymous, then " empiricists " are covertly employing just that " psychologistic " criterion of necessary truth which they so emphatically repudiate. It turns out, then, that " *S* is true by implicit linguistic rules " means nothing else but " *S* expresses a proposition which cannot be conceived to be false." To revert to an illustration already used: from the fact that a person verbally agrees with our assertion " when two bodies of different temperature are brought into contact the warmer body grows colder and the colder body grows warmer " we cannot infer that he means by " warmer " and " colder " what we mean, since he would, on the basis of relevant perceptions, make precisely the same assertion if he meant by " warmer " what is ordinarily meant by " colder " and by " colder " what is ordinarily meant by " warmer." Suppose, then, we wanted to make sure that he meant by these words just what we mean by them, by asking him whether a piece of ice is colder or warmer than a bowl of steaming soup, and to our surprise he replies that it is warmer. We would surely infer that he means by " warmer " what we mean by " colder," rather than abandon the presupposition that similar physical stimuli produce similar sensations in all similar organisms. But thus we are explaining a verbal denial of a sentence *S*, not in terms of disbelief of the proposition conventionally expressed by *S*, but in terms of deviation from linguistic conventions relevant to *S*. Nevertheless *S* would be said to express a contingent proposition, for no other reason than that the falsehood of that proposition is conceivable. Why not frankly confess, then, adherence to the old " psychologistic " criterion of necessary truth employed by Hume, according to which *p* is necessary if not-*p* cannot be conceived (whether or not it be formally self-contradictory) ? Sometimes philosophers try to avoid the suspect " psychologistic " language " *p* cannot be conceived to be false " by saying instead " it is impossible to *describe* a situation in which *p* would be false." Thus it is alleged to be impossible to describe what it would be like for a surface to be simultaneously blue and red all over, or for an event to both precede and follow the same event. But if I were asked to describe what it would be like for a piece of ice to feel hot, all I could do would be to repeat the very sentence " the piece of ice would feel hot," since " feeling hot " is an expression that can be defined only ostensively, not verbally. Similarly, all I could do in reply to the above questions would be to repeat the sentences, since the descriptive terms contained in them are unanalyzable. And thus the enemies of the psychologistic criterion will find themselves pushed back to the suicidal question, " but could you *imagine* situations in which these sentences would be true "?

To conclude " *p* is impossible " from " *p* is unimaginable " is of course illicit if the unimaginability of p is due to one's failing to have a simple concept constituent of p, or if there is reason to believe that the attempt to imagine p fails only because of limited experience (e. g. let $p =$ dogs sometimes hear sounds whose pitch exceeds the highest pitch audible to the human ear. This proposition is easily thinkable but it is unimaginable, owing to the particular anatomy of the human ear). But anybody can see that the sense of " imagine " in " I can't imagine a dog singing a Mozart aria " is different from the sense of the same word in " I can't imagine a surface being blue and red all over." If the fact that our imagination finds itself thus frustrated is no warrant for denying the existence of such a state of affairs, then one might as well argue that the unthinkability of x being both red and not red (at the same time) does not warrant the conclusion that nothing *is* simultaneously red and not red—which would be questioning the law of contradiction as a law of " being." But if we deny of a thing which can significantly be characterized as red (i. e. an extended thing, whether physical surface or sense datum) that it is both red and non-red, we have already denied that it is both red and blue, since to say that x, an entity of which " red " is significantly predicable, is non-red is to say that x has some color other than red. To hesitate in such a case to infer nonexistence from unimaginability would, therefore, be sheer intellectual perversity. For one could not even *consistently* say " though it is unimaginable, it may exist." No doubt it was this sort of reflection which led Hume to set up imaginability as the measure of " absolute " possibility; and once the relevant meaning of " imaginable " is circumscribed by excluding the case where it is lack of experience (lack of " impressions " giving rise to simple ideas) that limits the imagination, there is no objection to the imaginability criterion simply because there is no alternative to it.

C. *Analyticity and Criteria of Adequacy*

Let us turn our attention, now, to a second, perhaps more precise, sense of the expression " true by implicit definition." The view might be taken that a statement could be known to be analytic (in the strict sense) even though, for the time being at least, no explicit definitions can be constructed that would show the statement to be analytic (the way " all unmarried men are unmarried " shows itself as analytic). One might plausibly maintain that while he may be unable to construct an explicit definition of a term T contained in statement p which would show p's analyticity, he might nevertheless understand the meaning of T well enough to be able to say: no definition of T could be adequate unless it enabled a logical demonstration of p. This would amount to declaring p as a *criterion of adequacy* to be satisfied by a definition of T. Since " p is analytic " means " p is logically demonstrable with the help of adequate definitions," the election of p as a criterion of adequacy for proposed explications of T is, indeed, equivalent to declaring it as analytic. The following are examples of terms whose meanings it is difficult to explicate, and of corresponding criteria of adequacy which are much more easily produced than the definitions (explications) they are criteria of adequacy for:

law of nature	if p expresses a law of nature, then p is a universal implication
	if . . . . ,
	then p is not logically true
	if . . . . ,
	then p contains no individual constants essentially (this criterion is more controversial than the first two)
confirmation	if e confirms h, and h is logically equivalent to h', then e confirms h'
	if h entails e, then e confirms h (but not conversely)
cognitive significance	if S is cognitively significant, then either S or not-S is true
	if . . . . ,
	then not-S is cognitively significant
	if . . . . ,
	then the non-logical constants in S are cognitively significant.

One might think that once all the criteria of adequacy have been listed, a definition satisfying all of them is easily obtained by simply taking their conjunction. But notice that this form of definition would be possible only for the first of our three examples, since there each criterion of adequacy expresses a necessary condition for the predicability of the explicandum, such that if the list of criteria were exhaustive we would have a necessary and sufficient condition. A look at the other two groups shows that such a procedure would either lead to circular definition or to a compound statement that could in no sense be regarded as a " definition " of any term. The usual situation in philosophical analysis, indeed, is that the difficult labor only begins after the criteria of adequacy have been laid down; which would not be the case if a definition satisfying the criteria could always be produced in such trivial fashion.

Nevertheless, we cannot afford to ignore this " trivial " method of constructing definitions, since an advocate of the thesis that all necessary truth is analytic might avail himself of just this method in order to demonstrate the analyticity of our sample statement " temporal succession is an asymmetrical relation." We would surely have to grant him that no definition of " Sxy " could be adequate unless it entailed the asymmetry and transitivity of the relation. Now, an explicit definition satisfying these conditions of adequacy might be constructed indirectly by first constructing a set of postulates involving a free binary predicate variable R, and then defining the unique relation we wish to define as the unique relation satisfying this set. The difficulty in this procedure is, of course, that in general there is more than one model for a given set of abstract postulates; if there were not, then one of the essential purposes served by abstract postulational systems would be defeated. If R is characterized only in terms of formal properties, i. e. properties definable without reference to the nature of the entities in the field of R, then many distinct relations will satisfy the set of postulates. But if we add a postulate specifying the field of the relation by means of the predicate " event," a big step toward uniqueness will have been taken: [8]

(1) $(x)\ (y)\ [xRy \supset -yRx]$

(2) $(x)\ (y)\ (z)\ [xRy \cdot yRz \supset xRz]$

(3) $(x)\ (y)\ [xRy \supset (\exists z)\ (zRy \cdot xRz)\ ]$

(4) $(x)\ (y)\ [xRy \supset Ex \cdot Ey]$

---

[8] Alternatively, one could restrict the range of the bound variables to events, in which case the fourth postulate would be redundant.

(1) and (2) express the familiar properties of asymmetry and transitivity which, according to Russell's analysis of "order," any ordering relation must have. The reason why we cannot add a connexity postulate is that two events may be distinct yet not related by R: they may be simultaneous events happening at different places.[9] The loss of uniqueness due to the absence of such a postulate is, however, compensated by (3) which may be called a "density postulate" since it says that there is an element in the field of R between any pair of elements related by R. This postulate involves, to be sure, the idealization of events as instantaneous (without duration), but it is required to rule out interpretations of R in terms of such forms of temporal succession as "following after a long time" which satisfy (1) and (2). (4) finally limits the field of R to events; it also makes it impossible to interpret R in terms of *spatial* ordering relations, such as "above," for while events are no doubt in the fields of such relations, the latter comprise also *things*.

Nothing that has been said amounts, of course, to a proof that our postulate set has a unique model. And since it is likely that such a proof, if it could be constructed, would be based on some extralogical postulates, the following reduction of the a priori truth that succession is asymmetrical to a strictly analytic truth is suspect from the start anyway. That is, if we wish to prove that the explicit definition of succession as the *unique* relation satisfying our set is non-empty, we shall probably have to assume other extralogical postulates as a priori truths, and thus little will be gained by the attempted reduction. But be this as it may, granted the explicit definition: $xSy =_{df} (\exists' R) [F(R) \cdot xRy]$ (where "$F(R)$" means "R satisfies the set 1–4," and the accent within the quantifier means:

---

[9] One might think that succession is a strictly ordering relation, i.e. a relation which is asymmetrical, transitive, and connex, if its field is restricted to spatially coincident events, since events are identical if they coincide in their spatial and temporal coordinates. However, if the statement that events in the sense of mathematical physics are uniquely determined by the four coordinates determining a point in space-time were true, then it would be self-contradictory to speak of coincidence of *distinct* events. But it is not self-contradictory if we use "event" in the sense of "*kind* of event"—Whitehead's "eternal objects" ingressing into space-time. And since this is what one ordinarily means by "event," even succession limited to spatially coincident events can be used to construct an order in Russell's sense only among the *abstractions* called by the physicist "point-events" (uniquely determined by four coordinates), but not among concrete events given in sense experience.

there is exactly one R), the proof of analyticity is easily conducted: By the definition,

$$(xSy \supset -ySx) \equiv (\exists'R) \ (F(R) \cdot xRy) \supset -(\exists'R) \ (F(R) \cdot yRx).$$

The right-hand side of this equivalence expands, by the definition of " $F(R)$," into:

$$(\exists'R) \ [\cdot \ \cdot \ \cdot (xRy \supset -yRx) \cdot xRy]$$
$$\supset -(\exists'R) \ [\cdot \ \cdot \ \cdot (xRy \supset -yRx) \cdot yRx].$$

This conditional can be shown to be logically true as follows. Suppose that R_1 satisfies the antecedent; then $-yR_1x$. And suppose R_2 satisfies the negation of the consequent; then yR_2x. This is a contradiction if $R_1 = R_2$. But by the uniqueness assumption (incorporated into the explicit definition), $R_1 = R_2$. Now, if " $p \cdot q$ " entails a contradiction, then " $p \supset -q$ " is logically true.[10]

In our earlier discussion of the possibility of an explicit definition of temporal succession in terms of its converse, we focused attention on the question of circularity, and neglected the question whether such a definition could be said to *beg the question of analyticity*. Let us now take the reverse course. It would not, indeed, be terribly far-fetched to argue that the above definition is also circular, since nobody who did not already understand the words " before " and " after " could possibly understand the meaning of " event "; in other words, one could plausibly argue that the class of events can be defined only as the field of temporal relations. But this question will be disregarded now, and instead the matter of " begging the question " will be given attention.

There are definitions, frequently improvised in the heat of debate, which may be said to beg the question of the *truth* of a debated proposition. Thus, if I try to dispute your claim that all philosophers are impractical people by citing counter instances, and you then save your generalization by saying " but I would not call

---

[10] It should be kept in mind that the above attempt to construct an explicit definition of temporal succession which would justify the claim that the a priori truth in question is strictly analytic, is intended primarily as a devil's advocacy. In general, the attempt to convert a postulational (or " implicit ") definition into an explicit definition must fail for two reasons: (1) because postulate sets usually contain more than one primitive term (free predicate variable), (2) because such an explicit definition defines a *class* of structurally similar concepts which it is difficult, if not impossible, to prove to be a unit-class.

anybody a real philosopher unless he were impractical," your definition (or rather, partial definition—criterion of adequacy!) begs the question at issue (is the asserted generalization true?) if there is no evidence for its adequacy except the circumstance that it entails the truth of the debated generalization. Similarly, if the debated question is whether a given truth is analytic, a proposed definition would beg the question of analyticity if no good reason for accepting it could be offered to him who doubts whether that truth *is* analytic. For example, suppose it were debated whether the principle of the conservation of energy, in the form " the total energy of an isolated system is constant in time," is analytic. Then a definition of " isolated system " as " system whose total energy is constant in time " would beg the question of analyticity if no *independent* evidence could be produced that " isolated system " as physicists use the term is synonymous with the proposed definiens. If the question at issue, however, is, not whether *p* is analytic or empirical, but whether *p* is analytic a priori or synthetic a priori (the disputants being in agreement that *p* is a priori), it is not equally clear what could be meant by " definition begging the question of analyticity."

For a philosopher to say, " I am convinced that *p* is an *empirical* proposition, therefore I reject any definition which would make *p* definitionally true " does not seem unreasonable. But it seems queer to say, " I grant that *p* is a priori, but I refuse to accept any definition which would make *p* analytic, since I hold that *p* is *synthetic* a priori "; for one thus seems to hold, on the one hand, that " *p* " is true by virtue of its meaning (" a priori "), and , on the other hand, to refuse to accept a demonstration of what one holds to be the case. Does not explication amount to making implicit meanings explicit, and thus to *proving* that a given sentence expresses a necessary (a priori) proposition? To take a simple illustration: suppose a philosopher maintained, following Poincaré, that the principle of mathematical induction is a synthetic a priori truth. Insofar as he maintains that it is an a priori truth, he holds it to be true by the very meanings of the terms " zero," " successor," and " finite cardinal " (presupposing, of course, the customary meanings of the logical terms involved) . But Russell defined finite cardinals as numbers satisfying the principle of mathematical induction, so that the latter is an obvious tautology on his definition. Would it not be a strange defense of Poincaré's position against the logicist thesis to say that the logicist definitions simply beg the question of analyticity? This would be just like defending the claim that " if $x = y$, then $y = x$ " is, while a priori, not deducible from logical truths, by rejecting Leibniz' definition of identity *just because* it enables a formal proof of this proposition.[11] Indeed, it would seem that *any* a priori truth could be defended as synthetic by this method of refusing to recognize the legitimacy of the only possible instrument of defeat (cf. above, Chap. 2, C). It might be replied that, nevertheless, if the question at issue is whether *p*, admitted by both parties to be a necessary proposition, is deducible from logical truths, a relevant definition ought to be defended as adequate without prejudging the issue. But the trouble is that *the* method of proving the adequacy of an explication is just to show that it satisfies presupposed criteria of adequacy, and this is to show that it enables a formal proof of sentences involving the term to be explicated which are intuitively recognized as expressing necessary truths.

D. Simple Predicates and the Synthetic A Priori

However, the argument from " begging the question of analyticity " with respect to necessary truths becomes more reasonable if it takes this form: it is pointless to declare *p*, containing *T*, as analytic by electing it as " criterion of adequacy," if there are good reasons for doubting that a definition of *T* satisfying the criterion could ever be constructed. Since we suppose the philosopher who puts forth this defense of the *synthetic* truth of *p* to agree that *p* is true by the very meaning of *T*, his reasons for doubting that the promised goods (proof of analyticity of *p*) can be delivered can be only that *T* is *unanalyzable*. It used to be emphasized, in the earlier days of logical empiricism, that the concept " undefinable," just like the related concept " unprovable," is relative to a deductive system, such that it is meaningless metaphysics to speak of " absolutely " unanalyzable or simple concepts. Accordingly a defense of synthetic necessary truth based on the notion of " absolutely unanalyzable predicates " would hardly have received a fair hearing in those days. But this very notion plays a fundamental role in Carnap's recent explication of the concept of *logical truth*

---

[11] If $x = y =_{df} (f)(fx \equiv fy)$, then " $x = y \supset y = x$" follows from "$(p \equiv q) \supset (q \equiv p)$," a tautology of the propositional calculus.

in terms of the concept of " state description " (cf. above, Chap. 6) . As will be seen presently, I am referring to the implications of the requirement of " logical independence " (cf. above, Chap. 1) .

Since a state description is intended as a description of a possible world, any two components of it must be mutually consistent. To say that " Pa " and " $-Qa$," e. g., are mutually consistent is to say that " Qa " is not deducible from " Pa ." But we can be sure of this *a priori* (i. e. without empirical investigation of the truth-values of the atomic statements) only if we can be sure that Q is not a defining element of P. Generally speaking, then, we can be sure that a given set of atomic statements satisfies the requirement of logical independence only if we can assume that the predicates chosen as primitive are simple or unanalyzable (as was explicitly noted by Carnap in " On the Application of Inductive Logic ") . As a matter of fact, it has been pointed out that if a relational predicate like " warmer " is logically complex in the sense that from " warmer (a, b) " other (nonequivalent, factual) statements are logically deducible [" not-warmer (b, a) "; " if warmer (b, c) , then warmer (a, c) "], then it cannot be used as a primitive predicate in state descriptions. In discussing possible ways of solving this difficulty created by " logically structured " relational predicates, Carnap suggested a form of language in which only *qualitative* primitive predicates occur and corresponding relational predicates are defined in terms of the qualitative predicates. " For example, let the following five predicates be taken as primitive: ' P_1 ' for ' cold,' ' P_2 ' for ' cool,'' ' P_3 ' for ' lukewarm,'' ' P_4 ' for ' warm,' ' P_5 ' for ' hot ' . . . . On this basis, the predicate ' W ' for ' warmer ' can now be introduced by the following definition: ' Wxy ' for ' $(P_5 x \cdot P_4 y) \vee (P_5 x \cdot P_3 y) \vee \cdots \vee (P_2 x \cdot P_1 y)$ ' (The definiens is a disjunction of ten components; each component contains two predicates, the first having a higher subscript than the second) ." [12] Since in such a language " warmer " is not a *primitive* predicate, there can be no state descriptions, in this language, containing the conjunctions " $Wa, b \cdot -Wb, a$ " and " $Wa, b \cdot Wb, c \cdot Wa, c$," which violate the requirement of logical independence.

But suppose this " solution " were countered with the objection that now " $P_1(a) \cdot -P_2(a)$ " becomes a subconjunction of possible

[12] " The Problem of Relations in Inductive Logic," *Philosophical Studies* (Oct. 1951) , pp. 77-8.

state descriptions which likewise violates the requirement of logical independence, since evidently "*a* is hot" entails, by its very meaning, "*a* is not warm,"[13] just as "*Wa, b*" was argued to entail by its very meaning "*—Wb, a*." Carnap is aware of this difficulty and tries to dispose of it by introducing the concept of a *family of related properties*: "Suppose that two or more properties are related to each other in the following way: every individual must necessarily have one and only one of these properties; and this is a matter of logical necessity. That is, it follows from the meanings alone; it is not merely a contingent law of nature for which the occurrence of counter-instances remains always possible. We speak in this case of a *family of related properties*" (*Logical Foundations of Probability*, p. 76). Predicates $P_1 \cdots P_5$, used to define "warmer," are an example of such a "family." Now, since Carnap evidently holds that "P_1x" is logically equivalent to "$-P_2x \cdot -P_3x \cdots -P_5x$," and similarly for any other member of the family, a conjunction like "$P_1x \cdot -P_2x$" would be illegitimate as part of a state description, since if P_2 is a primitive predicate, then P_1, being negatively definable in terms of P_2, is not, and conversely; generally speaking, for predicates belonging to the same family, if 'P_i' is primitive, then 'P_r' $(r \neq i)$ cannot be primitive. Carnap considers, indeed, the alternative of taking whole families as primitives and redefining a state description as a description of each individual in terms of exactly one member of each such family; but this alternative is not relevant to the present discussion.

It should strike the thoughtful reader that in the above quotation the sentence "S_1 and S_2 are incompatible by virtue of their meanings alone" seems to be used synonymously with the sentence "the incompatibility of S_1 and S_2 is a matter of logical necessity." Indeed, if Carnap is right in saying that "P_1x" could be *defined as synonymous with* "$-P_2x \cdots -P_5x$," then, of course, "P_1x" formally entails "$-P_2x$," or "$(x)(P_1x \supset -P_2x)$" is strictly analytic. However, nothing is easier to show than that the proposed definiens could not possibly be an *explicating synonym* for the definiendum. For one thing,

[13] Strictly speaking, where Carnap writes "P_1x" he ought to write "P_1x, t," since "x" is used as a thing-variable, and the statement that a thing has a given quality is incomplete without a specification of the time at which it has the quality. If, on the other hand, the individual variables range over space-time regions, no such completion is required.

it is conceivable both that a person understood the definiendum without understanding the definiens and that, conversely, he understood the definiens without understanding the definiendum. For example, it is conceivable that a man, living in a climate with extreme temperatures, might be acquainted with the qualities "hot" and "cold" but not with intermediate degrees of temperature, and in that case he would not understand the complex definiens for "P_1." If it be replied that for him "hot" would be synonymous with "not-cold," we ask in return what would happen to his analytic disjunction "either hot or cold" if he subsequently moved into a moderate climate and acquainted himself with the qualities "cool" and "warm"? Could it plausibly be maintained that the revised disjunction "either hot or warm or cool or cold" which he would now assert would not really contradict the first disjunction, because "hot" and "cold" would now mean different qualities for him? Not so, for this would be maintaining that if two people A and B are acquainted with n, respectively $n-1$, members of a family of related properties, then none of the corresponding primitive predicates would have the same meaning for them! But would anyone wish to maintain that when a child comes to learn, say, the meaning of "green" after having learned the meanings of, say, "blue" and "red," the latter predicates change their meanings for him?

And that a person, being acquainted with the $n-1$ qualities whose names are mentioned in the definiens but being unacquainted with the n'th quality, might understand the definiens without understanding the definiendum is too obvious to require argument. One might, indeed, object that understanding the meaning of an expression "P," and having the concept P, are entirely different things that have been confused in the foregoing discussion; that the question one ought to answer in order to determine whether the *proposition* expressed by "$(x)\ (P_1 x \supset -P_2 x)$" is analytic is not whether anyone who understands "P_1" would understand "$-P_2 \cdot -P_3 \cdots -P_n$" and conversely, but whether the *concept* expressed by the definiendum is identical with the concept expressed by the definiens. Indeed, this is the proper way of formulating the question, but it is evident that the answer to this question again is negative. For if the concepts were identical, then the proposition expressed by "$(x)\ (P_1 x \vee P_2 x \vee \cdots \vee P_n x)$" would be logically necessary; yet it is logically possible that there should exist colors of which we have no concepts, because we have never seen them (and therefore have not named them). I conclude that Carnap has made an indefensible assertion in saying that " (x) $(P_1x \supset -P_2x)$ " is *logically true*, though he is, of course, right in denying that this is merely a contingent proposition. For " true by virtue of meanings " is not equivalent to " true by virtue of explicating definitions." To say of a statement that it is analytic in the strict sense is to say that once it is expanded into primitive notation it is seen to have the form of a logical truth; this is the only intelligible meaning of the dictum that " analytic truth is truth by virtue of logical form." But since " P_1 " and " P_2 " *already belong to the primitive notation*, the above implication would itself have to be a substitution instance of a logical truth if it were analytic—which it is not.

In just the same sense in which the relational predicate " warmer " must be regarded as epistemologically primitive, i. e. as not admitting of explicative definition in terms of qualities (such as the definition suggested by Carnap), the relational predicate " earlier " (and its converse " later ") must be so regarded. Here Carnap's device of adopting only qualitative predicates as primitives is inapplicable anyway, since there are no temporal *qualities* which correspond to temporal relations the way there are thermal qualities corresponding to thermal relations. To suppose that temporal positions (coordinates) could serve the role of such qualities would be delusion, since in assigning such a position to an event one assigns to it a definite *distance* from some event arbitrarily chosen as zero point of the time scale. Moreover, coordinates cannot occur in a qualitative (nonmetrical) language. Therefore the kind of qualitative language which Carnap calls " thing language " (which term is no doubt intended in such a way that qualitative statements about *events* are likewise possible in such a language) is either so poor that *changes* cannot be described by means of its resources, or else it contains a primitive relational predicate " earlier." If the latter, the language will presumably contain axioms specifying the logical structure of this relation (asymmetry, transitivity),[14] but such axioms are necessary propositions which are not strictly analytic. Logical empiricists will be reluctant to call them " synthetic a priori " because of the metaphysical connotations of this term. But I do not see that insight

---

[14] There are some sketchy remarks on this problem in § 15 of Carnap's *Logical Foundations of Probability*.

into the logical structure of empirically given relations requires a metaphysical explanation any more than apprehension of formal entailments. The *epistemological* significance of the admission that we know many propositions that are "synthetic a priori" in the specified sense is, as far as I can see, nil.[15]

E. Can a Contingent Proposition Become Analytic?

I hope to have thrown into full sight the first horn of the dilemma I claimed any apostle of the disjunction "either analytic or contingent" to be caught in: if "analytic" is used in the strict sense, then the disjunction is not exhaustive, since we must allow for synthetic necessary truths. Let us, then, turn again to the wider and looser sense of "analytic," viz. "true by virtue of meanings" (which, as we saw in Chapter 5, is the only acceptable sense of "a priori"). I propose to exhibit the second horn of the dilemma, viz. non-exclusiveness of the disjunction, by arguing that there is no reason why analytic truths in this sense could not be produced by electing highly confirmed contingent propositions as "criteria of adequacy." To begin with, let us once more scrutinize the dictum that *S* expresses a broadly analytic truth if and only if anybody who honestly denied *S* (and who made no relevant deductive mistake) would interpret *S* to express a different proposition from the one normally expressed by it. Now, consider the statement "if anybody honestly denied *S* (and made no relevant deductive mistake), then he would not interpret *S* to mean *p*." Is this implication itself intended as factual or as logically necessary? On the first alternative, it would simply assert that *as a matter of fact p* is universally believed. As already pointed out, this could be the case if *p* were a highly confirmed contingent proposition; hence, if the implication were intended as factual, the second horn of the dilemma would already be established. Suppose, on the other hand, it were intended as logically necessary. This is to suppose that the statement "somebody honestly denies *S* (and makes no relevant deductive error) but nevertheless interprets *S* to mean *p*" is self-contradictory. And this in turn is equivalent to supposing that "somebody believes not-*p*" is self-contradictory. But as far as I can see, this supposition

[15] Cf. my note "Once More: Colors and the Synthetic A Priori," *Philosophical Review* (Jan. 1957).

is true if *and only if* not-*p* is itself explicitly self-contradictory, in other words, if *and only if* *p* is analytic*k*: " *X* believes that *p* and not-*p* " (not to be confused with " *X* believes (at one time) that *p* and believes (at another time) that not-*p* ") entails " *X* believes that not-*p* " which entails " *X* does not believe that *p* " (cf. Chap. 7) . With regard to a self-consistent proposition, however, it cannot be self-contradictory to suppose that somebody believes it, no matter how improbable such a supposition may be. We thus come to the following conclusion: if the mentioned criterion of broadly analytic truth is a logically necessary implication, then it is not a criterion of broadly analytic truth but only of trivially analytic truth.

But I do not wish to limit myself to demonstrating merely the *logical possibility* that contingent propositions might be made " true by implicit definition " by electing them as criteria of adequacy. I proceed to show that this is actually a common procedure in science, amounting to *concept formation on the basis of empirical generalization*. Consider a definition of " equilibrium," as predicated of rigid bodies, as meaning " that state of a rigid body in which the vector-sum of the forces and the algebraic sum of the torques acting on it is zero." It logically follows from this definition that a lever is in equilibrium if the ratio of the suspended weights is the inverse of the ratio of the corresponding lever arms. It would, of course, be unbelievably naive to suppose that this proposition was discovered deductively by exploring the consequences of a definition constructed out of the clear sky. What happened, in the actual development of physics, was rather that to begin with " equilibrium " was only ostensively defined, or verbally defined as the *qualitative* concept " state of rest," such that it was a question of fact what the quantitative conditions of " equilibrium " in this qualitative sense are. Then a quantitative definition of the same term was constructed so as to satisfy the mentioned generalization from experiment. A closely similar example of this kind of concept formation is the definition of " force " as meaning " mass × acceleration." In the statement of Aristotelian physics (recognized as false— not self-contradictory!—since Galileo) that a body cannot move unless an external force keeps it moving, the term " force " had a qualitative, ostensively defined meaning. Galileo discovered, by an ingenious combination of experiment and dialectic, that external forces cause bodies to acquire and lose speed, so that no external force is required to *maintain* a speed once acquired. This suggested to Newton a quantitative definition of "force" (for a body of constant mass, the resultant of the forces acting on the body is proportional in magnitude, and identical in direction, to the body's resultant acceleration) which would *satisfy* Galileo's law, known as the "law of inertia": if $F = k \cdot a$, it follows that if $a = 0$, then $F = 0$.

Now, the standard objection to the claim that thus contingent propositions of physics *become*, in the process of physical concept formation, analytic truths,[16] is that it involves a confusion of "sentence" and "proposition." If an identical sentence expresses at one time a synthetic proposition p_1 and at another time an analytic proposition p_2, then p_1 must be different from p_2—so the objector will say. There is much to be said in favor of this view, and it appears particularly plausible if it is illustrated in terms of the process of redefining names of natural kinds, which is so common in the natural sciences. For example, one first establishes by experiment that a solid element like silver or gold has such and such a density and such and such a melting point, and then adds these quantitative properties as defining properties to the qualitative properties originally connoted by the terms "silver" and "gold." Relative to the original qualitative definition, the sentence "silver has density d" meant "anything with qualitative properties $P_1 \cdots P_n$ has density d," and relative to the later definition the same sentence means "anything with $P_1 \cdots P_n$ *and density d* has density d": obviously the sentence now expresses a different proposition, since the subject "silver" now has a richer intension (though its extension must remain the same if the generalization which led to its redefinition is true). Perhaps this form of redefinition by increase of intension (connotation) is less common than redefinition by *exchange* of qualitative intension for quantitative intension. The latter would mean that "silver" is redefined to mean "element with density d, melting point m, atomic weight w, etc., such that the statement "silver has $P_1 \cdots P_n$," formerly analytic, becomes synthetic. Here again it is obvious that the same sentence expresses a new proposition, since the subject-term has completely changed its intension.

[16] Cf. the detailed discussion of such transformations in my *The A Priori in Physical Theory*, esp. Pt. I. chap. 3.

It seems, then, that even though definitions of empirical, descriptive concepts are guided by empirical generalizations in somewhat the same way as explications of concepts inviting philosophical analysis are guided by criteria of adequacy, the two procedures are significantly disanalogous: what is formally deducible from the definition of the empirical concept is not, it seems, the empirical generalization which led to the definition, whereas a criterion of adequacy, being a sentence expressing a *necessary* proposition, can without contradiction be said to be deducible from a definition.[17] Yet, the disanalogy seems more clear-cut than it really is. It ought to be noticed that when I gave illustrations apparently supporting the view that if one token of S expresses a synthetic proposition and another token of S an analytic proposition, then they express different propositions, I chose cases where the *explicit definition* of a constituent term of S was changed. But what if a term which so far has been used without explicit definition comes to be provided with an explicit definition for the first time? Is its meaning then being changed? This surely would be a paradoxical claim since explicit definitions of a term already in use frequently, though not always, claim to be formulations of what was implicitly meant by the term all along. Consider the following simple illustration. A man discovers that closed curves presenting the qualitative appearance of circularity and normally called "circle" have the property (P) that all the points they contain are equidistant from a given point. If he then asserts, on the basis of this discovery (a discovery it is, that a given visual appearance is connected with a given quantitative property), "all circles have property P," this sentence surely expresses for him a synthetic proposition.[18] It is asserted on the evidence "a has P, b has P · · · and n has P," where a, b · · · n are ostensive proper names of circles. Should he now announce the

---

[17] Pedants may object to the locution "deducing a sentence *from* a definition," on the ground that definitions do not occur as premises in the object language but are rules of substitution. However, here as elsewhere this expression is intended as shorthand for "deducing a sentence from a logical truth with the help of a definition." For example, with the help of the definition "bachelor = unmarried man," "all bachelors are unmarried" is deducible by substitution of descriptive constants from the logical truth "$(x)(f)(g)[fx \cdot gx \supset gx]$."

[18] It is not, however, a proposition about linguistic usage, since it would still be true that this kind of visual appearance is connected with P even if it had never been named.

explicit definition " circle $=_{df}$ closed curve with property P," the same sentence would, of course, henceforth express an analytic proposition as used by him. But how could one consistently maintain that " circle " as occurring in the sentence expressing an analytic proposition has a *different meaning* from " circle " as occurring in the sentence expressing a synthetic proposition, *and* that the constructed definition explicates the meaning the word has had all along?

The reply might be made that when the term was used pre-analytically, it connoted only a certain shape and no metrical property; that even though anything with such a shape objectively had the metrical property, the metrical property was not thought of when the word " circle " was applied to the shape. But if is is held on this ground that the definition, in transforming the originally synthetic sentence into an analytic one, must have *changed its meaning*, then precisely the same ought to be said with respect to philosophical explication and criteria of adequacy. Let S be a sentence containing a term T to be explicated, and p the proposition expressed by it when it was laid down as criterion of adequacy (i. e. before an explicatum for T was constructed). Let T' be the explicatum, S' the sentence resulting if the explicandum is replaced with the explicatum, and p' the proposition expressed by S'. If the meaning of T' is different from the meaning of T, then p' is different from p. But then we cannot infer from the fact that p' is analytic that p is analytic. But if to satisfy the criterion of adequacy S is to prove, on the basis of the explication of T, that p is analytic, it follows that the criterion of adequacy could not be satisfied at all.

I see no way of avoiding this uncomfortable conclusion except to abandon the premise that the explicandum is not *in the relevant sense* synonymous with the explicatum. By the relevant sense of " synonymous " I mean, of course, the sense in which the synonymy of T and T' is a necessary condition for the identity of p and p'. If a scientist says, for example, " e confirms h," he surely is not *thinking* of such a complicated concept as an inductive logician might provide as explicatum for the classificatory concept of confirmation (e. g. Hempel's explicatum, involving the notion of the " development " of an hypothesis with respect to individual constants),[19] and in this psychological sense explicandum and explicatum are, of course, not synonyms. But there must be a philosophically relevant sense of "synonymous" in which synonymy of T and T' is presupposed by the identity of p and p' and in which T and T' *could be* synonyms no matter how complicated T' may be. An attempt to clarify that sense of "synonymy" which is relevant to philosophical analysis will be made in Chapter 10, where it will be seen that the sharp notion of synonymy must be replaced by a notion of degree of synonymy if philosophical analysis is not to pursue a self-contradictory goal. What this brief excursion into the problem of the nature of explication was intended to establish is the following: If we apply the term "synthetic" to self-consistent propositions which are not logical truths, and we take explications to establish an *identity* of concepts, then we are forced into the contradictory conclusion that the same *proposition* (not *sentence*) could be both analytic and synthetic.[20] I hope to be able to show in later chapters how this unacceptable conclusion may be avoided by gradualizing both the notion of synonymy and the analytic-synthetic distinction.

"But," the reader may protest impatiently, "surely the sort of sentences elected by philosophers as criteria of adequacy, in the sense that a materially adequate definition must render them formally provable, never express *synthetic* propositions; in fact it would be self-contradictory to say that they did. What, then, is the analogy between philosophical explication and physical concept-formation guided by empirical generalizations, considering that the latter clearly are synthetic propositions? Surely, you cannot maintain that such statements as the one concerning the quantitative conditions of physical equilibrium ('equilibrium' ostensively defined), or as 'the amount of work ("work" ostensively defined) a body does against a resisting force is equal to the body's displacement multiplied by that component of the force which is equi-directional with the displacement' are *implicitly analytic*, i.e. translatable into logically true statements with the help of explicative definitions, the way criteria of adequacy such as you cited are implicitly analytic." A detailed answer to this objection must be postponed to Chapter 11. For the only way of satisfactorily

---

[19] Cf. C. G. Hempel, "Studies in the Logic of Confirmation," *Mind* (1945).
[20] This thesis will be further supported in Chap. 9.

answering it is to show that the analytic-synthetic distinction has no clear meaning as applied to propositions involving what will be called "open concepts"; and that physical constructs which are genetically based on qualitative, ostensive concepts, yet not explicitly definable in terms of the latter, are just such "open concepts." The whole problem is all one with the problem of reduction sentences, and will occupy us at length in Chapter 11.

The position arrived at may be strengthened by two additional considerations. (1) The only other interpretation of the dictum that the axioms of a deductive science, like Newtonian mechanics, "implicitly define" the terms referring to the subject matter of the science would be this trivial one: the axioms are pragmatically a priori in the sense that, being so highly confirmed and deductively supporting such a vast edifice, they would not be abandoned by the scientist except as a very last resort. (2) If the "empiricist" still wishes to maintain a strict dualism between "implicitly analytic" and "genuinely factual" statements, he will have to fall back on the very "psychologistic" criterion of necessary truth which he spurns: he will have to say that, after all, the falsehood of any generalization of physics is *conceivable*, but that an implicitly analytic statement is such that it cannot be conceived to be false.

The alternative is still open to him who holds the disjunction "either analytic or empirical" to be exclusive to say: "Well, if the physical concepts are defined in terms of sentences which originally expressed factual truths, then these sentences are simply emptied of factual content." He will then have to hold that when an empirical science becomes axiomatized, its axioms implicitly defining the primitive concepts of the science, then none of the *laws* which have been incorporated into the deductive system have factual content any longer; the factual content will be displaced to the applicative singular sentences, like "*this body* is now in equilibrium," or "this is a Newtonian particle" (the axioms and theorems of Newtonian mechanics being all true analytically). This interpretation is particularly difficult to maintain if the subject matter of the axiomatized science is microcosmic, such as atoms or electrons, since such postulated entities cannot be ostensively referred to. A more serious criticism, perhaps, is that it does not by any means seem self-contradictory to speak of theoretical or deductive explanation of "laws," where "laws" are universal propositions with factual content.

Be this as it may, further, and perhaps more compelling, reasons for questioning the exclusiveness of the disjunction " either analytic or empirical " will emerge before long (specifically in Chapter 11, where it will be shown that the concept of " reduction sentence " cuts across the allegedly sharp boundary between the analytic and the empirical).

A. Analytic-Synthetic, and the Question of Indefinables

RECENT skepticism with regard to the analytic-synthetic distinction—a distinction so vital for analytic philosophy that its collapse
would reduce much of the latter to nonsense—has been inspired
mainly by the lack of a clear criterion of *synonymy*. Since it is
difficult if not impossible to define a strict meaning of " analytic,"
as a more inclusive concept than " logically true," without using
" synonymy " in the definiens, analyticity will indeed be problematic to the extent that synonymy is. Thus Quine, presupposing
presumably that " logical truth " admits of unproblematic, precise
definition (a presupposition which was challenged above, Chap. 6),
defines an analytic statement as a statement that " can be turned
into a logical truth by putting synonyms for synonyms," [1] and then
laments the fact that nobody has yet stated a clear criterion for
determining whether two expressions of a natural language, both
in actual use (or at least composed of expressions in actual use)
and not deliberately constructed for purposes of abbreviation, are
synonymous.

However, the difficulty with the concept of analyticity to be discussed in this chapter is a different one; it is a difficulty which few
of those who use the analytic-synthetic distinction with great confidence seem to be aware of. Quine's definition of " analytic," cited
above, suggests that the sentences which, though they are not
logically true, are characterized as analytic contain *definable* descrip-

[1] " Two Dogmas of Empiricism," *Philosophical Review* (Jan. 1951), p. 23. There is
a curious inconsistency between Quine's acceptance of " logical truth " as a reasonably
clear concept and one of his criticisms, in the cited paper, of Carnap's explication of
" analytic in *L* " in terms of " semantic rules of *L*." For Quine complains that Carnap
only tells us *which* are the semantic rules of *L*, leaving us in the dark about the
meaning of " semantic rule "; yet Quine himself is perfectly satisfied with a definition
by enumeration of " logical constant," which likewise leaves us in the dark about the
meaning of the term.

tive terms. I am not referring to the circumstance that in speaking of "putting synonyms for synonyms" Quine seems to restrict application of the concept "analytic" to sentences whose descriptive terms admit of *explicit* definitions. One could easily accommodate definitions in use (contextual definitions) and stay within the spirit of this conception of analyticity by broadening the definition thus: S_1 is analytic if it is translatable into S_2, where S_2 is synonymous with S_1 and S_2 is a logical truth (then "if John is Peter's brother, then John and Peter have common parents" would be analytic even though "brother of" is not *explicitly* definable in terms of "male" and "parent"). What I am concerned to show in this chapter is that there is a class of sentences which make unsuspected trouble for the analytic-factual dualism, because they contain descriptive terms (predicates or names) which do not admit of verbal definition but only of so-called ostensive definition.

Consider a statement of phenomenological [2] acoustics like "within a given octave, D lies between C and E." Nobody who recognizes necessary truths at all will deny that this is a necessary truth, but if it is asserted that this statement is simply *true by definition*, the question is surely pertinent and pressing what could be meant here by "true by definition." The descriptive terms to which "by definition" would have to refer are: three one-place predicates designating the kind of properties of sound-events we call "pitches," and a three-termed relational predicate of the second level, designating a relation between pitches. Now, to say flatly that these predicates do not admit of verbal, but only of ostensive definition, would hardly be illuminating. We do not want to imitate the well-known pseudo-argument of Moore's *Principia Ethica*: this predicate cannot be defined *because* it stands for a simple, unanalyzable quality. For to the extent that the premise that Q is simple admits of justification it can hardly mean anything else than the conclusion to be proved, viz. that it is impossible to explain the meaning of "Q" by using other words designating familiar concepts. The concept of absolute unanalyzability has, perhaps justifiably, fallen into disrepute especially among analytic philosophers close to logic who take the relativity to deductive systems of the concepts

---

[2] By prefixing this adjective I mean to exclude references to the physical correlates of sounds (frequencies and amplitudes of air waves) as irrelevant to the questions of meaning analysis at issue.

" definable," " undefinable," seriously. The difficulty besetting the notion of unanalyzability [3] emerges forcefully if we employ the fog-splitting formal mode of speech and translate " Q (the quality) is unanalyzable " into " ' Q ' (the name of the quality) cannot be verbally defined." What precisely does such a statement claim? That it is impossible to produce a synonym, in the same language, for " Q "? But obviously the validity of a philosophically significant claim cannot depend upon the accidental circumstance whether the language contains, or does not contain, several synonyms designating the same quality. However, as suggested in Chapter 3, a definition of verbal indefinability which will make it significant and reasonable to predicate this semantic property of a descriptive term is the following: no description, used as a synonym for " Q ," could convey the meaning of " Q " to a person who was not already acquainted with instances of Q. Even this definition, however, calls for further refinement, since in one sense of " the meaning of ' Q ' " it is no doubt always possible to explain the meaning of " Q " to somebody unacquainted with the quality referred to: one can produce a description having the same *denotation* as the name of the quality and having a *sense* [4] grasped by the instructed person. Thus one might explain the meaning of the color term " orange " to a person who had never seen the color by using the description " the color resulting from a mixture of yellow and red, and which is inter-mediate between yellow and red." But the reply made by those who maintain that colors are logically unanalyzable (whatever their causal complexity may be) would be that the mentioned description had a different sense than the predicate " orange "; if it had not, the statement " orange results from a mixture of yellow and red and is intermediate between these colors " would be a bare tautology. At the risk of incurring the accusation that I am poisoning logical analysis with " psychologism," I suggest that by the *sense* of " orange " —which allegedly cannot be reproduced by some such description as given—can be meant only the word's disposition to produce a mental image of the quality. The assertion of indefinability (or better, unanalyzability, since there are no doubt conventional senses of

[3] Cf. above, Chap. 3, D.

[4] I am here using Frege's terminology, which expresses the distinction of meanings of " meaning " that is also expressed by the pairs " extension-intension " (Carnap) , " denotation-designation " (Morris) , " denotation-connotation " (Mill) .

"definable" in which terms designating allegedly unanalyzable qualities are clearly definable)[5] reduces, then, to the statement of a psychological law which is subject to empirical test: a description uttered in order to produce in the hearer a mental image (an "idea," in Hume's terminology) of the quality Q is unable to produce that effect unless the hearer has already perceived an instance of Q.[6]

Let us now return to the statement "D lies between C and E," which is equivalent to the conjunction "D is higher than C and E is higher than D." It would surely be contrary to the intentions of most philosophers who operate with the analytic-synthetic dichotomy if it turned out that it depends on psychological facts whether a statement is analytic. It was one of the often blemished defects of Kant's original definition of "analytic" ("the *thought* of the predicate is, though confusedly, contained in the *thought* of the subject") that the concept defined was psychological, not logical (cf. above, Chap. 2, B). But it now turns out that the modern semantic terminology—one speaks of semantic rules, rules governing applications of signs, not of "thoughts" associated with signs—does not succeed in emancipating logical analysis from psychology. We are told that if "D" or "C" is synonymous with a description such that substitution of this description turns "D is higher than C" into a logical truth (something like "a pitch which among other things is higher than C is higher than C"), then the statement is analytic. And we have seen that in the relevant sense of "synonymous" this condition of synonymy is satisfied if and only if a description denoting the same pitch as "C" (or "D") has the power to make a person imagine the pitch even if it has not been heard before by that person. The reference to prior acquaintance with the quality, it is important to note, cannot be avoided. If by saying that a given name is synonymous with a given description were meant simply that the description had the power to produce (i. e. usually did produce) an idea of the quality designated by the term, and this concept of synonymy (as a relation between designative expressions) were used to define analyticity, then even a statement like "orange is the color of the dress Mrs. X invariably

---

[5] See, on this point, R. Robinson, *Definition* (Oxford, 1950), chap. 3, § 3.

[6] For a discussion of difficulties surrounding the notion of *simple* (unanalyzable) descriptive concepts, see above, Chap. 3, D.

wears on Sundays in the summer time " could be argued to be analytic—for a person who had the relevant information or beliefs. In denying to this statement the status of an *analysis* we assert just that one who completely grasped the sense of the description which is the predicate of the statement nonetheless would not grasp the sense of " orange " with the help of this statement unless he were acquainted with what the description *denotes*. Suppose I wanted to define " anger " for somebody who had never felt that emotion before, and I did it by saying " anger is what you would feel if somebody called you ' lover of your sister.' " It will be agreed that this is only a directive to the person for finding out what " anger " means but not an analysis, since the statement by itself could not convey the sense of " anger " to somebody unacquainted with this emotion. In this respect the statement differs from a statement like " a father is a man who has children " which would be accepted as an analysis precisely because a person grasping the sense of the definiens would thereby come to know the sense of " father " whether or not he be acquainted with instances denoted by the term. These illustrations should make it clear why I take the assertion that there are no *explicating synonyms* for words like " blue," " hot," " tone of pitch *C*," to mean that only prior acquaintance with instances of the designated qualities could bestow on descriptions of these qualities the power to evoke mental images of the qualities.

The question, then, of whether " *D* is higher than *C* " is analytic reduces to the question of whether there is a description containing " higher than *C* " as a component whose sense is identical with the sense of the pitch-symbol " *D*," i. e. such that a person who grasped the sense of that description could *ipso facto* imagine (get an auditory image of) the pitch though he had never heard it before. " Pitch exactly one second higher than *C* " might be a candidate to this title, assuming that the person for whom " *D* " is defined that way grasps the senses of the constituent terms " second," " higher pitch," " *C* " by virtue of ostensive definitions. If the psychology of imagination provides experimental evidence against such possibilities of imagination, we shall have to say that the psychological evidence makes it improbable that the statement is analytic (although, *nota bene*, it is inconceivable that anybody could conceive what it would be like for the statement to be

false! The synthetic a priori again!)   Before exploring further
the implications of this unorthodox position, however, let us stop
and convince ourselves that there is really no alternative to this
" psychologistic " criterion of analyticity.

It will surely be admitted that the simple characterization of
analytic truth as truth by definition requires to be clarified by
specifying the relevant sense of the ambiguous word " definition."
If we apply the concept of analytic truth to sentences of a formalized
language containing definitions that can simply be looked up, then
the question whether a given sentence is analytic (in that language)
can be decided by formal procedures alone. But our problem here
is the application of the concept of analytic truth to natural languages; here the definitions we are in search of are not rules of
substitution explicitly written down but are in some sense implicit
in linguistic behavior. When we ask with respect to a natural
language " is S analytic? " we ask " could we, *preserving customary
meanings*, construct definitions of the descriptive terms of S which
would turn S into a logical truth? " [7]   In this enterprise formal logic
alone does not get us far; we are involved in explication of meanings,
the distinctively philosophical business as lately recognized by the
progressive philosophers. We countenance such questions as " does
the definition ' orange is the color resulting from the mixture of
red and yellow ' express the customary meaning of the color term
' orange ' ? " If the quoted definition were acceptable as an analysis,
then it would not express a factual truth; and since it is surely
a question of fact what color results from the mixture of two given
colors, such a definition would not refute the claim that orange,
and colors in general, are logically unanalyzable qualities. But
while *necessary* truth of the statement " ' A ' and ' B ' have identical
denotation " is no doubt a necessary condition for the synonymy
of ' A ' and ' B ' (whatever the correct analysis of " necessary truth "
may be), it is not a sufficient condition.[8] If ' A ' and ' B ' are
synonyms relative to a class of language-users L and a context of
usage U, then anybody who grasped the sense of ' B ' as used by

[7] In this entire discussion it is assumed for the sake of the argument that the concept
of logical truth is itself unproblematic. For a detailed challenge of this assumption,
see above, Chap. 6.

[8] It follows that the definition of " P and Q are identical properties " as meaning
" P and Q have *necessarily* the same extension " is inadequate.

members of L in U would *ipso facto* grasp the sense of 'A' as used by the same people in the same context. But consider the expressions " shade of blue exactly intermediate between shades b_1 and b_3 " and " b_2," intended as the name of the shade thus described. Whether Hume's famous surmise was right or wrong, it is at any rate conceivable that a person who grasped the sense of the description (which implies according to Hume's genetic psychology that he had actually seen instances of the shades b_1 and b_3) did not grasp the sense of the name " b_2," i. e. could not imagine that shade, nor identify it if presented with a set of shades containing it. Conversely, we may suppose a person capable of imagining the shade designated by " b_2 " because he had seen instances of it, but ignorant of the senses of " b_1 " and " b_3 " (though grasping the senses of descriptions denoting those same shades, like " shade of blue just noticeably darker than b_2 "). He would grasp the sense of " b_2 " but be unable to grasp the sense of the description " shade of blue intermediate between b_1 and b_3." It is then conceivable that these expressions, a description and a name denoting an identical quality, fail to be synonyms. Nevertheless the statement asserting that their denotations are identical is a necessary truth. The serial position of a given shade of a color (i. e. the fact that it is darker or lighter than such and such other shades of the same color) could hardly be conceived to be other than it is in " this actual universe." Therefore the necessity of the statement " the denotation of 'A' is identical with the denotation of 'B' "[9] is not a sufficient condition for the synonymy of " A " and " B."

There seems to be no escape from the conclusion that such necessary propositions about color shades and pitches are synthetic for some sign interpreters. A person may not be able to imagine pitches

[9] To prevent a serious misunderstanding, I should point out that the statement " the (present) denotation of 'A' is identical with the (present) denotation of 'B' " is here so meant as to entail no statements about the (contingent) usage of the expressions " A " and " B." I might, to take an analogy, express the proposition that $4 = 2 + 2$ metalinguistically as " the number denoted by '4' is identical with the number denoted by '$2 + 2$' "; but from the fact that a metalinguistic expression is *used* to *mention* the number it does not follow that the statement is a contingent statement about expressions. Thus the statement " the individual named 'a' has property B " is no more about 'a' than is the statement " a has property B." Notice that this view is incompatible with Russell's theory of descriptions. See my article " Synonymy, Identity of Concepts and the Paradox of Analysis," *Methodos*, 7 (1955), 25-6.

he has not heard; the only way to acquaint such a person with the senses of pitch names is, not the method of relational description, but the method of ostensive definition. But this is to say that for him there are no explicating synonyms of pitch names, that to him pitch names can be defined only ostensively. In other words, assuming that he understands the interval-designation "major third" by virtue of ostensive definition and understands the pitch name "*C*" likewise by virtue of ostensive definition, the verbal definition "*E* is the pitch a major third above *C*" would not enable him to anticipate that pitch, would not provide him with a "criterion in mind" (to borrow Lewis' term) for identifying a subsequently heard pitch as *E*. The following question must now be faced: if analyticity in the present sense is, as argued, a *pragmatically relative* concept (i. e. "*S* is analytic" is short for "*S* is analytic for sign interpreter *I*"), could it be that one and the same proposition (not sentence) is for different interpreters both analytic and synthetic? It is almost a truism of contemporary semantics that if one and the same sentence is in different contexts of usage both analytic and synthetic it is because it expresses different propositions in those different contexts, i. e. has different (referential, descriptive) meanings.[10] The assertion that one and the same *proposition* may, relative to different interpreters, be both synthetic and analytic will, therefore, sound wildly paradoxical. But it remains to be seen whether the notion of synonymy which was argued to be involved in the semantic notion of analyticity does not in fact lead to this unsuspected consequence.

Let us revert to Hume's famous missing shade of blue. Hume may well have been right (but whether or not he was right is irrelevant to the point to be made, since all that needs to be established is a possibility) in saying that the relational description "shade exactly intermediate between shades b_1 and b_3" is capable of evoking an *idea* of the denoted shade prior to sensory acquaintance with it. In the terminology used above this means that the description might, for a person with the relevant power of visual imagination, be an explicating synonym for the shade's name "b_2." It has often been said that simple qualities, like a color shade, do not admit of analysis, just because they are simple, and of course

[10] Cf. above, pp. 231 f.

the statement would not have been made unless it had been intended as more than a tautology. But how it could be interpreted as an informative statement is by no means clear. If the meaning of " simple quality " is explained denotatively, by producing examples, what should prevent me from including in the list along with colors and sounds, shapes, like circularity, squareness? What could be meant by characterizing the latter qualities as complex, and thus excluding them from the list, except that their names admit of explicating synonyms in the sense explained, viz. that descriptions are available which have the power to produce images of those qualities in the minds of persons who had never sensed them? [11] If so, the argument " there could be no explicating synonym for this name, because the name designates a simple quality " is, indeed, question-begging. Now, consider the sentence " b_2 lies halfway between b_1 and b_3 " as interpreted by I_1 who learnt the meaning of " b_2 " with the help of this very sentence, and the same sentence as interpreted by I_2 who lacks the kind of visual imagination which Hume credited all of us with and who consequently grasps the meaning of " b_2 " only by virtue of ostensive definition. It is evident that after the two interpreters learnt the meaning of the name, the one by verbal means the other by ostensive means, the name had the same meaning for them, viz. the disposition to evoke a mental image of the same shade of blue.[12] Hence the proposition expressed by the sentence for the two interpreters is one and the same. It can hardly be denied that sameness of meaning of a given linguistic

[11] Cf. above, p. 241.

[12] The analysis of "meaning" as a dispositional property of signs, which can be traced in rudimentary form in Berkeley and Hume, may be found in C. W. Morris, "Foundations of the Theory of Signs," in the *International Encyclopedia of Unified Science, 1*, No. 2, and worked out with far greater finesse in C. L. Stevenson's *Ethics and Language* (New Haven, 1944), chap. 3. Here as elsewhere the material mode of speech is dangerous: the statement that the meaning of a descriptive sign is its disposition to produce some ideational response (like a mental image) has provoked critics of the dispositional theory of meaning to object that, after all, the word " stone " means stones, or the property of being a stone, and not a psychological disposition. But whatever the shortcomings of the theory may be, it does not appear to have such absurd consequences as that all descriptive terms have psychological meanings if it is put formally, as a contextual definition of " meaning ": " blue " means, for interpreter I, the color blue $=_{df}$ perception of " blue " causes I to imagine blue objects. If the semantic statement that a term means such-and-such is a causal statement of psychology, it does not follow that *what* is meant by the term (the term's " referent ") is something psychological.

expression for different interpreters is compatible with differences in the methods by which that meaning has been learned. One person may learn the meaning of "square" ostensively. another person may learn it through the verbal definition "right-angled, four-sided, rectilinear and equilateral figure," provided he has previously been acquainted ostensively with the meanings of the defining terms. If their subsequent verbal behavior shows that they can correctly identify squares as figures called "squares," we have evidence that these different methods of learning have led them to associate an identical meaning with the word. It cannot be disputed, therefore, that our sample sentence "b_2 lies halfway between b_1 and b_3" expresses the same proposition for both I_1 and I_2. Yet the consequence is inevitable that for I_1 the proposition is analytic (for I_1 "the shade halfway between b_1 and b_3" is an explicating synonym for "b_2") and for I_2 the same proposition is synthetic (for I_2 "b_2" has no explicating synonym).[13] Thus the old criticism, going back to presemantic days, of the Kantian analytic-synthetic distinction (which, be it noted, was applied by Kant primarily to "judgments," not to sentences) as being relative to psychological conditions, cannot be simply exorcized as a symptom of "psychologism." The fashionable semantic formulation in terms of "synonymy" has turned out to be no less "psychologistic" than Kant's formulation in terms of "implicit thoughts." If we think of analyticity as an intrinsic property of propositions (along the line of thought developed above, pp. 186-8), the statement that one and the same proposition is both analytic and synthetic will strike us as nothing less than a contradiction. But the foregoing analysis just led to a concept of analyticity which is relative to powers of imagination, such that "p is analytic for I" is a statement of psychology, not of logic. If we want to operate with an objective concept of analyticity, we first have to provide a criterion of *identity of attributes* which would justify such assertions as that, regardless of associations of ideas with words, the attribute *square* is identical with the attribute

---

[13] There may be good reasons for holding that "analytic" and "synthetic" are not properly predicable of propositions, but only of statements, i. e. sentences *as meaning* definite propositions. One might agree so to use "statement" that the same (type) sentence would be different statements in different uses. In this terminology, the surprising conclusion above could be expressed by saying that the same *statement* (not just *sentence*) may, relative to interpreters with different learning backgrounds, be both analytic and synthetic.

equilateral rectangle, while the attribute *orange* is not identical with the attribute *intermediate between yellow and red*. But I hope to show in the next chapter that, in order to escape from the paradox of analysis, we must give up the notion of complete identity of analysandum and analysans entirely, in favor of a notion of degree of synonymy. Indeed, the difficulty just exhibited throws the problematic character of the notion of synonymy or identity of attributes into full light.

Lest it be thought that these difficulties could be avoided by offering a criterion of synonymy which is not formulated in psychological terms, it should be added that such nonpsychological criteria are illusory. The famous logical criterion of synonymy, which seems to hold out hope if superficially viewed, is the Leibnizian *salve veritate* test: " *A* " and " *B* " are synonyms if they can be substituted for each other in any sentence without changing the truth-value of the sentence. It is obvious that if the sentences upon which the test of substitutability is performed all belong to an *extensional* language, the test fails. If, for example, the equivalence " for every *x*, *x* has a heart if and only if *x* has a kidney " is *factually true*, then the predicates " has a heart " and " has a kidney " would be *salva veritate* interchangeable in all extensional sentences, i. e. sentences whose truth-value depends only on the extensions of the descriptive terms.[14] The proposed test is at all plausible, therefore, only if applied to a language containing modal terms, like " logically necessary." If in the modal sentence " it is logically necessary that for every *x*, if and only if *x* has a heart then *x* has a kidney " I substitute " has a heart " for " has a kidney," I obtain a true sentence and thus effect a change of truth-value, since the sentence upon which the substitution was performed is obviously false. The test, then, seems to work after all. Yet success is here bought at the price of circularity. We set out to test synonymy *in order* to test analyticity. But in order to carry out our test we have to know the truth-value of the modal sentence. And if " logically necessary " means " analytic," then to say that the modal sentence is true is to say that the sentence to which the modal operator applies is analytic. Thus we are back where we started.[15]

---

[14] The test is, of course, meant to apply only to sentences in which these predicates are *used*, not to metalinguistic sentences in which they are mentioned, like " he said ' this organism has a heart.' "

[15] Cf. Quine, in " Two Dogmas of Empiricism ": " So we must recognize that inter-

From what has been said so far it can easily be inferred that the following class of sentences containing simple predicates, which most philosophers would regard as expressing necessary propositions, cannot be strictly analytic.[16] It is the class of sentences resembling the famous one (discussed *ad nauseam* ever since the Vienna Circle launched the linguistic approach to the concept of logical necessity) "nothing is ever simultaneously red and blue all over." We have a predicate designating a determinable quality Q, like "colored," and predicates designating determinate forms of Q, Q_1, Q_2, $\cdots$, Q_n, like "blue," "red," etc., and we assert confidently a proposition of the form "no space-time region can be characterized by both Q_i and Q_r, where $i \neq r$." That no sound-event can be characterized by two distinct noncompound pitches is another member of the same class. There is a temptation to construe these propositions as strictly analytic through tacit conventions concerning the ranges of the variable in terms of which they are expressed. Thus we might state " $-(\exists x)$ (g-sharp $(x) \cdot$ b-flat (x)) " and explain that the values of x are tones. Being asked how one is to decide whether what one hears at a given moment is one tone or more than one tone, we would presumably reply that a sound event is to be called "one tone" if it is characterized by just one pitch. It is in order to circumvent such question-begging formulations of the propositions under analysis, that a variable ranging over bare space-time regions was used above (that is, extended events, not point-events which are logical fictions that should not be mentioned in a phenomenological language) instead of a variable ranging over events already qualitatively characterized. Now, according to the conception of analyticity here examined, we would have to find explicating synonyms for the predicates designating such deter-

changeability *salva veritate*, if construed in relation to an extensional language, is not a sufficient condition of cognitive synonymy in the sense needed for deriving analyticity . . . If a language contains an intensional adverb 'necessarily' in the sense lately noted, or other particles to the same effect, then interchangeability *salva veritate* in such a language does afford a sufficient condition of cognitive synonymy; but such a language is intelligible only if the notion of analyticity is already clearly understood in advance." For an excellent discussion of the *salva veritate* criterion, see also Benson Mates, "Synonymity" (in *Meaning and Interpretation*, Univ. of California Publications in Philosophy, 1950, reprinted in L. Linsky, ed., *Semantics and The Philosophy of Language*). The whole problem of synonymy is discussed in greater detail in the next chapter.

[16] Cf. above, pp. 224-8.

minate forms of determinables if we wish to prove that these propositions are analytic. But the only form of the required synonyms
which would insure the desired reduction to logical truth is that
of a conjunction of negative predicates: $Q_1 = -Q_2 \& -Q_3 \& \cdots -Q_n;$
$Q_2 = -Q_1 \& -Q_3 \cdots -Q_n$ etc. Arguments against such negative definitions (intended as analyses) were presented in the preceding chapter,
to which I would like to add one that seems especially conclusive:
if "$-Q_2 \cdot -Q_3 \cdots -Q_n$" is an explicating synonym for "Q_1," then,
with equally good reason, "$-Q_1 \cdot -Q_3 \cdots -Q_n$" must be held to
explicate the meaning of "Q_2." But if both are explicating synonyms, then neither is, since the conjunction of the two definitions
is a vicious circle. And if only one member of a family of codeterminate predicates is held to be thus explicable, then the paradoxical
conclusion follows that of two perfectly similar incompatibility-
statements, like " nothing can be both blue and red " and " nothing
can be both red and green," one may be analytic and the other not.[17]

B. Truth by Ostensive Definition

We turn now to a further difficulty besetting the doctrine of
orthodox logical empiricism—that the traditional hazy distinction
between a priori and empirical truth is clearly explicated in terms
of the analytic-synthetic distinction. Specifically, the difficulty lies
in the description of analytic statements as statements true by
virtue of what they mean and *therefore* factually empty. It arises
from a semantic notion which may be termed " truth by ostensive
definition." One might suppose that in the expression " ostensive
definition " the word " definition " clearly does not mean what it
means in the expression " verbal definition," since a gesture of
pointing is part and parcel of an ostensive definition. But actually
ostensive definitions of descriptive predicates can have the form " let
this word be used as a synonym for that complex expression," just
like verbal definitions. Just as I say " let ' bachelor ' be a synonym
for ' unmarried man ' " I might say " let ' blue ' be used as a synonym
for ' the color of this paint.' " It is presupposed, indeed, that our

---

[17] An attempt to prove that such statements of incompatibility are strictly analytic,
by Hilary Putnam (" Reds, Greens and Logical Analysis," *Philosophical Review*, April
1956) , was published after the above had been written. See also my reply " Once more:
Colors and the Synthetic A Priori," and Putnam's rejoinder " Reds and Greens Again:
a Reply to Arthur Pap," *ibid.*, Jan. 1957.

language already contains a word designating a determinable, like color, which enables a relatively unambiguous formulation of the intended meaning of " blue." Such words perform the function of identifying the quality which is being pointed out. And it might be objected that obviously nobody could understand the meaning of " color " *before* understanding the meanings of " blue," " red," " yellow," etc.; and that therefore the ostensive definition thus formalized is in a sense circular. But while it must be granted that the meaning of a determinable predicate would hardly be grasped by a person ignorant of the meanings of *any* determinate predicates falling under it, it does not follow that such understanding presupposes acquaintance with the meanings of *all* determinate predicates falling under it. Hence no given ostensive definition of the specified form *need* be circular. A more important peculiarity of formalized ostensive definitions is the occurrence of an indicator term (" this ") in the *definiens*. Indeed, this is the characteristic feature of ostensive definitions. Unlike verbal definitions, they serve their purpose only if they are uttered in a definite perceptual situation. But it would surely be unreasonable to withhold the title " definition " from these fundamental semantic rules on this ground. Thus Einstein defines simultaneity of spatially distant events in terms of contiguous simultaneity, and the meaning of " contiguous simultaneity " can be grasped only through experienced simultaneity of perceptions. If the definiens " the light rays propagated from the places of the physical events arrive simultaneously at the midpoint " were expanded into epistemologically primitive vocabulary, one would come upon an ostensive definition of " contiguous simultaneity ": " two events are contiguously simultaneous if they stand in the temporal relation illustrated by *these* events," where the meaning of " these events " would be demonstrated by some such experiment as sounding two distinguishable notes simultaneously. Thus the indispensable indicator terms would appear in the definientia of our verbal definitions anyway if we built the latter up directly in terms of the primitive vocabulary of the observation language instead of using, for purposes of economy, further abbreviations in the definientia. In other words, what Russell has called (*Human Knowledge*, Pt. IV, chap. 2) a " minimum vocabulary " for a descriptive language must include at least one indicator term. This holds regardless of whether the reduction basis for the language of science be phenomenalistic or physicalistic. For coordinate descriptions of the spatiotemporal locus of events presuppose an identification of the origin of the coordinate system employed, and therefore the origin of some coordinate system must be identified by means other than coordinate description.

Now, let " a " be a logically proper name of some such standard object as the rod by pointing at which we define " having a length of exactly one meter." Let " P_1 " be the predicate ostensively defined, and " P_2 " the determinable, second-level predicate (like " color," " temperature," " shape ") which exercises the selective function above explained. The atomic statement " a has the property P_1 " can now easily be shown to be translatable, with the help of the ostensive definition of " P_1 " in terms of " a ," into a logical truth. In the notation of symbolic logic the ostensive definition reads:

$$P_1(x) = (P) [P_2(P) \cdot P(a) \supset P(x)].$$

This definition gives rise to the logical equivalence:

$$P_1(a) \equiv (P) [P_2(P) \cdot P(a) \supset P(a)],$$

which makes it evident that the atomic sentence " $P_1(a)$ " is analytic. Since this atomic sentence entails the existential sentence " $(\exists x) P_1(x)$," and no analytic sentence can entail anything but further analytic sentences, existential sentences with an ostensively defined predicate, like our sample sentence " something is blue," [18] turn out to be analytic. The analyticity of this kind of sentence becomes evident also if, assuming a finite domain of individuals, we resolve the existential sentence into a truth-function with atomic sentences as disjunctive components: if at least one member of a disjunction is analytic, then the whole disjunction is analytic, but the disjunction " $P_1(a) \vee P_1(b) \cdots \vee P_1(n)$ " clearly satisfies this condition.

" Analytic atomic sentence " sounds, indeed, almost self-contradictory if one considers (a) that atomic sentences were intended by the logical atomists (Wittgenstein, Russell, and others) as sentences expressing the simplest kinds of *facts*, or making explicit the factual content of the logically complex sentences we find in

---

[18] The reader should bear in mind that " is " in the context of the logical constant " there is " is tenseless, does not refer to the *present* time. If the question, here involved, whether any existence assertions are analytically provable is raised, " existence " is understood to mean " existence at some time," not " existence now."

natural languages ("imperfect" languages to the extent that logical complexity is usually concealed by grammatical simplicity); (b) that it was intended to be the very nature of atomic sentences that the meanings of their constituents, viz. a logically proper name and a simple predicate, are unanalyzable. But if the predicates of atomic sentences are meaningful at all, they must be ostensively definable. Unfortunately no attention seems to have been paid by the logical atomists to the consequences of the formalization of these ostensive definitions. As we have seen, one of the consequences which reduces the concept of "atomic sentence" to a self-contra-diction is that atomic sentences, intended as the ultimate basis of descriptive language, are analyzable into general sentences of the higher functional calculus! Another consequence is that at least one nonequivalent atomic sentence is logically entailed by each atomic sentence, viz. the analytic atomic sentence referring to the ostensive standard; hence it cannot be maintained that all atomic sentences are logically independent of one another.[19]

The point is sufficiently important to deserve further elaboration. It is tempting to counter the foregoing demonstration of the analytic character of existential statements involving primitive descriptive predicates cynically: "You have managed a splendid reductio ad absurdum of your formalization of ostensive definitions. Ostensive definition is a learning process which should never have been called 'definition,' as your own confusion testifies; you have been snared by a word!" Indeed, there are serious objections against formalizing ostensive definition. It is difficult to see how, if "*a*" is a logically proper name and "*P*" any descriptive predicate, "*Pa*" could be an *L*-determinate, i. e. analytic or self-contradictory statement. If nothing is said about the "nature" of *a*, but *a* is identified only by its spatiotemporal locus, how could any observable property be either necessitated or excluded by the nature of *a*? It is tempting, therefore, to lay down, as an adequacy condition for definitions of

[19] Other difficulties connected with the requirement of logical independence for atomic sentences were discussed above, pp. 225-8. I might add here that the concep-tion of atomic sentences as devoid of logical relations to other atomic sentences just because of their logical atomicity seems to presuppose that *determinable* predicates, like "colored," are analyzable: for surely "*a* is red" entails "*a* is colored," hence it would have to be denied that the latter sentence is atomic. And we have already pointed out (p. 155) that it is at least as plausible to hold that "colored" is unanalyzable as that "red" is.

descriptive predicates "P," that they should be compatible with the synthetic character of all atomic statements containing "P." [20] Yet, if such an adequacy condition is imposed on the reconstruction of natural language, should it not be imposed on the reconstruction of scientific discourse likewise? But the so-called coordinative definitions for the quantitative concepts of physics give rise to perfectly analogous counterintuitive consequences. Is it not logically possible that the rod r, described by its spatial location, should not be rigid, i. e. keep its length constant in space and time? Is it not logically possible that the pendulum which has been selected as standard of time equality and which we may suppose to be described in terms of properties that are irrelevant to its function as measure of time, should not oscillate at a constant period? Thus ostensive definitions of simple qualitative concepts and coordinative definitions of the quantitative space and time concepts stand and fall together with respect to the logical state of affairs here spotlighted. What kind of definition does Reichenbach mean when he says that some rod (the standard measuring rod) must be *defined* as rigid if questions of the form " is x a rigid rod " are to admit of verifiable answers? Evidently he means the following sort of definition: x is rigid $=_{df}$ if x has length l, as measured by standard rod r, at any given time and place, then x has length l, as measured by r, at any other time and place. On the basis of this definition the statement "r is rigid" reduces to the tautology "r has, as measured by itself, the same length at all times and at all places." This is a tautology, since measurement of length (within a given reference-frame—relativity considerations are irrelevant to the present topic) consists in establishment of congruence and any rod is of course congruent with itself. But now we face the following difficulty: in terms of the intuitive meaning of " constant length," the statement that any given rod has a constant length, no matter whether it be r or some other rod, is contingent. But according to the coordinative definition, "r has a constant length " is not contingent. Must we not reject the definition, then, as failing to explicate the intuitive meaning of " constant length "? Reichenbach would presumably

---

[20] It should be kept in mind that sentences whose subjects are definite descriptions, or abbreviations of such, are not atomic in the sense in question. " The Queen of England is a woman " is surely analytic—whatever Russell may say—but it is not an atomic sentence, since the subject is not a logically proper name.

reply that no criterion of *intuitive* adequacy should be imposed on definitions of physical concepts. Once such a criterion is enthroned, one could also object to Einstein's definition of distant simultaneity, on the ground that it is intuitively a contingent proposition that the speed of light in the positive direction is the same as the speed of light in the negative direction, whereas it becomes analytic on that definition. Similar considerations apply to the definition of the "direction" of time in terms of entropy states: the later states of a closed system are the states of higher entropy. Here again, a sentence which erstwhile expressed a contingent law in terms of an intuitive concept of time-direction has become analytic.

It may be recalled in this connection that Russell once objected to a classical attempt to avoid the Newtonian concept of absolute motion by defining "uniform motion" as motion with constant velocity *relative to some selected body* (Neumann's "body alpha"; cf. *The Principles of Mathematics*, § 465), on the ground that such a definition would make the question whether that body itself moved uniformly meaningless. Notice that whether "*r* has constant length" is meaningless or analytic depends on whether it is postulated that congruence is a logically reflexive relation (i. e. such that statements of the form "*x* is congruent with *x*" are analytically true), or that meaningful statements result from the function "*x* is congruent with *y*" only if names of *different* rods are substituted for "*x*" and "*y*." Russell evidently made the latter sort of decision with respect to "uniform motion." Had he made the other decision, then he would have argued that in terms of the intuitive meaning of "uniform motion" any statement of the form "*x* is in uniform motion" (where *x* is a body) is contingent, not analytic. Perhaps it would be advisable to rule that if a predicate "*P*" is defined in terms of an individual constant "*a*," then *a* is not a value of "*x*" in "*Px*." But one who is convinced of the meaningfulness of "*Pa*" according to the intuitive meaning of "*P*" might then retort that *a* is in relevant respects so much like the admitted values of the variable (in the context of "*Px*"), that a definition from which it follows that "*P*" cannot have the same meaning in "*Pa*" as it has in "*Pb*" (assuming that *b* is one of the values) is inadequate.

But it is not my purpose to take sides in this controversy now. My purpose was merely to construct a *tu quoque* argument: the counterintuitive consequences of formalized ostensive definitions are exactly duplicated by the outlined counterintuitive consequences of coordinative definitions which according to some logical empiricists are indispensable for the logical reconstruction of physics. If we adopt the suggested ruling that if a predicate is defined with reference to a particular, then it is not in the defined sense applicable to that particular, we can indeed escape from the admission of analytic atomic statements. But is it not plausible to object to such a stipulation that the selection of a given particular as "standard" is partly guided just by the belief that it has the property to be defined?

In developing his philosophy of logical atomism, Russell emphasized that what he means by a "logically proper name," a name strictly devoid of connotation and denoting what is logically simple, is never a name of a physical object, like "this piece of white chalk," but a name of a private sense datum. Accordingly the kind of atomic sentence which he and the other logical atomists had in mind cannot be found in a physical language but only in a sense-data language.[21] There may be some who think that for this very reason the claim here made, that if we admit ostensive definitions using names of particulars, then there are analytic statements asserting existence, contrary to the principle of logical empiricism that "analytic statements say nothing about the world," is untenable. But it actually makes no difference if these "indubitable existential statements," as I have elsewhere called them,[22] are taken to assert the existence of a certain kind of sense data. For a philosopher who maintains that no conclusions about existence are deducible from logic alone obviously extends this claim to the existence of sense data as much as to the existence of physical objects.

The idea that ostensive definitions give rise to analytic truths has been challenged by Waismann, in the series of articles "Analytic-

[21] A sense-data language capable of accommodating atomic sentences, it should be noted, would be utopian also for the reason that its predicates would have to have absolutely determinate meanings. "Red," for example, designates not just one color but a class of colors of close resemblance (the various "kinds" of red, as we call them). In that case "this is red" would be analyzable into a complex general sentence containing a predicate-variable: $(\exists f)$ (shade of red $(f) \cdot f(a))$.

[22] "Indubitable Existential Statements," *Mind* (July 1946). My thesis was criticized by C. D. Rollins, in "Are There Indubitable Existential Statements?" *Mind* (Oct. 1949). I replied to his criticisms in "Ostensive Definition and Empirical Certainty," *Mind* (Oct. 1950).

synthetic," in *Analysis* (Dec. 1949, Dec. 1950, Jan. 1951, and later issues). Speaking of the arguments leading to the conclusions " some things are red," "some rod is exactly one meter long," which according to my account are based on the use of ostensive definitions as transformation rules in the same way in which verbal definitions are used as transformation rules in order to demonstrate the customary sort of analytic statements (the " all bachelors are unmarried " sort), Waismann says that " the logic of the argument can plainly be followed even by a blind man who is entirely unacquainted with the colour red and therefore in no position to grasp the content of any ostensive definition of this sort. That tends to show that the ostensive definition is quite irrelevant, that it does not really enter into the argument " (*Analysis*, Dec. 1950, p. 37). And a few lines below he writes:

> Indeed, what matters is, *not* the connection between the *word* " metre " and the *actual* standard in Paris (. . .), or between the *word* " red " and the actual *specimen* of the colour (. . .), but solely the *verbal description* of this connection. It is only the latter which is needed to transform any of these sentences into truisms. That is why a person who has never come across a metre or never seen the colour red can still argue that the standard metre has the length it has, or that the sample has the colour it has. So what is really needed in transforming any such sentence into a truism is no more than a *verbalization* of the actual process of the ostensive definition. This verbal description, however, *cannot take the place* of the definition itself, i. e., it cannot act *in lieu* of the definition. If that were so, it would be the easiest thing in the world to make a blind man understand what white is simply by telling him that it is the colour of snow; which is too good to be true.

I propose to show, now, that contrary to Waismann's claim, truth by ostensive definition *is* analogous to truth by verbal definition in the respects relevant to my argument. Waismann urges the distinction between the verbal description, capable of functioning as transformation rule in a formal proof, " white is the color of snow," and the ostensive definition, involving the act of looking at snow, which conveys the meaning of " white " to seeing, but never to blind, people. Even a blind person could " see " the necessary truth of the sentence " snow has the color which it has," which shows, says Waismann, that only the syntactic rule " ' white ' is substitutable for ' the color of snow,' and conversely," not the ostensive definition, is essential to the proof of analyticity. But the distinction between *syntactic* and *semantic* rules, which Waismann is calling attention to (without using these particular terms) , is equally applicable to the " bachelor = unmarried man " variety of definitions, and it could accordingly be said that semantic interpretation of the descriptive terms is unnecessary for the proof of analyticity of *any* analytic statement. Just as the blind man knows that necessarily snow has the color which it has—more accurately, that snow has the kind of property called by seeing people " color " which it has—so the man ignorant of the meaning of " bachelor " as well as of the meaning of " unmarried man " (let him be a foreigner familiar with the syntax of the English language but unable to interpret a part of the latter's descriptive vocabulary) knows that necessarily all bachelors are bachelors, or all unmarried men are unmarried men. So Waismann's assertion that " a person who has never seen the color red can still argue that the sample has the color it has " may be countered by the equally valid assertion that a person ignorant of the meaning of " unmarried man " can still argue that the man before him has whatever property—designated by the word " unmarried," which he does not understand—he has. The point may be clarified by distinguishing explicitly between " sentence " and " proposition." An ostensive definition of " red " in the sense of a semantic rule, a rule enabling people to grasp the meaning of " red," is indeed unnecessary for convincing people that the sentence " this specimen (the ostensive standard) is red " expresses some, whichever it may be, analytic proposition;[23] for this purpose the syntactic rule of substitution " red = the color of this specimen " (what Waismann called " the verbalization of the process of the ostensive definition ") suffices.[24] But for the knowl-

---

[23] According to Carnap's convention for the use of " proposition," there is only one analytic (*L*-true) proposition. But apart from Carnap's purposes of formal system-construction there is no good reason for accepting that convention. It is plausible to regard propositions differing in their constituent descriptive concepts as distinct even if they are both analytic, e. g., that all fathers are men, and that all horses are animals.

[24] Even this claim must be qualified to become tenable. We cannot say that any sentence which is translatable into the form " all *A* are *A* " is analytic unless we assume a rule of *univocal* substitution of descriptive terms for variables (two tokens of the same type must have the same meaning) , which is, after all, a *semantic* rule.

edge that *the* proposition actually expressed by the sentence is analytic, the *semantic* rule (involving perceptual confrontation with the color) is needed, simply because otherwise one would not know which proposition it is used to express. And *mutatis mutandis*, exactly the same holds for the sentence " all bachelors are unmarried." It is one thing to know that a sentence written out in primitive notation expresses an analytic proposition (given a univocal language, only syntactic rules are required for this knowledge), it is another thing to know that the proposition which the sentence expresses is analytic: the latter knowledge presupposes a grasp of the relevant proposition, hence complete interpretation of the sentence (unless the latter has some vacuous constituents), and hence acquaintance with the meanings of the descriptive terms.

There is a further relevant respect in which ostensive and verbal definitions are analogous, contrary to Waismann's claim of disanalogy. It must surely be admitted that it would be impossible to convey to a person who has never seen something white the meaning of " white " by telling him that whiteness is the color of snow. We must agree wtih Waismann that such a description is not an explanation of what " white " means but rather a " *precept* which instructs you what you are to do in order to gain such an experience " (*loc. cit.*, p. 37; see also p. 241 of this chapter). This impossibility, however, is empirical, not logical. That sense impressions of colors and other sense qualities are causally necessary conditions for corresponding " ideas " (memory images), a proposition of fundamental importance in the epistemologies of Locke and Hume, is a well confirmed empirical proposition but not a necessary proposition. The evidence indicates that blind people cannot imagine colors, but it is by no means inconceivable that they could. We have already belabored at length the point that it is entirely a question of psychology whether a given relational description has the power to produce a mental image of a quality not yet perceived. But consider, then, a verbal definition like " a cube is a regular solid bounded by six square faces." Is it an a priori certainty that a person familiar with the meanings of the constituent terms of the definiens but unacquainted with cubes would by hearing or reading this definition be empowered to imagine a cube or at least to identify a cube as such when first confronted with one? Surely, this is again a factual question of psychology. Suppose, now, that the definition failed to produce an image of a cube in a person who had never seen cubes, just as the description " the color of snow " fails to produce an idea of whiteness in a person who has never seen snow or any other white things. Why would not this be a sufficient reason for denying the analyticity of " all cubes have six faces " (relative to interpreters lacking the relevant power of imagination), if the fact that understanding the description " the color of this " does not guarantee understanding what " blue " means [25] is a sufficient ground for denying the analyticity of " this is blue "? It appears, therefore, that Waismann's objection to " analytic truth by ostensive definition " is based on a purely *syntactic* concept of analyticity; and since what is here at issue is a *semantic* concept, it is irrelevant.

C. Logical and Pragmatical Contradiction

Let us return to the analytic existential sentence " $(\exists x)$ blue (x) " (keeping in mind that in the context of the problem under discussion it is irrelevant whether this sentence be taken to assert the existence of a certain kind of sense data or of a certain kind of physical objects) and ponder the implications of the claim that it is both analytic and " about reality." It will at once be objected that if the sentence were analytic in the sense of Carnap's pure semantics (called there preferably " *L*-true "),[26] then it would have to be true in all possible worlds. But surely a world not containing the color blue is possible! Yet, the following clarification ought to mitigate the paradox. The assertion here made is not that a world in which there are (" there are " is intended as the tenseless logical constant!) no blue objects or sense data is logically impossible. What is claimed to be logically impossible is rather a world in which nothing is blue and in which one can meaningfully *talk about* blue objects though " blue " means what it means through ostensive definition only. It is easy to see that understanding the meaning of a sentence which contains the purely denotative word " this " necessarily involves confrontation with the extralinguistic object denoted by " this " (unless, of course, " this " refers in the context

[25] Just suppose that a person had acquired understanding of " color " by seeing all colors except blue, and shortly before identifying the referent of " this " by touch operations lost his vision.

[26] Cf. above, Chap. 6.

of the discourse to an object *described* in a previous sentence).[27] But then it ought not to surprise after all that a sentence which asserts the existence of a blue object and which means what it means to the speaker only by virtue of his confrontation with a blue object, could not conceivably be false unless it meant something else.[28] "But," it will be protested, "is it not undeniable that, given the conventional usage of ' blue,' ' nothing is blue ' is by no means self-contradictory, while, given the conventional usage of ' bachelor,' ' some bachelors are married ' *is* self-contradictory? How, then, can the contradictories of these statements be analytic in the same sense? " Yet, superficial appearances notwithstanding, the two sentences are in the same boat. "Nothing is blue " is self-contradictory in the sense that it is transformable into a self-contradictory sentence with the help of the ostensive definition " blue is the color of this," and " some bachelors are married " is self-contradictory in the sense that it is transformable into a self-contradictory sentence

---

[27] It may appear as though the sort of precise descriptive language which Carnap has called "coordinate language" would free language from this dependence on pragmatic context since unambiguous coordinate descriptions would take the place of " this": " this thing is blue " would give way to " position (x, y, z, t) is blue." But this is a deception since, on pain of infinite regress, one would have to use " this " anyway in order to identify the *origin* of the coordinate system relative to which the coordinate descriptions mean what they mean (cf. p. 251).

[28] In his essay " Ueber das Fundament der Erkenntnis," Schlick mitigated his radical dualism between analytic and factual statements (which latter he also called " synthetic," a question-begging terminology still perpetuated by Carnap and the other logical empiricists) by noting an important analogy between analytic statements and " Konstatierungen," i. e. basic sentences that are absolutely certain: in both cases, he held, *understanding* the sentence, in other words, grasping the proposition which the sentence is used to express, coincides with *verification*. This, according to Schlick, is due to the presence of indicator terms (" this," " here," " now ") in basic sentences, interpretation of which consists in confrontation of the " reality " which the sentence is about. Schlick's *apperçu*, however, was thrown out rather tersely without the sort of careful elaboration it requires (for a more careful statement of Schlick's thesis in recent years, see A. J. Ayer, " Basic Propositions," in *Philosophical Analysis*, ed. M. Black). To mention some of the difficulties: if what the basic sentence is about is a transient sense datum of observer *O*, and understanding it means to be " confronted " with its subject, how could anyone besides *O* understand it? But Schlick himself notes that " Konstatierungen " are not strictly speaking asserted at all, rather they are experiences which give rise to (corrigible) physical statements; in that case it is obscure what " understanding " could mean in this context. And when Schlick asserts that it is impossible to understand an analytic sentence without knowing that it is analytically true, he is either, again, using " understanding " obscurely, or else gives the word the sort of question-begging definition which was criticized above, p. 123 n.

with the help of the verbal definition " a bachelor is an unmarried man." True, a universe without blueness in it is logically possible; but such a universe could not contain an ostensive definition of " blue " giving to " blue " the meaning it now has. If the sentence " nothing is blue " were honestly asserted in such a universe, it could not, therefore, express the proposition it now expresses. Similarly, the sentence " some bachelors are married " could be true, but in a universe in which it were true either the word " bachelor " or the word " married " would not mean what it now means (given the same syntax of the English language as in this universe) , and the sentence accordingly would not express the proposition it now expresses. That the *proposition* expressed by " something is blue " is contingent while the proposition expressed by " all bachelors are unmarried " is necessary, is of course granted. But neither sentence can be denied without assigning to it a different meaning from its present meaning (which shows, incidentally, that, as argued in the preceding chapter, it does not follow from the fact that anybody who denied S would assign a meaning other than the usual meaning to S that S expresses a necessary proposition) .

After all these explanations, which were intended to remove the air of paradox from our thesis, we are still left with a curious puzzle. We must, it seems, countenance propositions which cannot be expressed in any language if they are true, and which necessarily become false the moment they are verbally expressed; for such is the proposition that nothing is blue, if " blue " admits only of ostensive definition. This state of affairs is puzzling, since it suggests something like a causal dependence of the truth-value of propositions upon the event of their verbal expression. It is noteworthy, however, that a puzzle of this kind already found implicit recognition in semantics when attention was called to so-called *pragmatic* contradictions. It will turn out that the latter, just like the proposition that nothing is blue, are propositions which might be true if they were not verbally expressed but are necessarily false if they are verbally expressed. Consider the sentence " I am not speaking now," spoken by somebody at some time. It has been said [29] that such a sentence is pragmatically, but not formally contradictory: we can infer from the fact that the sentence is uttered (a " prag-

[29] A series of short articles on pragmatic contradictions was started in *Mind* by D. J. O'Connor's note " Pragmatic Paradoxes " in 1948.

matic" situation, in the terminology of contemporary semiotics) that it is false, but we cannot infer this conclusion from its syntactic form. But in the first place, let us emphasize again that the logical concept of self-contradiction, in the sense in which a self-contradiction is a necessarily false statement, is a semantic, not a syntactic concept. For one thing, if a self-contradictory sentence contains defined terms, like "some bachelors are married," formalization (i. e. replacement of descriptive terms with variables) will not necessarily disclose its self-contradictoriness. And secondly, even if we confine ourselves to sentences written out in primitive vocabulary ("some men that are not married are married"), the form of the sentence shows it to be self-contradictory only if we make the semantic assumption that different tokens of the same type have the same meaning. The contrast between "formal" and "pragmatic" contradiction would, then, be more clearly defined thus: a proposition is formally contradictory if it can be shown to violate the law of contradiction by analyzing it, without reference to such pragmatic situations as are called "assertion of the proposition." A proposition is pragmatically contradictory if the event of asserting it necessarily falsifies it. Thus if the proposition that I am not speaking now is asserted by me, or the general proposition "nobody is speaking now" (where "now" names the moment of assertion) by anybody at all, it follows necessarily that it is false. In the same way, as we have shown, given the assumption that the concept "blue" is acquired only by ostentation, the proposition that nothing is blue would be necessarily falsified by the event of its assertion (notice that "asserting the proposition that nothing is blue" means, not "uttering the sentence 'nothing is blue,'" but "uttering the sentence 'nothing is blue,' or a synonymous sentence, with its present significance").

Two comments are in order before discussing the reason why such negative existential statements as "nothing is blue" (tenseless "is"!) are pragmatic contradictions, viz. the occurrence of indicator terms in the expansion into primitive vocabulary of the sentence expressing the proposition. It might be pointed out that pragmatic contradictions are reducible to formal contradictions, in the following way. To say that the event of my asserting "I am not speaking now" necessarily falsifies the proposition expressed by the sentence, is to say what would perhaps be more clearly expressed by saying " the propositions that I am not speaking now and that I am at the same time speaking the sentence ' I am not speaking now ' are mutually contradictory." Indeed, a proposition of the explicit form " p and not-p " is easily derivable from the conjunction of these propositions, since " I am now speaking the sentence ' I am not speaking now ' " entails " I am speaking now." There seems to be nothing wrong with this analysis of the concept " pragmatic contradiction " in terms of the concept " formal contradiction "; but it remains the case that propositions are, from the semiotic point of view, significantly divisible into two classes, those whose truth-value is independent of whether or not they are asserted (orally or graphically), and those that do not enjoy this independence. Further examples of *pragmatically reflexive* sentences [30] are (*a*) nothing that I assert is true, (*b*) no proposition is ever verbally expressed. (*a*) cannot be said to be simply self-contradictory, like " all propositions are false." For the latter proposition, intended as the kind of self-referential proposition forbidden by the theory of types, can be shown to imply its own contradictory (and thus to be self-contradictory) without any reference to the event of its assertion. But it would be logically possible for (*a*) to be true

[30] It should be noted that not all of the so-called " semantic " paradoxes are due to what is here called " pragmatic reflexiveness." The Grelling-Weyl paradox concerning the heterological-autological distinction, e. g., can be developed without assuming any empirical premise (unless the semantical rule that " heterological " uniquely designates the property *heterological* be construed as an empirical statement), and a fortiori without assuming an assertion-event. In this respect it is like the purely logical paradoxes (such as the Russell paradox) and unlike the liar paradox. That the liar paradox rests on such a premise becomes evident if we take as the paradox-generating sentence " the only sentence on this page is false " (written assertion) or " the only sentence uttered by me during time-interval t is false " (oral assertion) : in order to derive a contradiction, an empirical premise identifying the referent of the definite description is needed. This pragmatic factor in the liar paradox is concealed by the often used formulation " this sentence is false." But such a formulation is a poor one, since a paradox cannot be taken seriously unless it is based on an apparently meaningful statement, and " this sentence is false " would even pre-analytically be condemned as meaningless unless " this sentence " refers to a sentence other than the one in which it occurs. O'Connor, in discussing the difference between semantic and pragmatic paradoxes, overlooks this difference between the liar paradox and paradoxes of the type of the Grelling-Weyl paradox, for he classifies the liar paradox as a semantic paradox, and says of this type of paradox that they " can be made manifest by a formal proof that, where p is the proposition in question, p is equivalent to not-p " and that they arise from *semantic* relations exclusively (" Pragmatic Paradoxes and Fugitive Propositions," *Mind*, Oct. 1951).

provided it is not asserted by the person "*I*" refers to. On the other hand, the event of asserting (*a*) falsifies it inevitably, since if the assertion of (*a*) were true there would be at least one assertion made by myself which is true, which is to say that the proposition asserted is false; given, then, that (*a*) is asserted, (*a*) is false if true; hence, given that (*a*) is asserted, (*a*) is necessarily false.

The second comment is that pragmatic contradictions as here defined must not be confused with similarly peculiar propositions which are nonetheless of a different sort. In connection with (*a*), pragmatic contradictions have already been distinguished from self-referential propositions which give rise to contradiction independently of pragmatic premises. The distinction is easily grasped if we compare (*c*) no proposition is true, with (*d*) no proposition is known to be true. (*c*) is a self-referential proposition which implies its own falsehood by virtue of its content alone. But (*d*) is readily seen, if only attention is confined to what it *says*, to be logically possible, since it is logically possible that there should be no knowers, organisms capable of what Russell calls "propositional attitudes." Is (*d*), then, an example of a pragmatic contradiction? Not quite, for from the event of its being asserted alone it does not *logically follow* that it is believed. If the person who asserts (*d*) does not believe (*d*), then he does not know (*d*) to be true (since "*X* knows that *p*" entails "*X* believes that *p*"). Therefore (*d*) might still be true even though it is asserted. Therefore (*d*) illustrates another class of pragmatically reflexive propositions, similar to but different from the kind of propositions here labeled "pragmatic contradictions." A proposition may be such that the event of its assertion makes it highly probable that it is false. The proposition expressed by "it will rain tomorrow but I do not believe it" is of this kind: my saying "it will rain tomorrow" makes it highly probable that I believe the proposition asserted, and hence makes it highly probable that the second conjunct of the asserted conjunction is false—and hence that the conjunction itself is false. And the assertion of (*d*) would make it highly probable that (*d*) is believed, hence that at least one proposition is believed. And since "at least one proposition is believed" would be compatible with "no proposition is known to be true" only if it were logically possible that no proposition is true—which is not logically possible—

the assertion of (d) would make it highly probable that (d) is false.[31]

Let us return to " I am not speaking now." It can be urged, as will be shown presently, that its contradictory " I am speaking now " is *analytic* in just the sense in which " something is blue " was argued to be analytic, despite the embarrassing undeniable fact that nothing is more easily conceived than that the proposition expressed by it should be false, viz. that the person denoted by " I " should not be speaking at the time denoted by " now." We saw that " a is blue " (where " a " is the logically proper name of some fictitious standard patch) is transformable into a logically true sentence by substituting for " blue " the description " the color of a." But similarly, substitution of the description " the speaker of this sentence token " for " I " turns " I am speaking now " into the logically true sentence " the speaker of this sentence token (= the sentence token spoken here-now) is speaking now." If it should be considered desirable to eliminate vague indicator terms as far as possible, we may substitute for " here " and " now " coordinate descriptions, so as to obtain a logically true sentence of the form " the speaker of the sentence-token spoken at place P and time t speaks at time t." One might object that this sentence implies the uniqueness of the sentence token described, which is a contingent fact (if P is a spatial region it is conceivable that two sentences are uttered in region P at time t) and therefore cannot be logically true. But this objection confuses the condition of appropriate usage of a sentence with the truth-condition of the sentence. If more than one, or no, sentence were spoken at the specified time at the specified place, the sentence referring to the spoken sentence would not be false but inappropriate; it could not be said to be false any more properly than, say, an interrogative sentence could be called false. Russell's theory of descriptions takes, indeed, uniqueness and exis- tence of the denotatum of a given description as truth-conditions of elementary sentences containing the description as grammatical subject. But this is just a shortcoming of Russell's theory of descrip- tions. According to that theory, no substitution instance of the law of identity " $(x)(x = x)$ " can be logically true if the expression sub- stituted for " x " is a definite description. Thus " the king of

---

[31] This argument is based on the weak definition of " p is known " as " p is believed, and is true."

England is the king of England " could no more count as a logical truth than " the speaker of the sentence spoken at *P* at *t* speaks at *t*," if the objection based on Russell's theory of descriptions were sound: it implies that there is a king of England, which is a factual proposition.[32]

The problem of deciding whether a statement containing indicator terms is analytic or not is tricky, because the question whether a given indicator term or proper name is *synonymous* with a given description is even less well defined than the corresponding question for two predicates. If an indicator term merely denotes and has no sense (intension), how could it significantly be said to be synonymous with another expression in any other sense than that of identical denotation? But identity of denotation cannot be a source of analytic truth. Consider again " *a* is blue," where *a* is the (fictitious) ostensive standard with reference to which " blue " is ostensively defined as " the color of *a*." One could plausibly argue that the description " the color of *a* " could not be synonymous with " blue," since a person might be unacquainted with the particular *a* (in fact this particular might not exist), in which case he would not understand the description (" *a* " is supposed to be a *logically* proper name!), and still might understand the meaning of " blue." On this ground one might reject our claim that " *a* is blue " is analytic. But we have already countered this objection by emphasizing that " analytic," defined in terms of synonymy relations that are not arbitrarily stipulated, is an elliptical term of pragmatics, short for " analytic for interpreter *I*." All that has been asserted, accordingly, is that " *a* is blue " is analytic for an interpreter who was taught the meaning of " blue " by the ostensive definition referring to *a*. It is readily shown that similar conclusions apply to " I am speaking now." One might argue that " *I*," even as used in the sentence token " I am speaking now," cannot be synonymous

[32] Notice that Russell's theory of descriptions leads to the consequence that the law of identity is a logical truth only if the following rule of substitution of individual constants is adopted as a partial definition of " logical consequence ": " $f(a, b \cdot \cdot \cdot n)$ " is a logical consequence of " $(x_1)(x_2) \cdot \cdot \cdot (x_n)f(x_1, x_2 \cdot \cdot \cdot x_n)$ " provided " $a, b \cdot \cdot \cdot n$ " are logically proper names—not if they are descriptions; which is tantamount to saying that logically true substitution instances of the law of identity " everything is identical with itself " cannot be expressed in a natural language! Detailed discussion of this problem is omitted here since it is discussed elsewhere, in my article " Logic, Existence, and the Theory of Descriptions," *Analysis* (April 1953).

with the description "the speaker of this sentence token" since this sentence token might not have been spoken, in which case the description would fail to denote, and still "*I*" would denote the same person. But it surely cannot be denied that "*I*" as used in the context "I am speaking now" has the disposition to call the interpreter's attention to the present speaker, and may in this causal sense be said to function, relative to the relevant interpreter, as a synonym for "the speaker of this sentence." In the same way "this," as used in a sentence of the form "this *S* is *P*," may be said to be synonymous for the interpreter with "the object here-now pointed at," and therefore "this object is here-now pointed at" is analytic for the interpreter. It is, indeed, conceivable that the object which was in fact pointed to should not have been pointed to at that time, but in such a "possible universe" the relevant token of the expression "this object" could not have the same meaning it has in the actual universe. What characterizes the pragmatically necessary propositions here called attention to is just that they might be false, but could be false only in a universe which did not contain the pragmatic situation involved in their verbal expression.

D. Conclusion

It is hoped that in the course of this discussion the initial air of paradox surrounding the claim that there are propositions whose truth-value depends on whether or not they are verbally expressed has been dispelled, and that it has become clear why the conventional doctrine of analytic truth, conceived as a property of statements, not of extralinguistic propositions, has the troublesome implications that have been revealed: the concept of analytic truth has actually been constructed with regard to one type of statement to the neglect of other types of statements,[33] and nonetheless it was assumed that the range of significant application of the concept coincided with the totality of statements. The puzzle that "something is blue" seems, on the one hand, to be analytic, and on the other hand to be factual in that it asserts what conceivably might not be the case, is perhaps comparable to the puzzle of whether a given fraction is odd or even: "odd" and "even" are defined as contradictory

[33] For example, all the statements in terms of which Kant discussed the analytic-synthetic distinction were universal and devoid of singular terms (except perhaps "space is three-dimensional"—if "space" is a singular term!).

predicates of integers and hence are not predicable in the same sense of fractions. The idea of analytic truth is the idea of truth provable by logic alone on the basis of *interpretation* of a given sentence. This interpretation is conceived as a mental event which does not presuppose " looking at the world "—except of course that part of the world which is the very sentence to be interpreted. Hence the view that knowledge of analytic truth is not knowledge about the world. It has, of course, been recognized that some facts must be observed if one is to arrive at an interpretation of a given sentence which justifies its classification as analytic: the linguistic facts consisting in such-and-such verbal usages. Accordingly it has been recognized that statements of the form " *S* expresses an analytic proposition " are, indeed, factual, since they are derived from factual premises describing linguistic behavior. It would be conceded as a rather trivial point that an analytic sentence (indeed, any sentence of a natural language) would not mean what it means if it were not for contingent facts of linguistic usage. Yet, it could not be allowed consistently with the doctrine that analytic truth is factually empty truth, that there are sentences which would not mean what they mean if it were not for certain *extra-linguistic* facts, such as the existence of blue objects, or the occurrence of pains. To put it in the form of a terse summary: according to the conventional empiricist doctrine " sentence *S* means proposition *p* " is, indeed, a factual statement, call it " *M* "; but, the conventional doctrine holds, *if S asserts a fact, then the truth of S is not deducible from the truth of M alone; such a deduction is possible only if S is analytic, and if S is analytic it asserts no fact.* What I have endeavored to show is that, if only we accept, as surely we must, the semantic principle that the formation of empirical concepts (or the genesis of descriptive language) involves ostensive definitions at some point, there are sentences which clearly refute the above generalization of semantics.

CHAPTER 10. *Analysis and Synonymy*

A. *The Classical Notion of " Real Definition "*

A RECURRENT theme of the preceding discussions has been the inadequacy of the neat division of true propositions into strictly analytic and empirical, maintained by the very philosophers who by inaugurating the analytic method in philosophy forged the semantic tools which help us nowadays to see flaws in their own doctrines. A new, especially formidable, difficulty with this " empiricist " doctrine emerges as we ask what kind of propositions analyses themselves are. If they are empirical generalizations about linguistic usage, then analytic philosophy is an empirical science, indeed a branch of sociology (the pity being, then, that analytic philosophers excogitate in the armchair what they ought to establish by experimental methods). But the alternative of construing them as strictly analytic propositions is likewise unsatisfactory since, as argued already (above, p. 105), it leads to the paradox of analysis, a paradox to which I want to give in this chapter the serious attention it deserves: the only way in which " $A = B$," where " A " represents the analysandum and " B " the analysans, could be shown to be strictly analytic would be by substitution of " A " for " B " (or " B " for " A ") into an instance of the law of the self-identity of concepts or attributes. Such a substitution, however, could be justified only by the claim that " A " and " B " are synonymous, in which case " $A = B$ " would be synonymous with the trivial identity " $A = A$." Schlick tried to escape between the horns of this dilemma by denying that philosophical analysis is an activity aiming at grounded assertion of propositions: there is no special kind of propositions, besides empirical and analytic ones, which it is the business of philosophers to establish; philosophical analysis is an activity of *clarifying*, not of *validating*, propositions. But while we can understand, in a vague way, what Schlick had in mind, we can hardly rest satisfied with his solution of the difficulty. The fact is that the vast majority of analytic philosophers, before as well as after Schlick, did and do make claims, *qua* philosophers, to the effect that such-and-such propositions are true. Schlick himself asserted such "philosophical" propositions as "a causal statement means the same as a statement of regular sequence," "a cognitively meaningful statement is the same as a statement which is in principle verifiable," "an a priori truth is the same as a tautology." Indeed, since it never occurred to him to interpret these statements as empirical generalizations that might be refuted at any time by contrary instances, he was committed by his own principle to classification of such statements as strictly analytic; yet, as we have already noted in Chapter 5, any proof of their strict analyticity would be question-begging. Some philosophers, particularly advocates of a linguistic theory of necessary truth (cf. above, Chap. 7), try to avoid this paradoxical consequence by refusing application of the term "proposition" to such statements and construing them instead as linguistic recommendations.[1] In the following discussion, however, I shall asume that to assert the correctness of an analysis is different from making a linguistic recommendation (e. g. "please, don't apply the expression ' a priori truth ' to anything except tautologies "), and examine afresh the problem which I think was dodged rather than solved by Schlick.

The question whether, and if so in what sense, an analysis can be said to be correct or incorrect, is the form which the old problem of *real definition* has taken in contemporary analytic philosophy. The linguistic-recommendation-theory of philosophical analysis (maintained mainly by disciples of Wittgenstein) is affiliated with the view that all definitions are nominal in the sense that they express decisions as to the usage of a word and thus cannot significantly be said to be true or false; while the view of G. E. Moore that analysis is of *concepts* and *propositions* (not words and sentences) and terminates, if it is correct, in assertion of a necessary proposition [2] is in some striking respects (to be spotlighted presently)

---

[1] See, e. g., Alice Ambrose, "Linguistic Approaches to Philosophical Problems," *Journal of Philosophy* (April 24, 1952).

[2] While Moore himself has confessed, with the disarming frankness so typical of him, to be anything but clear about the nature of analysis as he himself practiced it, the view here attributed to Moore is surely implicit in the one essay in which he writes, in part, *about* analysis: "Russell's Theory of Descriptions," in *The Philosophy of Bertrand Russell* (Library of Living Philosophers, ed. P. A. Schilpp). Russell's theory of descriptions is there evaluated as the claim to be a correct analysis of descriptive

reminiscent of the Platonic-Aristotelian view of real definition as formulation of the *essence* of a concept.

Particularly clear examples of what Plato and Aristotle regarded as real definitions are analytic definitions of visualizable geometrical figures: " to be a circle is to be the locus of all points equidistant from a given point," " to be an ellipse is to be the locus of all points P such that the sum of the distances of P from two given points (called the "foci") is constant." If anybody maintains (and there are many who do maintain it) that anybody but a philosopher corrupted by the ancient myth of real definition means by the word "definition" either a rule as to how a given word is to be (or will be) used (stipulative definition) or a generalization about the actual, antecedent usage of a word (dictionary definition), he must be blind to the truth of one or the other of the following propositions:

(a) The above sentences about geometrical figures are properly called definitions (they are so called by geometricians who have never heard of the "myth" of real definition) .

(b) These sentences are not about the *words* "circle" and "ellipse." If they were, then a correct translation of them into another language would have to reproduce the quoted English words "circle" and "ellipse." Since, on the contrary, a correct translation into, say, German of the definition of the circle would begin "ein Kreis zu sein . . ." it is evident that the sentence cannot be interpreted as a report of the usage of the English word "circle." This obvious argument is usually countered by admitting that what is defined is not just the English word "circle" but the entire class of words synonymous with "circle." One difficulty with this theory is that it presupposes that we know what the intended sense of "synonymous" is (does the class, e. g., include the definiens of the English definition of "circle"?) , whereas the clarification of the concept of synonymy has turned out, in recent analytic philosophy, to be as difficult a matter as the clarification of the concept

phrases, and the question whether the analysis is correct is formulated by Moore as the question whether propositions of the same form as the following are correct: " the proposition that Scott is the author of Waverley *entails and is entailed by* the proposition that one and only one man wrote Waverley, and that man was Scott." To assert that p is logically equivalent to q is to assert precisely that the proposition that (if and only if p, then q) is necessary. And modal propositions, as was argued above, pp. 119 f., are themselves necessary if true.

of correct analysis itself. But a more tangible defect, as it were, of the theory is that it tries to remedy the unplausibility of the view that in analyzing our intuitive concept of a circle or of an ellipse we generalize about *one* language, by having us believe that we generalize about *all* languages. If, to be sure, the statement " any definiendum, in any language whatever, which is a synonym for ' circle ' is used in that language as a synonym for whatever definiens in that language is a correct translation of the English definiens " is meant to be *analytic*, in the sense that the foreign terms D_1 and D_2 are acceptable as correct translations of the English definiendum and definiens only if D_1 and D_2 are themselves synonymous, then nothing has been added to the more restricted generalization about English usage, and we are back where we started. We must admit, then, that the expression " to be a circle " functions, analogously to the propositional expression " that x is a circle," as name of an *intension* or *attribute*.[3]

(c) These sentences are used to assert *necessary connections* of attributes, not empirical generalizations about particulars characterized by the attributes. We may, indeed, be wrong in thinking that as assertions of this kind they are true. It may turn out, for example, that if two attributes can be distinguished at all, one qualitative and the other quantitative, then the only warranted assertion is that of an *empirical* connection of a given kind of shape with a given quantitative property, and that if not, then we have only two *expressions* standing for an identical attribute; in the latter case the statement of necessary connection dissolves into a contingent metalinguistic statement to the effect that two expressions are used synonymously. But as long as the sentences are uttered with the described intentions, we must recognize that there is an identifiable sense of the word " definition " corresponding to the—to be sure, confused—classical notion of real definition, which calls for analysis. In other words, whatever the correct analysis of the analysandum " real definition " may turn out to be, we must at least recognize the existence of the analysandum.

(d) To say that two expressions " A " and " B " are used synonymously is different from saying that the concept intended by " A "

---

[3] As a matter of fact, the same arguments which were brought, in Chap. 7, against the dictum that a proposition is a class of sentences, are applicable, *mutatis mutandis*, to the kindred dictum that a concept is a class of synonymous terms.

is identical with the concept intended by " *B*." The latter proposition is not about the expressions " *A* " and " *B* " at all, though the concepts which it is about are described, semantically, as the meanings of " *A* " and " *B*." The difference is like the difference between " Mr. X has a wife who has just borne a child " and " the wife of Mr. X has just borne a child." The speaker's belief that the woman who is the subject of his assertion is married to Mr. X leads him to describe her in that particular way, but if this belief turned out to be false, the proposition he intended to assert might still be true: it will be true provided the woman mistakenly described as the wife of Mr. X did give birth. Similarly, facts of usage lead one to formulate an analysis in the particular way one formulates it, but it does not follow that the analysis is an assertion about usage.[4] " To be a father is to be a male parent "—to use a highly uninteresting example of analysis lest the interestingness of the example detract attention from the semantical point to be driven home—is not correctly interpreted by the earthy statement of descriptive semantics " ' father ' is used synonymously, by English-speaking people, with ' male parent.' " To be sure, anybody who understands the meaning of " father," as well as the meanings of " male " and " parent," will be observed to be willing to apply the latter two predicates to any object to which he is willing to apply the first predicate, and conversely. But this very proposition is necessary, not contingent: for if a person were found saying " X is male and is a parent, but is not a father " or " X is a father but not a parent " or " X is a father but not male," one would unhesitatingly conclude that he does not attach the conventional (biological) meanings to these words.

A type of question characteristic of analytic philosophy is the following: which of a specified set of terms are *definable* in terms of which? Or, which is the smallest subset of a given set of terms that is sufficient to define all the other terms in the set? Or, is " *A*," within a specified logical system, definable in terms of " *B*," or " *B* " in terms of " *A*," or perhaps both? These questions presuppose, to be sure, that the relevant terms have fairly fixed meanings in their everyday or scientific usage. But given these empirical presuppositions, the questions of definability are to be

---

[4] Cf. A. Pap, " Synonymy, Identity of Concepts, and the Paradox of Analysis," *Methodos*, 7 (1955) , 25-6.

answered *a priori*, not by any sort of interviewing of people with representative speech habits. The proposition, e. g., that all concepts of kinship relations that happen to be the meanings of predicates of the English language are definable in terms of just the concepts *male*, *female*, and *parent* is knowable *a priori*, by reflecting on concepts. So is the proposition that the primitive concepts of arithmetic are definable in terms of logical constants alone; so is the proposition that whereas " parent " is definable in terms of " ancestor " within the lower functional calculus, the definition of " ancestor " in terms of " parent " requires, as first discovered by Frege, the resources of the higher functional calculus (i. e. quantification over a predicate or class variable). Any definition, then, which is a correct answer to such a question of definability is far more like a necessary proposition than like a stipulation or an empirical proposition about synonymous usage.

Now, the central difficulty with the concept of real definition is how we can maintain *both* that the definition expresses a *necessary* proposition and that definiendum and definiens stand for *distinct* attributes. In a necessary proposition of the type " if x is red, then x is colored " we have distinct attributes indeed (and, as was pointed out earlier, there is not even an obvious sense in which the attribute " colored " is a *component* of the attribute " red "), but there is only a one-way entailment, whereas a real definition purports to express a mutual entailment, a logical equivalence. Propositions of the type of " whatever has size, has shape, and conversely " assert mutual entailments and involve distinct attributes, yet those attributes are unanalyzable, whereas a real definition is supposed to be an analysis of an attribute. Finally, propositions of the type " if and only if x is an equilateral triangle, then x is an equiangular triangle " assert a mutual entailment and involve distinct and analyzable attributes; yet the entailment in this case is a *systemic* one, i. e. one attribute can be deduced from the other only with the help of extralogical postulates in the system in which " triangle " is defined. One cannot discover that an equilateral triangle must be equiangular, or that a circle must have the maximum area compatible with its perimeter (as compared with all other possible closed figures), by just analyzing the attributes " equilateral triangle " and " circle " (cf. above, p. 202) ; in this sense Kant would call such necessary connections *synthetic*. We thus find ourselves hard pressed to find examples of mutual entailments holding between distinct but analyzable attributes in a *nonsystemic* sense of "entailment"; yet this is the sort of necessary proposition which a real definition is claimed to be. Notice that we cannot argue that a given analysans may be distinct from the corresponding analysandum—though logically equivalent to it—because it contains descriptive concepts which are not contained in the analysandum, without begging the very question at issue: the *expression* denoting the analysans will, to be sure, have constituents not to be found in the expression denoting the analysandum, but the question is precisely whether the *concept denoted* could be distinct from the analysandum if the analysis is correct.

B. *The Paradox of Analysis*

The difficulty pointed up is none other than the famous *paradox of analysis*, which has been vaguely perceived by several philosophers who were puzzled about the concept of identity (how can *two* entities be said, without contradiction, to be identical?) but has been precisely formulated and precisely discussed only recently since G. E. Moore formulated it. Let X be analysandum, Y analysans (it is immaterial whether we take as values of X propositional functions or propositions satisfying the analyzed propositional function). If the analysis is correct, then X is identical with Y; but in that case the proposition expressed by "$X = Y$" is identical with the proposition expressed by "$X = X$"; in other words, if the analysis is correct, it is trivial. Now, it is true that as the paradox has been stated it is not specifically a paradox of analysis, but more generally a paradox of identity: a statement of identity, whether the identified entities be concrete or abstract, cannot, it seems, be both true and informative (nontrivial). Thus we might ask: if a proposition of the form "$p \vee q$" is identical with the corresponding proposition of the form "$-(-p.-q)$," how can the equivalence "$p \vee q \equiv -(p.-q)$" be more informative than the trivial equivalence "$p \vee q \equiv p \vee q$"? And if the number 4 is identical with the number $\sqrt[3]{64}$, how can the equation "$4 = \sqrt[3]{64}$" be more informative than the trivial equation "$4 = 4$"? Since Frege made the famous and important distinction between sense and denotation, it has come to be realized that there is no way out of this paradox unless we leave the material mode of speech and discuss the problem in a semantic metalanguage. Thus Frege pointed out [5] that it is both true and informative to say that the *distinct* symbols " 4 " and " $\sqrt[3]{64}$ " denote the *same* number, and that unlike the trivial equation " $4 = IV$ " this equation is informative because the two symbols differ in sense.

That the recent construction of semantic metalanguages has made a clearer and more refined discussion of the problem of real definition (or analysis) possible, cannot be denied. It must be pointed out, however, that if we replace the ontological mode of speech " X and Y are identical concepts (or attributes) " by the semantic mode of speech " ' X ' and ' Y ' are synonymous expressions," we only reformulate, do not solve, the problem—even though something has been gained by avoiding the contradictory form of expression " two things are identical (and so not two) ." The burden is now placed on the semantic term " synonymous." The paradox of analysis reappears in semantic formulation if we grant the following principle: let S_1 be a sentence containing expression X, and S_2 the sentence resulting from S_1 if X is replaced by a synonymous expression Y; then S_1 is synonymous with S_2. To see that this principle leads straight to our paradox we only need to take as S_1 a sentence expressing an analysis, as X the expression denoting its analysandum, and as Y the expression denoting its analysans; thus if " father " is synonymous with " male parent," then to say that a father is a male parent is to say nothing more informative than that a father is a father! It has been claimed, by Alonzo Church,[6] that the paradox admits of easy solution if we observe Frege's distinction between *sense* and *denotation*. The expressions " being a father " and " being a male parent " denote, as they occur in the sentence " being a father is the same as being a male parent," *concepts* (attributes, universals) , and accordingly the truth of this sentence requires the identity of these concepts. But any designative expression has, according to Frege, both denotation and sense. Now, just as in the arithmetic equation " $2 + 2 = 4$ " the left-hand and right-hand symbols denote an identical number yet have different senses,

[5] See " On Sense and Nominatum," transl. from the German, in Feigl and Sellars, *Readings in Philosophical Analysis*.

[6] *Journal of Symbolic Logic* (Dec. 1946) , review of a controversy concerning the paradox of analysis between Max Black and M. G. White.

so " being a father " and " being a male parent," while denoting the same concept, have nevertheless different senses. It is clear that the substitutivity principle formulated above is tenable only if " synonymous " means " having the same sense "; for declarative sentences denote truth-values (as shown by Frege in the cited essay), and there is no guarantee that replacement of a component of S_1 by an expression of equal denotation will not affect the truth-value of S_1;[7] but if so, then the principle cannot be used to derive the paradox of analysis.

Church's solution seems to me unsatisfactory for two reasons. In the first place, the paradox of analysis is derivable in such a way that the sense-denotation distinction is irrelevant to it. We start out from the principle of the substitutivity of identity: if $x = y$, then, if for " x " in any sentence S " y " is substituted, the truth-value of S remains unchanged (notice that the concept here involved is invariance of truth-value, not invariance of meaning). Then the analysis " the attribute brother = the attribute male sibling " allows us to derive the counterintuitive conclusion (II) " the proposition (the attribute brother = the attribute male sibling) = the proposition (the attribute brother = the attribute brother) " from the logically true premise (I) " the proposition (the attribute brother = the attribute brother) = the proposition (the attribute brother = the attribute brother) ." [8] Further, if we take as S a sentence like " so-and-so knows that the attribute brother = the attribute brother," the same principle allows us to infer " so-and-so knows that the attribute brother = the attribute male sibling." It is obvious that this inference cannot be logically valid, for if it were logically valid in this case it would be logically valid for all analyses of concepts, including analyses which it is very difficult to know.

Secondly, Church's solution is superficial, since it uses the Fregean term " sense " *without interpretation*. If " sense " is so used that the mere syntactic fact that one expression is elementary while the other is composed of words establishes that the expressions have different senses, then " having the same sense " simply will not

[7] This could, indeed, be guaranteed for an extensional language, but in such a language analyses in Moore's sense could not be formulated, and hence the paradox of analysis could not be derived. Cf. pp. 284-5 of this chapter and my article " Synonymy, Identity of Concepts, and the Paradox of Analysis."

[8] Cf. C. Lewy's review of Carnap's *Meaning and Necessity*, in *Mind* (April 1949), p. 236.

do as an analysans for " synonymous." What if a person had been
brought up first to use the complex expression " male parent " and
then were trained to use " father " as an abbreviating synonym?
Would it still be the case that for him " to be a father " and " to be
a male parent " have different senses? I should think not. And if
the criterion of difference of sense of expressions " X " and " Y "
is that the identity statement " $X = Y$ " should be informative, then
the proposed solution begs the question. As long as " sense " remains
an abstract primitive term of a semantic theory, only " implicitly
defined " by the postulates of the theory, the " sense-denotation "
distinction is really useless for solving the paradox of analysis. But
in which direction should we look for a genuine solution?

The problem of solving the paradox of analysis is all one with
the problem of explicating relevant senses of " synonymous," or of
clarifying the concept of identity as applied to attributes and other
abstract entities. And this is also what the problem of real definition
reduces to. The connection between the old problem of real definition and the modern problem of synonymy may be made still clearer
by showing that Aristotle's notion of *essence*, as something formulated
in real definitions, is closely similar to the modern notion of an
adequate *analysans* designated by an expression which is, in some
suitable sense, synonymous with the expression designating the
analysandum. An important distinction made by Aristotle in his
theory of the five predicables, important especially for his influential
theory of scientific ($=$ demonstrative) knowledge, is the distinction
between *essence* and *property*: the attributes " being the locus of
all points equidistant from a given point " and " having a maximal
area for a given perimeter " are both convertibly predicable of the
circle (which means, in the modern terminology, that these two
predicates have the same extension as the predicate " is a circle "),
yet the first, says Aristotle, is the essence of the circle while
the second is demonstrable on the basis of the essence.[9] As the
Aristotelian notion of self-evident axioms of a deductive science,
expressing the " essence " of the subject matter of the science, came

[9] " Demonstration " here means " systemic demonstration," i.e. demonstration with
the help of extralogical axioms of the system in which " circle " is defined. One
cannot deduce the mentioned property with the sole help of the explicit definition
of " circle," the way one could thus deduce the proposition " any triangle formed
by two radii of a given circle and the chord subtending the arc of the sector, is
isosceles."

to be discredited, so did naturally the essence-property distinction: it might conceivably be more fruitful, said the formal logicians, to define " circle " in terms of what Aristotle regarded as a property, and then what for Aristotle was the essence would be deflated into a mere property. However, it seems that the very same distinction which was outlawed by scientists and mathematicians has been offered an honorable refuge by such analytic philosophers as Moore. It is a demonstrable property of cubes, and only cubes, to have twelve equal and perpendicular edges, yet Moore and many of us would refuse the title of analysans to this property on the ground that this simply is not what we *mean* by "cube." According to what was, earlier in this book, called the "epistemic" criterion of adequacy of analyses, it must be impossible to know, or verify, that the analysandum applies in a given case without knowing, or verifying, that the analysans applies.[10] And clearly we do not ordinarily verify that x is a cube by counting the edges of x. But thus the requirement of epistemic adequacy may be an excellent analysis of what Plato and Aristotle meant by the requirement that the definiens of a real definition should express the essence of the universal defined. We might formulate the requirement more precisely as follows: an adequate analysans must be designated by an expression which is synonymous with the expression standing for the analysandum, in a sense of "synonymous" which is, at least partly, specified by the following postulate: if " X " is synonymous with " Y," then it is impossible to know the proposition that X applies in a given case without knowing the proposition that Y applies [11] in that case. Thus Moore would say that one cannot know that x is a cube, in the ordinary sense of "cube," without knowing that x is bounded by square faces, and square faces only, but that one could know that x is a cube without knowing how many edges x has.

But we encounter a serious difficulty in trying to reconcile this criterion of epistemic adequacy with a famous principle earnestly asserted by Moore himself: that it is possible to know, and know for certain, that a proposition is true without knowing its analysis! It is perhaps easier to see that this claim is correct than that it

---

[10] The requirement is formulated by Moore in "Reply to My Critics," *The Philosophy of G. E. Moore.*

[11] "Application" is here meant as the nonsemantic relation between a concept and an instance of the concept whose converse is exemplification or instantiation.

conflicts with the criterion of epistemic adequacy.[12] Most of us, for example, have no idea of how the concept of twoness might be correctly analyzed (most of us, after all, are no students of mathematical philosophy), yet we know, on the basis of simple counting, such propositions as "I have two legs." But is it plausible to maintain that in knowing this proposition we know the proposition "there is an x and a y, such that x is distinct from y and both x and y are legs of mine, and for any z, if z is a leg of mine, then z is either identical with x or with y"? It would, to be sure, be irrelevant to argue against Moore that if the analysans is fairly technical, as it is in most philosophically interesting cases of analysis, like the above example, then a person who knows that the analysandum applies might in fact be unable to understand the meaning of the analysans-expression and therefore be ignorant of the truth-value of the proposition expressed by means of the analysans-expression. For the same argument could be used to prove that knowing the proposition expressed by the English sentence "my father is rich" does not entail knowing the proposition expressed by the German sentence "mein Vater ist reich," since there are people who understand English but do not understand German. The point is that "X knows that the proposition expressed by S is true" does not entail "X knows what proposition is expressed by S," just as "X knows that Mary's husband is ill" does not entail "X knows who Mary's husband is."[13] However, a serious objection against Moore can be put forth if it is granted that it is impossible to know the truth-value of a proposition which contains one or more concepts with which one is unacquainted; for philosophers often analyze familiar concepts with the help of technical concepts with which people who are able to use the analyzed concepts correctly are not familiar.[14] Thus ordinary people may be quite unfamiliar with

---

[12] Richard Robinson confesses, in *Definition*, p. 174, that he finds this criterion unacceptable, "for it seems to me that if this were true there would never be any difficulty in analyzing anything." It may well seem so, but whether this evidently false consequence *does* follow from the requirement is a subtle question which Robinson has unfortunately not discussed.

[13] For a more detailed discussion of the analysis of sentences of the form "X knows that $g((\imath x)fx)$," and of its relevance to the problem of synonymy, see my article "Synonymy, Identity of Concepts, and the Paradox of Analysis."

[14] It is important to distinguish here "being acquainted with the concept C" and "understanding what the expression 'C' means." A man might not know what "red" means yet have a concept of redness, the behavioral criterion of his having the concept

the mathematical concept of limit, and accordingly with the concept of random sequence which von Mises defined with the help of the limit concept (and by this I don't just mean that they do not know how the *word* "limit" is used in mathematical contexts, the way one might be said to be ignorant of the usage of a word belonging to a language one does not know); yet they know, for example, the proposition that the sequence of increasing even numbers, 2, 4, 6, 8 · · · is not a random sequence (but an "orderly" sequence). Consistency would, therefore, require Moore to defend the *prima facie* unplausible view that it is possible to have a cognitive attitude (such as belief or knowledge) toward a proposition while being unacquainted with some of the constituents of the proposition. Is not this view as unplausible as the view that a blind man might well know the truth-value of a proposition about colors?

Clearly, all these difficulties are connected with the fact that no complete criterion has been specified for the use of sentences of the form " p and q are one and the same proposition "; and since the semantic analogue of this sentence is " sentences S_1 and S_2 are synonymous (in some relevant sense)," we see again that to clarify the notion of analysis and to analyze the relevant sense of " synonymy " amounts to one and the same problem. Specifically in connection with the criterion of epistemic adequacy, a question never explicitly discussed by Moore but surely crucial for an evaluation of his criterion is, whether identity as predicated of propositions is substitutive in nonextensional contexts, i. e. contexts of modal sentences, sentences about beliefs and other " intentional acts." That identity as predicated of individuals is not generally substitutive is well known. That King George wished to know whether Scott was identical with the author of *Waverley* does not entail that King George wished to know whether Scott was identical with Scott, as Russell pointed out long ago. And other logicians (especially Quine) have more recently pointed out that " it is necessary that the morning star is identical with the morning star " does not entail " it is necessary that the morning star is identical

---

being his ability to discriminate objects with respect to redness. It is obvious that such an ability to discriminate objects with respect to a property does not presuppose understanding of any language, and therefore even animals can (verifiably) be said to have concepts, though probably of qualitative properties and relations of things only.

with the evening star," even though the morning star is identical
with the evening star. But, now, supposing that $p = q$, does "X
knows that p" entail "X knows that q"? It should be noted that
a negative answer to this question is by no means entailed by
Russell's statement about King George's cognitive desires, reported
above. For even on Carnap's weak criterion of propositional identity, viz. L-equivalence,[15] the propositions "Scott is identical with
Scott" and "Scott is identical with the author of *Waverley*" are
not identical, since one is a tautology and the other factual
(assuming that "Scott" is not a definitional abbreviation for "the
author of *Waverley*"). However, Moore's criterion of epistemic
adequacy is precisely equivalent to an affirmative answer to this
question: to say that p cannot be identical with q unless one cannot
know that p without knowing that q, is equivalent to saying that
"$p = q$" entails that "X knows that p" entails "X knows that q."
And then one faces, of course, the paradox of analysis in the
epistemological form: if $(p = q)$, then $(p = p) = (p = q)$, and
since everybody knows that $(p = p)$, it follows that everybody
knows that $p = q$. But Moore stipulated this entailment without
offering a reason for accepting it. And one might well argue that
the stipulation is unreasonable precisely because it precipitates the
paradox of analysis.

C. *The Interchangeability Test of Synonymy*

Let us examine, now, what contemporary analytic philosophers
have to say by way of explicating the troublesome, but for analytic
philosophy central, notion (or notions) of synonymy. It is best
to begin by showing that the old concept of substitutivity *salva
veritate* (which goes back to Leibniz) is really quite useless as an
analysans in Moore's sense. The primary reason why it is useless
is not the fact, often pointed out, that by this criterion any two
terms with identical extension (like "man" and "featherless biped") would be synonymous in an extensional language. Indeed,
as Benson Mates has pointed out,[16] it is quite reasonable to regard
extensionally equivalent terms as synonyms *in an extensional lan-*

---

[15] See *Meaning and Necessity*, § 6.

[16] "Synonymity," in *Meaning and Interpretation*, University of California Publications in Philosophy, 25 (reprinted in Linsky, *Semantics and the Philosophy of Language*.)

guage: for if it is impossible to construct a sentence whose truth-value would change if one term were substituted for the other, then there is no way of proving that the terms are not synonymous, and one would have to transcend the given language if one wished to challenge their synonymy. The primary reason is rather that the criterion is implicitly circular, especially if it is applied to a language sufficiently rich to make the conduct of philosophical analysis possible. The circularity is hidden in the tacit assumption that the truth-value of a statement can be determined independently of knowledge of synonymy relations. To see that this assumption is not generally valid, suppose someone familiar with the meaning of "male parent" yet ignorant of the meaning of "father." Observations of other people's ways of speaking suggest to him the hypothesis that "father," as used by those people, is simply a synonym for "male parent." How would the *salva veritate* criterion help him to test his hypothesis? He would have to verify that statements of the form "x is the father of y," occasionally made by his neighbors, keep their truth-value unchanged if for "father" "male parent" is substituted. But then he has to know their truth-value to begin with, and if he does not know which of the expressions whose meanings he understands "father" is synonymous with, he obviously has no way of finding this out. Further, as N. Goodman has pointed out (*The Structure of Appearance*, Cambridge, Mass., 1951; p. 7), among the contexts in which "A" has to prove interchangeable *salva veritate* with "B" is the very identity-sentence "$A = B$"; but if its truth-value were known independently of the substitution test—which is required if the test is to be noncircular—the latter would be unnecessary! It may well be the case that invariance of truth-value with respect to synonymy transformations follows from the very meaning of "synonymy," but by Moore's own criterion of epistemic adequacy, as I have chosen to name it, this property of synonymous expressions cannot be part of a correct analysis of the concept of synonymy. The kind of circle here involved may be compared to the circle contained in the epistemically inadequate analysis of "logically valid inference" which was incidentally mentioned in Chapter 6: a logically valid inference is an inference which, after reduction to primitive notation, exhibits the form of an inference which invariably leads from true premises to a true conclusion. If this definition were operational in the sense that it

prescribed a method for determining logical validity, then knowledge of logical validity would presuppose knowledge of the truth-
values of empirical propositions—and logic would not be a " pure "
science. But since our knowledge of a good many empirical propositions is *inferential*, it would be difficult to complete the prescribed
test of valid inference without running into a circle.

Now, the formulation and testing of analyses is possible only
in a nonextensional language, specifically a language containing
names of propositions. To see that this is indeed the case we only
need to ask ourselves whether analyses could be expressed in an
extensional metalanguage containing the term " synonymous " and
names of expressions of the object language. In such a language
analyses would be expressed in the form " ' X ' is synonymous with
' Y.' " But while this form may be appropriate for dictionary
definitions it cannot be appropriate for analyses, for two reasons.
(1) As Moore has pointed out,[17] such a statement might be understood and known to be true by one who is ignorant of the meaning
of both " X " and " Y ": just suppose that " X " and " Y " did mean
the same and that so-and-so believes this because an authoritative
dictionary says so! And it would be absurd to claim that one knew
the correct analysis of the meaning of " X " while being ignorant
of the meaning of " X." (2) Just like entailment statements, statements of analyses are not about expressions of a given language,
which can be shown by means of the translation device already used
in our discussion of entailment (above, p. 200) : if " the concept
father is identical with the concept *male parent* " (S_1) were correctly
rendered by " ' father ' is synonymous with ' male parent ' " (S_2) ,
then it would be correct to translate this analysis into, say German,
as follows: " ' father ' ist gleichbedeutend mit ' male parent ' " (S_3) .
To put it more explicitly: if two sentences of a given language are
synonymous, then their correct translations into another language
must themselves be synonymous sentences. But the correct translation of S_1 into German is " der Begriff *Vater* ist identisch mit dem
Begriff *maennlicher Elter*," and surely this sentence is not synonymous with S_3. We are thus led to the semantic formulation " ' x is
a father ' means (designates) *that x is a male parent* ' (which is
immune against the first objection but not against the second) , or

[17] " Russell's Theory of Descriptions," in *The Philosophy of Bertrand Russell*, ed.
P. A. Schilpp, pp. 199 f.

to the nonsemantic formulation "*that x is a father* entails, and is entailed by, *that x is a male parent*," or alternatively perhaps "the propositional function that *x* is a father is identical with the propositional function that *x* is a male parent." What is here called a "name of a proposition" is the expression formed by prefixing "that" to the sentence which designates the proposition (analogously for names of propositional functions, like "that *x* is a father"; alternatively, participial expressions, like "Jack *being* a father," may be used as names of propositions).[18]

That a language which is adequate for the expression of analyses must contain names of propositions, used in statements of entailment and designation and other statements about propositions, is further evident from the fact that the concept of entailment is used either directly in formulating an analysis or in the process of testing an analysis. For example, suppose a simple behavioristic analysis of propositional belief were offered, as follows: *A* believes that $p = A$ is disposed to respond affirmatively to "p." One would of course reject it on the ground that neither is the analysans entailed by the analysandum nor is the analysandum entailed by the analysans: it is *possible* that *A* believe that p yet not respond affirmatively to "p" because he does not understand that particular sentence; and it is likewise possible that in responding affirmatively to "p" he should be lying. It should be clear, then, that if the *salva veritate* criterion is to have any relevance to the philosophical use of the notion of synonymy, it must be applied to a nonextensional language, a language containing such modal operators as "necessary" and "possible." Now, if the nonextensional language in question also contains verbs designating propositional attitudes (belief, doubt, etc.), then interchangeability *salva veritate* is, indeed, a demonstrably necessary and sufficient condition for synonymy.[19] And if logical equivalence of analysans and analysandum were itself a

---

[18] The major error of the thesis of extensionality (cf. above, Chap. 6) is precisely the confusion of quoted sentences, intended as *names* of sentences, with that-clauses intended as *names of propositions*. What has probably promoted this confusion is the habit, due to the desire for typographical convenience, of using quotes ambiguously sometimes to designate the quoted sentence and sometimes to designate the proposition designated by the quoted sentence. Just compare "'all men are mortal' is a declarative sentence" with "'all men are mortal' entails 'there are men.'"

[19] See, on this point, the articles already cited: by Benson Mates, "Synonymity," and by W. V. Quine, "Two dogmas of empiricism."

sufficient condition of adequacy for analyses, then there would have to be no further worry about the analysis of synonymy: synonyms would be simply terms which are interchangeable in any sentence of such a rich nonextensional language in which they are used (not mentioned). But by Moore's criterion of epistemic adequacy no analysis can be adequate unless it indicates a method for verifying whether the analysandum applies in a given case. It is easily shown, however, that the attempt to verify synonymy on the basis of inter-changeability *salva veritate* is even more glaringly circular in a nonextensional language than it is in an extensional language. If I am to verify that " father " and " male parent " are synonyms by verifying that they are universally interchangeable in a nonexten-sional language, then I must know in particular that the statement " it is necessary that a father is a male parent " is true, just as the statement " it is necessary that a father is a father " is true. But how could the truth of the first, the nontrivial modal statement be established independently of determining that " father " and " male parent " are synonyms? Indeed, if " necessary " here is meant in the sense of " strictly analytic," then the word " synonymous " would explicitly appear in the definitional expansion of the modal statement!

D. *Synonymy and Logical Equivalence*

Having examined the interchangeability test of synonymy and found it ineffective, let us turn to the attempts made by Lewis and Carnap to provide adequate analyses of the concept of synonymy with the help of the concept of *logical equivalence*.[20] Both Lewis and Carnap use the concept of *intension* as their basic instrument of analysis. There are, to be sure, differences in their use of this term. Thus Lewis defines the intension of a predicate *explicitly* as the class of predicates entailed by applications of the given predicate. Carnap defines " intension " only in context, or what he explicitly defines is only the phrase " same intension ": two predicates " P " and " Q " have the same intension if the equivalence " $(x) (Px \equiv Qx)$ " is analytic (L-true). Carnap thus leaves the question open whether intensions are to be regarded as classes of logically equivalent expres-

---

[20] The following is in part reprinted from my article " Synonymity and Logical Equivalence," *Analysis* (March 1949). Cf. Carnap, *Meaning and Necessity*, §§ 14, 15, and Lewis, *An Analysis of Knowledge and Valuation*, chap. 1.

sions or as nonlinguistic *designata*; while Lewis treats intensions definitely as classes of verbal expressions and uses a special term ("signification") for nonlinguistic *designata*. But in this context such differences are negligible and the similarity of their approaches is more important. "Intension" is defined (whether explicitly or in context) in terms of logical equivalence, and thus indirectly "synonymy" is defined in terms of logical equivalence. I propose to show, now, that this procedure is fatally circular.

Let me begin with Lewis' concept of "equivalence in analytic meaning." Sameness of intension is a necessary but insufficient condition for two expressions to be equivalent in analytic meaning. If they are both complex, then their corresponding constituents must have the same intension (an example used by Lewis is the pair of complex expressions "circular hole" and "round excision"). This conception helps Lewis, indeed, to clarify the sense in which terms of universal intension (like "round square") as well as terms of zero intension (like "square or not square") fail to have the same meaning: they are usually built up with the help of descriptive terms in such a way that corresponding constituents are far from being logically equivalent. But what if one of the two logically equivalent expressions is elementary, as in "square = equilateral rectangle"? Lewis' answer is that, if so, logical equivalence is also a sufficient condition for synonymy. Now, the above is an example of an *explicative statement*, and consistently with the conditions laid down for equivalence in analytic meaning, Lewis regards explicative statements as a species of *analytic* statements. It would seem to follow that in order to determine whether the explicative statement "a square is an equilateral rectangle" is true, we have to determine whether it expresses a logical equivalence, an analytic truth; for to say that it is a correct explication is to say that "square" is synonymous with "equilateral rectangle." Now, however, the vicious circle looms large. To show that "a square is an equilateral rectangle" is analytic, it must presumably be derived by substitution of descriptive terms from the principle of identity "$(x) (P) (Px \equiv Px)$." Now, which definition is to lead to the substitution instance "a square is a square" if not the very definition "square = equilateral rectangle" which is to be proved as adequately equating identical meanings? To propose demonstration of logical equivalence as the test of synonymy is, therefore, to put the cart before the horse (cf. above, p. 105).

A similar, though better hidden, circularity seems to me involved in Carnap's explication of the concept of synonymy in terms of what he calls " intensional isomorphism." Carnap stipulates *L*-equivalence of sentences as the symmetrical and transitive relation by which propositions are logically constructed, i. e. two sentences are to designate the same proposition if they are logically equivalent. Obviously, according to this usage of " proposition," two sentences may express the same proposition without being synonymous. First, any two *L*-true sentences, and any two *L*-false sentences, are logically equivalent: Carnap consequently speaks of *the L*-true, and *the L*-false, proposition. Secondly, if an explicative statement, like " to be a father is to be a male parent," is true, it expresses a logical equivalence but is itself logically equivalent to the trivial identity obtained on replacing the *analysans* by the *analysandum* (" to be a father is to be a father "). Carnap should say, in accordance with his convention for the use of the word " proposition," that " to be a father is to be a father " expresses the same proposition as " to be a father is to be a male parent " (which has been called the " paradox of analysis "); so the task remains to explicate the sense in which the two sentences, though logically equivalent, fail to be synonymous. Now, Carnap's concept of intensional isomorphism corresponds to Lewis' concept of equivalence in analytic meaning insofar as two complex expressions, like " $7 > 5$ " and " $Gr(7, 5)$ " are said to have the same intensional structure if corresponding constituents, like " $>$ " and " Gr," down to the elementary constituents, are *L*-equivalent.[21] There is an important difference, however, since Carnap does not allow an elementary expression to be intensionally isomorphic with a compound expression (one made up of subdesignators, like " male parent "). Thus Lewis' explication of synonymy leads to the conclusion that " father " *is* synonymous with " male parent " (provided the explicative statement " to be a father is to be a male parent " is correct), while Carnap's explication entails the very opposite. What we need, however, is an explication of that sense of " synonymous " in which a correct analysis can be said to express synonymy without being either trivial (" a father is a father ") or a mere dictionary translation (" father " $=$ " Vater ").

---

[21] Carnap widens the use of " *L*-equivalent " in such a way that this semantical term is predicable not only of sentences but of other designative expressions, like predicates and descriptions, as well.

So far I have merely shown that Carnap's concept of intensional isomorphism fails to provide a criterion of a correct and nontrivial analysis; which, indeed, would be a relevant criticism only if Carnap had claimed that it did. I proceed to explain why Carnap's explication of synonymy lands one in a fruitless circle once one attempts to use it in order to test synonymy. Take the above illustration (used by Carnap) of the pair of synonyms " $7 > 5$ " and " $Gr\,(7, 5)$." In order to show that the matrices " $\cdot\cdot > \cdot\cdot\cdot$ " and " $Gr(\,\cdot\,\cdot,\,\cdot\,\cdot\,\cdot)$ " are L-equivalent, I have to show that the identity of the truth-values of the schematized statements *follows from the semantic rules.* Indeed, this can easily be shown by referring to the semantic rules " ' $\cdot\cdot > \cdot\cdot\cdot$ ' means that $\cdot\cdot$ is greater than $\cdot\cdot\cdot$ " and " ' $Gr(\,\cdot\,\cdot,\,\cdot\,\cdot\,\cdot)$ ' means that $\cdot\cdot$ is greater than $\cdot\cdot\cdot$." Now, if all this analysis takes place within a language *system* as envisaged by Carnap, then the semantic rules are simply conventions and there can be no question of their cognitive justification. However, if the test of synonymy is to be applied to expressions in a natural language, then the whole procedure is circular since the semantic rules would themselves be statements of synonymy. That is, in order to know that " $\cdot\cdot > \cdot\cdot\cdot$ " means that $\cdot\cdot$ is greater than $\cdot\cdot\cdot$, I would have to know that " $\cdot\cdot > \cdot\cdot\cdot$ " is *synonymous* with " $\cdot\cdot$ is greater than $\cdot\cdot\cdot$," and continued reference to semantic rules would lead to an infinite regress. Clearly, the analysis of synonymy in terms of a concept of logical equivalence defined with reference to language systems fails to help those who want to apply semantic analysis to natural languages.

Carnap claims that his concept of intensional isomorphism, which he proposes as explicatum for the concept of synonymy, easily solves the paradox of analysis (cf. *Meaning and Necessity*, pp. 63-4) . The sense in which " father " is not synonymous with " male parent " but is synonymous with " *père* " (or, if we must stay within one language, with " daddy "—cognitively at any rate), is just intensional isomorphism. Is the solution quite so easy? Notice that no elementary predicate can be intensionally isomorphic with a compound predicate. But how, then, has Carnap explicated the sense in which the analysandum-expression and the analysans-expression of a correct analysis are synonyms? In his framework of semantic concepts it is impossible to justify the claim that " cube " is synonymous with " regular solid bounded by square faces " but not synonymous with " cube with twelve edges," for in either case the extensionally equivalent expressions are *L*-equivalent, and according to Carnap the sense of "synonymy" in which a correct analysis states a relation of synonymy is none other than *L*-equivalence. One is, indeed, tempted to say that Carnap's solution is irrelevant to the problem raised by the paradox of analysis, since this problem consists in the explication of the sense in which an analysis asserts an *identity* of concepts while according to Carnap an analysis only asserts an *L*-equivalence.

E. *Solution of the Paradox of Analysis*

My own proposed solution of the paradox is simply that the principle of substitutivity does not hold without restriction for analytic synonyms. Universal interchangeability of analytic synonyms is actually an essential premise without which the paradox of analysis cannot be derived. For without it we could not derive from the identity (I) the counter-intuitive consequence (II) (see p. 277). What, again, makes this consequence so unacceptable, The way it is usually put is that, if it were true, then all analysis would be trivial; but an equally forceful way of showing its absurdity is to point out that if it were true, then one could not fail to know the analysis of any concept. For, " I know that to be a father is to be a father " would entail " I know that to be a father is to be a male parent " (cf. p. 282), and the entailing proposition is undoubtedly true.[22] Now, since this consequence cannot be derived if universal interchangeability of analytic synonyms, even in *nonextensional* contexts, is denied, a restriction of the rule of interchange is just what is called for. Once this restriction is made, we cannot infer from the analytic synonymy of " brother " and " male sibling " that I entails II, since this inference would require interchange of analytic synonyms in an obviously *nonextensional* context: if in " the proposition that *p* is identical with the proposition that *p* " we substitute for " *p* " in its first occurrence a statement which has the same truth-value as " *p* " but is not logically equivalent to it, we clearly change the truth-value of the statement as a whole.

[22] In all strictness, one should rather say that " I know that to be a father is to be a father " expresses no proposition at all (cf. Chap. 7, on propositions as objective constituents of possible beliefs), and is in this sense meaningless. The paradox in question would then take the form that it is meaningless to speak of knowledge of the analysis of a concept. But I do not think this modification affects the soundness of my solution of the paradox.

(It should be noted, however, that in denying that q *follows* from p, one is not denying that q *may* be true when p is true. Thus I am not denying that interchange of analytic synonyms *may* leave the truth-value of a nonextensional sentence unchanged).

A charge which this solution is likely to bring forth, like so many solutions of so many paradoxes, is that it is purely *ad hoc*. But it may be answered by pointing out (1) that the proposed restriction kills at one stroke many similar paradoxes concerning analytic synonymy, and (2) that it is perfectly natural since it has already been recognized that substitutivity of identity must be limited in nonextensional contexts. (1) The following cognate paradoxes would all arise if the restriction were not made: anybody who is in doubt whether being a rectangle entails being a parallelogram is in doubt whether being an equiangular parallelogram entails being a parallelogram; if to say that to be a father is to be a male parent is to express an analysis of a concept, then to say that to be a father is to be a father is to express an analysis of a concept; etc. (2) it is well known that, for example, L-equivalent designators (in Carnap's terminology) are not interchangeable in a special kind of nonextensional context, viz. the context of statements about propositional attitudes: thus my knowing that $4 = 2 + 2$ does not entail my knowing all L-true equations of arithmetic about the number 4. Since for Carnap analytic synonyms are L-equivalent designators, the proposed restriction is in fact quite continuous with the discussion of limited interchangeability of L-equivalent designators in *Meaning and Necessity*, § 13 (similarly with Quine's theory of nondesignative occurrences of designative expressions,[23] and Frege's theory of " oblique " modes of speech [24]).

[23] In Quine's terminology an expression occurs " nondesignatively " in a given context if in that context it is not accessible to the rule of substitutivity of identity. For example, the descriptions " the morning star " and " the evening star " occur non-designatively in the statement " it is not logically necessary that the morning star = the evening star," since otherwise the apparent falsehood " it is not logically necessary that the morning star is self-identical " would be deducible. To be sure, this " paradox " is easily solved without limiting the substitutivity of identity if one accepts Russell's theory of descriptions, for on the latter the conclusion " it is not logically necessary that the morning star = the morning star " is true! But this type of solution is not applicable to a very similar paradox likewise formulated by Quine: it is necessary that $9 = 9$; $9 =$ the number of planets; but it is not necessary (it is a contingent fact) that $9 =$ the number of planets. Here the modal premise is undeniable.

[24] Cf. " On Sense and Nominatum," Feigl and Sellars.

And what do we have to offer by way of explicating the notion of analytic synonymy which has been illustrated by such simple pairs as " father—male parent," " square—equilateral rectangle "? It seems to me that for this purpose it is sufficient to indicate how analytic synonymy differs from (a) intralinguistic stipulated synonymy, (b) intralinguistic reported synonymy, (c) interlinguistic translational synonymy. And this is no great problem at all. It differs from all, first and foremost, in the respect that it is primarily a relation between concepts, not expressions. This is obvious from the reasons already given (cf. pp. 271-4), to which we may add that no analytic philosopher could seriously believe that the knowledge he grinds out " in the armchair " could be better attained by empirical linguists working in the field. I do not see that the claim that the discovery of adequate analyses of meanings properly belongs within the province of empirical linguistics is any less paradoxical than would be the claim (which such a cynic would likewise have to make were he only consistent) that logicians should seek the linguists' help in trying to decide which propositions entail which. Now, while nobody is likely to confuse a statement of analytic synonymy with a statement of synonymy of kind (a) or kind (c), there is a danger of confusing it with such statements of intralinguistic synonymy as may be found in Webster's dictionary. It may be useful, therefore, to show once more where the difference lies.

Like entailment statements, statements of analyses are, if true, necessary, and accordingly could not be invalidated by such contingent facts as changes of linguistic usage. Indeed, the criticisms made in Chapter 7 of the linguistic theory of necessary propositions are applicable almost *mutatis mutandis* to what might be called, analogously, the linguistic theory of analysis. Suppose the English word " square " came one day to be used in the more general sense of " parallelogram." Would the entailment statement " being a square entails being equilateral "—which expresses a partial analysis of the meaning of " square "—then be invalidated? Of course not. What would be invalidated would be only the undoubtedly contingent statement " the conventional English designation for the concept *square* is (at all times) the expression ' square.' " It should be a sufficient refutation of the linguistic theory of analysis to point out that if it were sound, then it would be impossible to distinguish logic from empirical linguistics (except as botany is distinguishable, as a branch, from biology). For a statement of logical entailment, like " that all *a* are *b* and some *a* are not *c* entails that some *b* are not *c*," would then have to be regarded as an empirical generalization about the usage of the English logical constants " all," " some," " not," etc. Why is it, however, that even philosophers who recognize the autonomy of logic as a pure a priori science are tempted to accept the linguistic theory of analysis? The reason may well be that analysis of concepts, unlike formal logic, is intimately interwoven with a preliminary empirical study of linguistic usage. Before we can proceed to the analysis of a given analysandum we must identify the latter, in other words, we must carefully define the problem of analysis. But such identification cannot take the simple form of producing a linguistic expression and saying that we wish to analyze the meaning of this expression. The reason is obviously that usually there is no such thing as *the* meaning of a given expression, expressions being multiply ambiguous. Identification of the analysandum then will consist in identification of relevant contexts of usage. The safest way of identifying these contexts is to *denote* instances of the analysandum as well as instances of other concepts designated by the ambiguous expresssion with which the analysandum in question should not be confused. Thus an analytical ethicist occupied with the analysis of the ethical concept of rightness might preface his analysis with the remark " the sense of ' right ' I wish to analyze is not the legal sense, the sense in which any act conforming to existing laws of the state is right, nor, of course, the sense in which answers to questions are said to be ' right ' (or ' wrong '), but rather the sense illustrated by such sentences as ' it is under no circumstances right to torture a sentient being,' ' mercy-killing is right (though legally wrong) .' "

Now, the same instances which are initially used to identify the analysandum may subsequently, after the analysis has been stated, be again referred to as material that confirms the analysis since they are likewise instances of the proposed analysans. And thus the error may insinuate itself that the analysis, being tested in terms of linguistic usages, is itself a generalization about linguistic usages. Let us denote by " C_1," " C_2," " C_3 " concepts that are designated by the ambiguous expression E in various contexts of usage, and suppose that C_1 is our analysandum. Then we identify C_1 by saying that it is the sense in which E is used when E is predicated of instances $x_1, x_2 \cdots x_n$. We then proceed to analyze C_1 and, since we cannot contemplate abstract ideas (or better perhaps, abstract images), concentrate attention on instances $x_1 \cdots x_n$ in doing so. Finally we test the analysans Y (by which we mean a concept, not an expression) by seeing whether it applies to $x_1 \cdots x_n$ as well as to further instances of C_1. This schematization shows that the only stage in the process of analysis at which linguistic expressions are *mentioned* (and not just *used*) is the initial stage of identification of the analysandum. The statement of the analysis, however, is a statement about C_1, not about E.

The final question about analytic synonymy to which an answer is overdue, is just in what sense analysandum and analysans are *identical* concepts. We have seen that the assumption of identity in the sense of universal interchangeability of their designations leads inevitably to the paradox of analysis. But if this were a good reason for denying the propriety of speaking of identity here, then it could hardly ever be proper to speak of identity; for even identity of individuals, as was pointed out, fails to be substitutive in certain non-extensional contexts. Thus suppose that "$a = b$" is an informative statement about individuals, like "the morning star $=$ the evening star." If its truth required that "a" and "b" are interchangeable in *all* contexts, then it could not be true: for while everybody knows that $a = a$, it is highly doubtful whether everybody knows that $a = b$. It would seem, then, that an explication of the identity in question must take the form of a specification of the contexts in which substitutivity obtains. The strongest identity that could reasonably be expected is, of course, substitutivity in all extensional contexts. But we shall see presently that often the identity is even weaker in that failure of substitutivity in some *extensional* contexts is not held a sufficient ground for rejecting an analysis; in other words, that Y may be acceptable as analysans for X even though these concepts do not have exactly the same extension. However, since the word "analysis" is so used by many analytic philosophers that it would be self-contradictory to say that analysandum and analysans differ in extension, it might be better to speak, with Carnap, of *explication* instead.

F. *Explication and Degree of Synonymy*

To test the correctness of an explication is to determine by formal deduction whether such and such antecedently specified *criteria of adequacy* are satisfied by the explication. If the explication has the form of an eliminative definition, then the proof of satisfaction consists in showing that substitution of explicatum for explicandum turns the criteria of adequacy into strictly analytic statements. To take a simple illustration: presumably a criterion of adequacy to be satisfied by an explication of the concept of propositional knowledge (i. e. knowledge in the sense of the word in such contexts as "I know that the earth is approximately a sphere") is "if p is known, then p is true." Now, if the explicatum is simply the conjunction "p is true, and p is believed on good grounds," then simple substitution turns the criterion of adequacy into the strictly analytic statement "if p is true and believed on good grounds, then p is true." But to lay down such a criterion of adequacy is actually equivalent to specifying a context in which explicandum and explicatum should be interchangeable not only *salva veritate* but, since criteria of adequacy are usually meant as necessary propositions, *salva necessitate* (let us call this "strong interchangeability"). Yet it often happens that an explication violates some criteria of adequacy which one would impose if one wanted the explicatum to be closely similar to the explicandum. As an example of an explication which produced an explicatum of relatively little similarity to the explicandum, consider Russell's explication of the concept of implication, as a relation between propositions, in terms of material implication. The important criterion of adequacy satisfied by the explication is: it is impossible that p implies q, if p is true and q is false; in other words, if p is true and p implies q, then q must be true. On the other hand, a criterion violated by the explication yet clearly satisfied by any *ordinary* usage of "implies" is: for any self-consistent p, there is a q such that p does not imply q and does not imply not-q. For a false proposition materially implies every proposition. Again, consider Russell's explication of natural numbers as classes of similar classes of individuals. Russell tacitly adopted Peano's five postulates of arithmetic as criteria of adequacy inasmuch as he aimed at a definition of "number," along with definitions of the other two of Peano's primitives, " zero " and " successor," which would turn those postulates into logical truths. It is well known, however, that Russell was but partially successful in this enterprise since the third postulate, asserting that distinct numbers have distinct successors, cannot be deduced from Russell's definitions of " number " and " successor " alone but only in conjunction with the axiom of infinity (at least the latter is required in a logistic system embodying the theory of types).[25] This postulate, therefore, constitutes an extensional context for the term " number " in which this term is not strongly interchangeable with Russell's explicatum. That is, since the axiom of infinity is a *contingent* premise (see above, Chap. 6) required for the demonstration of the third postulate in logicist interpretation, the interchange of the explicandum " number " with the explicatum " class of similar classes " in this context is not necessity-preserving (though it *may* be truth-preserving). The identity of explicandum and explicatum, then, falls short of the maximum degree that could reasonably be demanded.[26]

We have seen that the requirement of *complete* synonymy of analysandum and analysans expression (or, in the material mode of speech, complete identity of analysandum and analysans), in the sense of universal interchangeability in a nonextensional language, is impossible to fulfill, inasmuch as it leads inevitably to the paradox of analysis. The alternative course of requiring only a certain *degree of synonymy*, determined by specifying contexts of strong interchangeability in the form of adequacy criteria, brings us into substantial agreement with a thesis recently argued by Nelson Goodman that has produced quite a stir among some analysts. Here is a direct quotation of Goodman's contention:

it is commonly supposed that a satisfactory definition of syn-

---

[25] To see this, suppose there existed exactly five individuals. Since the number 5 is by Russell's definition the class of all quintets, it would be a unit class, having exactly one member. The number six, however, would be the null class, and so would all the numbers greater than five. The numbers 5 and 6, then, would have an identical successor (the null class), yet they are distinct numbers since 5 is, by our existential hypothesis, a unit class, while 6 is the null class (see below, p. 387).

[26] Carnap mentions, in § 3 of *Logical Foundations of Probability*, the similarity of explicatum to explicandum as a requirement to be satisfied by an explication, and notes explicitly that " close similarity is not required, and considerable differences are permitted." He does not, however, discuss the question of how degrees of such similarity might be measured.

onymy must meet two requirements: that some predicates be synonymous with others, and that either of a pair of synonyms be replaceable by the other in all non-intensional contexts without change of truth-value. But we have seen that these two requirements are incompatible. The sound course seems to be to construe degree of synonymy as, so to speak, degree of inter-replaceability. . . . and to recognize that the relation of exact synonymy between diverse predicates is null [" On Likeness of Meaning," reprinted from *Analysis* in *Semantics and the Philosophy of Language*, ed. Linsky, pp. 73-4].

I wish to emphasize, however, that I agree neither with (a) his completely *general* thesis, nor with (b) his arguments in support of it, nor with (c) his tentative suggestion that if synonymy is a gradated relation, *it follows* that logical necessity is likewise a matter of degree. (a) It should be remembered that the assumption of universal interchangeability of synonyms " X " and " Y " generates a paradox only if the assertion " I *know* that to be an X is to be a Y " is assumed to be significant (nontrivial) ; but this it is only if " X " and " Y " are analytic synonyms, not if they are stipulated or translational synonyms. Using the old example again, suppose that " square " is introduced into the language as an abbreviation for " equilateral rectangle," having had no antecedent ostensive usage. In that case the assertion " I know that to be a square is to be an equilateral rectangle " is not one bit less trivial than the assertion " I know that to be a square is to be a square." If it seems less trivial it is because it is confused with the entirely different assertion about knowledge of linguistic usage, " I know that ' square ' is synonymous with ' equilateral rectangle.' " (b) Goodman argues in effect that the criterion of adequacy generally laid down for an analysis of a sharp concept of synonymy (i. e. a concept which allows us to say that either a pair of terms are synonymous or they are not, the way in which either a statement is true or it is not) , viz. interchangeability in all extensional contexts, cannot be satisfied by any pair of distinct terms, and that therefore it is pointless (or obscure) to speak of distinct terms as being sharply synonymous. But he has succeeded in the proof of this startling proposition only by changing the meaning of " extensional interchangeability." He introduces the concept of *secondary* extension of a predicate, meaning the extension of a compound of the predicate, and then proves that if by "extension" we mean the sum of primary and secondary extension, then distinct terms cannot have the same extension. Thus he argues that triangle descriptions form the primary extension of the compound "triangle description," and thus a secondary extension of the predicate "triangle," and that similarly "trilateral description" has as its extension a secondary extension of the term "trilateral"; and that since the class of triangle descriptions includes the description "triangle that is not trilateral" which is not included in the class of trilateral descriptions, "triangle" and "trilateral" differ in secondary extension. But actually Goodman has proved nothing more alarming than that distinct terms are—distinct, which I propose to show as follows. Why does Goodman say that "triangle that is not trilateral" is a triangle description yet not a trilateral description? If by "triangle description" he meant "description *of* a triangle," then the only way he could deny that triangle descriptions coincide with trilateral descriptions would be by denying that "triangle" is synonymous with "trilateral"—for if these are synonyms, then "description of a triangle" is synonymous with "description of a trilateral," and thus "triangle description" and "trilateral description," being themselves synonyms, would have to have the same extension. But if Goodman *assumes* in his proof that "triangle" and "trilateral" are not synonymous, then he begs the question. The other alternative is that "triangle description" is meant as a purely syntactic term, viz. "description containing 'triangle' as first term." But then to say that "*P*-description" and "*Q*-description" have different (indeed, nonoverlapping) extensions is equivalent to saying that a description which has "*P*" as first term does not have "*Q*" as first term, which is equivalent to saying that "*P*" is distinct from "*Q*." And then the theorem that all distinct terms differ in secondary extension is just an impressive way of stating the triviality that all distinct terms are distinct. There is no reason, therefore, why any analytic philosophers should be shaken by Goodman's discovery.[27]

(c) At the end of his paper, Goodman points out that since analyticity is defined in terms of synonymy, the view that synonymy

[27] See also A. F. Smullyan, "ϕ-Symbols," *Analysis* (Jan. 1951).

is gradated entails that analyticity is gradated; the same point was made earlier, more explicitly, by White in " Analytic-Synthetic: an Untenable Dualism " (reprinted in Linsky, *Semantics and the Philosophy of Language*). Now, since we have seen that solution of the paradox of analysis requires abandonment of *identity* of analysandum and analysans in favor of *similarity* of varying degrees, we implicitly already assented to this consequence. A philosopher like C. I. Lewis who, it will be remembered, emphasized that analytic statements in the epistemologically interesting sense of " analytic " are based on explicative definitions, could succeed in conceiving of the analytic-synthetic distinction as a sharp one only by not seeing the problem raised by the expression " identical meanings." However, we must take sharp issue with an unwarranted assumption which the entire trio of analytic " gradualists "—Goodman, Quine, White—seems to share: that what holds for the analytic-synthetic distinction also holds for the necessary-contingent distinction—presumably for the excellent reason that the distinctions are one and the same. Thus Goodman concludes his revolutionary paper with the conjecture: " thus, at least according to the suggested interpretation of ' analytic,' no non-repetitive statement will be analytic. The most we can say is that it is more, or less, nearly analytic. This will be enough to convince many of us that likewise a non-repetitive statement is never absolutely necessary, but only more or less nearly so." In the first place, we should clearly distinguish between (strictly) analytic and logical truths.[28] As the concept of synonymy does not enter into the definition of " logical truth " at all, and as logical truths are necessary propositions, it cannot be validly inferred from the gradualistic character of analyticity that logical necessity is itself a matter of degree. Consider, e. g., the syllogistic principle " if all a are b and all b are c, then all a are c." Synonymy relations, expressed by contextual definitions of logical constants, help us to show (not, though, without the help of another logical principle, viz. the tautology of propositional logic " $p \cdot q \supset r \equiv p \cdot -r \supset -q$ ") that this syllogistic principle is equivalent to the principle of the OAO syllogism " if all a are b and some a are not c, then some b are not c," but then the validity of neither principle can be said to be grounded in synonymy relations at all. In fact, since presumably

[28] Compare the terminology introduced above at the end of Chap. 5.

any logical principle would remain valid if it were written out in primitive notation, it cannot be said that logical truth even partly depends on synonymy relations. Secondly, if it is admitted that most criteria of adequacy are themselves necessary statements, then the claim that in all cases the necessity of a statement can be known only on the basis of the synonymy of certain expressions can be shown to involve a circle. For, as we have shown, analytic synonymy can be defned only in terms of satisfaction of specified criteria of adequacy; hence, if we argued, to repeat an earlier illustration, " it is necessary that if p is known, then p is true, for ' p is known ' is synonymous with ' p is true and . . . ' ", we would naively beg the question. This conclusion might, indeed, be avoided by refusing to grant to criteria of adequacy the status of *assertions*, and interpreting them instead as postulates of the form " produce for explicandum X an explicatum Y of such a kind that X and Y are L-interchangeable in contexts of the following kind."

This, indeed, seems to be Carnap's attitude toward criteria of adequacy, for he calls the latter *conventions*. But the untenability of this position is easily shown. Suppose someone decided to lay down the following criterion of adequacy for an explication of the concept of truth: p is true if and only if p is universally believed. We would reject the criterion at once on the ground that we understand the meaning of " true " pre-analytically with sufficient clarity to see that " true " and " universally believed " need not have the same extension. It is pre-analytically evident that " p is true " does not entail anything regarding cognitive attitudes that such-and-such minds may have toward p, although in *saying* " p is true " one *expresses* belief in p. Anybody who adopted that criterion, the Carnapians would surely admit, could not mean by " true " the explicandum in question. This, however, is equivalent to saying that the explicandum is that meaning of " truth " according to which " p is true " does *not entail* that p is universally believed. The analyst specifies his explicandum X by stating entailments " being a case of X entails . . . .". Most criteria of adequacy are nothing else than such pre-analytically evident entailment statements, and hence are necessary propositions. It follows that nothing less than the conventionalist theory of necessary truth (criticized above, Chap. 7) is needed to justify the characterization of criteria of adequacy as " conventions." That it is a matter of convention which necessary propositions containing the explicandum are *selected* as criteria of adequacy, is not denied (cf. below, p. 421).

It ought to be concluded from these considerations that whatever good reasons there may be for a revolutionary theory of entailment as a relation admitting of degrees, the gradualistic character of the concept of analyticity which is defined in terms of the concept of analytic synonymy is not a sufficient reason for it. Nevertheless we shall see in the next chapter, which deals with the problem of reduction of concepts, that a good deal may be said in favor of such a "gradualism." Once the fiction of a "language system" is laid aside, the distinction between necessary truth and empirical truth appears somewhat less than clear-cut. This we have observed on several occasions already, particularly in Chapter 8. The kind of statements which are especially critical for that distinction, and which will occupy our attention in the ensuing chapter, are statements connecting what have been called different "language strata": implications from theoretical constructs to publicly observable things and events, and from publicly observable things and events to private sense data.

CHAPTER 11. *Reduction and Open Concepts*

A. Probabilistic Reduction

SINCE the time when Carnap published his classical contribution to the analysis of scientific language, "Testability and Meaning" (TM) (*Philosophy of Science*, 1936-37), it has come to be widely recognized among philosophers of science that explicit definition of theoretical concepts on the basis of "observables" is not possible, at least not within the framework of extensional logic. In TM Carnap initially explained the need for a different type of meaning-specification, viz. introduction of new descriptive terms by means of *reduction sentences*, in connection with the problem of defining dispositional predicates, like "soluble." His argument was that if an explicit definition of dispositional predicate "*P*," of the form: $Px = (t)(\text{if } Qx, t, \text{ then } Rx, t)$, where Q is a test operation and R the corresponding test result, is used, one is faced with the para-doxical consequence that "*P*" would be predicable of anything that is never subjected to the test operation. If instead a reduction sentence of the form: $(t)(x)(\text{if } Qx, t, \text{ then } (Px \text{ if and only if } Rx, t))$, is used, this paradox—e. g. a piece of iron is soluble in water pro-vided it is never immersed in water—is avoided; this was one of Carnap's chief reasons for developing the theory of reduction sentences. But since the mentioned paradox merely arises from the interpretation of "if-then" in the sense of material implication, Carnap's argument is not conclusive. For one might argue that reduction sentences need to be used only as long as one fails to analyze the meaning of "if-then" involved in conditionals expressing causal connections (synthetic "nomological" conditionals). As among others Reichenbach has emphasized, one of the criteria of adequacy of an analysis of nomological implication is just that the falsehood of the antecedent should not entail the truth of the implication. In view of this objection, it would be a pity if TM should have conveyed the impression that the mentioned " paradox of material implication " (a false proposition materially implies any proposition) is the basic reason, or even the only reason, for using reduction sentences to specify the meanings of theoretical terms, such as dispositional predicates, that do not designate directly observable qualities. It is conceivable that once we have a correct analysis of nomological implication [1] we could analyze dispositional predicates such as " soluble," " fragile," in terms of nomological implications, or sets of such, connecting test operations and test results, and thus could revert from reduction sentences to explicit definitions. Carnap's argument from the paradox of material implication establishes no more than that reduction sentences are needed if the language employed for " logical reconstruction " is extensional and thus suffers from the shortcoming that no causal statements of ordinary language and scientific language are translatable into it; and in such a language one had better not attempt to talk about dispositions and causal connections in the first place. However, there is an argument in favor of such *incomplete* meaning specification of theoretical terms—the meaning of " P " is defined by the above reduction sentence only relative to test condition Q—which does not rest on the preference for an extensional interpretation of " if-then."

Let " C," suggesting "construct," stand for a predication of a theoretical construct, like " at time t, electrical current of intensity I flowed through this wire," and " if Q_i, then R_i " for some conditional of the language of observables (e. g. " if at t this wire is connected with an ammeter, the pointer of the ammeter will be deflected at t so-and-so much ") in terms of which it is tested. It is tempting to construe some such conditional as a definition of the construct, and in this way to achieve an easy translation of the construct language into the language of observables. This kind of logical reconstruction—" naive phenomenalism," as we might call it— is surely inadequate, since a) it would be perfectly gratuitous to select this rather than that test-conditional for purposes of definition, b) the

---

[1] Whether such an analysis can be given in an extensional language is a question beyond the scope of this discussion. I have dealt with it in the articles " Reduction Sentences and Disposition Concepts " (*The Philosophy of Rudolf Carnap*, ed. P. A. Schilpp, forthcoming) , " Extensional Logic and Laws of Nature" (*Proceedings of the Second International Congress for Philosophy of Science*, Zürich, 1954) , " Disposition Concepts and Extensional Logic " (*Minnesota Studies in Philosophy of Science*, 2, 1958) ; and in my book *Analytische Erkenntnistheorie* (Vienna, 1955) , esp. chap. IV, C.

meaning of a given construct can hardly be exhausted even by a finite set of such conditionals. Since nevertheless empiricists would not abandon the idea of reducing in some sense the language of constructs to the language of observables, the distinction was made between a *closed* and an *open* reduction: if no *C*-statement strictly follows from ever so large a set of experimental data (in line with the idea that a hypothesis predicating a construct can only be confirmed, not completely verified) and no finite set of such conditionals, therefore, can be construed as a *translation* of the *C*-statement, at least any *C*-statement entails an unlimited set of such test conditionals (let us call them " *P*-conditionals," the letter " *P* " suggesting " phenomena "). But the crucial issue is not at all whether a *C*-statement is logically equivalent to a finite or to an infinite set of *P*-conditionals. Both positions evidently assume that at least one *P*-conditional is analytically entailed by a *C*-statement, and it is this assumption which even a superficial glance at scientific procedure must lead one to challenge. The challenge is perfectly straightforward: if *C* entailed, say, (if O_1, then R_1), then verification of " O_1 and not-R_1 " would logically compel rejection of *C* as false, even if all the other conditionals entailed by *C* turned out to be true. This surely does not correspond to scientific procedure. What the scientist would do in such a situation is rather to weigh the amount of disconfirmation of *C*, due to the falsification of one consequence, against the amount of confirmation of *C* due to the verification of the other consequences.[2]

The point here emphasized is not the trivial one that in the hypothetical situation just described the experiment corresponding to the first *P*-conditional would be repeated in the hope that either the belief in " O_1 " or the belief in " not-R_1 " would be revealed as an error, experimental or observational. For the argument here is constructed on the assumption that the first *P*-conditional is really false and all the others true. It will no doubt be said, at this point, that the whole difficulty is a spurious one which can be easily resolved by replacing entailment with probability implication: " given *C*, P_1 with probability p, and given P_1, *C* with probability q (where p and q differ as a rule)," is, of course, perfectly compatible with " *C*, but not P_1." Perhaps *probabilistic reductionism*

[2] For an illustration, see below, p. 310.

is a good name for this reconstruction of the language of theoretical constructs, and what seems to augur well for it is that we must resort to it even when we try to translate sentences from the ordinary "thing language," as Carnap calls it, into an artificial sense-data language.[3] In order to deduce from a physical statement conditional predictions of sense data (conditional, that is, upon specified operations of the organism), a number of "normal" physiological and environmental conditions must be assumed: normal visual apparatus, specified conditions of illumination, etc. These normal conditions correspond, to refer back to the attempted reduction of the construct language to the laboratory language of observables, to such states of affairs as establishment of proper connection between wire and ammeter. However, this theory involves a delicate problem which, to my knowledge, has not been squarely faced yet. On the macroscopic level, I can know that given conditions $C_1 \cdots C_{n-1}$, R is not certain, because cases of $C_1 \cdots C_{n-1}$ and not-R (nonfulfillment of condition C_n being responsible for not-R) are *observable*. Of course, it would not be possible to know that these conditions were realized even though the usual result did not occur unless there were *independent* tests for the presence of those conditions. And such independent tests might in turn be described by probability implications connecting physical conditions with sense data. Yet, it is difficult to see how one could even distinguish the cases "given R, C is probable" and "given R, C is certain" unless the meaning of "C" were specified by an analytic equivalence describing what *conclusive* evidence for C would be like. It does not seem sensible to deny that R makes C certain unless one is prepared to specify what data *would* make C certain. It is commonly assumed that, on the level of the thing language at least, meanings are not specified by means of probability implications, but that, on the contrary, a statement of the form "on evidence e, h is probable to degree p" can be significant only if the meanings of "h" and "e" are specified independently.[4] To illustrate: if the statement "if this is a watchdog, he will bark when a stranger approaches the house" is intended as analytic of the meaning of "watchdog," then one will have to conclude with analytic certainty that the term "watchdog" is inapplicable to the animal if the predicted reaction fails to occur.

---

[3] Cf. Lewis, *An Analysis of Knowledge and Valuation*, Bk. II; and sec. *C* below.

[4] See, e.g., D. Rynin, "Probability and Meaning," *Journal of Philosophy* (1947).

If this conditional, however, were a probability implication, one could at best conclude " probably it is not a watchdog," and the question whether the term " watchdog " is finally applicable or not would have to be decided by an independent test. This trend of analysis seems, however, to lead into the following dilemma: since such independent tests (independent, that is, of any observational data) obviously cannot be specified for constructs, we either must abandon the attempt of interpreting the construct language by means of the language of observables, or else we must revise our notion that meanings are not specifiable by probability implications but only by strict entailments.[5] One of the main trends of the following discussion will be the adoption of the latter alternative.

B. *The Method of Open Concepts in Physics*

That a conditional " if *P*, then *Q* " must be devoid of factual content, i. e. such that it could not be contradicted without self-contradiction, if it amounts to a (total or partial) analysis of the meaning of " *P*," is usually taken for granted. Indeed, to say " *Q* forms part of the very meaning of ' *P* ' " seems to be synonymous with saying " to predicate ' *P* ' together with ' non-*Q* ' would be a contradiction in terms." For this reason a phenomenalist who claims that the meaning of a physical statement is to be analyzed in terms of sense-data statements seems to be committed to the view that any physical statement *entails* analytically sense-data statements—although he need not claim that a finite conjunction of such entailed sense-data statements would in turn entail the corresponding physical statement. However, the axiom that to specify the meaning of a term *T* by verbal means is to state a number of strictly analytic implications about *T* cannot stand once we admit the method of

[5] Those readers who keep up with epistemological literature may feel at this point that the ensuing discussion is likely to be a repetition of familiar arguments. For Reichenbach argued long ago, in *Experience and Prediction*, that the logical relation between existential hypotheses and confirming observation sentences is not an equivalence (in fact, Reichenbach denied that even an infinite set of observation sentences is ever equivalent to an existential hypothesis), but a " probability connection," i. e. a mutual probability implication. It seems to me, however, that Reichenbach was unaware of the semantic implications of his theory of probability connection, as evidenced by his rigid adherence to the frequency interpretation of probability. It is in the discussions of these semantic implications that the reader may find some novelty (see esp., sec. D).

reduction sentences as a proper method of meaning specification. Consider a reduction pair: if Q_1, then (if Q_2, then Q_3) ; if Q_4, then (if Q_5, then not-Q_3). As Carnap pointed out (TM, p. 444), such a pair has a factual consequence, viz. not-(Q_1 and Q_2 and Q_4 and Q_5), and therefore must be admitted to have factual content [6] in spite of serving to specify (incompletely) the meaning of " Q_3." Strictly speaking, the (demonstrable) assertion that a reduction pair, and a set of convergent [7] reduction pairs or convergent bilateral reduction sentences (henceforth abbreviated: R_b-sentences) are conjunctions with factual content, does not commit Carnap to the view that each member of such a conjunction is a factual statement, since all that follows is that *at least one* member is factual. But it would be arbitrary to grant factual character to one member of such a set and treat the other as analytic. In fact, it is part of what is meant by a reduction sentence (henceforth abbreviated: R-sentence) that the three predicates involved are logically independent, i. e. none is explicitly definable in terms of the others. We could, of course, arbitrarily designate one member of the pair as a meaning rule and the other member as a factual statement: it is not self-contradictory to suppose that an instance of $Q_1 \cdot Q_2 \cdot -Q_3$ be found if $-Q_3$ can be inferred from $Q_4 \cdot Q_5$, and it is not self-contradictory to suppose that an instance of $Q_4 \cdot Q_5 \cdot Q_3$ be found if Q_3 can be inferred from $Q_1 \cdot Q_2$. But this way of splitting the reduction pair into an empirically refutable factual statement of the object language and a (partial) semantic rule of the metalanguage (with regard to which it does not make sense to speak of " refutation ") , is clearly contrary to the spirit of Carnap's theory of reduction. If so, then the concepts " having factual content " and " being factually empty " which logical empiricists, including Carnap, have always intended as contradictories are not applicable in the original sense to sentences whose predicates are but partially (or " conditionally ") defined; and it is, in that case, misleading to apply the same semantic concepts to such sentences. It is true that Carnap explicitly *extends* the

---

[6] At the present time, Carnap prefers to formulate reduction sentences as " meaning postulates " devoid of factual content, by using the form:

$$- (Q_1 \cdot Q_2 \cdot Q_4 \cdot Q_5) \supset [(Q_1 \supset (Q_2 \supset Q_3) \cdot (Q_4 \supset (Q_5 \supset -Q_3)].$$

For an epistemological discussion of the method of meaning postulates, cf. Chap. 14.

[7] By " convergent " reduction sentences I mean reduction sentences describing alternative tests for the presence of the same property.

meanings of " analytic " and " synthetic " in such a way as to make these semantic concepts applicable to sentences whose predicates admit of reduction but not of explicit definition. Yet, this extension of the meaning of " analytic " is confusing since according to the original meaning of the term it is characteristic of analytic sentences that they are empirically irrefutable, while according to the generalized meaning an analytic sentence may be empirically disconfirmable. This will become clear as we turn our attention to the special case of reduction pairs which Carnap calls " bilateral " reduction sentences.

In the case of an R_b-sentence the " representative " sentence (i. e. sentence representing the factual content) degenerates into $-(Q_1 \cdot Q_2 \cdot Q_1 \cdot -Q_2)$ which is a tautology, and hence this kind of R-sentence is said to be factually empty. Now, this sounds plausible enough if we think of an *isolated* R_b; for to refute $Q_1 \supset (Q_2 \equiv Q_3)$ we require a case of $Q_1 \cdot Q_2 \cdot -Q_3$ or of $Q_1 \cdot -Q_2 \cdot Q_3$, and if the only basis for asserting Q_3 is $Q_1 \cdot Q_2$, and the only basis for asserting $-Q_3$ is $Q_1 \cdot -Q_2$, then neither of those cases can occur. However, Carnap himself recognizes that, apart from the paradox of material implication which precludes explicit definability of disposition concepts in an extensional language, the main reason for using R-sentences is the desire to leave concepts " open " for application in new contexts. Isolated occurrence of a reduction pair or of an R_b-sentence is therefore the exception, and occurrence within a system of convergent R-sentences (converging, that is, to the open concept) is what the very purpose of R-sentences would lead one to expect. As a matter of fact, it would seem that if an R-sentence occurs isolated, like the famous R-sentence for " soluble " and similar R-sentences for dispositional predicates of the qualitative thing language, this indicates that we have to do with a closed concept serving merely the purpose of shorthand, which would be explicitly definable were we only permitted to use the concept of causal implication in the definiens.[8] Carnap sees clearly that what may be called the " systemic " occurrence of R-sentences is the rule, as the following citation shows:

in most cases a predicate will be introduced by either several

---

[8] Nevertheless such an explicit definition could not assume the simple form " $Q_3 = Q_1 \rightarrow Q_2$ " (where " $\rightarrow$ " symbolizes causal implication), for reasons discussed in " Reduction Sentences and Disposition Concepts," and " Disposition Concepts and Extensional Logic," *loc. cit.*

reduction pairs or several bilateral reduction sentences. If a property or physical magnitude can be determined by different methods then we may state one reduction pair or one bilateral reduction sentence for each method. The intensity of an electric current can be measured for instance by measuring the heat produced in the conductor, or the deviation of a magnetic needle, or the quantity of silver separated out of a solution, or . . . We may state a set of bilateral reduction sentences, one corresponding to each of these methods. The factual content of this set is not null because it comprehends such sentences as e. g. 'If the deviation of a magnetic needle is such and such then the quantity of silver separated in one minute is such and such, and vice versa' which do not contain the term 'intensity of electric current,' and which obviously are synthetic [TM, pp. 444-5].

Like a reduction pair, such a set of convergent R_b-sentences is said to have factual content because factual statements not containing the "introduced" term are deducible from it (if the set consists, e. g., of the two R_b-sentences: $Q_1 \supset (Q_2 \equiv Q_3)$, and $Q_4 \supset (Q_5 \equiv Q_3)$, then such a consequence is: $-(Q_1 \cdot Q_2 \cdot Q_4 \cdot -Q_5)$). But it should now be obvious that the "theorem" of the factual emptiness of R_b-sentences holds only for isolated R_b-sentences, and so only for those of them that really involve closed concepts. If "$Q_1 \supset (Q_2 \equiv Q_3)$" is accompanied by "$Q_4 \supset (Q_5 \equiv Q_3)$," it makes good sense to say "even though $Q_1 \cdot Q_2$ was verified, it is probable that $-Q_3$," for this probability judgment could be supported by the evidence $Q_4 \cdot -Q_5$. And since a set of convergent R_b-sentences is never constructed all at once, but, as Carnap himself observes, new R-sentences for the same term are laid down as new discoveries are made, R-sentences are rarely *introduction* sentences at all. Indeed, it is just because the reduced term does have antecedent meaning that an R-sentence can without paradox be said to function both as meaning rule and as expression of an empirical law.

It must be admitted that a scientific language containing reduction sentences, conceived as partial definitions, could be formalized in such a way that the requirement that no empirical propositions should be deducible from definitions (or analytic statements) alone would be satisfied. In the spirit of Bridgman's "different operations define different concepts" one might use different symbols for constructs defined by different R_b-sentences: $Q_1 \supset (Q_2 \equiv Q)$; $Q_4 \supset (Q_5 \equiv Q')$. The extensional equivalence "$Q \equiv Q'$" would then take the place of Carnap's "representative sentence" with factual content: $-(Q_1 \cdot Q_2 \cdot Q_4 \cdot -Q_5)$, but it is not deducible from the conjunction of the R_b-sentences.[9] Yet, if this method were used, one would in effect operate with closed concepts; the only reason for using R-sentences, and not explicit definitions, then, would consist in the "paradoxes" of material implication. Since it is my aim to show that the method of open concepts is appropriate for growing empirical sciences, regardless of whether scientific propositions be expressed in an extensional language or a language containing modal connectives, I shall disregard this way of reconciling R-sentences with the analytic-factual dichotomy.

As an illustration of what is here called "the method of open concepts" consider the following positive R-sentence for the expression "x has a larger mass than y": if equal forces act on x and y (where the equality of the forces may be supposed to be determined independently), then, if the acceleration imparted to x is smaller than the acceleration imparted to y, then x has a larger mass than y. It seems, indeed, strange to say that this sentence (which is a consequence of Newton's second law of motion) serves at once as a partial definition of the expression "x has a larger mass than y" and as formulation of an empirical law that can be used for predictions. And, admittedly, this would be a self-contradictory claim if no independent test for the assertion "x has a larger mass than y" could be specified. But it is of the very essence of an R-sentence that it is only *one of several* R-sentences for the same predicate, and those other members of the same set describe the independent tests. What I predict from the information concerning the state of motion of x_1 and y_1 after they were acted on by equal forces is, for example, that there is a body z such that x_1 will balance $y_1 + z$. One is tempted to object: "Well, you cannot have your cake and eat it too. If the latter statement, concerning the behavior of x_1 and y_1 in a statical experiment, defines the meaning of the expression under discussion, then the first statement, concerning the behavior of x_1 and y_1 in a kinetic experiment, is purely factual and

---

[9] This kind of reconstruction has been suggested to me by Professor H. Mehlberg.

in no sense about the meaning of the expression. You can, indeed, regard both statements ' $\tan(x) = \sin(x)/\cos(x)$ ' and ' $\tan(x) =$ opposite cathete/adjacent cathete ' as definitions of ' $\tan(x)$,' but that is because they are logically equivalent. But our propositions about the comparative masses of x_1 and y_1 are not logically equivalent. From the proposition ' there is a body z such that x_1 balances $y_1 + z$ ' you cannot logically deduce the proposition of kinetics ' if equal (unbalanced) forces act on x_1 and y_1, then x_1 will receive a smaller acceleration than y_1.' If you insist, I shall even permit you to use in one context of inquiry the first proposition as a definition and the second as an empirical law, and in another context the second as a definition and the first as an empirical law; but to say that in one and the same context one and the same proposition is both a definition and an empirical law is just hopeless confusion."

Let us be clear about the implications of this position which *prima facie* looks quite reasonable and clear-headed. The un-doubtedly correct observation that the statical and kinetic proposi-tions cited (which we may think of as being supplemented by corresponding propositions concerning the conditions of equality of two masses) are not logically equivalent implies that the meaning of " larger mass " defined by the first proposition is different from the meaning of " larger mass " defined by the second proposition; so that the *concept of mass* defined by kinetic laws is simply different from the concept of mass defined by static laws. Analogous remarks apply to all quantitative physical concepts which stand in a network of functional relations, i. e. which are such that their values can be determined through alternative routes of measurement. The proposition " if so-and-so much heat per second is generated in an electrical conductor through which current flows, then a magnetic needle near the conductor will undergo such and such a deviation " is factual; therefore the concept of intensity of electric current defined in terms of thermal effects is different from the concept of intensity of electric current defined in terms of magnetic effects. According to a strictly operationist criterion of identity of concepts, then, the physicist is defining a new concept whenever he claims to *redefine* an old concept on the basis of discovery of new laws. But is it just sheer love of ambiguity, then, which induces him to preserve the old terminology and thus to suggest that, e. g., the " thing " which he now measures in terms of molecular velocities is still the same thing as he formerly measured by the mercury thermometer? A more plausible account of scientific procedure would be to say that the scientist deliberately works with *open concepts*, where an open concept is a concept incompletely defined by reduction sentences with predictive content.

In order to clarify the distinction between open and closed concepts, let us explore the alternative interpretations a scientist could give of the following hypothetical situation: a body z_1 is found such that x_1 balances $y_1 + z_1$, and on the basis of this observation the scientist declares that the mass of x_1 is greater than the mass of y_1; but when x_1 and y_1 are successively suspended on a spring scale kept at constant altitude, x_1 produces a smaller deformation of the spring than y_1; and when x_1 and y_1 are acted upon by unbalanced forces which are equal by a statical criterion (they are capable of balancing each other), x_1 accelerates more than y_1. We may assume that this is an anomalous experience in that past experience has shown that determination of comparative masses by static and by kinetic methods lead to consistent results. If the scientist decides to operate with closed concepts and to use either of the statical propositions as an explicit definition of " x has a larger mass than y," then he will regard the surprising outcome of the kinetic experiment as irrelevant to the truth of the proposition " x_1 has a larger mass than y_1." If at another time x_1 should again, as one would expect on the basis of correlations observed in the past, offer more resistance to a change of velocity than y_1, and at still another time the anomalous behavior should be repeated, the scientist may well discontinue altogether operating with the concept of mass, defined as indicated, since it would appear to have lost its *predictive value*: nothing is gained by interpreting the static experiment by saying " x has a larger mass than y " instead of simply reporting bare observations (the lever inclined toward the side where x was placed), if no unique predictions can be derived from such an interpretation. But, of course, to abandon further use of the concept is totally different from rejecting its predication as false or at least improbable. If, on the other hand, the method of reduction or open concepts is used, the following comment on the experimental results would be perfectly in order: " there is no doubt that this beam balance is reliable and that x_1 outweighed y_1 on it; but the results of the other two experiments make it improbable that x_1 has a larger mass than y_1."

As this illustration shows, in using open concepts the scientist operates with a system of convergent reduction sentences (convergent, that is, from different fields of possible experimentation to the same open concept) which check each other. The scientist's use of the *same term* in all these different contexts indicates, not negligent ambiguity which it would be useful to resolve, but his belief in the consistency of such a system of convergent reduction sentences: the system is consistent if it never happens that the reduced term is predicable on the basis of one member of the system and not predicable on the basis of another; or, if the term be a functor, if different members of the system always lead to consistent values of the designated magnitude. We shall see presently that it is in terms of such consistency that the *identity* of open concepts is to be defined.

Carnap points out (TM, p. 449) that what motivates the scientist to specify meanings by reduction sentences instead of laying down explicit definitions is the desire to leave open the field of application of the term beyond the field already investigated. For example, if we laid down an explicit definition by which statements about degrees of temperature are synonymous with statements about reactions of mercury thermometers when brought into contact with the substance to which the degree of temperature is ascribed, we would preclude application of the term "temperature" to, say, the sun. Carnap's technical explanation, however, of the disadvantage of such explicit definitions seems inadequate.

Now we might state one of the following two definitions:

(D_1) $\qquad\qquad\qquad Q_3 = (Q_1 \cdot Q_2)$

(D_2) $\qquad\qquad\qquad Q_3 = (-Q_1 \vee Q_2)$

If c is a point of the undetermined class, on the basis of D_1 '$Q_3(c)$' is false, and on the basis of D_2 it is true. Although it is possible to lay down either D_1 or D_2, neither procedure is in accordance with the intention of the scientist concerning the use of the predicate 'Q_3.' The scientist wishes neither to determine all the cases of the third class positively, nor all of them negatively; he wishes to leave these questions open until the results of further investigations suggest the statement of a new reduction-pair; thereby some of the cases so far undetermined become determined positively and some negatively [*ibid.*].

Carnap's argument is clearly based on the concept of material implication, and thus the impression is again created as though reduction sentences were a temporary device which could be disposed of once we have an analysis of nomological conditionals. However, if a physicist were to lay down the definition " (temp (x, t) $= y°) = if$ a mercury thermometer is brought into contact with x at time t, *then* the top of the mercury will coincide with the mark y at $t + dt$," he would obviously intend " if, then " in the sense of nomological implication. If so, the truth of the implication does not follow from the falsity of the antecedent. If for x we substitute the sun and for t any time at all, the antecedent turns into a description of a physical impossibility. But the physicist would hardly say that therefore the sun has any temperature whatsoever on the basis of this operational definition. Rather he would say it does not make sense to speak of the temperature of the sun in the operationally defined sense.

At any rate, the situation is this: when the physicist speaks of the temperature of the sun, he surely does not mean to predict the result of hypothetical operations with mercury or gas thermometers; this will be admitted regardless of whether or not one holds it to be meaningless to speak of what would happen if such a thermometer were brought into contact with the sun. It follows that if such an operational definition explicates the meaning with which " T " is used in contexts of limited temperature ranges, then in extrapolating beyond those limited ranges one uses the same symbol either *without meaning* or with a *different meaning*. This dilemma becomes especially apparent if we turn from extrapolation to high temperatures to extrapolation to low temperatures, and take a fresh look at the old question of whether it is meaningless to speak of a temperature below the absolute zero. If the operational definition of temperature in terms of the gas thermometer were a true statement of synonymy, then the hypothesis that a substance has a temperature lower than $-273°$ C would assert that if thermal contact were established between the substance and a gas thermometer the latter would be found in a state of negative volume and negative pressure—which is surely nonsense. But on the other hand, strong reasons can be adduced for the meaningfulness of the hypothesis that temperatures lower than the absolute zero occur. It is, after all, a contingent fact that the pressure coefficient (or the coefficient of volume expansion, which has the same value) for gases has the value it has. And at any rate this value (1/273) has been verified only for a limited range of temperature variation. It would seem significant, then, to entertain the possibility that complete shrinkage of a gas has not yet occurred when it reaches −273°C.[10] But then again, one might plausibly argue that in entertaining such a possibility we must be thinking of some other way of measuring temperature than with the gas thermometer as presently calibrated. Therefore a strict operationist who holds, with Bridgman, that different operations define different concepts, would be justified in saying that in the hypothesis " T might sink below the absolute zero " the symbol " T " must have a different meaning than the meaning explicated by the gas laws.

But that this second horn of the dilemma, the view that in extrapolating a physical law beyond the experimental range of its variables we change the meanings of the variables and thus really talk about different physical magnitudes, is no easier to take than the first, it is not difficult to show. Consider the hypothesis about the sun's temperature again. This temperature is usually calculated by means of the Stefan-Boltzman law relating the absolute temperature of a surface to its intensity of heat radiation (I) in conjunction with the law that I is inversely proportional to the square of the distance of the surface from the heat source. That is, after the value of I at the sun's surface has been calculated by means of the latter law, the Stefan-Boltzman law is applied to calculate the value of T at the sun's surface. But as this value of T is outside the range to which the " operational " definition of " T " refers, the " T " in the conclusion of the mathematical deduction has a different meaning from the " T " in the premises (both the proposition of measurement about the temperature of the earth's surface and the

---

[10] We may disregard in this discussion the fact that there would be no gas anyway at such a low temperature, on account of condensation; for the question is what suppositions are *meaningful*, and it is surely meaningful to suppose that a substance could survive the gaseous state at such low temperatures.

Stefan-Boltzman law) of the mathematical deduction. Now, since the terms in the conclusion of a valid argument must have the same meaning which they have in the premises, we are led to this consequence: if the conclusion has any physical significance at all, then it does not follow from the premises which are the sole ground of its credibility!

Our problem, then, is to formulate a criterion of *identity of meaning* of a physical functor in different contexts of application; in other words, a criterion for determining whether a symbol like " *T* " stands for the same physical magnitude in different contexts of application. Carnap's theory of reduction sentences suggests this solution: if the symbol is a " nodal point," to use a suggestive metaphor, of a system of convergent reduction sentences, then it has the same meaning in all the contexts described by the various members of the system, provided the system is consistent. Thus, suppose that on the basis of measurements of the pressure of a thermometric gas we obtain the result: $T(A, t_0) > T(A, t_1)$, and that on the basis of measurements by means of a mercury thermometer we obtain the same result. Then we have confirmed the consistency of the reduction system converging to " *T*," and thus we have (partially) justified our identification of the meanings of " *T* " in these different contexts, or our claim that what is measured by these different methods is the same magnitude. Similarly, if a physicist finds in terms of Mach's action-reaction test (measurement of mutually induced accelerations) that two bodies have equal mass, and subsequently verifies that they produce equal strains on a spring-scale kept at constant height (which proves equality of the gravitational forces acting on the bodies), he confirms the hypothesis that the magnitude measured in these two ways (in terms of impact forces in one experiment, in terms of gravitational forces in the other experiment) is one and the same.

However, the method of extrapolating numerical laws involves the employment of the same physical functor in contexts of *measurement* and in contexts of *calculation*. And how could it be maintained that the functor has the same meaning in the two kinds of contexts? It must be conceded that to say, with Bridgman, that it still has " operational " meaning in the contexts of calculation since calculations, after all, are also operations, is tantamount to reducing the operationist theory of meaning to a truism. Nevertheless, if we closely observe the reasons for which a physicist believes that in calculating the sun's temperature and mass he comes to know the values of the *same magnitude* which is measurable in other contexts (though these calculations cannot be verified by direct measurement), we shall find that the same *criterion of physical consistency* is presupposed. If the extrapolated law leads to consistent calculations, the extrapolation is considered justified, and the variables of the equations are said to represent the same magnitude no matter whether their values can be determined by direct measurement or by calculation only. In this connection it is important to distinguish two kinds of test of a physical equation, which may be called the *correspondence test* and the *consistency test* respectively. The correspondence test of the physical equation $y = f(x)$ consists in the three steps: measurement of x, calculation by means of the equation of the corresponding value of y, measurement of y in order to test the calculation. But if the calculated value of y lies outside the experimental range of y, the correspondence test is obviously unavailable. All that can be done is to determine whether different calculations of y from different bases yield consistent results. Thus the mass of the sun was calculated, in Newtonian astronomy, on the basis of the centripetal acceleration of a revolving planet, according to the equation (deducible from the second law in conjunction with the law of gravitation): $a = G \cdot M/r^2$. Now, it is logically conceivable that as the calculation is repeated on the basis of different values of a and r, corresponding to the different orbits and periods of revolution of the various planets, inconsistent values of M are obtained. If this happened, the law of gravitation would have failed the consistency test (provided, indeed, that the trouble is not blamed on the general laws of motion), and the extrapolation of the concept of mass to celestial bodies would be suspect. If, on the other hand, calculations of M on the basis of optical data, viz. spectral displacements of the light emitted by atoms on the surface of the sun (which according to the general theory of relativity are due to the sun's gravitational field), should corroborate the calculations based on mechanical data, the extrapolation would be further justified. The same holds, of course, for extrapolations to microscopic contexts, as when we speak, e. g., of the mass of an atom, or of an electron (think of the extrapolation of the law of conservation of mechanical energy to the motion of electrons, which led to the calculation of the mass of an electron). The main point is that a concept like mass is, by the physicist, left open not only for further experimental contexts but also for calculational contexts in which no correspondence test is feasible; and that the attribution of an identical property (uniformly called "mass") to bodies outside experimental reach, like the sun or the electron, is justified to the extent that the extrapolation of experimentally confirmed laws survives the described consistency test.[11]

The claim that in a theoretical science the theories themselves are used to define the theoretical concepts and do not forego the status of "factual propositions" because they are (incomplete) definitions, will appear untenable to those who are accustomed to separate factual propositions neatly from definitions and consequences of definitions. But such a bifurcation of scientific discourse becomes untenable once it is recognized that theoretical constructs are implicitly defined by postulates which together with statements connecting some constructs with observables (sometimes called "rules of correspondence") entail empirically testable consequences. For in this conception the postulates of a scientific theory serve the double function of partially defining theoretical constructs and of being instrumental, in cooperation with the rules of correspondence (which may have the form of explicit definitions or of reduction sentences), to prediction of empirical laws and observable facts. To illustrate, consider the kinetic theory of gases. There occur in its postulates the constructs "molecule," "velocity of a molecule," "mass of a molecule," "number of molecules." None of them can be said to be operationally definable. The velocity of a molecule is of course explicitly definable in the usual way, but length of molecular displacement is obviously not definable in terms of measurements of length the way length of displacement of a tennis ball, say, is so definable. Similar comments apply to the other constructs; thus "the volume of this gas consists of n molecules" hardly means "if the molecules were counted—i. e. correlated one by one with the numerals beginning with '1' and taking after each numeral its immediate successor—the correlation would be completed with numeral 'n.'" However, the constructs receive a partial

[11] For further illustrations of the method of open concepts in physics, see my article "Reduction Sentences and Open Concepts," *Methodos*, 5 (1953), from which pp. 313-18 have here been reprinted with kind permission of the editors of *Methodos*.

interpretation in terms of observables as follows. They enter into the explicit definitions of complex constructs which are either directly connected with observables or are connected within the theory with other constructs that are so connected. Thus the instantaneous pressure of the gas against a given area of the containing wall is defined, within the theory, as the number of molecules hitting some point or other within that area at a given instant times the rate of change of momentum undergone by a single molecule as it bounces back from the wall, divided by the area. Since momentum is defined as mass times velocity, it is clear that gas pressure is thus theoretically defined in terms of the constructs in question. But this theoretical definition of gas pressure is supplemented by an operational definition in terms of manometer readings. It is because of this operational definition, of course, that differences in assumptions about average molecular velocities and numbers of molecules entail differences in observational consequences. Since what statements involving the theoretical constructs entail with regard to the domain of observable fact depends on both the logical and mathematical relations of the constructs to other constructs (fixed by the theory) and on the operational definitions, it is clear that the postulates of a partially interpreted deductive theory are both implicit (and incomplete) definitions of the constructs and hypotheses that are indirectly confirmable by observational findings—which is to say that the analytic-synthetic distinction in the usual sense is not applicable at all. Secondly, consider "average kinetic energy of a gas molecule." This again is a complex construct explicitly defined, within the theory, in terms of the primitive constructs. It is connected by a postulate with absolute temperature (the absolute temperature of a gas is proportional to the average kinetic energy of its molecules, i. e. $m\bar{v}^2/2$, where $\bar{v}^2$ is the sum of the squares of all possible molecular velocities divided by n, the number of molecules, and m the mass of a molecule). But absolute temperature is also operationally defined; there is, for example, a rule of correspondence which enables us to deduce from the statement that the absolute temperature of a gas has increased that the mercury in a thermometer in thermal contact with the gas has risen. And such observations are then indirectly relevant to the hypothesis that the average velocity of the gas molecules has increased.

Note that in order for the theory to have empirical content, and thus to deserve to be called " scientific theory " as contrasted with a pure, uninterpreted calculus whose postulates cannot significantly be called true, false or confirmed, it is sufficient that _some_ of its constructs be empirically interpreted; by calling it partially interpreted we mean that not all of the theoretical terms are directly connected with observables by rules of correspondence.[12] Further, even what we ourselves have called, following prevailing terminology, an operational definition of a physical magnitude is not a complete interpretation in terms of operations of measurement. It consists only of a finite set of rules for translating comparative or metrical statements about ,the magnitude into the language of laboratory observations, but the variable which is chosen to represent the magnitude ranges over infinitely many real numbers, and to the difference between many of these values (e. g. an irrational number and a rational number which is a very close approximation to it) no observational difference can correspond at all.

Now, in terms of this conception of physical magnitudes as non-operationally defined within the theory in terms of mathematical relations to other physical magnitudes (illustrated above in terms of the kinetic theory of gases) it is easy to define what is meant by saying that a quantity which is only computable with the help of theories and a quantity which is directly measurable are yet values of one and the same physical magnitude, like " mass " or " temperature " or " length ": it means that the mathematical relations of the functor to other physical functors, expressed by the equations of the theory, are the same. If we follow H. Margenau's terminology in calling these equations, like the equation linking temperature to kinetic energy, or the equation linking mass to force and acceleration, " constitutive " definitions of the magnitudes in question, we may say that the functor has the same constitutive definition, and in that sense the same " meaning," whether or not the statement applying it to a particular body or space-time region is such that

---

[12] On partial interpretation of a scientific theory, see Carnap, " Foundations of Logic and Mathematics," _International Encyclopedia of Unified Science, 1_ (no. 3) ; " The Methodological Character of Theoretical Concepts," in _Minnesota Studies in Philosophy of Science, 1_ (1956) ; Hempel, " Fundamentals of Concept Formation in Empirical Science," _International Encyclopedia of Unified Science, 2_, no. 7; H. Margenau, _The Nature of Physical Reality_, New York, 1950; R. B. Braithwaite, _Scientific Explanation_, Cambridge, 1953 (esp. chaps. I-III) .

it could be *directly* inferred with the help of a rule of correspondence from statements describing observations. In this sense of "meaning" (conceptual meaning, if you wish), "mass" means the same in "mass of an electron," "mass of the sun," and "mass of a brick."

The most important result of these considerations for our topic is this: since it is the laws or theories themselves which, jointly with rules of correspondence of whatever form, determine the meanings of theoretical terms, it is hopeless to try to reconstruct a scientific theory dualistically as a system of statements some of which are analytic and some of which have factual content. Take, for example, the equation relating the average velocity of the molecules to the absolute temperature of the gas. Since temperature is measurable independently of any assumptions about the micro-states of a gas (or a body in any state of aggregation), there is, as it were, independent access to this variable, and it is therefore wrong to say the equation in question is purely analytic, just an explicit definition of temperature in terms of micro-magnitudes. The equation definitely is " in principle falsifiable " by experience: if Boyle's law, for example, should be refuted by future measurements (even as an approximative law), the physicist *might* decide to give up this equation and to retain the other assumptions of the kinetic theory. On the other hand, the equation fixes conceptual meanings of theoretical quantitative terms in the manner of a postulate, and is in that sense "analytic." The point is that the analytic-synthetic distinction in the usual sense is not applicable at all.[13]

C. Reduction of Thing Language to Sense-data Language (Phenomenalism)

Let us now turn to the qualitative thing language and see whether a similar method of open concepts prevails on this level of language. Thanks to the clear discussion of the logical relations between statements in the thing language and statements in the sense-data language by C. I. Lewis, R. Chisholm, and R. Firth,[14] the central

[13] This is lucidly argued also by Hempel, in " A Logical Appraisal of Operationism," *Scientific Monthly* (Oct. 1954).

[14] Cf. R. Chisholm, " The Problem of Empiricism," *Journal of Philosophy, 19* (1948); C. I. Lewis, " Professor Chisholm and Empiricism," *ibid.*; R. Firth, " Radical Empiricism and Perceptual Relativity," *Philosophical Review* (April and July, 1950).

issue can be formulated without many preliminaries. In criticizing Lewis' form of phenomenalism, as carefully expounded in *An Analysis of Knowledge and Valuation*, Bk. II, Chisholm advanced the argument from perceptual relativity. Let "*P*" stand for the statement "this is an apple" and "*S*" for the sense-data conditional: "if sense-data of biting in region *R* (in perceptual space) occur, then in all probability an apple-like [15] taste sensation will occur." Lewis' form of phenomenalism may be illustrated by the assertion that *P* entails *S*. The qualification "in all probability" is inserted in order to take account of abnormal conditions (e. g., insensitivized organs of taste, when the organism suffers from a cold) which might disrupt the sequence of sense-data even though *P* is true. Chisholm, now, challenges the claim that *P* entails *S* as follows: It is conceivable that abnormal conditions (*C*) should exist very frequently such that even the less than 100 per cent correlation asserted by *S* would fail to hold even though *P* is true. Substitute, for example, for "*C*," "the person who bites into the apple suffers from a continuous cold insensitivizing his taste organs." The proposition "*P* and not-*S*," therefore, might conceivably be true, and this possibility contradicts the entailment asserted by Lewis. Lewis counters Chisholm's argument by pointing out that the alleged inconsistency is always verbal, on account of the ambiguity of probability statements like *S*, i. e. the evidence relative to which the correlation of apple-biting and apple-like taste is probable is different from (in fact, incompatible with) the evidence relative to which the correlation is improbable. Thus the consequents of the conditionals "if *P*, then *S*" and "if *P* and *C*, then not-*S*" are only verbally contradictories. Firth argues, successfully I think, that Lewis' reply to the argument from perceptual relativity fails (mainly because in order to complete the probability statements Lewis has to introduce *physical* terms into their antecedents) although it is a step in the right direction. Firth grants Lewis the point that acceptance of the facts of perceptual relativity does not convict the phenomenalist of inconsistency and that the appearance of inconsistency is due to ambiguity, but he differs from Lewis in locating the ambiguity elsewhere, viz. in the physical statement *P*. That "this is an apple" entails *S*

---

[15] This circumlocution must be employed because the sense-data language contains no predicate which designates the taste without referring to the kind of object with which the taste is normally associated.

would, indeed, be perfectly consistent with " this is an apple, and not-*S*," if " apple " were used in different senses, and Firth argues that this is the case.

At this point a presupposition will be challenged which all the parties to the dispute share, viz. that if phenomenalism is an analysis, or program of analysis, of the meanings of physical statements, then physical statements must *analytically entail* sense-data statements in a sense in which analytical entailment is sharply contrasted with factual implication. But let us first see whether Firth's theory of ambiguity is really plausible within the framework of this common presupposition. The question is how the phenomenalist claim that *P* entails *S*, along with *S'*, *S''*, etc. can be reconciled with the fact that the phenomenalist hesitates to reject *P* even though *S* turned out to be false owing to such abnormal conditions as a prolonged lack of coordination of visual and tactual sense, insensitivized taste organs, etc. Firth's solution is that when we say " still, *P* must be true," we are really defending a different, though closely related, proposition *P'*, defined by *S'*, *S''*, etc. but not entailing *S*; and in defending *P'* we express our expectation that *S'*, *S''*, etc. will remain true even though *S* failed. The context of Firth's discussion makes it clear that a psychological criterion of entailment is tacitly adopted: to say that sentence *P* entails *S* would seem to mean that *P* is associated with a *firm expectation* of the high correlation asserted by *S*.[16] Indeed, it should be obvious that " entailment " could not, in a discussion of this kind, designate the formal concept employed in formal logic. If we had definitions (explicit or contextual) of the predicates of the thing language in terms of expressions of the sense-data language, we could, relative to those definitions, speak of a *formal* entailment from *P*-statements to *S*-statements. But such reductive definitions, which the phenomenalist claims can be constructed in principle, would first have to be shown to be adequate explications of the meanings of physical statements; hence, it would be circular to operate with a formal concept of entailment in this context.[17] But once it is realized that the proposition expressed by

[16] " In the extreme case . . . we should have *all* the expectations expressed by *P* *except* the one expressed by *S*. And if we were to express these expectations in physical language, we should do so by asserting a physical statement which is, we may say, ' closely related ' to *P*—in this case a statement which is identical in meaning with *P* except that it does not entail *S* " (*Philosophical Review*, July 1950, p. 321.)

[17] Cf. my *Elements of Analytic Philosophy*, chap. 17, e, and this book, below, Chap. 13.

a *P*-sentence is altogether a function of the expectations associated with the latter, Firth's theory of ambiguity becomes subject to psychological tests. Suppose that a person with originally normal coordination of visual and tactual sense has developed firm perceptual habits, as they may be called, by virtue of which a visual sense datum (S_v) stimulates expectation of a tactual sense datum (S_t) but that he then suffers a brain injury which destroys the coordination. And let conditional predictions of S_t and S_v be members of the family of *S*-conditionals entailed by *P*. Does the psychological evidence at all warrant Firth's assertion that from the time when S_t fails to be correlated with S_v, the sentence *P*, whose vocal or subvocal utterance we may suppose to be caused by S_v, will fail to be associated with an expectation of S_t? Or, to repeat the illustration used above, we all know that when we suffer from an acute cold our sense of taste is numbed, so that in this abnormal condition the usual correlation between visual and taste sensations fails; but don't we nevertheless continue to expect the corresponding taste sensations?

A further objection to Firth's theory of ambiguity arises from a consideration of the *social tests* for *P*-statements which, strangely, are nowhere mentioned in his discussion. Suppose that, biting into what looks like a lemon and failing to experience a sour taste, I am utterly baffled because, as it is the first time I suffered from a severe cold, I have had no opportunity yet to learn from experience that there is a correlation between severe colds and insensitivized taste organs. What I would undoubtedly do in order to find out whether it is nonetheless a real lemon, is to gather the testimony of other observers regarding its taste. Now, according to Firth's theory, when I say " still, it is a lemon," the word " lemon " does not refer to the lemon-like taste at all. But how can this account be reconciled with the fact that the evidence which led me to make this assertion consisted of other people's reports about their taste sensations? The reply might be made that in the new usage of " lemon," " *S* " is replaced by a similar sense-data conditional referring to the correlation of biting and tasting as experienced by other people. But as one, notoriously, cannot perceive other people's sense data, such statements would not belong to a pure sense-data language at all (personal pronouns denote logical constructions, according to phenomenalism!) and the translation of the *P*-statement into predictions of sense data would have come to naught.

In the light of what has been said about the psychological meaning of "entailment," it should not be difficult to see what is wrong with the mentioned presupposition "shared by all the parties to the dispute." No opponent of phenomenalism denies that sense data (or, if this term have misleading connotations, perceptions) constitute the ultimate *evidence* for or against *P*-statements; what he denies is that the *meaning* of a *P*-statement could be expressed in sense-data language.[18] Presumably he holds, then, that any implication from a *P*-statement to an *S*-statement is a *factual* implication, like an implication from a statement describing a mental state to a statement describing a form of behavior that is symptomatic of that mental state (e. g. "if a man feels hot, then he wears light clothes"). The phenomenalist who attempts to answer the argument from perceptual relativity is not just defending the claim that *P*-statements *imply* *S*-statements but that they analytically entail the latter.[19] But *is there a safe behavioristic criterion for distinguishing factual implication from analytic entailment?* Suppose that the sour taste I experience when I bite into a lemon inevitably causes me to shudder. Could it not, in that case, be argued with equal plausibility that in saying "there is a lemon" I express my expectation that if I were to bite into it I would shudder as that if I were to bite into it I would taste a sour taste? If so, just what would be the intended distinction if one maintained "if I bite into *x*, then I shall taste a sour taste" is a *logical* consequence of "*x* is a lemon" while "if I bite into *x*, then I shall shudder" is only a *factual* consequence of the same *P*-statement? It would seem, then, that the entire contrast between what *P*-statements analytically entail (not by virtue of explicitly formulated definitions, be it noted again, but by virtue of habits of expectation) and what they factually imply, lacks a clear meaning; and it is therefore idle to dispute

[18] For some philosophers, indeed, the repudiation of phenomenalism means the repudiation of the thesis that *P*-statements are equivalent to *finite* conjunctions of *S*-statements (cf. for example, P. Marhenke, "Phenomenalism," in *Philosophical Analysis*, ed. M. Black). But this is not the kind of phenomenalism here under discussion. The issue discussed by Lewis, Chisholm, and Firth is whether even a single *S*-statement could be said to be entailed by a *P*-statement.

[19] ". . . we are concerned only with an experimental situation in which a *logical* consequence of *P* is thought to have been refuted. The phenomenalist can consistently admit, of course, that *P* might be saved if any of its supposed *natural* consequences were refuted" (Firth, *loc. cit.*, p. 326).

the question whether the argument from perceptual relativity refutes or is consistent with phenomenalism. The *R*-sentences connecting physical predicates with sense-data predicates are probabilistic; and if the physical predicates are not *completely defined*, the question whether the *S*-statement is an analytic or a factual consequence of the *P*-statement has no meaning. To add an illustration: the statement that a physical object x is red implies with probability that a sense datum of looking at x is accompanied by a red sense datum. It is obvious that the latter *S*-statement is implied only with probability by "x is red," since various organic and environmental conditions must be fulfilled if an objectively red thing is to appear red. Suppose, now, that the question were raised of whether "a sense datum of looking at x is probably accompanied by a red sense datum" follows *analytically* from "x is red." The question evidently presupposes that there is a complete analysis of "x is red" relative to which the *S*-statement either is or is not formally deducible from "x is red"; but this presupposition is unfounded.

D. *Degrees of Meaning*

It should be obvious that a semantic analysis of natural languages cannot abstract from the *pragmatic* dimension of semiotic situations; if "meaning" refers to psychological or behavioral dispositions of sign-users and sign-interpreters, it stands for a three-termed relation involving sign, designatum, and *interpreter* (the locus of what C. W. Morris calls the "interpretant," i. e. the disposition to take account of the designatum, which is actualized by the perception of the sign). While this may be a commonplace, I doubt whether its implications have been sufficiently realized by philosophical analysts of natural language. One of its implications is that the concepts "*L*-consequence" and "*F*-consequence" which are relative to a formalized language with explicitly formulated semantic rules cannot be applied in the semantic-pragmatic analysis of a natural language.[20] In view of what might be called the "intensional vague-

---

[20] Morris' characterization of *descriptive semantics* as the empirical study of the semantic rules governing signs in actual use which *abstracts from the pragmatic dimension* of semiosis is highly confusing; especially considering that on the very same page on which he says that semantics abstracts from pragmatics, he also says that semantic rules ". . . are not ordinarily formulated by the users of a language . . . they exist rather as habits of behavior"! (*Foundations of the Theory of Signs*, p. 23).

ness " of most descriptive terms, i. e., the flexibility of habits of application with regard to them, consisting in uncertainty as to exactly which properties a thing must have in order for the term to be applicable to it, it is advisable to introduce a comparative (not necessarily metrical) concept of *degree of meaning* into the semantic-pragmatic analysis of natural language; and a gradation of the concept of meaning entails of course a corresponding gradation of the concept " analytic statement." If " S " represents a declarative sentence and " p " a state of affairs, then degree of meaning p is related to reluctance of withdrawing S after an assertion of S as follows: the greater the degree to which " S " means p, the smaller the reluctance with which " S " will be withdrawn (or " not-S " will be asserted) in case p is disbelieved as a result of subsequent observations. To illustrate, consider the following possible properties of a chair: (a) having at least three legs, (b) capable of seating just one person, (c) having a back. Correspondingly let us construct the functions: " chair " means (for a fixed individual) (a) to degree x; " chair " means (b) to degree y; " chair " means (c) to degree z. I would conjecture that x is the highest and z the lowest degree. In that case the reluctance with which a person will call an object " chair " if he believes it to lack (a) is greater than the reluctance with which he will call it " chair " if he believes it to lack (b), and still greater than the reluctance with which he will apply the word to a thing he believes to lack (c).[21]

According to this conception, to ascribe a certain meaning to a descriptive term (and derivatively to a descriptive sentence) is to ascribe to the users of the term a certain *disposition* with regard

[21] The present suggestion of replacing the dichotomous concept of meaning underlying the analytic-synthetic dichotomy, with a continuum of degrees of meaning, was anticipated long ago by Max Black, in his study " Vagueness," in *Philosophy of Science*, 1937. He there attempted to generalize the laws of logic (specifically, the law of the excluded middle) so as to make them applicable to vague predicates. In order to do so, he replaces the function " L is applicable to x " with the more complicated function " L is applicable to x with degree m/n " which is defined as follows: the limit approached by the ratio of the number of applications of L to x (m) to the number of applications of non-L to x (n) as the number of discriminations of x with respect to L and the number of observers increases indefinitely, is m/n. This gradation of the relation of *denotation* (application) naturally suggests a similar gradation of the relation of *connotation*. For a similar approach to the semantic analysis of empirical class terms, see A. Kaplan and F. Schott, " A Calculus for Empirical Classes," *Methodos* (1951).

to its application. The above analysis in terms of a person's reluctance to withdraw a claim when faced with apparently disconfirming evidence can easily be reformulated in terms of dispositions of people to apply a term to an object x if they believe x to have such and such properties. In an attempt to dispel the skepticism entertained by Quine and others towards the possibility of giving a verifiable sense to statements about " intensions," Carnap has recently [22] suggested the following tentative analysis of " intension ": F is the intension of " Q " for $X =_{df} X$ has the disposition to (apply " Q " to an object y if and only if y has property F). This is similar to the above analysis, except that beliefs are not mentioned. But it is easy to show that ". . . if and only if y has property F " should be replaced by ". . . if and only if X believes that y has property F." [23] For people may misclassify things because they make false judgments about their properties while making no mistakes about the conventional meanings of the predicates they apply to them. Thus I may apply the word " sugar " to salt, not because I think " sugar " means salt, but because I expect the white and granular substance before me to taste sweet. If the statement " ' sugar ' means for me sugar " [24] entailed that I apply the word " sugar " to a thing y only if y is sugar, then I could not make this sort of mistake. Let us take a close look, now, at the statement: X applies the word " sugar " to y if and only if he believes that y is sugar. What sort of connection is meant by " if and only if " ? Since, as we have pointed out,[25] an extensional explicit definition of disposition concepts is not possible, it cannot mean material equivalence. Take, for instance, any two empty predicates like " unicorn " and " goblin," and assume that X does not believe that there are unicorns or that there are goblins. Then " unicorn " and " goblin " would have the same intension for X if the " if and only if " of the definiens of our contextual definition of " intension " meant material equiva-

---

[22] " Meaning and Synonymy in Natural Language," *Philosophical Studies* (April 1955).

[23] This is recognized by Carnap, in " On Some Concepts of Pragmatics," a reply to Chisholm's " A Note on Carnap's Meaning Analysis," both in *Philosophical Studies* (Dec. 1955).

[24] Notice that this semantic statement is not a tautology. It only looks like a tautology, because both metalanguage and object language happen to be English. Nobody would suppose that the translation of it into, say, a German metalanguage is tautologous: " ' sugar ' bedeutet fuer mich Zucker."

[25] See the references given in p. 303 n.

lence. It cannot mean logical equivalence either, for a statement of logical equivalence is L-determinate (cf. above, Chap. 5, D) whereas statements of the form " F is the intension of ' Q ' for X " are factual. Besides, how could the assumption that X believes that y has property F *logically entail* that X applies this rather than that word to y? Which word X will apply depends not only on his beliefs but also on his linguistic training—apart from the consideration that a person may hold a belief which he is capable of expressing verbally without *actually* so expressing it. Is X's belief that y has F, then, a *causally sufficient* condition for his applying " Q " to y, if " Q " means F for X? Obviously not. At least certain stimulus-conditions must be fulfilled if X is to apply " Q " to y, e. g. that X is asked to characterize y. Further, X must be motivated to be truthful, he must not be afraid to say what he believes, etc. It should be obvious that there is no psychological law to the effect that whenever a person believes that a given object y has a given property F and is stimulated in a particular way, then he will utter a particular sentence, say " y is F "; nor is there a law that would justify the assignment of maximum probability to a hypothesis about a belief of a person on the evidence of a particular linguistic response of that person. But if so, then the defined concept of intension would be empty if the " if-then " of the definiens meant a strictly causal implication.[26] In order to get a practically applicable concept of intension, we should mitigate the requirements and require only a reasonably high *probability implication* from the existence of a belief together with the occurrence of a suitable stimulus (such as a question) to the occurrence of a linguistic response, and conversely. Meaning would then be explicated as a disposition whose degrees are measured by the degrees of the corresponding probability implications. Thus, if from the fact that X applies the word " lemon " to y we can infer with high probability that X believes that y tastes sour, then we can say " lemon " means that sense-quality for X to a high degree. We cannot, then, significantly ask whether the implication " if A is a lemon, then

---

[26] It would be a mistake to suppose that the above considerations merely establish that hypotheses about intensions could not be conclusively verified if the definiens were meant as a strictly causal implication (or equivalence). For if a defining causal implication does not hold for any values of the free variables of the definiens, then the defined disposition concept is not applicable to any ordered set of values of the free variables of the definiendum.

A tastes sour " is analytic or synthetic for *X*; this question pre-supposes that we can apply a dichotomous concept of meaning to natural language.[27] The question is to be replaced by the in prin-ciple decidable question to what *degree* the implication is analytic for *X*.

This gradation of the concept of meaning seems to be implicit in the method of meaning specification by reduction sentences, though Carnap never drew this consequence. For a systemic reduction sentence (cf. p. 308) for a predicate " Q_3 " does not formulate a precise truth condition for sentences of the form " Q_3x." We cannot say that by virtue of " $Q_1 \supset (Q_3 \equiv Q_2)$ " the directly verifiable con-junction " $Q_1 \cdot Q_2$ " expresses a sufficient condition for " Q_3," and the directly verifiable conjunction " $Q_1 \cdot -Q_2$ " a sufficient condition for " $-Q_3$," in the sense that such observations would justify the respective conclusions no matter what else may be observed. For, as was explained, the possibility that the system of reduction sen-tences is inconsistent cannot be precluded a priori. Suppose that the above reduction sentence is accompanied by " $Q_4 \supset (Q_3 \equiv Q_5)$." Then we may say that $Q_1 \cdot Q_2$ entails Q_3 [28] to the degree that, having verified $Q_1 \cdot Q_2$, we would be reluctant to withdraw Q_3 in the face of the observational evidence $Q_4 \cdot -Q_5$. Being asked what he means by the construct " Q_3," the scientist who operates with open concepts could do no better than specify the various *degrees of entailment* (or " weights," if this term be preferred) from the various reduction bases to the construct in question.

It has been argued that a semiotics that takes proper account of the openness of descriptive concepts should replace the dichotomous concepts of meaning and analyticity by comparative, if not neces-sarily metrical, concepts. Since C. W. Morris, a noted pioneer in semiotics, has attempted to define analyticity in behavioristic terms as a dichotomous concept, it may not be amiss to show how his attempt fails. Morris defines " analytic implicate " as a dyadic rela-tion between signs (not propositions or concepts, nonsemiotically conceived), in terms of a concept of " degree of generality " which in turn is based on the concept " sufficient condition ":

[27] By " dichotomous concept " I mean the same as Carnap means by " classificatory concept " (see *Logical Foundations of Probability*, § 1). My term seems to me more suggestive.

[28] For the sake of typographical convenience, the predicates are used to represent the atomic statements in which they might occur.

Degree of generality is a matter of the interrelationship of significata. "Colored" is more general than "red" since the conditions for something being a denotatum of "red" are sufficient to insure that that something meets the conditions for being a denotatum of "colored," while the significatum of "colored" is such that it can denote something without "red" denoting it. A sign which is more general than another sign, or of equal generality with it, is an *analytic implicate* of the other sign; in this sense "colored" is an implicate of "red" [*Signs, Language, and Behavior*, p. 22].

The basic term, used to define other semiotic terms but itself undefined, is "sufficient condition." What does Morris mean by the sentence "the conditions for something being a denotatum of 'red' are sufficient to insure that that something meets the conditions for being a denotatum of 'colored'"? We can simplify this sentence in terms of Morris' explanations, given elsewhere, that "conditions determining the denotation of predicate 'P'" means the same as "property designated by 'P'" and that "x is a denotatum of 'P'" means the same as "'P' is predicable of x." We thus obtain "'x is red' expresses a sufficient condition for what is expressed by 'x is colored.'" But since Morris nowhere indicates his intention to depart from the ordinary usage of "sufficient condition," we must assume that this is in turn simply a more elaborate way of saying "for any x, if x is red, then x is colored." A simple if-then statement, however, does not *assert* an analytic or logical implication (it is not a modal statement, in other words, although it might be made the subject of a true modal statement). Morris' definition of "analytic implicate," therefore, is either circular, viz. in case "sufficient condition" is intended in the narrower sense of "logically sufficient condition," or else it is too wide, in effect simply a definition of "implicate" which would fit if for "red" and "colored" we substituted logically independent predicates such that the extension of the first is part of the extension of the second. The reader can easily convince himself that the same criticism applies to the semiotic explication of L-implication given by Morris later in his book, in the chapter on "Formators and Formative Discourse" (sec. 4): "Formative ascriptors which denote if their antecedent ascriptors denote will be called *analytic*." This somewhat cryptic definition seems to imply that formative ascriptors are conditional sentences (otherwise " antecedent " would be obscure), and although not all ascriptors, in Morris' terminology, are declarative sentences, an application of the definition to this subclass of ascriptors yields the following consequence: if " if p, then q " is true provided that " p " is true, then " if p, then q " is analytic. But actually the definiens " if p, then (if p, then q) " only implies the *truth* of " if p, then q," not its analyticity. In order to make it imply " $p \dashv q$ " (using Lewis' symbol of strict or analytic implication), the definiens would have to be changed to " $p \dashv (p \supset q)$ "; but thus the definition would be saved at the cost of circularity.

E. *The Physicalistic Reduction*

In section A of this chapter it was pointed out that the chief reason given in TM for the use of R-sentences instead of explicit definitions was the paradox of material implication according to which any conditional statement, interpreted as a material implication, is true if its antecedent is false. It may not be wasted effort to remind the reader why this is a poor argument in support of the method of reduction sentences. It is a commonplace by now that the meaning of " if-then " in a counterfactual statement of the kind " if this piece of sugar were immersed in water, then it would dissolve " is not the meaning of " $\supset$ " (the sign for material implication), since on this extensional analysis *any* counterfactual conditional would be true just by virtue of being counterfactual. Hence, as was stated at the beginning of this chapter, Carnap's argument merely proves the indispensability of R-sentences in a language of logical reconstruction which suffers from the shortcoming that no causal statements of ordinary and scientific language are translatable into it; and in such a language we had better not attempt to talk about dispositions and causal connections in the first place. But unfortunately Carnap's various statements about reducibility and definability in connection with the physicalism issue do not even possess the virtue of consistency. In TM there is a passage which makes it sufficiently clear that the reason why Carnap asserts physicalism only in the sense of reducibility of psychological terms to terms of the physical language, not in the sense of translatability from one language to the other, is again the paradox of material implication. For "positivism," in the older form maintained in the *Logische Aufbau* where it was argued that physical statements are logically equivalent to conjunctions, whether finite or infinite, of sense-data statements, is rejected on the following ground: the analysans of the analyzed physical statement, like "there is a table in this room at time t," would be a conjunction of formal implications of the form "$(x) [Px \supset Qx]$," where the antecedent describes a perceptual operation, like looking in a given direction, and the consequent a resulting sense impression. But each of these conjuncts would be true if there were no values satisfying their antecedents, i. e. if there were no observers around performing the relevant perceptual operations, in which case the analysans would be true, even though the analyzed physical proposition might be clearly false (cf. TM, pp. 464-6). As may be expected, Carnap applies the same argument, *mutatis mutandis*, to the thesis of physicalism by saying: "Here a remark analogous to that about positivism has to be made. We may assert reducibility of the terms, but not—as was done in our former publications—definability of the terms and hence translatability of the sentences" (*ibid.*, p. 467).

As we turn, however, to the admirably concise statement of Carnap's views about the language of science in *Logical Foundations of the Unity of Science*, we find that the argument in favor of physicalistic reducibility, in contrast to translatability, is by no means equally clear (the TM argument is, for the reason stated, unconvincing, but it has the virtue of clarity). I quote the key passage in which Carnap states his reason for denying definability ("definability" is used as a synonym for "translatability"):

Let us take as an example the term "angry." If for anger we knew a sufficient and necessary criterion to be found by a physiological analysis of the nervous system or other organs, then we could define "angry" in terms of the biological language. The same holds if we knew such a criterion to be determined by the observation of the overt, external behavior. But a physiological criterion is not yet known. And the peripheral symptoms known are presumably not necessary criteria because it might be that a person of strong self-control is able to suppress these symptoms. If this is the case, the term "angry" is, at least at the present time, not definable in terms of the biological language.

It is clear that a behavioristic necessary and sufficient criterion of anger, which Carnap rightly says is not known (suggesting moreover a reason for holding such a criterion to be impossible), would be described by a stimulus-response sentence, the customary form of behavioristic operational definitions. So, a *definition* of anger in terms of behavioristic concepts would take the form: angry (x, t) $\equiv [S(x, t) \supset R(x, t)]$, where the antecedent of the definiens describes a stimulation of organism x, and the consequent describes the resultant response. The term " angry," indeed, is ambiguous in that it sometimes refers to an introspectable feeling and sometimes to a temporarily unactualized disposition to such mental states: " he got me so angry that I felt like knocking him down " illustrates the first usage and " you'd better not speak to him now while he is still angry at you " illustrates the second usage, since the speaker only predicts that a feeling of anger would be produced by appropriate stimuli (such as seeing, or being reminded of, the object of anger) without implying that the person even thinks of the object of his anger at the present moment (and one could hardly feel angry toward x without thinking of x). But it is nevertheless certain from the context of the above quotation that Carnap there means " anger " in the dispositional sense, for he compares a " state " of anger with a " state " of being electrically charged. Now, according to the argument of TM about definitions of dispositional predicates, definitions of this kind are, on account of the " paradox " of material implication, inadmissible and must be replaced by bilateral reduction sentences, such as: $[S(x, t) \supset (\text{ang}(x, t) \equiv R(x, t))]$. If Carnap, therefore, were consistent with his reasoning in TM, he would have used the above argument from our ignorance or even the nonexistence of a physical necessary and sufficient criterion, to establish the conclusion that no physicalistic *bilateral* reduction sentences for psychological terms can be constructed, not that no physicalistic *definitions* can be constructed. The argument, thus recast, would say that only " $[S(x, t) \supset (R(x, t) \supset \text{ang}(x, t))]$," the so-called *unilateral* reduction sentence, is a plausible form of behavioristic reduction sentence for the term " angry," since the possibility of " strong self-control " shows that no specific response could be considered as a necessary condition (or more exactly, conditionally necessary condition, the necessity being conditional upon the occurrence of the stimulus S) for anger.

But even if we replace in Carnap's argument "definability" by "bilateral reducibility," we are left with a serious confusion. It is argued in TM that any bilateral reduction sentence is analytic. The proof is to be found in TM, p. 444, and the theorem is restated on pp. 451-3 in the context of the presentation of a complete criterion of analyticity, covering sentences containing defined descriptive terms as well as sentences containing terms introduced by reduction pairs. The point is briefly this: the content of a reduction pair $Q_1 \supset (Q_2 \supset Q_3)$, $Q_4 \supset (Q_5 \supset -Q_3)$ can be expressed by a "representative sentence" S: $-(Q_1 \cdot Q_2 \cdot Q_4 \cdot Q_5)$, which logically follows from the pair. For the special case of a reduction pair called "bilateral reduction sentence" S reduces to $-(Q_1 \cdot Q_2 \cdot Q_1 \cdot -Q_2)$, which is clearly analytic, devoid of factual content; hence the R_b-sentence, whose content S expresses, has no factual content. Now, as pointed out in section B, above, this theorem seems plausible if we consider the function of R_b-sentences to be strictly *introduction* into a scientific language of a predicate (usually a dispositional predicate) without antecedent meaning, i. e. for whose applicability we know no tests other than the test described by the given R-sentence. But at the same time we had to recognize that the theorem also has its unplausible side, since, as Carnap admits, we may have a whole set of R_b-sentences for the same predicate. It obviously does not happen that the same predicate is *all at once* introduced by several R_b-sentences. Carnap is well aware that in the growth of a scientific language R-sentences (even bilateral ones) are laid down instead of complete definitions in order to leave the concepts *open* for new domains of application. But in that case R-sentences for a predicate will later, after its "introduction," be formulated which cannot again be characterized as "introductions"; rather the predicate for which a new test is formulated now has an antecedent meaning. Yet, all these added R-sentences are equally analytic according to Carnap's theorem.[29] To get a concrete example of the possibility

[29] Notice that Carnap's theorem has the paradoxical consequence that a conjunction of analytic sentences can have synthetic consequences. According to the present view, the only effective solution of this paradox consists in the recognition that the concepts "analytic" and "synthetic" are not applicable at all to statements involving open concepts, and it would seem that Carnap has clouded the issue by applying these terms in contexts in which they are not significantly applicable (though he explicitly speaks of a *generalized* concept of analyticity). Hempel, on the other hand, who calls attention to this paradox in his penetrating paper "The Concept of Cognitive Significance:

here abstractly described, just consider an R-sentence of the type:
$S(x, t) \supset [(\text{Temp}(x, t) = z) \equiv (F(\text{Temp})(y, t) = z)]$ (x ranges over measured objects, y over thermometers; S is the operation of establishing thermal contact between x and y, $F(\text{Temp})$ is some function of temperature, like length), involving functors and expressing one physical magnitude as a function of another by which it may be measured. Later the physicist discovers several more functional relations of the "introduced" magnitude to other magnitudes, and each of these discoveries of further necessary and sufficient conditions for the truth of sentences applying the introduced functor may again be formulated by R_b-sentences. Suppose, now, that such a system of R_b-sentences turns out to be inconsistent in the sense defined in sec. B. In that case the physicist will argue "probably one of these functional laws is false"; but according to Carnap's theorem, such an inference is nonsensical, since "on evidence e, p is probably false" makes no sense if p is analytic.

But let us, in this context, ignore the difficulty just discussed, and make the contrary-to-fact assumption that there can be only one R_b-sentence for a given predicate (or functor). It will be seen that Carnap's conception of R_b-sentences does not accord with his quoted statement about the reducibility of "angry" to physicalistic terms. Suppose I were asked how I discovered Carnap's paradigm of an R_b-sentence, the one for "soluble," and I replied "by experimenting with soluble substances, which is the only way to discover the necessary and sufficient conditions of solubility." Such an answer would of course betray a complete misunderstanding of the *semantic* function of the reduction sentence, the fact that it specifies conditions of predicability of "soluble," and that experimental investigations are accordingly irrelevant to its discovery as well as validation. But when Carnap speaks of the conditions of bilateral reducibility of "anger" (see the above reformulation of his argument), he unmistakably refers to an empirical inquiry—not into verbal habits such as the common usage of "angry," but into correlations between an *independently identifiable* mental state and

a Reconsideration," *Proceedings of the American Academy of Arts and Sciences, 80,* no. 1, seems to think that it dissolves if one properly relativizes the concept of analyticity to a deductive system (partially interpreted). I have stated my reasons for rejecting Hempel's solution of the difficulty in "Reduction Sentences and Disposition Concepts," *loc. cit.*

physiological or behavioral states. If we knew a physiological criterion (read: necessary and sufficient criterion), he says, we could formulate an R_b-sentence, but unfortunately no such criterion is so far known. Yet we know what we mean by "angry," in spite of our ignorance of the physiological criterion, and the day we are relieved of this ignorance, physiologically oriented psychologists will not "introduce" a new term without antecedent meaning on a physiological reduction basis the way it may be imagined that some time in the past people might have introduced "soluble" on the basis of occurrent terms, had language developed by construction instead of by natural growth. They would simply state an empirical psychophysical law. Carnap, then, has not been faithful to his conception of R_b-sentences as semantic rules devoid of factual content, and this ambiguous usage of such a fundamental methodological term naturally confuses the issue between psychophysical dualists who refuse to be intimidated by the accusation that they believe in ghosts and the supposedly more tough-minded logical behaviorists (or physicalists).

Although Carnap, as just shown, is somewhat ambiguous and inconsistent in his application of the theory of reduction sentences to the logical analysis of scientific language, he deserves credit for having clearly seen that this method of partial specification of meaning is employed in the empirical sciences and that consequently the concept of "definition" in the sense of complete, final determination of meaning is unsuited for such logical analysis. But this insight is not shared by all logical empiricists, as a paper by G. Bergmann on "The Logic of Psychological Concepts" (*Philosophy of Science*, April 1951) unmistakably shows. Bergmann claims that a psychological concept like "seeing green" is definable (in use) in terms of a stimulus-response sequence in just the same way in which a physical construct like "electrical field" is definable (in use) in terms of a subjunctive conditional "if an electroscope were placed at P at t, then the leaves of the electroscope would diverge." Let us refer to these definitions in use, which have the identical form "$p \equiv (\text{if } q, \text{then } r)$," as D_s and D_f respectively. Bergmann is aware of the objection which was raised, in sec. A, against the D_f type of definition of physical constructs, viz. "that it does not do justice to all we mean by 'electric field' . . . that there are many other 'tests'; that the description of any one of these could equally well

serve for R (read: the definiens); and that this very fact, together
with other laws about electric fields, belongs to the meaning of
'electric field'" (*loc. cit.*, p. 99). But his answer is anything but
convincing: the opposition is simply accused of the elementary confusion between a (metalinguistic) statement about the meaning of
"electric field" (that's what the definition is) and (object-linguistic)
true or probable statements about electric fields. In a way this easy
answer begs the central question at issue, which is just whether the
analytic-synthetic distinction as usually construed by logical empiricists is applicable to the theoretical language of physics. Bergmann gives no evidence of being aware of the really serious reason
behind the objection from the "surplus meaning" of constructs:
that, on the reconstruction of the theory of electrical fields proposed,
the degree of confirmation of the existential hypothesis about the
electric field relative to the electroscopic evidence would be a
maximum, so that a negative outcome of all other possible tests
could have no tendency whatever to diminish the credibility of the
existential hypothesis but would instead logically compel us to
abandon all the physical laws about the electric field defined as
proposed. In symbols: if E_d is the defining evidence (behavior of
the electroscope), and $E_1{}^p \cdot E_2{}^p \cdots E_n{}^p$ the sum-total of evidence
confirming H by virtue of physical laws, we would have the paradoxical theorem that

$$c(H/E_d) = c(H/E_d \cdot E_1{}^p \cdots E_n{}^p) = c(H/E_d \cdot -E_1{}^p \cdot -E_2{}^p \cdots -E_n{}^p) = 1.$$

But apart from this point, which was discussed at greater length
in sec. B, there is something dangerously misleading in the suggestion, implicit in the formal analogy of D_f and D_s, that the concept
of "seeing green" is related to behavioristic stimulus-response
concepts in just the way the concept "electric field" is related to
the mentioned "observable" concepts of experimental physics.
Bergmann is not unique in making such a comparison. Many
psychologists would say that explaining stimulus-response sequences
in terms of such "hidden" mental events as seeing green is just
like explaining the behavior of the electroscope in terms of such a
hidden reality as the electric field. And if they feel uncomfortable
about the "unobservables" thus postulated, they soothe their con-
science in Bergmann's fashion by saying: "Well, we do not really
pretend to *explain*; we merely *describe* in terms of a shorthand

concept the sequence observed." But has it escaped Bergmann's and the behaviorists' notice that while "electric field" is clearly a dispositional concept, "seeing green" does not describe a disposition but an event, and that a term describing a kind of event cannot possibly be synonymous with a dispositional term? That a sentence asserting the occurrence of an event, in other words, cannot be synonymous with a conditional sentence expressing a law, since the latter type of sentence does not assert nor entail that anything actually happens at a given time at all? From the subjunctive conditional "if stimulus S acted on organism O at time t, then O would respond in fashion R at t" you cannot deduce what *actually* happens at t. Yet, when we say "O sees green at t" we are describing an event we believe to be happening at t; not so when we assert the existence of an electric field at a given place at a given time. I conclude that Bergmann succeeds in producing his startling proof of logical behaviorism only by overlooking a semantic distinction of the first importance, the distinction between categorical statements asserting occurrences and hypothetical statements expressing dispositions or laws. In fact, it follows from Bergmann's proposed definition scheme that if we have good evidence for the relevant behavioristic law "for any t, if S acted on O at t, then O would respond in fashion R at t," then we have good evidence for believing that O is seeing green all the time! Just as we have good evidence for believing that sugar is always soluble in water if we have good evidence for the law "for any t, if a sample of sugar is put into water at t, then it dissolves at t." To make the point concretely, suppose that the following behavioristic conditional is used as definiens for "O sees green at t": if a signal is flashed at t and O has been instructed, in a language he understands, 'press the buzzer the moment you see green,' then O presses the buzzer at t. If, now, the signal is flashed at various times, and each time O, who received the relevant instruction, presses the buzzer, we can conclude by ordinary induction that the universal conditional obtained from the definiens by universal quantification over the time variable is probably true. But this is equivalent to what would ordinarily be expressed by saying "probably O is always *disposed* to see green when stimulated in this way," not to "probably O always sees green." Only if it were reasonable to conclude from the conjunctive evidential statement ("the signal was flashed at t_0 and O pressed the buzzer at t_o, and the signal was flashed at t_1 and O pressed the buzzer at t_1, etc.") that it is probable that the stimulation occurs at other times also, would it be reasonable to conclude that O probably always sees green; whereas the reasonableness of the inference to " probably O is always disposed to press the buzzer when stimulated in the described way" does not presuppose the reasonableness of this inference. What may be defined in terms of such a test conditional, therefore, is not the occurrent concept "seeing green" but rather the concept " being disposed to see green when stimulated in such and such a way." Furthermore, it is hard to see how any behavioristic definiens could be extensionally equivalent to the definiendum without being circular. The circularity of the above definition is concealed by the proviso ". . . in a language he understands . . .". Actually this means ". . . is instructed to press the buzzer if he sees green, by means of a sentence which he interprets to mean that he should press the buzzer if he sees green . . ." !

The first criticism of the kind of behavioristic definition proposed by Bergmann, viz. that what is defined is a disposition, not a kind of event, cannot be answered by the familiar statement (which is reasonable enough) : " Well, you must concede to the psychologist, as you do to the physicist, the right to construct useful concepts even if the definitions do not preserve the usual meanings of the terms defined." For the term for which the definition is proposed is clearly intended as a term designating a kind of *event*; but thus the criterion of adequacy is inevitably imposed that predications of the defined term should, according to the definition, be assertions of the occurrence of an event. It is a mistake to suppose that just because the possible tests of an hypothesis h are described by conditionals linking realizable test conditions to observable reactions, therefore h must describe a *dispositional* state, such as an electric field of specified magnitude in a certain space-time region. Consider a physical hypothesis like " at time t electrical current of intensity I flows through this wire." The method of testing it is, like the method of testing the hypothesis about the electric field, properly described by causal conditionals, but what the hypothesis asserts is the occurrence of an event, albeit an event that is not as directly observable as, say, the deflection of a galvanometer needle. To put it in formal terms: the possibility of deriving a causal conditional statement from an hypothesis " Px " indicates that P is a disposition *only* if the conditional statement is *analytically* derivable, so that we can say it partially explicates the meaning of "P." If the deduction is mediated by a *law*, then "P" may still be perfectly non-dispositional, i. e. designate a state which is properly described as an event. Thus suppose we have an R_b-sentence for "P": $O \supset (P \equiv R)$. By virtue of it, "$O \supset R$" is derivable from "P." But if "P," far from being *introduced* into the language by means of the R_b-sentence, has a background meaning relative to which the latter was suggested by empirical regularities, then this is not an analytic derivation at all.[30] Let us apply this consideration to Bergmann's example "seeing green," replacing definition in use by (incomplete) reduction: if x (who is assumed to be honest) looks at a colored object and is asked what color he sees, then (x will reply 'I see green' if and only if he sees green). This statement is obviously not analytic: just suppose that x does not speak English! The statement still remains disconfirmable if along with the honesty condition we put into the antecedent "x speaks English"—as well as further "other things being equal" provisos, e. g. willingness to cooperate with the experimentor: for he might utter a different sentence. Hence a *semantic* condition must be imposed: he utters some sentence synonymous with those tokens of "I see green" that refer to himself. But I am afraid that even so it will not be self-contradictory to suppose that all the test conditions are fulfilled, the response occurs, and yet he does not see green (which is to say that the R_b-sentence is not analytic, for otherwise its consequence "$O \cdot R \supset P$" would have to be analytic): it is logically possible that S, the actually uttered sentence, is synonymous with "I see green"—more accurately: with those tokens of "I see green" that would be uttered by x if he knew English—in the sense of expressing the same proposition, but that the proposition which both of these sentences express is not the proposition that the speaker sees green but some other proposition. The required condition, therefore, is not just that he utter a sentence expressing the same proposition as the relevant tokens of "I see green," but that he utter a sentence

---

[30] It may seem to the reader that I am contradicting here my own advocacy of "gradualism" insofar as I use the dichotomous concept of analyticity in the above argument. But the contradicton is apparent only, for the statement that "if p, then q" is analytic in the dichotomous sense can be translated into the "gradualistic" meta-language: "q" is entailed by "p" to the highest possible degree.

expressing the proposition that he sees green. Thus analyticity would be ensured at the price of circularity: " seeing green " crops up in the allegedly physicalistic reduction basis.

I would like to illustrate the distinction between psychological *dispositions* and *events*, which is obliterated when it is claimed that the meanings of " mentalistic " terms can be specified by explicit operational definitions, or for that matter by reduction to physicalistic terms, further in terms of an operational definition of " expectancy," given by Tolman, the outstanding exponent of operational behavior theory. His definition is reformulated as a reduction sentence by Meehl and MacCorquodale:

> If x is deprived of food and x has been trained on path P and x is now put on path P and path P is now blocked and there are other paths which lead away from path P, one of which points directly to location L, then (x runs down the path which points directly to location L if and only if x expected food at location L).[31]

It will surely be admitted that such a reduction sentence is subject to revision; specifically, the psychologist may have forgotten to take some " inhibiting " variable into account. Now, the very statement that a rat who expects food at L and who satisfies the antecedent may nevertheless not run towards L because of some historical fact other than the learning background specified (e. g. would the response necessarily occur if the rat had also been deprived of sex mates for a long time?), can be reasonably made only because of the mentalistic background meaning of " expectation." To say that as introduced by reduction sentences into psychological theory the term is nevertheless dispositional, is confusing. If one insists on using " dispositional " so liberally, one will simply have to invent another term meaning what " dispositional " usually means. The point may be illustrated as follows: it makes good sense to say " this rat has at t the disposition (to run toward L *if* the path to L is not blocked and it smells food at L)." Such a proposition may be inferred from historical facts about the rat such as the distance of

---

[31] William K. Estes and others, *Modern Learning Theory* (New York, 1954), p. 179. The authors' replacement of definitions by reduction sentences is motivated by their insight into the openness of psychological constructs, in the sense explained above, Secs. A, B.

time *t* from its last feeding and absence of other " deprivations " that may set up conflicting " drives." But the inductive evidence for the dispositional statement need not include observation of the rat's actual behavior at *t*, specifically its running toward *L*; whereas such overt behavior at *t* is an essential part of the evidence for the hypothesis that a certain kind of expectation *occurs* at *t*. Briefly: " the rat expects at time *t* food at place *L* " is surely different from " the rat will expect food at *L* at time *t* *if* it has suffered food deprivation, and no other deprivations, before *t*."

This illustration suggests the following criterion for the dispositional character of a psychological state. Suppose that historic information about an organism is sufficient to warrant the hypothesis that a given " intervening variable," in the terminology of Tolman and other behavior theorists, has at the present time a given value for the organism in question; for example, we derive a present value of hunger drive from a knowledge of the time of food deprivation (and perhaps also knowledge about other kinds of deprivation that might set up conflicting drives). Then the intervening variable has dispositional character. A good analogy from molar mechanics is " potential energy ": if we know how much work was done to get the body into its present position (and we know its mass), then we can determine its potential energy (degree of magnetization is a similar example of what might be called historically conditioned quantitative dispositions). But if we further require information about a stimulus variable, then the intervening variable has occurrent character. Thus, in order to tell how strongly a rat expects at *t* food at place *P*, it would surely not be sufficient to have the historic information; one would also have to know how strongly the rat's smell organs are stimulated by " stimulus energy " coming from *P* at *t*.

Let us return to Bergmann's challenging thesis. Strangely enough, he proceeds in a section entitled " Other Minds " to make an admission which amounts to an unconditional surrender of what seems to be a (if not the) central thesis of the whole paper. He concedes to " common sense " that the conditional statement (law) " if stimulus *S* acts on *O*, then response *R* occurs " does not at all mean what we (including perhaps the behaviorist in non-professional moments) mean when we say " *O* sees green "; in other words, that the statement " if *S* causes *R*, then *O* sees green " is by no means a tautology. But in the section headed " Behaviorism " he had explicitly confessed himself to behaviorism in the sense in which to be a behaviorist is to maintain the following thesis: " All concepts of the science of psychology can be defined by means of the class of undefined concepts that enter into the definitions of physical science, i. e., the names of some immediately observable characters of physical objects." Surely, the only way to reconcile this thesis with the mentioned concession to common sense is to construe " can be defined by means of . . ." not in the philosophically interesting sense of " can be explicated by means of . . ." but in the trivial sense of " can be arbitrarily stipulated as synonyms for . . .". When Russell, to present an analogy, contended that the concepts of arithmetic are definable in terms of the concepts of logic, he was naturally understood to claim that such definitions preserve the usual meanings of the arithmetical expressions. If he had merely asserted that it may in certain contexts be useful to employ arithmetical terms in senses other than the customary ones, his assertion would not have invited philosophical controversy. *Mutatis mutandis*, the same holds for the behaviorist claim that psychological concepts are definable in terms of physical concepts.[32]

F. *Degree of Entailment and Psychophysical Dualism*

Our discussion of phenomenalism ended with the observation that the time-honored controversy about the analysis of statements about physical objects must necessarily remain inconclusive because it is formulated in terms of the distinction between analytic entailment and factual implication, a distinction which has no clear meaning as applied to statements involving open concepts. It was also suggested that a proper formulation of *R*-sentences (proper, that is, from the viewpoint of their applicability to growing empirical sciences) results in *gradated* entailment-statements and that in the context of discourse involving open concepts it is more appropriate

[32] Perhaps Bergmann would reply that regardless of the mentalistic connotations of psychological terms, behavioristic definitions are forced upon the psychologist by the postulate of public verifiability of scientific statements. This argument is, however, based on a failure to distinguish conclusive verifiability and confirmability, as I have tried to show in my article " Other Minds and the Principle of Verifiability," *Revue Internationale de Philosophie* (1951) , no. 17-18. See also A. J. Ayer's recent paper " Our Knowledge about Other Minds," reprinted in Ayer, *Philosophical Essays*, New York, 1954.

to speak of "degree of entailment" than of purely analytic as opposed to purely factual statements. What remains to be shown, now, is how a dissolution of the physicalism–dualism controversy along similar lines may be possible. But first a few more words may profitably be said about "degree of entailment." Consider the simple implication " if *x* is a lemon, then *x* is sour" (*S*). Is it analytic or synthetic? It would be naive to try to answer this question by looking for an explicit definition of " lemon " and then determining whether sourness was entailed by it; for even if the assumption of explicit definability were warranted, the adequacy of a proposed definition would be judged precisely by asking whether such conditionals as " if *x* is a lemon, then *x* is sour " would be analytic or synthetic under it. If, for example, a man should be convinced that it is self-contradictory to speak of a non-sour lemon, in other words, that *S* is analytic, he would for that very reason reject a definition of " lemon " from which *S* is not deducible. Suppose, then, we interpret analyticity as a pragmatic concept according to which " *S* is analytic for *A* " means something like " *A* would firmly refuse to call something a lemon unless he believed it to be sour." I think that in this sense *S* is not analytic for most English-speaking people, for circumstances are conceivable under which they would be strongly inclined to classify *x* as a lemon even though *x* is not sour: just suppose that *x* resembles things ordinarily called " lemon " in all respects except the taste; probably most people would describe this anomalous situation by saying " there seems to be a kind of lemon that is not sour " ! According to what was earlier called the " either-or " pattern of semantic analysis,[33] one would conclude that sourness is not logically connoted by " lemon " or deducible from the definition of " lemon "—in other words, that *S* is synthetic. But this alternative is equally unplausible since, just as it is conceivable that we should classify the described *x* as an instance of a new species of lemon (a decision analogous to the decision to classify those Australian swimming birds that are swanlike except for being black as a species of swans), so it is conceivable that we should invent a new class term standing for a new species of fruit coordinated with the old similar species called " lemon " (a decision analogous to refusing the name of, say,

[33] Cf. above, p. 112.

"zinc" to a hypothetical metal to be discovered on Mars which is exactly like zinc except that it has a different atomic weight). The trouble with either alternative—to call S analytic or to call it synthetic—is that it presupposes that "lemon" is a precisely defined class term, that we can draw a sharp line between those properties differentiating lemons from other kinds of fruit that are "logically connoted" by the class term and those which lemons have contingently.[34] Since, on the contrary, such class terms are intensionally vague (see above, pp. 326-7), the sharp concept of logical connotation had better be replaced by a continuous concept "term T connotes property P to degree x." We might ask, for example, whether people would more readily refuse application of the term "lemon" to a mature fruit which is not yellow than to a mature fruit which is not sour; and if the answer is affirmative, "lemon" (or "mature lemon") might be said to connote yellowness to a higher degree than sourness.

But, if it is possible that a lemon fail to be sour, in the sense that the complex of qualities connoted by "lemon" which is usually compresent with sourness might be present in some instance without sourness, then S cannot be interpreted as expressing an entailment in the ordinary sense. It is best interpreted as a probability implication, but a probability implication of altogether different kind from those referring to the exactly bounded classes of formal logic. Similarly, a term like "furious" stands for a correlation of an emotion with bodily symptoms of the emotion, such as fiery eyes, but situations are conceivable in which we would apply the term "furious" to a smiling person; a definite kind of facial expression may be connoted by this psychological term to a high degree, yet it is not connoted to the maximum degree. Therefore, "if x is furious at time t, then x does not smile at t" ought to be interpreted as the same kind of probability implication. Yet it is only by means of such probability implications that the differential meanings of such terms can be explicated.[35]

---

[34] This "rational animal–featherless biped" dualism, as it might be called, exerts a dangerous charm especially on formal logicians who operate with the fiction of exactly defined properties determining exactly bounded classes and overlook that it is a fiction if the class term in question acquired its connotation, not through stipulated definition, but through ostensive definition. See, in this connection, the penetrating discussion of "ostensive concepts" in S. Körner, *Conceptual Thinking*, chaps. 5-7.

[35] "Differential" meanings are here contrasted with "generic" meanings, such as

The very application of the method of reduction of terms which Carnap mentions show that the connections between the reduced terms (which in the case of a logically reconstructed natural language have usually antecedent meanings and are not, therefore, strictly "introduced" by the reduction sentences at all) and the terms of the reduction basis are probability connections and not deductive connections. This emerges clearly from his discussion, already commented on in the context of a different problem, of behavioristic reduction of psychological terms in *Logical Foundations of the Unity of Science*. Speaking of the possibility of behavioristic reduction of a term like " angry," Carnap says (*op. cit.*, reprinted in Feigl and Sellars, *Readings in Philosophical Analysis*, p. 419) :

> It is sufficient for the formulation of a reduction sentence to know a behavioristic procedure which enables us—if not always, at least under suitable circumstances—to determine whether the organism in question is angry or not. And we know indeed such procedures; otherwise we should never be able to apply the term " angry " to another person on the basis of our observations of his behavior, as we constantly do in everyday life and in scientific investigation. A reduction of the term " angry " or similar terms by the formulation of such procedures is indeed less useful than a definition would be, because a definition supplies a complete (i. e., unconditional) criterion for the term in question, while a reduction statement of the conditional form gives only an incomplete one. But a criterion, conditional or not, is all we need for ascertaining reducibility.

Carnap here says that we know behavioral symptoms which are sufficient conditions, but none which are sufficient and necessary conditions, for the presence and absence, respectively, of a state of anger. But clearly we cannot assert with any greater confidence that the presence of a given behavioral symptom is invariably accompanied by the presence of anger than that the absence of such a symptom is invariably accompanied by the absence of anger. Since the correlation between behavioral states and mental states is neither

---

" fruit " in the case of " lemon," " emotion " in the case of " furious." Notice that the intensional vagueness of " lemon " and " fruit " notwithstanding, the nuclear intensions, so to speak, of these terms are definite enough to permit the statement that " x is a lemon " entails " x is a fruit."

one-many nor many-one (i. e. many-many), we can only assert probability implications no matter whether a sufficient condition or a necessary condition for a given mental state is in question. Just as the possibility of strong self-control, mentioned by Carnap in the same article, makes it difficult to find a behaviouristic term which expresses a strictly necessary condition for anger, so the possibility of putting on an act makes it difficult to find one that expresses a strictly sufficient condition.

Now, the way in which this concept of degree of entailment is relevant to the psychophysical problem, specifically the physicalism–dualism controversy, has already been implicitly indicated. It was hinted above that just the way names of natural kinds like " lemon " connote a correlation of qualities (and let us postpone scrutiny of the meaning of "correlation" for just a while), so names of mental states like " fury " connote a correlation of a feeling with bodily expressions and behavior. According to the " either-or " pattern of semantic analysis we ought to distinguish clearly the meaning of " fury " (the logical connotation of the word), which is an intro-spectable emotion, from the logically contingent accompaniments of the mental state, such as a red face and a trembling voice. The psychophysical law " whenever x is in mental state M, then x exhibits bodily and behavioral expressions B " is, on this view, clearly a contingent proposition. But the question whether this is indeed a contingent proposition may be like the question whether " all lemons are sour " or " all (mature) lemons are yellow " is a contingent proposition. As we saw, one can adduce reasons for classi-fying such propositions as contingent and also reasons for classifying them as necessary. And we argued that the trouble comes from treating " lemon " as a closed concept and hence attempting to apply the dichotomy necessary-contingent (analytic-synthetic) whereas the continuous concept " degree of connotation " ought to be applied. Similarly, the question about the logical status of the psychophysical law presupposes that a term like " furious " either is or is not definable in terms of behavior. But such terms are not " introduced " into a natural language through verbal definition. They come to mean what they mean by learned association with *both* introspect-able (mental) states and bodily and behavioral expressions. We should not therefore ask *whether* the latter are logically connoted but instead *to what degree* they are connoted by the psychological term. It may be that the degree to which the introspectable feeling is connoted is much higher than the degree to which any given " expression " of the feeling is connoted. Thus it may be that a person would not retract the autobiographical statement " I am furious " even if it were pointed out to him that he exhibits all the symptoms of a relaxed, contented man, since he finds the emotion undeniably present. On the other hand, there are names of emotions, like " love " perhaps, which connote public symptoms to a higher degree; this means that if one is convinced by others that one's behavior differs from the characteristic behavior of people who are " in love," one would more readily retract the introspective judgment.

It is important that the relevant meaning of " correlation," in the statement that such psychological terms as " fury," " love," " disappointment " stand for a correlation of introspectable states and publicly observable " symptoms " of those states, be understood. What exactly do we mean when, ridiculing the concept of substance in the footsteps of Berkeley and Hume, we say " names of natural kinds stand for nothing but a correlation of qualities " ? One might think that the question is answered easily enough by the definition:

' K ' stands for the correlation of qualities $Q_1 \cdots Q_n = df$

x is a member of $K \equiv Q_1x$ and $Q_2x \cdots$ and Q_nx.

But this analysis illustrates precisely the confusion of closed concepts, like " square," " cube," with open concepts. The fact, if we may bore the reader by pointing it out once more, that one might under circumstances classify an object as a lemon even though it lacks one of the characteristics which all objects usually called " lemon " have, shows conclusively that the analysis is inadequate. Just as the presence of no part of the correlation entails the presence of the remaining part of the correlation, so the implication from a proposition of the form " $x \in K$ " to a proposition of the form " Q_ix " cannot be generally construed as entailment. For example, if we found several cases of " Q_2x and $Q_3x \cdots$ and Q_nx and not-Q_1x," it might be reasonable to classify thenceforth objects of this sort as members of K even though previous experience justified the claim that the group $Q_2 \cdots Q_n$ is a sign of Q_1.[36] For exactly similar reasons it would be unplausible to analyze a psychological statement like " he is furious " into the *conjunction* of a mentalistic statement, which the statement's subject alone can know with certainty to be true or false, and behavioristic statements such as "he is speaking in a loud, trembling voice, clenching his fists, and his eyes spit fire." It is obvious that none of the behavioristic or even physiological symptoms is a logically necessary condition for the occurrence of the emotion, as it should be on the conjunctive analysis. But even the claim that at least the occurrence of the subjective experience is a logically necessary condition is highly doubtful, since it simply cannot be predicted what the verbal reaction of a man would be if he did not experience the " feeling " of fury at all, yet discovered to his amazement that his outward behavior and expression as well as the physiological processes in his body were those normally associated with a feeling of fury. He *might* say " I must be in a state of fury, though it is a very special kind of fury," or he *might* say " this is not fury, I must invent a special name for this kind of psychological condition—though it is, in its physical aspect, just like fury."

Radical physicalism, as propounded in the early articles by Carnap and Hempel on the logical analysis of psychology,[37] has been largely abandoned on the ground that the relation between physicalistic and mentalistic statements is not that of analytic entailment. And we have seen that the contemporary thesis of reducibility of psychological terms to physicalistic terms is perfectly compatible with the dualists' insistence that psychophysical correlations are *contingent* (cf. p. 337). But while this recognition of contingency has been a most salutary reaction against radical physicalism, the denial of analytic entailment, as the foregoing analysis has aimed to demonstrate, shares with the assertion of analytic entailment an untenable premise: the " either-or " of the tidy analysts. This untenable premise seems to me to underly a particularly tidy and subtle defense of the thesis of contingency by C. Lewy in the article " Is the

[36] Should the objection arise in the reader's mind that the described situation is nothing but the well known phenomenon of redefinition in the light of new experience and as such is compatible with the criticized analysis of " correlation," he is referred to the answer already given above, pp. 112-16.

[37] See particularly the incisive—incisively erroneous—discussion in Hempel's " The logical analysis of psychology," reprinted in English transl. in Feigl and Sellars, *op. cit.*

Notion of Disembodied Existence Self-contradictory? " (*Proceedings of the Aristotelian Society*, new ser., 1942-43). Consider Lewy's claim that " when I say ' Smith feels happy ' I am *not*, even partly, referring to the behavior of his body; that is to say, the behavior of his body is not a part of the *meaning* of the statement ' Smith feels happy.' His bodily behavior is my *evidence* for this statement, but not a part of its meaning" (p. 66). The argument by which Lewy supports his claim consists in affirming that evidently no conjunction of the form " x is happy but x is not in bodily (or behavioral) state B " is self-contradictory. And since to say that " p and not-q " is not self-contradictory is precisely equivalent to saying that p does not analytically entail q, the assertion made amounts to an appeal to the self-evident fact that a given proposition p does not analytically entail a given proposition q. Lewy admits elsewhere that a psychological statement like " Smith is happy " may well *causally imply* statements about Smith's body, but emphasizes that this is irrelevant to the question at issue, which is whether there is an analytic connection between the statements. But Lewy nowhere raises the question what the criterion of distinction between causal implication (or, more generally speaking, factual implication) and analytic entailment is, if the predicated term means what it means, not by virtue of stipulated definition, but by virtue of the untidy process of meaning specification called " ostensive " definition. Is Lewy denying that perception of the word " happy " is associatively connected with memory images of facial expressions and ways of behaving, and maintaining that *only* memory images of *feelings* are thus connected with the word? To reply that the term " associative connection " blurs the crucial distinction between logical connotation and logically inessential imagery would be to dodge the issue, since to explain this distinction *is* to explain the distinction between what the predication analytically entails and what it factually implies. Indeed, if we reflect on what is involved in ostensive definition of such psychological terms we shall find that it is most unlikely that bodily " symptoms " of the feeling should fail to be connoted. Suppose that " happy " is predicated of x with the intention of teaching x the meaning of " happy," and suppose that the bodily state of x which suggests to the teacher that x is at this moment happy is B_1. By an elementary rule of ostensive definition, the teacher should predicate the same term again of x or some other person when B_1 is absent, otherwise x might interpret "happy" to mean B_1. Similarly, to prevent interpretation of "happy" to mean B_2, the teacher must find a state of happiness associated with B_3, and so on. To simplify the matter, let us make the contrary-to-fact assumption that the only subject of predication used by the teacher in the process of teaching x the meaning of "happy" is x himself; this assumption simplifies our problem, since we thus need not bother with analogical inferences to other minds to be drawn by x (though the teacher himself could hardly refrain from them!). Is it not obvious, now, that the set of bodily states which are interpreted by the teacher as symptoms of happiness must, however dissimilar, have *some* (physical) similarity? If they had not, what should induce the teacher to interpret all of them as signs of a feeling of happiness? The reply that the only requisite similarity is the relational similarity of being at one time or other associated with a feeling of happiness in the teacher himself would be confronted with all the difficulties besetting the analogical theory of the origin of beliefs about other minds.[38] If this argument is correct, then the word "happy" must come to be associated with a memory image of a certain kind of bodily state along with a memory image of a certain kind of subjective feeling. And if so, the meaning of the claim that only the latter is analytically entailed by "x is happy," not the former, remains obscure.

If, in opposition to a tradition of semantic analysis which seems entrenched in both positivistic and antipositivistic camps of analysts, we countenance the suggested concept of *degree of entailment*, we may find that the distinction in question could be explicated as a vague distinction along the line of pragmatic analysis suggested above in sec. D. In order to give some color to the problem under discussion, let us invent a tale of a man born physiologically blind who miraculously exhibits all the outward signs of ability to discriminate colors. The first reaction of people who hear him call green meadows "green," red lips "red," blue ribbons "blue," and who find to their amazement that, on being asked to identify the blue-haired woman out of a group of elegantly dressed society women, he gives the right answer, is to suspect that all the objects to which he applies the same color predicate have some quality in

[38] For a weighty critique of this theory see C. D. Broad, *The Mind and Its Place in Nature*, chap. 7.

common which could be recognized by senses other than the visual (such as a distinctive smell, e. g.). But let us assume that the most careful investigation of the sensible qualities of these objects flatly refutes that hypothesis. What would they say then? One alternative would be to abandon the highly confirmed generalization that color vision presupposes the possession of those physiological organs which congenitally blind men are said, by definition of " blind," to lack. Lewy would probably say that such a decision is possible (and even reasonable) precisely because no physiological proposition is analytically *entailed* by the proposition that a given person can see colors. However, it can hardly be denied that we might alternatively stick to the well-confirmed psychophysical law and make the *ad hoc* hypothesis that the mentioned objects do have sensible qualities other than colors in common, qualities which only blind people can sense and whose extensions strangely coincide with the extensions of specific color qualities. What we would say obviously depends on how firmly we believe in the psychophysical law. And we might say that the more we incline to stick to the law, resorting to *ad hoc* hypothesis in the face of an apparent exception, the greater the degree of entailment expressed by the law.

Generalizing from this hypothetical case, " degree of entailment " might be roughly explicated as follows. Let "A-B" represent a law of correlation from kind of event A to kind of event B; and let e_1 be evidence which makes it probable (to some degree) that an instance a_i of A is present, and e_2 evidence which makes it probable (to some degree) that the corresponding instance, b_i, of B is not present. Then, assuming that $\text{Prob}\,(a_i/e_1) = \text{Prob}\,(\bar{b}_i/e_2)$, the degree to which A entails B is measured by our inclination to conclude that a_i is absent (and thus to save the law) or that b_i is present (and thus alternatively to save the law), the evidences to the contrary notwithstanding. Now, suppose in particular that A-B is a psychophysical law such as " whenever a sensation of seeing blue occurs, then a neurological event N occurs simultaneously." And suppose that e_1 is introspective evidence, to which the person owning the sensation will naturally ascribe considerable weight. In assuming, therefore, the above equation of probabilities we assume that e_2 is weighty physical evidence against the occurrence of the normally correlated event N. Some philosophers may say that the person possessing the introspective evidence has no choice but to reject the psychophysical law, since it would not make sense for him to say " It seems to me that I see blue, but it is not true that I see blue ": it is meaningless to say " it seems to me that p, but p is nevertheless false " if p is what Ayer has called an " incorrigible sense-statement " about the speaker's sense-data. However, this argument overlooks that at the time when a person who is struggling to make up his mind as to what is reality and what appearance, weighs e_1 against e_2, the mental event in question is *past*, and in view of the fallibility of memory it is not meaningless to say " I seem to remember distinctly that I saw blue, but perhaps my memory deceives me." If we, then, apply the suggested definition of " degree of entailment " to this case, we would say that seeing blue entails, for the introspecting subject X, the occurrence of N to the degree to which X would be inclined to question his memory if such a situation were to arise.

The feeling that to speak of *degrees* of entailment expressed by psychophysical laws is just as absurd as to speak, say, of degrees of primeness of numbers, is not justified. In particular, it does seem that some psychological terms connote bodily states to a much higher degree than others. Consider the following sentences: (1) I am congenitally blind ("blind" meant as a physiological term); (2) I can see colors; (3) I desire to learn astronomy; (4) I read books on astronomy; (5) I desire at present to drink water, and this desire is stronger than any other desire I have at present (here "strongest desire" is meant in the sense in which one can judge by introspection which is the strongest desire, not in the behavioristic sense of "desire most likely to issue in action"); (6) If I should have the opportunity to drink water now, and believed that the offered drink was water, I would. It will be noticed that sentences (2), (3), and (5) describe mental events or dispositions, while the remaining sentences belong wholly or partly to the physical language. According to the type of position illustrated by Lewy's none of the sentences of the first group analytically entails, or is analytically inconsistent with, any sentences of the second group. But is it not plausible to say that (5) entails (6)? If I announced the desire described by (5), were thereupon offered a glass of water yet refused to drink (even though I firmly believed that the glass contains water), would not such behavior be regarded as *logically conclusive evidence* that I was lying? At any rate, if confronted with such a situation, one would rather try out every conceivable *ad hoc* hypothesis (such as " he was lying when he told us about his strongest desire," or " he does not believe that the glass contains water," or " his reported desire must suddenly have been outweighed by a conflicting desire, such as the desire to get us puzzled ") than admit the truth of the premise about the strongest desire. And what is more, the introspecting subject himself would become doubtful of the validity of his introspective analysis if he caught himself in such unexpected behavior. By the suggested pragmatic criterion of degree of entailment, this simply means that (5) does entail (6) to a very high degree, a degree which is higher, I should think, than the degree to which (1) entails the negation of (2), and much higher, of course, than the degree to which (3) entails (4).

G. Degree of Entailment and Degree of Confirmation

Those philosophers who are accustomed to what may be called the " dualistic " method of logical reconstruction, viz. the method of dividing a network of scientific statements whose nodal points are descriptive concepts ("temperature," " mass," " electric field " in physics, " belief," " expectation," " hunger " in psychology) into analytic ones that are definitive of the concepts, and synthetic ones that are empirically confirmable and disconfirmable, may launch the following protest against the " gradualism " here argued for:

The facts which you cite as reasons for abandoning the dualistic method are well known, but can be fully reconciled with the use of the dualistic method. We contend that *at any given stage* of the development of a scientific system the nodal concepts have *definite meanings*, while admitting that new empirical discoveries make *changes of definition* advisable. Take, e. g., a disposition concept like " vaporization point." At a stage of experimental physics when the dependence of the degree of temperature at which changes of states of aggregation occur on the atmospheric pressure is not suspected, " K has vaporization point z " is explicitly defined as " if at any time the temperature of a sample of K were raised to z, then it would vaporize." Now, since we mean by a " disposition " a property which is invariant within a given ultimate natural kind (e. g. any two samples of pure water should have the same vaporization point), the stipulation of this definition is indeed motivated by the belief in the following empirical regularity: if x and y are samples of the same ultimate natural kind (in the sense in which "iron," but not "metal," denotes an ultimate natural kind), and there is a time at which x vaporizes after its temperature was raised to z, then y vaporizes at any time at which its temperature is raised to z. But owing to the effect of atmospheric pressure on the value of z, this empirical generalization is found to be false. Hence the definition is modified by including in the antecedent the condition of standard atmospheric pressure. Relative to the original definition, "K has vaporization point z, but some samples of K vaporize at a temperature different from z" is self-contradictory. Relative to the modified definition, this statement is not self-contradictory; indeed it is probably true.

The best way to answer this objection is to ask by which criterion it is determined that the simple explicit definition expresses the *definite meaning* which the dispositional predicate allegedly has at time t_o. As explained in sec. D, the relevant *pragmatic* concept of meaning is itself a disposition concept. Roughly, to say that the defining conditional expresses what the scientist means by "vaporization point" at t_o is to say that he is at t_o disposed to assert "K has vaporization point z" if and only if he believes that K satisfies the conditional. But since a dispositional predicate is intended to designate a property which is invariant within a given ultimate natural kind, such a statement about the scientist's linguistic disposition just is not true. In order to bring out the fact that even now he is not irrevocably determined to assert "K has vaporization point z" if the relevant observations should cause him to believe that K satisfies the defining conditional, and that therefore a probabilistic reduction sentence is a more faithful expression of his attitude than an explicit definition, we only need to ask him what *he would say* if it turned out that different samples of the same kind (where sameness of kind is established independently of sameness of vaporization point) vaporized at different temperatures. If he replies that he would still stick to the hypothesis that the kind has a constant vaporization point, this proves that the meaning he attaches to the dispositional predicate (or functor) has that "openness" which makes application of the analytic-synthetic dichotomy unsuitable.[39]

---

[39] For more detailed discussion of the "openness" of disposition concepts, see my articles "Disposition Concepts and Extensional Logic" and "Reduction Sentences and Disposition Concepts," *loc. cit.*; also A. W. Burks, "Dispositional Statements," *Phi-*

The concept of *probability* which is involved in probabilistic reduction sentences is a pragmatic concept and thus radically different from both the frequency concept and the logical concept which Carnap calls " degree of confirmation "—indeed the difference is so great that it may be advisable not to use the term " probability" in this context; " degree of entailment " or " degree of analyticity " would be less misleading. Suppose we specify the meaning of a disease name "D" probabilistically by assigning to a hypothesis of the form "x has D at t " (h) various probabilities relative to various symptoms $S_1, S_2 \cdots S_n$. Take, e. g., the statement " Prob $(h/S_1) = p$." If this were a frequency statement, it would assert that the limiting relative frequency, in a sequence of increasing random samples, of people who have D at a given time t within the class of people who exhibit S_1 at t is p. Now, such a statement is significant only if the truth-value of an hypothesis of the form of h can be ascertained independently of verification of S_1, which does not seem to be the case if the meaning of "D" is partially specified in terms of S_1. It may be replied that all that is presupposed by the frequency interpretation is that the substitution-instances of h can be assessed as probable or improbable relative to the symptoms $S_2 \cdots S_n$. But here precisely the same difficulty arises all over again. If in order to determine empirically Prob (h/S_2) I am referred to Prob (h/S_3) and so on till I reach eventually Prob (h/S_n), then I will simply return to the question of the value of Prob (h/S_1) —which is the question that started us on the merry-go-round. Now, since statements about a degree of confirmation of an hypothesis relative to observational evidence, in Carnap's sense, are L-determinate and the probability statements under discussion are semantic statements, the interpretation in terms of degree of confirmation may seem more plausible. But actually the same difficulty arises in connection with this interpretation. $c(h/e)$ is determined by the ratio of some measure of the class of state descriptions (Z) in which (h and e) holds to the corresponding measure of the class of state descriptions in which e holds. But Carnap defines "p holds in Z" in such a way that it means nothing else than "Z formally entails p" (e. g. p holds in Z if it is a subconjunction of Z). Suppose, now, to illustrate the difficulty, that the language of pathology contains

losophy of Science (July 1955) ; and R. Carnap, " The Methodological Character of Theoretical Concepts," *Minnesota Studies in Philosophy of Science, 1.*

primitive predicates designating symptoms $S_1 \cdots S_n$ (e. g. coughing, urinating excessively, perspiring), in terms of which we construct pathological state descriptions that describe possible pathological states of a given organism in observational terms; and we now wonder in how many of these Z a hypothesis of the form " x has disease D," where " D " is a probabilistically introduced construct, holds. Clearly none of our Z formally entail, and none are formally incompatible with, such an hypothesis. All we can say is that such-and-such state descriptions make the hypothesis probable to such-and-such a degree. And the Carnapian explication of " logical probability ",[40] therefore, sends us on a merry-go-round if we want to determine the symptom-disease probabilities, just as did the frequency interpretation.

It will not help either to incorporate statements of the form " $c\,(h/S_i) = p$ " into the language of pathology as meaning postulates. Under the influence of Kemeny and Bar-Hillel, Carnap found it necessary to bring his explicata for " L-truth " and " degree of confirmation " into better agreement with the explicanda by introducing primitive predicates into a language in the context of postulates delimiting their possible interpretations: e. g. " warmer " is introduced as a relational predicate designating an empirically given and *necessarily asymmetrical* relation. A state description, then, was reconceived as a conjunction of atomic statements (and negations of atomic statements, in case not all the members of a family of co-determinate properties are represented in the language by predicates) which not only conforms to the formal laws of contradiction and excluded middle but moreover to the meaning postulates; that is, if a state description is to be a description of a possible world, then there must be no state descriptions that are incompatible with any meaning postulate. Let us say, therefore, that the function of meaning postulates is to restrict the class of Z in L (e. g., by virtue of the mentioned meaning postulate for " warmer," there is no Z containing a subconjunction of the form " warmer $(x, y) \cdot$ warmer (y, x) ").[41] But how can a statement like " Prob $(h/S_1) = p$ " perform this function, considering that a Z is a singular statement and no singular

---

[40] For the details of this explication, see Carnap, *Logical Foundations of Probability*. See also below, p. 406.

[41] Cf. above, p. 225.

statement is incompatible with a probability statement, whether limiting-frequency statement or logical-probability statement?

These considerations lead to the conclusion that " degree of entailment," involved in partial meaning specification, is a *pragmatic*, not a semantic concept. The pragmatic concept essentially involved is " degree of willingness to assert h if such and such observational evidence is found," as explained above in sec. D. An interesting question which arises immediately is whether such attitudes with respect to predications of constructs when relevant observations are made are reducible to expectations of correlations of the observed symptoms with as yet unobserved symptoms. If such expectations are themselves based on observed correlations of symptoms (e. g. S_1 is accompanied by S_2 in 80 per cent of the cases), then every degree of entailment would *correspond* to a statistical probability statement of the observation langauge, i. e. the language used to describe and predict observations.

Perhaps it will be suggested that a weight attached to a symptom as indicator of a disease can be given a frequency interpretation involving anticipation of an as yet unspecifiable micro-explanation of the symptom cluster. Let θ be a property variable ranging over micro-states of an organism—i. e. not directly observable states of the cerebro-neural system and the body cells that cause the occurrence of a symptom cluster. Then " $P(h/S_1) = p$ " means, according to this suggestion:

$$(\exists \theta) \ (P(\theta x/S_1 x) = p),$$

where the probability is a straight frequency (" θx " reads: organism x is in micro-state θ). The frequency interpretation here may seem plausible, since we have " independent access " to micro-states of an organism, e. g. we can verify the presence of certain kinds of germs in the organism without first observing " symptoms." But how can we specify a value of p *before* knowing the specific micro-property that causes the occurrence of the symptom cluster? If we have already found the value of p for a specific value of θ, we can of course derive the above statement by existential generalization with respect to that value of θ. But it will be agreed that such a probability implication (to be distinguished from the assertion of the existence of a certain kind of probability implication) does not explicate the meaning of " $P(h/S_1) = p$," since the scientist assigns weights to the hypotheses before he finds a specific micro-explanation. It is therefore more plausible to regard as the statistical basis of the degree of entailment some kind of inter-symptom correlation, and micro-property—symptom correlations are rather *explanations* of the initially verified intersymptom correlations.[42] The exact mathematical form of such correlations, however, and the functional dependence of degrees of entailment upon the latter, is a problem for specialists that lies beyond this foundational inquiry.

[42] On probabilistic meaning specification see also A. Kaplan and F. Schott, "A Calculus for Empirical Classes," *Methodos* (1951).

CHAPTER 12. *Pragmatics and the Meaning of Entailment*

A. *The Problem of Interpreting Logical Constants*

A FUNDAMENTAL distinction made in the contemporary theory of signs ("semiotics") and frequently used in philosophical analysis is that between the *pragmatic* and the *semantic* dimension of meaning. It would not be surprising if the kind of pragmatic analysis of material entailment (i. e. entailment holding between propositions of such a kind that some descriptive terms occur essentially in the entailment statement) [1] as a gradated relation—elaborated in the preceding chapter—aroused the complaint that what one expects a theory of entailment to be is a semantic analysis, not a pragmatic analysis. That a judgment of the form "*p* entails *q*" *expresses* a firm belief in the conditional proposition "if *p* then *q*," manifesting itself in stubborn refusal to admit the truth of *p* (respectively the falsehood of *q*) if one is convinced of the falsehood of *q* (respectively the truth of *p*), the critic might say, is obvious, but such a commonplace cannot satisfy our desire to know what the *semantic* meaning of "entailment" is, i. e. what is being *asserted* when we say "*p* entails *q*." That what is *asserted* by a sentence is not, in general, identical with what is *expressed* by the sentence is easily illustrated: if I say "it will certainly rain within minutes" I express a firm expectation of rain, but my assertion is not *about*

---

[1] It is advisable to predicate "essential occurrence" only of expressions, not of concepts. It would not make sense, e. g., to speak of logically true *propositions* as a proper subclass of analytic propositions, characterized by the inessential (vacuous) occurrence of descriptive concepts. For an analytic, yet not logically true, sentence of the form "all *A* are *B*" expresses the same proposition as the logically true sentence "all *CD* are *B*" if the concept designated by "*A*" is identical with the concept designated by the complex expression "*CD*." Thus we would arrive at the contradiction that the same proposition is logically true and not logically true. This consideration shows, incidentally, that in terms of Quine's definition of "logically true" no sense can be attached to statements of the form "*S* expresses a logical truth," where it is the proposition expressed that is characterized as a logical truth.

my mental state at all; if it were, then subsequent rain would not verify my assertion unless it were further the case that I actually believed what I said.

In view of the possibility of such, not obviously unreasonable, complaints it is best to begin by taking a close look at the distinction between pragmatic and semantic meaning. Since anybody who consciously uses a linguistic sign undoubtedly expresses some mental state or other by his usage, the pragmatic dimension of meaning may be said to be present in all linguistic sign behavior. On the other hand, semantic meaning is present only in what is alternatively called the assertive, cognitive, communicative, or referential use of language. It does not make sense, for example, to speak of the semantic meaning of interrogative or imperative sentences.[2] It is true that we can distinguish " what did he intend by asking that question, what was his purpose? " from " what did his question mean anyway? " But to speak of the *semantic* meaning of, say, the question " do universals exist? " is really to speak of the semantic meaning of the corresponding declarative sentence (" universals exist "). The point may be succinctly stated by saying that semantic meaning is primarily a property of declarative sentences, and that the semantic meaning of a declarative sentence consists in the *truth-condition* of the sentence: S means (semantically) that p, if and only if S is true if and only if p. The pragmatic meaning of S, on the other hand, consists in whatever mental states cause the utterance of S and are caused by the latter in sign interpreters.[3] The two kinds of meaning may coincide in certain cases, as in honest autobiographical reports of immediate perception: if I honestly report " I feel hot," then the event which conclusively verifies this sentence, viz.

---

[2] Imperatives are sometimes said to have both *cognitive* and emotive meaning because the total reaction to an imperative has a cognitive as well as a practical component, viz. understanding of the utterance and compliance or refusal to comply with the command; indeed, the cognitive reaction is causally presupposed by the practical reaction. But " semantic " meaning in the restricted sense explained in the text should not be confused with such cognitive meaning.

[3] It is, of course, clear that the pragmatic as well as the semantic meaning of S may be different relative to a user of S and relative to an interpreter of S. The pragmatic meaning of the sentence " I am miserable " relative to the sign user consists usually in a feeling of misery conjoined with a desire to make this mental condition known to others, but since it will rarely produce a feeling of misery in the listener, it rarely has the same pragmatic meaning to the interpreter. However, whatever problems may be raised by this relativity are irrelevant to the present discussion.

my feeling hot, is itself a cause-factor of the utterance of the sentence. But in general they are different, indeed necessarily different if the sentences are not autobiographical. If, for example, an interpreter *I* deems it relevant, in connection with the question whether the sentence " the presence of dark clouds makes it probable that it will rain shortly" is true, to consult a statistic of the relative frequency of rain following the appearance of dark clouds, but irrelevant to inquire into the strength with which people expect rain when they perceive dark clouds, then mental states or dispositions form no part of the semantic meaning which the sentence has as used by *I*.

If semantic meaning is thus defined as a property of entire sentences, it is not obvious what is meant by the semantic meaning of a *term*, such as a name or a predicate. While it may be difficult to define the distinction in question for names, it is not difficult to define it for predicates, however; for we can explain that when we speak of the truth-conditions of a predicate we mean the truth-conditions of *predications* of the predicate. Thus " ' dog ' means (semantically) a kind of quadruped " means " sentences of the form ' x is a dog ' are true only if x is a quadruped." Such semantic statements are, of course, informative only for people who already understand the metalanguage in which they are delivered. The semantic rule " ' dog ' means dog " cannot, for just this reason, be informative, although its translation into another metalanguage, say, " ' dog ' heisst Hund " can. In this respect there is no difference between interpretation of descriptive constants and interpretation of logical constants. A statement like " ' not-p ' is true if and only if ' p ' is not true " is, as an attempt at explanation of the meaning of " not," just as futile as " ' dog ' means dog." On the other hand, " ' $\sim p$ ' is true if and only if ' p ' is not true " corresponds to the informative semantic statement " ' dog ' heisst Hund," because here understanding of the metalanguage does not presuppose understanding of the object language to be interpreted (in this case a logistic calculus). That semantical interpretations of the logical constants of an artificial language can be given in just the same sense in which the descriptive constants of, say, English can be semantically interpreted if the metalanguage does not employ the same constants, it would be foolish to deny. However, the problem of interpretation here to be discussed concerns the contact between language and something extralinguistic. Here the analogy between interpretation of descriptive constants and interpretation of logical constants seems to break down: in the case of descriptive constants we can, after having reached the primitives, go on to ostensive definition, since there is something " in the world " which they designate. But what would it be like to show the semantic meaning of the primitive *logical* constants of a natural language, such as the English word " or " ?

It is well known that one cannot construct explicit definitions of logical constants which legitimize simple interchange of synonyms the way the definition " father-in-law = spouse's father " legitimizes such simple interchange. The specification of semantic meaning must here take the form of contextual definition. Thus " and " may be introduced into a logical system containing " not " and " or " as primitive logical constants by the contextual definition " p and q = not- (not-p or not-q) ." Here it is obvious that the statement of the semantic meaning of the term consists in a statement of the truth-conditions of sentences containing the term. In general, to specify the semantic meaning of a logical connective can mean nothing else than stating the truth-conditions of sentences containing the connective. Now, as long as we remain within the logical system we can be satisfied with definitional introduction of logical constants on the basis of the primitives of the system (like " not " and " or," or Sheffer's " not both ") in analogy to definition of descriptive predicates on the basis of primitive predicates in a descriptive system. But a significant disanalogy appears as we turn to the problem of *interpretation* of such systems. For this purpose it is sufficient to interpret the primitives, since the verbal definitions within the system automatically lead to interpretation of the defined terms once the undefined terms are interpreted. In the case of descriptive primitives, the interpretation takes the form of ostensive definition. But clearly this method of interpretation is unavailable for logical primitives: what could be meant by ostensive definition of " not," or " possible " ? Here the interpretation can take no other form than the specification of truth-conditions of sentences containing the primitives, usually in the form of truth-tables. But simple reflection on the meaning of a truth-table shows that unless the meanings of " not," " or," and " and " were already understood, no truth-table could communicate them; in other words, if such a truth-table were expressed as a contextual definition it would turn into a circular definition. We would obtain:

$$p \text{ and } q =_{df} \text{``} p \text{'' is true and ``} q \text{'' is true}$$

[or, negatively: not- (" p " is true and " q " is false) and not- (" q " is true and " p " is false) and not- (" p " is false and " q " is false)].

$$p \text{ or } q =_{df} \text{``} p \text{'' is true and ``} q \text{'' is true, or ``} p \text{'' is false}$$
$$\text{and ``} q \text{'' is true, or ``} p \text{'' is true and ``} q \text{'' is false}$$

[or, negatively: not- (" p " is false and " q " is false)].

$$\text{not-}p =_{df} \text{``} p \text{'' is false.}$$

In short, a truth-table for a dyadic connective says that *either* this *or* that *or* · · · that *conjunction* of truth-values of the components would make the compound statement true; and furthermore " false " can only be defined as meaning " not-true "; hence the circularity in the attempts to explain formally the meaning of " not," " or," and " and." The circle can, indeed, be temporarily broken by using as metalanguage some natural language other than English, but the circle will sooner or later be reinstated as one attempts to interpret the corresponding connectives of the metalanguage. Formal logicians will no doubt protest that the semblance of circularity vanishes once the distinction between object language and metalanguage is properly observed. The truth-table definitions are what Carnap calls *truth-rules* (though, for the reasons explained, they could with equal propriety be called " semantic rules ") and hence must be formulated by means of the metalinguistic term " true." Then the definition, for example, of " not " becomes: " not-p " is true if and only if " p " is not true. In this formulation it is clear that the defined " not " belongs to the object language and the " not " used in the definition [4] belongs, like " true," to the metalanguage. Similarly for the definitions of " or " and " and." This objection, however, I propose to answer by asking the objector how he would prove that the metalinguistic " not " on the right of the " if and only if " is not synonymous with the object-linguistic " not " on the left? It would hardly make sense to argue that just

---

[4] To be quite accurate, truth-rules and semantic rules are not *definitions* in the sense in which " definition " is used in formal logic, since definiendum and definiens must belong to the same language.

because they occur in different languages they are not synonymous, for an object language is commonly conceived as a part of its metalanguage, hence, synonymy being a reflexive relation, there must be terms in the metalanguage which are synonymous with some terms of the object language. But how it could be proved that the two tokens of " not " are not synonymous except by assuming that a term cannot be moved through the hierarchy of metalanguages without change of meaning (and thus to beg the question) , it is difficult to see. The same argument holds, of course, for a definition like: " p or q " is true if and only if " p and q " is true or " p and not-q " is true or " not-p and q " is true. Furthermore, the object language–metalanguage distinction becomes irrelevant to the question of circular definition if the calculus is strictly *propositional*, not *sentential*. If the variables " p " and " q " range over propositions, then the predications of truth and falsity have the forms " it is true that p " and " it is false that p," which sentences belong to the same language as " p." [5]

But even if a rigorous pure semanticist should succeed in proving that the definitions are not formally circular, it would surely remain undeniable that one could not satisfy the curiosity of one who wished to know the meaning of " not " by telling him " ' not-p ' means that ' p ' is not true," and similarly for the logical constants " or " and " and." Such " semantic rules " are no more informative than the semantic rule " ' dog ' means dog," to refer to our initial example. But since the (partly) nonverbal method of semantic interpretation called " ostensive definition " is not applicable to logical constants, it follows that it is not clear at all what could be meant by a semantic interpretation of the logical constants of the natural metalanguage in which an artificial calculus is interpreted. The same holds for that subclass of logical constants employed in systems of modal logic which are called " modal operators " and which are of particular interest in this discussion, since what is in question is a semantic analysis of the term entailment. If " possible " is used as modal primitive, then all the other usual modalities are, within the system, definable with the additional help of the extensional connectives. For example: it is necessary that $p =$ it is not

---

[5] For the distinction between the absolute and semantic concepts of truth, see above, p. 153 n., and the references there given. See also the author's " The Linguistic Hierarchy and the Vicious-Circle Principle," *Philosophical Studies* (June 1954) .

possible that not-p. The burden of semantic interpretation of the system of modal logic then rests on the term " possible." Ostensive definition is out of the question (what would it be like to point at, or experience, a possibility?) unless this simply means to give examples of statements of the form " it is possible that p " which are accepted as true. But if this were all that those who want a semantic interpretation of " entailment " would like to get, there would be no problem: we can easily produce entailment statements commonly accepted as true. We might, further, focus attention on the relevant sense of " possible " by the usual method of identifying the relevant analysandum connoted by an ambiguous expression: " we mean the concept of possibility illustrated by the statement ' it is possible that a man should live forever, but it is not possible that there should be round squares anywhere '; and let us call this concept ' logical possibility ' "—so we might say. Perhaps this process of interpretation is sufficiently analogous to ostensive definition of descriptive terms to be itself called " ostensive definition." In that case we would have to admit that logical primitives, like descriptive primitives, can be interpreted by ostensive definition, and the question would remain what more those who ask for a semantic analysis of " entailment "—distinguished from a pragmatic analysis—could reasonably demand if not such an ostensive definition of " possible " together with the usual explicit definition of " necessary " on the basis of " possible." [6]

The attempt to define " logical possibility " (to be distinguished from *illustrating* the concept) usually results in the statement " anything is logically possible which does not involve a self-contradiction (which is ' consistently thinkable,' in Lewis' phrase) ." But if we try to clarify further what is meant by " involving a self-contradiction " we get into trouble. If it means " reducible, with the help of adequate explicit definitions, to the form ' p and not-p,' " then the definition is too narrow. For example, one would want to say that the sentence " a has property P, but nothing has property P " expresses a logical impossibility, yet in order to deduce from this conjunction a statement of the form " p and not-p," we require the principle of existential generalization: " a has P " entails " some-

---

[6] Incidentally, in this discussion I am identifying entailment with Lewis' " strict implication." For a criticism of attempts to distinguish the two, see my paper " Strict Implication, Entailment and Modal Iteration," *Philosophical Review* (Oct. 1955) .

thing has *P*," the contradictory of "nothing has *P*." Explicit definitions might conceivably legitimize reduction of this principle to the
tautology "if *p*, then *p* or *q*," but then the latter would be required
for deriving the contradiction. If, however, the definition of "logical
possibility" is widened to read "a sentence expresses a logical possibility if no contradiction is derivable from it with the help of logical
truths," then we have a circular definition. For, according to the
conclusion of Chapter 6, "logical truth" is to be defined in terms
of "necessary truth," and any system of modal logic which is based
on "possible" as the sole modal primitive will presumably contain
an explicit definition of "necessary" in terms of "possible."

The *extensional* interpretation of the modalities which has been
suggested by such philosophers as Russell and Reichenbach [7] is
irrelevant to our problem since, though any state of affairs which is
possible in that extensional sense is also logically possible, the
converse does not hold: it is, for example, logically possible that a
man should be immortal regardless of whether there ever will be
immortal men or not; yet in the extensional sense this is not
possible since extensional possibility of a function ("*x* is a man
and *x* is immortal") simply means existence of values satisfying
the function. Furthermore, the extensional modalities do not even
have the same significance range as the intensional modalities, for
they are predicable of propositional functions only (this follows
from their definitions) while the intensional modalities are predicable also of propositions. It makes sense to say "it is logically
possible that all men are virtuous," but since "all men are virtuous"
does not express a propositional function, this sentence would
become meaningless if "extensionally possible" were substituted
for "logically possible." [8] Russell would probably reply that attribution of necessity to a proposition is elliptical. Suppose that a
statement *p* contains nonlogical constants $C_1, C_2 \cdots C_n$, and let
$X_1, X_2, \cdots X_n$ be corresponding variables. Then, on Russell's view,
"it is necessary that *p*" means that the propositional function

---

[7] Cf. B. Russell, *An Inquiry into Meaning and Truth*, p. 43; H. Reichenbach,
Elements of Symbolic Logic, § 23. For a more detailed treatment of this interpretation
of modalities, see O. Becker, *Untersuchungen über den Modalkalkül*, §§ 1, 2.

[8] The view that necessity is properly predicable of propositional functions only is
expressed by Russell also in "The Notion of Cause" (reprinted in H. Feigl and M.
Brodbeck, *Readings in the Philosophy of Science*, New York 1953), though this essay
is concerned with causal necessity only, not with logical necessity.

$F(X_1 \cdots X_n)$ which is abstracted from p by replacing the nonlogical constants with the variables (putting the same variables for the same constants) is true for all values of the variables. The analysis of " it is possible that p " would be similar except that the resulting function is asserted to be true for *some* values of the variables. But there are various objections to this analysis. In the first place, the analysis is applicable to modal statements of the form " it is necessary that p " only provided that p is a statement in primitive notation. Thus " it is necessary that all fathers are male " would be false, since " $(f)\ (g)\ (x)\ (fx \supset gx)$ " is false. And the transition to the true statement " $(f)\ (g)\ (x)\ (fx \cdot gx \supset gx)$," corresponding to the statement in primitive notation " all male parents are male," would have to be justified by pointing to the necessary character of the equivalence

$$\text{" } (x)\ (\text{father}\ (x) \equiv \text{parent}\ (x) \cdot \text{male}\ (x))\text{ " !}$$

Secondly, it would follow that if a given statement in primitive notation is necessary then any other statement of the same form is likewise necessary. This is nothing but the prejudice that all entailments and incompatibilities are formal, which we have already criticized (remember, e. g., " no surface is simultaneously blue and red all over " !). But finally: is it nonsense to apply the necessity operator to a logical principle, where a logical principle contains only *logical* constants and no free variables, such as

$$\text{" } (f)\ (g)\ (x)\ (fx \cdot gx \supset gx)\text{ " ?}$$

Is it not more plausible to hold that, on the contrary, the necessity of the substitution instances of a logical principle derives from the necessity of the logical principle itself?

B. Do Logical Words Only " Express " ?

The only kind of interpretation, therefore, which can reasonably be demanded of primitive logical constants—if it is not just the quest for illustrations of their usage—is a *pragmatic* one: all we can reasonably be expected to do is to describe the mental states with which the use of such constants is causally connected. We might say, for example, following Russell's discussion of the problem in *An Inquiry into Meaning and Truth*, that the use of " or " *expresses* indecision, the use of " not " rejection, disappointment of an expectation. Of course, the pragmatic metalanguage in which we discuss the pragmatic meanings of logical constants contains those very constants, but there can be no question of vicious circularity here, since we are not attempting to define them. According to Russell, logical words are distinguished by being indispensable only for expression of mental states, not for indication of facts: "Words are of two sorts: those that are necessary in order to indicate facts, and those that are only necessary in order to express states of the speaker. Logical words are of the latter sort" (*op. cit.*, p. 266). He does not, however, develop this suggestion; specifically, he does not apply the idea of the essentially expressive function of logical words to modal terms, such as "entailment" itself. One might argue in favor of such an extension of Russell's view as follows. If, as Russell contends under the evident influence of Wittgenstein, a complete description ("indication") of physical facts does not require the use of "not" and "or" (in other words, if atomic sentences are sufficient for this purpose), then it can presumably dispense likewise with "if, then," and with "if, then necessarily." The omniscient being who used language for the sole purpose of recording his boundless knowledge about the physical universe would not assert disjunctive statements, since he would know which alternative is true (disjunctive statements express partial ignorance). And the omniscient being, we may continue along the line of Russell's suggestion, would not assert negations, since "not-p" is a weaker assertion than the "but q" to which it is preparatory; after the totality of true atomic propositions have been asserted no additional information could be contained in negations. But then our omniscient being could not have any use for "if, then," or "if, then necessarily" either: these expressions are used for formulation of inferences, and so express expectations; but one who knows everything at once has no need for making inferences.

The discussion so far has aimed at a defense of the suggested pragmatic, gradualistic theory of entailment against the charge that the *semantic* meaning of "entailment" has not been clarified. We must now turn our attention to the distinction between *formal* and *material* entailment, for it might conceivably be contended that the theory, while being a plausible analysis of material entailment, is irrelevant to formal entailment. The reader may be reminded that "if p, then q" is said to express a material entailment if descriptive terms occur essentially in it, as e. g. in (1) " if anything is red, then it is colored "; (2) " if anything is a lemon, then it is sour "; (3) " if *x* is a bachelor, then *x* is unmarried." In a formal entailment, on the other hand, descriptive terms occur vacuously, as in (4) " if *x* is an unmarried man, then *x* is unmarried." To hold that the concept of degree of entailment is involved in *all* material entailments would be unplausible since not all material entailments involve open concepts. Thus (3) is based on an explicitly definable, though vague, concept and hence is transformable into a formal entailment. And there is likewise nothing gradual about the entailment expressed by (1), since there is no conceivable situation in which one might be inclined to affirm the antecedent but to deny the consequent.[9] The relevant contrast to receive our attention, then, is that between (2) and (4).

That there is nothing gradual about a formal entailment like (4) must be admitted. But might it not be the case that formal entailment is simply the upper limit of degree of entailment, in the same sense in which certainty is the upper limit of the continuum of probability degrees, such that the mental condition expressed by a judgment of formal entailment (or a formal inference) does not differ in kind from that expressed by a judgment like (2)? Now, while there is no objection to declaring formal entailments, like the *ponendo ponens* entailment, as entailments of highest degree if this merely means that one's reluctance to conjoin the antecedent with the negation of the consequent is maximal in the case of formal entailments, we would silently contradict the view expressed in earlier chapters (especially 5 and 7) if we did not also stress the differences. In some contexts of usage, " necessity " (and therewith " entailment ") does designate a property which some propositions are seen to have, either immediately or as a result of deductions. " Or," " not,", and all the logical constants of the lower functional calculus may be dispensable for the expression of *factual* knowledge, but what about knowledge of necessary propositions? And is a statement like " it is *necessary* that if the axioms $A_1, A_2, \cdots, A_n$ are true, then theorem T is true " just an *expression* of a mental state

---

[9] Notice that this is not to deny that one might have a concept of redness without having a concept of color. The latter is surely possible, since it is possible (logically, at any rate) that an organism should be capable of recognizing red objects as red yet incapable of recognition of any other color.

or an attitude, and no *assertion*? As already mentioned in Chapter 7, there is a striking analogy between the question of whether there are ethical propositions and the question whether there are necessary propositions, or between the question of whether ethical predicates designate properties, albeit " non-natural " ones, and the question of whether " necessary " is merely expressive or designates a non-natural property of non-natural entities. Indeed, one who feels compelled to postulate the existence of non-natural properties and relations may take a philosopher's failure to analyze " possible " and " entails " naturalistically simply as evidence of unanalyzability, not as evidence of there not being any property or relation to analyze. And the reason, he might say, why we are so reluctant to give up an entailment like the *ponendo ponens* entailment is simply that we *see* it to be true; just as an ethical intuitionist will say we disapprove of, say, cruelty toward innocent animals or children because we *see* the wrongness of such actions.

What is so obviously unsatisfactory about the pragmatic characterization of logical truths, like the *ponendo ponens* entailment, as those propositions which we are most reluctant to abandon when a discrepancy between our theoretical system and experience arises, is that not even a hint of an answer is given to the pressing question of *why* we should so tenaciously cling to just those propositions. If the answer is that abandonment of one logical principle would *entail* abandonment of all logical principles and therewith even of classical arithmetic and all the mathematical disciplines built on it, then the necessity of logical principles is presupposed in pretending to give a purely pragmatic characterization of logical necessity. It seems to me that the pragmatism which Quine wants to substitute for the analytic-synthetic distinction of logical empiricism is vitiated by this sort of inconsistency, since he admits that the revisions of the total system of assumptions—physical, mathematical, and logical— which are now and then " occasioned " by discrepancies between predictions and observations must be made *consistently* (see *From a Logical Point of View*, p. 42). On the other hand, the answer that this attitude results from an insight into the necessary truth of the principles of logic, where ." necessary " is a predicate resisting reduction to naturalistic predicates, leaves the " tough minded " empiricist profoundly uneasy. The most tempting of such naturalistic reductions is the linguistic theory. It is, indeed, so tempting that it may be worth the effort to point up its weakness once more.

C. *Formal Entailment and "Inconsistent Usage"*

What, then, is wrong with the theory that a formal entailment is undeniable simply because a denial of it is equivalent to a flatly *inconsistent usage* of terms? This characterization undoubtedly fits such formal entailments as (4), in general entailments of the form " if p and q, then p." But the latter not only constitute just a small subclass of formal entailments but, moreover, are useless entailments, in the sense that any deductive argument based on such an entailment would be circular, and hence this type of entailment is useless for purposes of proof.[10] Is there, on the other hand, a clear sense in which the denial of a formal entailment capable of supporting a proof, like " if p and (if p, then q), then q," would amount to " inconsistent usage? " Let us see. The conjunction of the antecedent with the negation of the consequent, viz. " p, and (if p, then q), and not-q," is, unlike " p and q and not-p," not explicitly self-contradictory. And if the deduction of a contradiction from the conjunction requires the use of formal entailments in turn, then " inconsistent " has been defined in terms of " formal entailment," and so definition of " formal entailment " in terms of " inconsistent usage " is precluded. As a matter of fact, in order to arrive at the explicit contradiction " (p and not-q) and not-(p and not-q)," we first have to legitimize the deduction of " not-(p and not-q) " from " if p, then q." If it could successfully be argued that this deduction is simply a case of substitution of definitional synonyms, such that no new entailment needs to be invoked, then assimilation of the *modus ponens* entailment to (3) would be justified. For the inference from " if p, then q " to " not-(p and not-q) " would then be just like the inference to " x is an unmarried man " from " x is a bachelor." But it seems to me obvious that the deduction in question is not a case of definitional substitution. To argue that it is, is to interpret " if, then " as the extensional connective symbolized by " $\supset$." But, as has often been pointed out, if

---

[10] I am not denying that the rule " q is deducible from $p \cdot q$ " is useful as an authorization of essential *steps* in a proof, but only that the entailment in question corresponds to what is ordinarily called " proof."

this interpretation were correct, then the *modus ponens* entailment could not be useful in the sense explained above. For knowledge of the truth of a contingent material conditional presupposes that either its antecedent be known to be false or its consequent known to be true. If the antecedent p is known to be false, then it cannot be used as a premise in order to prove q; and if the consequent q is known to be true already, then it requires no proof.[11] If, on the other hand, the conditional used as a premise is formally true, as in a mathematical proof, then the relation which one asserts to hold between its antecedent and its consequent is logical entailment, not material implication—as was emphasized by Lewis. It follows that if we recognize the intensional meaning which " if, then " has in any useful *modus ponens* inference (be it logical entailment or causal connection), then we must recognize that the entailment from " if p, then q " to " not-$(p$ and not-$q)$ " is not a case of " if p, then p." As a matter of fact, the negation of an intensional implication has the form " it is possible that p and not q "; and we need the axiom " what is the case is possible " (or " what is impossible, is not the case ") in order to proceed to " not both p and not-q " from " (if p, then q) ." It would be easy to show that in any other case of formal entailments capable of supporting noncircular proofs, the denial is not explicitly self-contradictory but formal entailments have to be presupposed in order to derive an explicit contradiction (as is especially evident in the case of categorical syllogisms). This is the basic reason why it won't do to define " formal entailment " in terms of " inconsistent usage of words."

The foregoing considerations (which are continuous with the more detailed discussion of theories of logical truth in Chapters 6 and 7) show that the widespread " nonpsychologistic " definition of formal entailment in terms of " inconsistent usage " is implicitly circular or else fits only those formal entailments which cannot justify *inferences*, as expressed in English by " since, therefore " and " because." Sometimes the position is taken that it is consistent obedience to linguistic conventions which *accounts for* the pragmatic apriority of logical truths, i. e. our determination not to give them up no matter what experience may be like. As an illustration I quote Nagel (" Logic Without Ontology," p. 199) :

---

[11] Cf. Russell, *Introduction to Mathematical Philosophy*, p. 153.

suppose, for example, " *A* " and " if *A*, then *B* " are asserted as true statements (the expression " if . . . then " being used in some one of the customary ways), so that the conclusion that " *B* " is true may be drawn in accordance with the familiar rule of *ponendo ponens*. Let us now imagine that as a matter of fact " *B* " is false and that we are therefore urged by someone to abandon the rule as a universal logical principle. Would not such a suggestion be dismissed as grotesque and as resting upon some misunderstanding? Would we not retort that in the case supposed " *A* " or " if *A*, then *B* " must have been asserted as true mistakenly or that if this is no mistake then the assertion of the falsity of " *B* " must be an error? Would we not, in any event, maintain that statements of the form: " If *A* and (if *A*, then *B*) then *B* " are necessarily true, since not to acknowledge them as such is to run counter to the established usage of the expressions " and " and " if . . . then " ?

Unfortunately Nagel does not tell us what precisely is to be understood by the crucial expression " running counter to established usage." If he means " inconsistent usage " in the sense in which an assertion of the form " *p* and not-*p* " involves inconsistent usage, then he is open to the criticism just developed. Or, is the criterion by which we are to recognize a violation of the established usage of " if-then " a denial of commonly believed conditional statements? This could hardly be Nagel's intention, since he would surely admit that *some* statements containing expression *E* can be denied without violation of established usage of *E*; a person may simply disbelieve a statement without misinterpreting it. Is the criterion, then, more specifically denial of *necessary* statements formulated in terms of the relevant expression? If it were, then Nagel's explanation of the necessary truth of the *ponendo ponens* principle would be circular. He might, indeed, fall back on the declaration that the meaning of " if-then " is *implicitly defined* by *modus ponens* jointly with other logical principles, such as the transitivity of implication, *modus tollens*, etc. But then he would be open to all the criticisms raised against this concept of " truth by virtue of implicit definitions " in Chapter 8; [12] specifically to the criticism that

---

[12] See also my article " Necessary Propositions and Linguistic Rules," sec. 5, in *Semantica* (Archivio di Filosofia), Rome, 1955.

no criterion of such truth has been formulated that would effectively differentiate necessary truths from firmly believed contingent truths.

D. *The Pragmatic Aspect of Entailment*

As to Nagel's undoubtedly correct claim that if the conclusion turned out to be false one would never question the principle of deductive inference but instead would re-examine the premises, this is exactly what I mean by saying that the formal entailment has the highest possible degree. However, in calling such principles " necessary " we seem not only to express the specified attitude but also to make a cognitive assertion, just as we make a cognitive assertion when we say of a given algebraic equation that it is identically true (true for all values of its variables).[13] Now, I have argued that the necessary-contingent distinction is vague, in the same sense that the bald-nonbald distinction is vague, the borderline area in which the vagueness manifests itself being constituted by conditional statements involving open concepts: if we are undecided as to whether property P is " essentially predicable " of A's, and thus whether " A " is applicable to an object lacking P, then we are undecided as to whether conditionals of the form " if anything is an A, then it has P " should be classified as necessary or as contingent, and this indecision seems indistinguishable from the sort of wavering we experience when asked whether a given vague term applies to a borderline case. But this is consistent with the view that the principles of formal inference, which do not involve descriptive concepts at all, are necessary absolutely, not just to a certain degree. It is true that the distinction between formal and material entailment is itself vague in the absence of an exact, general definition of " logical constant." [14] Suppose, however, that we restricted the extension of " formal entailment " to a class of entailments containing one or the other of a restricted set of logical constants, say, those of the propositional calculus, as the only essential constituents. It seems that formal entailments in such a precise sense of the word " formal," are, unlike material entailments involving open concepts, not subject to revision in the light of empirical data:

---

[13] Cf. above, Chap. 7, on " knowledge " of necessary propositions.

[14] Cf. above, Chap. 6, where doubts about the possibility of such a definition were expressed.

for they do not contain descriptive concepts, and hence not open concepts, as essential constituents. Revision of such material entailments as illustrated by (2) is nothing else than what is commonly called " redefinition in the light of experience," and this sort of thing cannot, of course, happen to logical constants. It was argued in Chapter 5 (pp. 112-16; see also p. 349) that when scientists define, for example, names of natural kinds in terms of empirically discovered properties, the " definition " amounts to a formal expression of high confidence in the empirical correlation of the properties originally connoted by the term (usually qualitative surface-properties) with the " defining " property. The definition is then a necessary truth of high degree in the sense that there is a high probability that the scientists would refuse that class term to a specimen that lacked the defining property (e. g. refuse the name " water " to a liquid that, though qualitatively like water, had a molecular structure different from H_2O). But it is not necessary to the highest degree, since discoveries are conceivable in the light of which one would say that the originally connoted properties are not, after all, reliable signs of the defining property (or vice versa), and hence would revise the definition (thus, if more and more accurately performed experiments revealed that the qualities originally connoted by " water " do not invariably co-exist with the structure H_2O, the chemist would abandon his definition of " water ").

It should be noted, then, that one may consistently replace the sharp analytic-synthetic distinction, which refers primarily to statements in which descriptive terms have essential occurrence, by a continuous, pragmatic concept " degree of entailment " and yet maintain that the necessary-contingent distinction is in *some* cases—notably in the case of logical principles—perfectly sharp. It should not be forgotten that in calling a distinction " vague " one is not saying that *all* relevant cases are borderline cases. Further, while I reject the view, exemplified by Nagel, that the distinction between logical truths and empirical truths can be made sharp by a *linguistic* interpretation of logical truths, I do agree with him in his rejection of the ultra-Millian theory,[15] which has currently recovered prestige

---

[15] I call it " ultra-Millian " because I have found no evidence that even Mill held it. Mill in fact held that the theorems of a deductive science are but *hypothetically* necessary, i. e. that it is only the implication from axioms to theorem, not the latter itself, which is *categorically* necessary: " When, therefore, it is affirmed that the conclu-

with some logicians, that even the principles of formal inference, along with the truths of arithmetic, are subject to the test of experience. Nagel is certainly right in saying that it would be " grotesque " to suppose that in any context of inquiry the empirical falsehood of a deduced proposition were interpreted as proof of the unreliability of the principle of formal inference involved. The view, in fact, that the principles of formal inference, like the *ponendo ponens* principle, and likewise the principles of mathematics, are subjected to empirical test whenever a system of empirical hypotheses is indirectly tested by deduction of directly testable consequences is logically absurd. Suppose, for example, that an Ultra-Millian contended that when the physicist tests the hypothesis that the instantaneous velocity of a freely falling body is proportional to the time of fall—by letting balls roll down a frictionless incline and seeing whether the distances are proportional to the squares of the times—he thereby also tests the integral calculus, since it is by integration that he deduces the testable consequence " $s = \frac{1}{2}gt^2$ " from the hypothesis " $v = gt$." Is it not obvious that it would be self-contradictory to blame a negative outcome of the test on the integral calculus if indeed the latter was used to deduce the tested consequence? For, unless one accepts the principles of deduction, leading from the tested hypothesis p to the directly testable consequence q, the test of q is not a relevant test of p at all. That is, the rejection of the mathematical law on the basis of disconfirmation of q would presuppose acceptance of p as true, but without the use of that mathematical law (or an equivalent one) p cannot be inferred from the observed facts. And if the principle of deduction allegedly tested is a logical principle like *modus tollens* (which is logically equivalent to the *modus ponens* principle), then any argument from a negative outcome of the test to its falsehood would presuppose it!

Those who, in a spirit of radical relativism, reject the notion of absolutely necessary logical truths, are likely to reply that the inconsistency they have been accused of can be resolved by properly distinguishing between object language and metalanguage. There is no inconsistency, they may say, in abandoning a " logically true "

sions of geometry are necessary truths, the necessity consists in reality only in this, that they correctly follow from the suppositions from which they are deduced " (*System of Logic*, bk. II, chap. 5, § 1) .

postulate of an object language L on the basis of an argument that involves an analogous rule of deductive inference formulated in the metalanguage of L. Thus there would be no formal inconsistency in an argument leading to the conclusion that some sentences of L do not satisfy the *modus ponens* principle though the argument may presuppose that all the sentences of the metalanguage of L satisfy an analogous principle. This defense of logical relativism (or "logical pragmatism")[16] might be countered in terms of the sentence-proposition distinction. The principle "for any propositions p and q, $p \cdot (p \supset q) \supset q$" is not about sentences at all, hence it would not make sense to split *modus ponens*, or for that matter any principle of formal, two-valued deduction, into duplicates for different language levels if propositions are taken as its subject-matter. Now, while there seems to me to be no harm in principle in talking—uninhibited by nominalistic strictures—about extralinguistic propositions (cf. above, Chap. 7, E), I realize that this move may not force the logical relativist to surrender. For both the ramified theory of types and the theory of language levels, which were proposed by logicians as alternative devices for avoiding semantical (or epistemological) paradoxes, deny us the right to speak of unitary, absolutely universal logical truths. Thus instead of the all-encompassing principle of deductive inference above, ramified type-theory would restrict us to "for all propositions p and q of order n, $\cdots$" and the theory of language levels would restrict us to: all substitution instances of the schema "$\ldots$" which result from the substitution of *sentences of L* for the sentential variables "p" and "q" are true. Yet even so, the feeling that there are logical truths that are *absolutely necessary* could be expressed in a manner that would not offend logicians whose painful encounters with paradoxes have made them suspicious of the dictates of "intuition." Instead of speaking of *modus ponens*, and other conventional logical principles, in the singular, we might speak of the "*modus ponens* family" and assert that some member of such a family must be present in any language in which reasoning processes can be expressed. And surely the corresponding assertion about physical laws would be indefensible, though a highly con-

[16] Cf. the critical discussion of the Carnapian kind of logical relativism, below, Chap. 14.

firmed physical law may be elevated to metalinguistic dignity by formulating it as a definition or a (*P*-) rule of inference.

To sum up: a semantic interpretation of logical constants, by rules connecting the constants with something extralinguistic, is impossible, since there can be no "ostensive definition" of the primitive logical constants. This might lead one to the view, represented by Russell in *An Inquiry into Meaning and Truth*, that such symbols have only *pragmatic* meaning, that they *express* states of the speaker (or writer), but do not "designate." Yet it cannot be denied that in saying " it is necessary that *p* " we sometimes make a genuine assertion about a proposition designated by " *p*." The property thereby ascribed to the proposition cannot be reduced to observable attitudes of people, such as unwillingness to abandon the proposition " come what will," or determination to stick consistently to a verbal usage once it is stipulated (in fact, we need the concept " necessary proposition " in order to define the concept " consistent usage "). On the other hand, there are contexts in which " entailment "—or " necessity " as predicated of implications—has only pragmatic meaning, especially the contexts of open concepts which were investigated in Chapter 11. Thus I cannot offer a grand, unified " theory " of necessary truth: there are contexts for which the pragmatic theory seems adequate and there are contexts for which the rationalistic theory seems adequate. If this sounds like weak eclecticism, I can only plead in self-defense that it should not, after all, surprise those who are sensitive to ambiguity to find the one word " necessary " functioning both expressively and cognitively—a duplicity of functions similar to that which complicates the analysis of such terms of ethical appraisal as " good " and " right."

CHAPTER 13. *Semantic Analysis of Natural Language*

A. "Absolute" Entailments and Contradictions

THAT what may be called an "absolute" concept of entailment (and a correlated "absolute" concept of self-contradiction) [1] plays a major role in the kind of analysis of natural language which dominates especially the English school of analysis will be revealed by just a cursory look at the relevant literature. It is constantly argued that *p evidently* entails *q*, that *r* is *evidently* self-contradictory, that the conjunction of *p* and not-*s* is *evidently* not self-contradictory and that therefore *p evidently* does not entail *s*. And it is no surprise that no attempt at *formal* justification of such judgments is made by those analysts: for such a justification would have to be based on definitions of the relevant expressions, yet it is precisely in order to *test* proposed definitions of the expression whose meaning is to be clarified that such judgments are made, and therefore their formal justification would be a circular enterprise. This raises the question, however, at least in the minds of the "formalists," whether such an "absolute" use of the concepts of entailment and contradiction is meaningful at all. Many a formalist in analytic philosophy is inclined to question the scientific respectability of this kind of analysis, for the very reason that it is based on alleged *intuitions* of logical relations between propositions. It will be my endeavor, in the following, to defend the absolute use of these fundamental logical concepts against the formalist charge, by showing that it is only through such "intuitive" judgments of entailment and compatibility that the formal method of analysis practiced by Carnap and his school has any relation to the professed aim of philosophical analysis: clarification of concepts in use. But first let us survey a sample of such "intuitive" judgments taken from more or less contemporary analysis.

[1] Cf. above, p. 85.

381

The contrary-to-fact conditional. The obvious reason why the concept of material implication must be distinguished from the concept of implication (sometimes called " causal," sometimes " nomological" implication) involved in a statement like " if I jumped out of this window, I would get hurt " is that the false-hood of its antecedent is a sufficient condition for the truth of a material implication. From this it follows that both the above contrary-to-fact conditional and the *intuitively incompatible* con-ditional " if I jumped out of this window, I would *not* get hurt " would be true if they were interpreted as material implications. The intuitive judgment of incompatibility may be expressed as an intuitive judgment of entailment as follows: " p is self-consistent " entails that " pCq " entails " not-$(pC$ not-$q)$ " (where " C " sym-bolizes causal implication) .[2] Accordingly all analysts working on the analysis of the contrary-to-fact conditional would stipulate this entailment as a criterion of adequacy which any analysis must satisfy. As pointed out, among others, by R. Chisholm,[3] the following simple analysis of " pCq " violates this criterion: there is a true statement S such that q is deducible from $p \cdot S$ but not from p alone or from S alone. For suppose we take as our S the formal implica-tion " (x) (x jumps out of this window $\supset x$ gets hurt) " and suppose that nobody ever jumps out of the specified window. Then S would be true, but " (x) (x jumps out of this window $\supset x$ does not get hurt) " would likewise be true. Therefore, if we take as " p," " q," and " not-q " respectively the singular statements " I jump out of this window," " I get hurt," and " I don't get hurt," we could prove both " pCq " and " pC not-q " on the basis of the proposed analysis.

The concept of law of nature. In the essay " Studies in the Logic of Explanation," [4] Hempel and Oppenheim define " law " via " law-like sentence," viz. as " true lawlike sentence " (it would probably better accord with usage to define a law as what is *expressed* by a true lawlike sentence) . A lawlike sentence has universal form, but this is not a sufficient condition for its lawlikeness. It must more-

[2] Some may prefer the stronger proviso that the antecedent be *physically* possible. See A. W. Burks, " The Logic of Causal Propositions," *Mind* (July 1951) .

[3] " The Contrary-to-fact Conditional," *Mind* (1946) , reprinted in Feigl and Sellars, *Readings in Philosophical Analysis.*

[4] *Philosophy of Science* (April 1948) , reprinted with omissions in Feigl and Brod-beck, *Readings in the Philosophy of Science.*

over have *unlimited scope*. For example, " all the apples now in this basket are red " is about a finite collection; it does not support the prediction " any apple that might be in this basket in the future would also be red "; hence this universal sentence is not lawlike. The authors recognize, indeed, that a sentence may be lawlike even though it has limited scope, e. g. " all the 16 ice cubes in the freezing tray of this refrigerator have a temperature of less than 10 degrees centigrade ": it would be reasonable to predict " any ice cube in . . . would have a temperature less than 10° C." But in this case we have what would ordinarily be called a special case of a law. The requirement of unlimited scope, which is to guide their subsequent systematic explication of " law," then takes the following form: if S is a *fundamental* lawlike sentence, then S has unlimited scope. In the form of an entailment: being a fundamental lawlike sentence entails having unlimited scope.

The concept of explanation. In the same essay the requirement, to be satisfied by an adequate analysis of " explanation," is laid down that the statements asserted in order to explain a given fact (the " explanans," in the authors' terminology) must be true. And since at least one of the statements that constitute the explanans is lawlike, the requirement implies that if L, a universal statement of unlimited scope, explains any fact, then L is true—not just highly confirmed. The alternative requirement of high confirmation is rejected on the ground that it implies that a given explanation may be correct at one time and incorrect at another time. So: it is intuitively evident that " L (jointly with statements of initial conditions) explains F " entails " L is true."

The next three illustrations are drawn from analytic ethics. We are all familiar with Moore's much debated argument against all forms of ethical naturalism, in *Principia Ethica*: no matter what naturalistic predicate " P " you take, " good " cannot be synonymous with " P "; for if it were, then the question whether something which has property P is really good would be meaningless, as meaningless as the question whether what is good is really good. Moore evidently meant that the question would be " meaningless " in the sense that a positive answer would be a tautology and a negative answer a self-contradiction. He held, then, that " good " is not synonymous with, e. g., " conducive to a balance of pleasure " *be-*

cause the functions " *x* is good and *x* is not conducive to a balance of pleasure " and " *x* is not good and *x* is conducive to a balance of pleasure " are not self-contradictory. If a hedonist had retorted " but they are self-contradictory *by my definition* of 'good,' " Moore would no doubt have replied that he was begging the question, the question being precisely whether such a definition is adequate in the sense of expressing what people mean by the word; which shows that Moore was operating with an absolute concept of self-contradiction.

The same moral is implicit in Moore's famous argument against one specific form a ethical naturalism, viz. ethical relativism. The analyses " ' *x* is right ' means ' I (the speaker) approve of *x*," and " ' *x* is wrong' means ' I (the speaker) disapprove of *x* ' " are incorrect, said Moore, because if they were correct then the judgments made by different persons that a given act is right respectively wrong would be compatible, but they are *evidently incompatible* (See *Ethics*, pp. 100 ff.) . Here one may be inclined to sneer: " What fruitless dogmatism! To Moore *A*'s statement ' *x* is right ' is evidently contradictory to *B*'s statement ' *x* is wrong,' and to the relativist the two statements are evidently compatible. How are they going to resolve their disagreement? " But I don't think the situation is quite so desperate. Disagreements about material criteria of adequacy, i. e. criteria relating to the degree of synonymy between explicandum and explicatum, are in fact likely to be *verbal* disagreements, in the sense that the proposed incompatible criteria of adequacy refer to *different explicanda*. And disputes, conducted pre-analytically in the language of explicanda, as to what entails what and what is compatible with what, have in that case the salutary effect of revealing ambiguities not so clearly noticed before. Thus Moore's disagreement with the relativists as to whether people really *disagree* when one says of an action that it is right and the other says of the same action that it is wrong provoked Stevenson into disagreement with Moore's tacit assumption that " disagreement " was an unambiguous term and to make the important distinction between disagreement in attitude and disagreement in belief explicit. The criterion of adequacy for analyses of " right," that " *A* is right " should express *disagreement* with the person who says " *A* is wrong," was thus diagnosed as ambiguous.

The point may further be illustrated in terms of Sir David Ross' views about the meaning of " right." Kant and Mill are commonly represented as having held incompatible views about the nature of moral rightness: according to Kant " x is (morally) right " entails " x springs from a good motive " (ethics of motives), according to Mill " x is (morally) right " is perfectly compatible with " x springs from a selfish motive " (ethics of consequences; utilitarianism). But Ross [5] makes the simple observation that we must distinguish two notions applicable to conscious acts, viz. moral goodness and rightness; that " x is morally good," indeed, entails a proposition about the motivation of x, but not so " x is right." Here again we have judgments of entailment and of compatibility, serving to focus attention on the concept to be explicated.

That disagreements about such entailments are verbal and hence, so far from being irresoluble conflicts of intuitive insight, simply signalize a difference of explicanda, seems to be demonstrable. For a true entailment statement, like " being red entails being colored " (S), expresses a necessary proposition. And by the very meaning of " intuitively necessary proposition," to say that S expresses an intuitively necessary proposition entails that whosoever seriously denied S would interpret S to express a different proposition.[6] To be sure, if the entailment statement is a complicated formal one, like " that x is red entails that if (if x is red, then x is round), then (if x is not round, then x is not heavy)," a person may reject it, not because he fails to grasp the intended meaning of any constituent expression, but because of an error in logical deduction. But such are not the pre-analytically asserted entailments that serve to identify the explicanda, in which the latter occur essentially. As an interesting confirming instance of this thesis, viz. that rejection by one philosopher of an entailment statement accepted by another indicates that they are talking about different explicanda, I shall cite Schlick's analysis of the concept of causality.

While it has been disputed by some that a cause must *precede* its effect, on the ground that cause and effect may be simultaneous, it is pretty generally accepted as a necessary proposition that no effect occurs *before* the event which causes it. Some writers, however,

---

[5] See *The Right and the Good*, chap. 1.

[6] For a detailed discussion of this point, see above. pp. 122-3, 210-11. The reader should keep in mind also the arguments advanced in Chaps. 5, 7, and 10 against the view that all entailment-statements are contingent statements about usage of expressions.

have regarded teleological causation as an exception to this principle: that type of causation, they hold, amounts precisely to a determination of the present by the future. It should be obvious that this is a verbal disagreement arising from confusion between an act of mental anticipation of a future event which contributes indirectly to the causation of the future event, and the future event itself: if I run in order to catch a bus, it is not the catching of the bus, an event which has not occurred yet, which causes me to run, but my *present* desire to catch the bus jointly with my belief that running is a necessary means to the fulfillment of that desire. Yet Schlick, in the essay "Causality in Everyday Life and Recent Science" (reprinted in Feigl and Sellars, *Readings in Philosophical Analysis*), does not challenge the claim that sometimes "the future determines the past" along this line. On the contrary, he accepts it, but points out that in this respect there is no difference at all between teleology and the sort of causal connections investigated by the physicist, since the scientific meaning of "causation" is "determination" and the latter is a symmetrical relation: the present position of a particle moving in accordance with mechanical laws determines its future positions, in the sense that the latter are predictable if one knows the former, but the calculations go equally well in the reverse direction. However, if the concept of determination thus refers to a symmetrical relation, it must be different from the concept of causation which is partially analyzed by the necessary proposition "if an individual event *a* causes an individual event *b*, then *b* does not cause *a*." [7] Indeed, while it makes sense and is true to say that a determinate change of the period of a simple pendulum kept at constant altitude *determines* a corresponding change of its length, it would hardly make sense to speak of the former variation as *causing* the latter variation.

B. The Process of Explication

The sort of intuitive judgments of entailment that have been sampled serve to identify the explicanda. But it would be a mistake to suppose that once the explicandum has been sufficiently

---

[7] This proposition should not be confused with the following proposition which, far from being necessary, is false: if an instance of *kind* of event *A* causes an instance of kind of event *B*, then no instance of *B* causes an instance of *A*.

identified in this way, the question whether a proposed explicatum is adequate easily answers itself. For whether a given explicatum satisfies those entailments (the criteria of adequacy) may be a complex question involving more than straightforward formal deduction. This may be illustrated by Russell's explication of the primitives of arithmetic in terms of logical constants. Any adequate explication of "(immediate) successor" (S) must surely satisfy the following conditions: S'is one-one and irreflexive. The condition of irreflexiveness can be expressed by the following entailment: Sx, y entails $x \neq y$. Accordingly, the meaning of this arithmetical primitive is pre-analytically clear enough to enable us to say that equations of the form $x = x'$ (i. e. x is its own successor) are all self-contradictory. But Russell's definitions seem to entail that if such equations are false at all they are so *contingently*, since the axiom of infinity, which is a contingent proposition (cf. above, Chap. 6), seems to be required in order to guarantee that all equations of this form are false: if, for example, no more than five individuals existed, the successor of 5 would, by Russell's definitions of the natural numbers, be the null class, and so would the successor of the successor of 5, so that we would have $6 = 6'$. However, as Russell noted, if it were not for the theory of types, the above condition would be demonstrably satisfied by his definitions without the assumption of the axiom of infinity. For we could conceptually construct as many distinct classes as desired which could in turn serve as the infinite set of elements needed to construct an infinity of distinct natural numbers, defined as classes of similar classes: beginning with the null class, we next construct the unit class whose only member is the null class; next, the class whose members are the foregoing classes; and so on. These constructions are forbidden by the theory of types which requires that the membership of a class be " logically homogeneous " (any two members of the same class must belong to the same type). But now the question whether Russell's explicata satisfy the above entailment is seen to lead to the question whether the theory of types is the only satisfactory solution of the logical paradoxes. There is an alternative solution due to J. von Neumann and Quine, the theory of " nonelements," [8] which legitimizes the mentioned conceptual construction of an

---

[8] See W. V. Quine, *Mathematical Logic.*

infinite set of entities, and accordingly makes it possible to prove that the relation of successorship is irreflexive independently of an *ad hoc* assumption of the axiom of infinity.

The conception of analysis outlined so far involves the steps (1) intuitive perception of the necessity of propositions by means of which the explicandum is, though not uniquely, identified (of course, such " perception " is inseparable from an *understanding of words*, especially in view of the inseparability of abstract thinking from verbal images);[9] (2) construction of an explicatum; (3) test of adequacy of the explicatum, consisting in formal demonstration of the pre-analytic entailments (criteria of adequacy) by substituting explicatum for explicandum. Through this last step the pre-analytic entailments are converted into explicitly analytic (logically true) entailments. To the extent that the demonstration is successful the explicatum may be said to be similar to the explicandum (cf. above, p. 296). But just as a scientific theory which deductively explains empirical laws that were antecedently confirmed may subsequently be found to imply false consequences, so an explication may, while satisfying the specified pre-analytic entailments, imply further theorems which are counterintuitive—propositions involving the explicandum which are either not necessary or even self-evidently false. In such a situation two alternative courses are open to the analyst: he may reject the explication and try to construct an explicatum which will not give rise to such counterintuitive consequences; in taking this course he manifests his desire to construct an explicatum which is *closely similar* to the explicandum, i. e. can be substituted for the latter *salva necessitate* (cf. above, p. 295) in a large number of entailment–statements. Or, he may frankly acknowledge the discrepancy between his explicatum and the explicandum and justify the technical concept he has constructed in terms of the good uses it can be put to (the logicians' construction of the concept of " material implication " is a good illustration of the latter course).

C. *The Requirement of Applicability*

An explication, then, " conforms to ordinary usage " to the extent that it satisfies pre-analytic entailments which serve to identify

[9] To say that the material conditions of adequacy do not identify the explicandum uniquely is to say that more than one explicatum satisfies them.

(partially) the explicandum. This concept of "conformity" is analogous to the concept of "satisfaction of a postulate set." For example, if an inductive logician asserts pre-analytically, i. e. prior to the construction of an explicatum, "if h is L-equivalent to h', then for any evidence e, $c\,(h/e) = c\,(h'/e)$," and "if e is L-equivalent to e', then for any h, $c\,(h/e) = c\,(h/e')$," he says as much as "by the concept of degree of confirmation which I am trying to analyze I mean a relation which, among other properties, has the property of satisfying these postulates." Now, besides the discussed pre-analytic entailments a criterion of adequacy which is often pre-supposed in analyses of concepts in use which aim at close conformity to "ordinary usage" is an *existential postulate*: there are instances of the explicandum; the latter is not an inapplicable concept. Suppose, for example, that an "avoidable" action (i. e. the kind of action for which people are morally and legally accountable) were defined as an action caused by a conscious choice which itself is a completely uncaused event. The definition entails, of course, that if every event has a cause then there are no avoidable actions. Suppose two philosophers who are both determinists, the first advocating this definition and the second rejecting it. Surely the latter could not convince the former of an error of analysis by pointing out that actions $a_1 \cdots a_n$ which clearly are avoidable would be unavoidable on this definition; he would simply be told that by this very definition $a_1 \cdots a_n$ are as unavoidable as all other actions. However, he might retort that no analysis of a predicate in use could be adequate if it entails the emptiness of the predicate. Thus a believer in determinism might reject an analysis of "avoidable act" which entailed that avoidable acts are partly undetermined, precisely on the ground that *it is certain* that there are avoidable acts. Again, a linguistic theory of necessary propositions which entailed that there are no necessary propositions (see above, Chap. 7) might be rejected by some for that very reason. Or, consider the analysis of "certainty," as predicated of empirical propositions, according to which such a proposition cannot be pronounced as certain until it has met all conceivable relevant tests. This analysis entails that "certainty" is altogether inapplicable to empirical propositions, and for this very reason "philosophers of ordinary usage," like Moore and Malcolm, have rejected it. Consider, finally, Goodman's startling demonstration (discussed in Chap. 10) that no two distinct terms are synonymous: would it not be natural to argue that if an analysis of " synonymy " entails that " synonymy " is an inapplicable concept, this is an excellent reason for rejecting the analysis?

But how can one know for certain that there exist instances of a given concept (where the concept is not a universal property like " round or not round ") before knowing the analysis of the concept? This is a serious question which ought to be taken seriously particularly by the philosophers of ordinary usage, since the belief that some such existential propositions are indubitable seems to be implicit in their analytic practice. Such a belief might, indeed, be justified by the following reasoning. In order to test an analysis of concept *C* we examine whether predications of *C* would keep their truth-value unchanged if for *C* its explicatum were substituted. This procedure implies that knowledge of the *truth-value* of a predication is possible independently of knowledge of the analysis of the predicated concept, since otherwise the alleged test of the analysis would be circular. But does it further imply that the analysis could not be pronounced correct unless the *truth* of some predications of *C* were known prior to the analysis of *C*? The philosophers of ordinary usage may argue that it does, on the ground that a pre-analytic predication of *C* could be recognized as false only by *contrast* to true pre-analytic predications of the same concept. And I think they are right on this point. Consider, for example, the claim made by a " skeptic " who has no analysis of " physical object " to offer, that we never see a physical object (but only sense data). How could such a philosopher answer the question under what conditions it would be true to say " I see a physical object " ? If he *can* answer this question, then he has an analysis, whether correct or incorrect, of the concept " seeing a physical object." But this assumption contradicts our hypothesis, which is that he allegedly knows *pre-analytically* that all propositions of the form " *x* sees at time *t* a physical object " are false. And if he cannot answer the question, then surely the only ground on which he could truly say " *x* is not seeing a physical object now " would be that the given situation contrasts in some relevant respect with situations which are *correctly* described as cases of seeing a physical object. To determine the meaning of *C* pre-analytically, in other words, involves specifying a set of *standard predications* [10] of C. If *p* is such a standard predication, then the assertion of the truth of *p* is part of the process of specifying the meaning of C. It is really a semantic assertion of the form " by C I mean a concept of which *x* is an instance," even though it is formulated nonsemantically, as a predication in the object language. It follows that in denying *p* one would interpret *p* to express a different proposition from the one it is intended to express, and in that sense *p* may be argued to function as a partial definition.

A recent illustration of this method of proving that there must be some correct predications of a concept which invites philosophical analysis is an attempted refutation of Goodman's startling thesis that no two terms are synonymous (or at least " completely " synonymous) by C. D. Rollins. Rollins accuses Goodman of violation of " the principle of non-vacuous contrast, which might be expressed: ' The contrast implicit in the definition of an expression, cannot be vacuous ' " (" The Philosophical Denial of Sameness of Meaning," *Analysis*, December 1950). He writes (p. 39) :

> Sameness of meaning is something which two words can have and often do have; and indeed if this were not the case there could be no point in saying that they never do. If it were not correct usage ever to say (truly) that two words have the same meaning, it would surely be nonsense for Goodman to say that they *never* do; for if his statement were literally true, there would never be, nor ever have been, a true application for its negation, and hence no *use* for the latter and consequently no use for the former.

Rollins is, indeed, somewhat dogmatic in saying that it would be *nonsense* to deny that two given words are synonymous if there were no pairs of words at all that are synonymous. After all, it is sometimes both significant and true to say that a given predicate determines an empty class. For example, those who deny the existence of synthetic a priori propositions could hardly be refuted in terms of Rollins' principle of nonvacuous contrast, by saying to them: unless there were some propositions which could truly be said to be synthetic a priori it would be nonsense for you to say

---

[10] The term " standard predication " is borrowed from C. J. Ducasse. See *Nature, Mind and Death* (LaSalle, Ill., 1951) , chaps. 4, 5.

that there are none. But Rollins could defend his claim by pointing out that an explicandum, such as "synonymy," is identified pre-analytically in terms of standard predications, and that therefore the denial of its applicability to any pair of distinct terms amounts to a denial of a necessary proposition, and is *in this sense* "nonsense." He might compare the expression "exactly synonymous" with the expression "exactly the same length" and contrast it with the expression "exactly the same facial appearance": in order to give a meaning to the latter expression we do not require standard predications involving this very expression; we may instead refer to identical copies of a given book, eggs that look exactly alike, cigarettes of a given brand that look and taste exactly alike, etc. Similarly we can ostensively define "facial appearance," and then we understand the compound expression "exactly the same facial appearance" prior to asserting the truth of any predication of it; hence it will not be nonsensical to deny that there are two people with exactly the same facial appearance. The expression "exactly the same length," on the other hand, is not *semantically* compound (though it is, of course, *syntactically* compound). That is, if we could ostensively define "length" without ostensively defining "same length" (which is actually doubtful since objects having the determinable property "length" also have other determinable properties such as weight and color, and relatively unambiguous ostensive definition therefore requires comparison with other objects which are identical with respect to one determinable and different with respect to another), and ostensively defined "exactly the same" in terms of objects having the same weight, the same color, the same temperature, etc., it would hardly be possible to derive from these ostensive definitions of the syntactic components a meaning of the syntactic compound. Rather "exactly the same length" must be ostensively defined *as a whole* in terms of a standard rigid rod (x and y have the same length, if the same length-value is obtained for them by means of measurement with the standard rod—whose length is constant by ostensive definition),[11] and then a statement like "no object has exactly the same length at two different times" would be either meaningless or self-contradictory.

[11] Cf. above, p. 253.

D. *A Sense in Which Existential Statements Can Be Necessary*

The assumption that some predications of a concept in use can be *known to be true* even though one may not know how to analyze the concept, underlies the method of analysis practiced by both the Moore and the Wittgenstein schools of analysis of natural language. Thus the skeptic who doubts whether there are physical objects, or whether there are physical statements which are absolutely certain, is put in his place by the argument from correct usage—"surely it is a correct usage of the expression 'absolutely certain' to say 'I have made absolutely certain that there is a table in this room now'"—but is this argument more than an *argumentum ad hominem*? How attack the skeptic if he replies, with Berkeley, "we must think with the learned though speak with the vulgar"? I think the only successful attack would be to point out that it is by means of standard predications that a term acquires its meaning pre-analytically, unless it be verbally defined prior to its predicative use; from which it follows that to deny such predications is to associate a different meaning with the term in question. The puzzle how one can know that "*Px*" is *true* if one does not know the analysis of *P*, is now easily solved.[12] If "*Px*" is a standard predication, then it is what we may call an *ostensive meaning rule* for "*P*," though but a partial one. It is therefore a case of articulating a concept rather than a case of applying a concept already articulated; accordingly it is possible to fail to *understand* such a statement but not to fail to *agree* with it. Suppose, to illustrate, that a philosopher prepared the ground for an explication of the term "mental event" by producing a list of examples of mental events pre-analytically recognized as such: thinking, desiring, remembering, feeling sad, suffering toothache, etc. If some other philosopher disagreed with the inclusion of the last item in the list, it could not be because he judges the proposition expressed by the first philosopher by the predication "suffering toothache is a mental event" to be false, but rather because he does not grasp that proposition, i. e. does not catch on to the concept which the list of standard predications was intended to identify. He may have mistaken a common property of the first three kinds of events—if indeed they may be called "events"—which is not possessed by the

---

[12] Cf. above, p. 279.

fourth kind of event, viz. nonspatiality (in the sense that such questions as " *where* is your present memory of your honeymoon? " are meaningless) , for the intended connotation of the term " mental event." Standard predications, then, are like sentences expressing (intuitively evident) necessary propositions in that they cannot be denied without being misinterpreted. Accordingly it might be argued that they cannot be " known to be true " in quite the same sense in which a statement which is not a meaning rule can be said to be known to be true. Indeed, we have seen already that if two analysts disagree with respect to material criteria of adequacy, this can only be because they have different explicanda in mind. To *deny* an ostensive (partial) meaning rule like " suffering toothache is a mental event " on the ground that its subject differs in certain respects from the subjects of the other ostensive meaning rules for the same term, is like denying a formal postulate on the ground that a given interpretation which fits all the other postulates of the set fails to fit it: we can significantly deny that a given interpretation satisfies all the formal postulates, but we cannot significantly deny, assert the falsity of, a formal postulate.

So far the respects in which ostensive meaning rules resemble nonexistential criteria of adequacy (criteria which do not entail the existence of instances of the explicandum) [13] have been called attention to: in either case we are dealing with sentences which cannot be denied without changing their intended meanings, and this is a mark of (intuitively evident) *necessary* statements. However, we should not fail to observe that there is also an important difference between the two kinds of necessary statements. It is none other than the difference between the sense in which " something is blue " and " whatever is blue, is colored " are *necessary* statements. And after the discussion in Chapter 9 it ought to be clear what is meant by saying that the former statement is *pragmatically* and the latter

---

[13] It is true that the logical relation between " thinking " and " mental event " is different from the logical relation between, say, " this blue object " and " blue ": thinking is a *species*, not an *instance*, of a mental event, and the statement of class inclusion " for any event *x*, if *x* is a thought, then *x* is a mental event " has no existential import. However, ostensive meaning rules for such determinable predicates as " mental " may still be said to entail existence of instances indirectly: the determinate predicates which are used to specify (pre-analytically) the meanings of determinable predicates acquire their meanings in turn through reference to instances (ostensive definition in the narrower sense; special case of standard predication) .

semantically necessary. If, to return to our last illustration, someone were to deny that there are mental events (which hypothesis, unfortunately, is not even contrary-to-fact), he could not, for the reasons explained, mean by " mental event " what is meant by those who affirm such existence. Again, when Goodman denies that there are pairs of synonyms he cannot mean by " synonyms " what is intended by this term by those who maintain that, e. g., " father " as a biological term is synonymous with " male parent." In this respect such existential statements are necessary, i. e. two people who are in agreement about their *meaning* cannot be in disagreement about their *truth.* On the other hand, the propositions expressed by these sentences are not necessary in the sense of being true in all conceivable universes: a purely material universe, i. e. a universe devoid of consciousness, will be granted to be conceivable by all except dogmatic idealists still adhering to Berkeley's " esse est percipi " as self-evident; and obviously we can conceive of a universe devoid of language, and even more easily of a universe in which there are no synonymous expressions. The sampled kind of propositions are, however, necessary in the sense that if they were false they could not be asserted, since on that supposition the concepts " mental event," " synonymy," " absolute certainty," " avoidability," etc., would never have been acquired by any mind. It is true that it can never be shown to be *logically* impossible that a given predicate should designate the concept which it designates even though it is not ostensively definable. For example, it is not logically impossible that a man should have the concept of *blue,* i. e. the ability to imagine and identify blue surfaces, even though there do not exist blue objects that could have produced blue sensations in him; accordingly it is not logically impossible that " blue " should mean the color blue without being ostensively definable. And similarly it is not logically impossible that a man using the sort of economic language mentioned above could describe conditions under which two terms *would* be synonymous if *there were* any synonyms. The concept " mental event," indeed, is in a different boat, because the concept of a purely material universe in which someone has a concept of a mental event is presumably self-contradictory. So we might be inclined to say that here is at least one expression of such a kind that from its ostensive undefinability it would *logically* follow that it does not designate the concept which it now designates.

But in spite of these important differences the existential statements in question may be said to be necessary in the sense that disagreements about them in *this* universe anyhow are bound to be *verbal*, i. e. rooted in differences of interpretation. That statements which are, in the specified sense, pragmatically necessary nonetheless express contingent existential propositions ought not to strike the reader as a paradox if he remembers the arguments of Chapters 8 and 9. Thus it was shown in Chapter 8 that a disagreement about a statement S may be strong evidence for the presumption that one of the disputants assigns an unusual meaning to S, not because the proposition usually expressed by S is logically necessary, but because it has such a high degree of empirical certainty that it is most unlikely that anyone would disbelieve it. As a matter of fact, though I have emphasized (especially in Chap. 10) that the test of analyses which is actually employed by analytic philosophers is better described as a *salva necessitate* test than as a *salva veritate* test, I would admit that among the adequacy criteria there may properly be included, along with pre-analytic entailments, contingent propositions involving the explicandum that have a high degree of certainty. The classical example of this is, of course, Russell's attempt to explicate the concepts of arithmetic in such a way that the *empirical application* of arithmetic is accounted for. There are infinitely many definitions of " 0," " number," " successor," which satisfy Peano's postulates. But if we add to the latter, say, " 0 is the number of feathers on the human body," we come considerably closer to the ideal of a unique explication.

E. Conformity to Usage and Introspection of meanings

We have seen that semantic analysis of natural language involves *intuitive* knowledge of necessary propositions, since the test of adequacy of a proposed analysis refers inevitably to propositions which are *pre-analytically* recognized as necessary. The position taken by many analytic philosophers of reputation that a proposition is either *demonstratively* known to be necessary, by demonstration that its negation is self-contradictory, or else not known to be necessary at all [14] actually implies that it is impossible to know

[14] See, e. g., the paper " Concerning Allegedly Necessary Nonanalytic Propositions " by W. Hay and J. Weinberg (*Philosophical Studies*, February 1951) , in which the authors

that any proposition is necessary. For, as we have seen repeatedly in the course of this book, the sort of demonstration which is asked for by those enemies of "intuition" involves the formulation of analyses, and the latter could not be known to be adequate if no propositions could be *pre-analytically* known to be necessary. To add just one more supporting illustration, suppose it were maintained that a proposition asserting the transitivity of an asymmetrical logical relation, such as proper class inclusion, is known to be necessary because its negation is demonstrably self-contradictory, while the mere "intuitive feeling" that an asymmetrical sensory relation like "darker" or "louder" is transitive does not warrant the assertion that this proposition *is* necessary. The former proposition is demonstrable, indeed, on the basis of the following definition of "proper class inclusion": A is properly included in B = there is a nonempty class C such that $A + C = B$. But this definition is either acceptable because it is intuitively evident that the two propositional functions entail one another—in which case the point is already conceded—or else it has to be justified deductively by showing that it entails that the relation has such-and-such properties, e. g. transitivity itself, and asymmetry. And in the latter case the propositions asserting that it has these properties must be known to be necessary independently of the definition in question, otherwise the justification of the definition would be circular.

If by the requirement of "conformity to ordinary usage" is meant the sort of demonstrable satisfaction of propositional functions containing the explicandum as "free variable" and abstracted from propositions pre-analytically judged as necessary or as true, which has been the subject of the foregoing discussion, it is of course imposed by the very definition of "semantic analysis." There are, however, two misinterpretations of the requirement to be guarded against. First, the expression "ordinary usage" suggests that semantic analysis of the sort practiced by analytic philosophers is an empirical study of contingent speech habits; which it clearly is not if the result of the analysis is a proposition that is translatable into other languages, and so is not *about* a particular language at all.[15] Secondly, it would be unreasonable to require *direct* con-

challenge the claim "that there are necessary propositions whose contradictories are impossible even though there is no way to exhibit this by deriving a self-contradiction by purely formal methods."

[15] Cf. above, pp. 181, 271-2.

formity to usage in the sense that the analysis should be confirmable by *introspection of meanings*. In other words, the requirement would be unreasonable if it meant that a negative answer to the question " is this what I (you) *have in mind* when I (you) use term T " would disconfirm a proposed analysis of the meaning of T. Who would maintain that whenever he identifies a figure as a circle he thinks of the concept of equality of length? Yet, this concept enters into the customary analysis of the concept " circle," and if it be held that for this very reason the analysis does not give the *meaning* of the term " circle," then it is obscure in what sense of " meaning " a somewhat complicated analysis could ever express the meaning of a term. Ewing objects to several philosophical theories, especially ethical theories, on the ground that " if we take ' meaning ' quite literally as signifying what the speaker consciously intends to assert, the analysis in question can be easily shown not to give the right account of our meaning " (" Philosophical Analysis in Ethics," *Philosophical Studies*, October 1950) ; accordingly he requires a philosophical analysis to be an introspectively testable statement about meanings in this " literal " sense of " meaning." But it is not as clear to me as it seems to be to Ewing what this literal sense is. Would Ewing say that a man could, by using sentence S, have " intended to assert " proposition p if p contains one or more concepts which he did not think of when he used S? If not, then an honestly introspecting man will have to confess that he did not intend to assert the proposition that there is a closed line all of whose points are equidistant from a given point on the blackboard when he said " there is a circle on the blackboard." And even more obviously, an analysis like that of " infinite class " as meaning " class such that there is a proper subclass of it to which it is similar " will not give " the right account of our meaning "; for most people, including mathematicians, do not always think of one-one relations, let alone the concept " one-one relation," whenever they judge a given class of numbers to be infinite.

Perhaps the concept of " meaning " relevant to philosophical analysis refers to a complicated kind of psychological disposition, but it surely is not so simple a disposition as the disposition to find by introspection the thought of the explicatum accompanying the use of the term in question. Such a misinterpretation of " meaning " is in fact responsible for frequent oppositions to proposed analyses, of the kind " I am sure this is not what I mean, though I can't tell exactly what I do mean, nor exactly what is wrong with your analysis; but after all, who are you to tell me what *I* mean? " A case in point is the opposition of *realists* to the phenomenalist analysis, in terms of subjunctive conditionals, of grammatically categorical statements about physical objects such as " this (physical) surface is green." The subjunctive conditional in question is the statement " if a visually normal observer looked at this surface under standard optical conditions he would see a green sense-datum " (or, if the sense-datum language be frowned on, " he would see green "). Now, it has been maintained that while this dispositional analysis, as it may be called, correctly renders the meaning of predications of smells and tastes upon physical objects, it is not a correct analysis of predications of colors. The statement " the unseen part of the surface of this apple is red," it is maintained, expresses the same kind of *categorical* proposition as the statement " my present sense-datum of an apple surface is red (I seem to see a red apple surface)." [16] But if the ground of opposition to the dispositional analysis is that no such conditional proposition is actually thought of when unseen physical surfaces are judged to have such and such colors, it is simply irrelevant. An analysis is not an introspective report, but an account of various pre-analytic uses of the analyzed concept; it is an adequate account to the extent that it demonstrates various intuitively necessary propositions involving the analyzed concept essentially. Thus " x is green at t " (where x is a physical surface) is held by " common sense " to be compatible with " nobody looks at x at t " and even with " several observers who looked at x at t did not see green." The dispositional analysis *demonstrates* that these propositions are compatible, or if you wish, justifies these common sense beliefs. To ask whether it expresses what people *have in mind* when they ascribe colors to physical surfaces is to judge analyses by an irrelevant criterion, as irrelevant as it would be to require that a physical theory describe what is perceptually observable as a condition of its acceptability as a correct explanation of empirical regularities.

---

[16] See, e. g., C. D. Broad's lecture " Berkeley's Argument about Material Substance," *Proceedings of the British Academy* (1942) , pp. 127, 131.

F. The Verificationist Conception of Analysis

After these critical observations on Ewing's "introspectionist" conception of analysis, let us take a look at a sharply contrasting conception, the "verificationist," adhered to by Schlick and Ayer. According to this conception we are to discover the meaning of a statement form (such as "*x caused y*," "*x* is *really* round," "*x explains y* "), not by introspecting "intentions," but by observing what we and other people do in order to *verify* instances of it: "the meaning of a statement is the method of its verification." This conception is reminiscent of what in Chapters 6 and 10 was called the "criterion of epistemic adequacy": the operation of counting edges is not normally part of the process of verifying that a given solid is a cube, hence "regular solid with twelve edges" is not part of a correct analysis of "cube"; we do not normally determine whether a form of argument is valid by determining empirically truth-values, hence the Tarski analysis of "validity" in terms of "model" is epistemically inadequate,[17] and so incorrect by the verificationist conception of analysis. However, the term "verify" in the maxim "in order to explain the meaning of a statement, describe what has to be done in order to verify it" suffers from a serious ambiguity owing to which the verificationist principle has perhaps produced as much confusion as clarification. This will now be explained.

It is obvious that there is a close connection between the (semantic) *meaning* of a statement and the *evidence* which would establish the statement as true. Thus if the discovery that a given woman has a child conclusively establishes the statement that she is a mother, then it is plausible to say that "she is a mother" *means* that she has a child. Nothing more sophisticated than this is expressed by the Wittgenstein-Carnap identification of meanings and *truth-conditions*. If any evidence which would establish that either "*p*" is false or "*q*" is true would establish the conditional "if *p*, then *q*," then "either not-*p* or *q*" expresses the truth-condition for "if *p*, then *q*," and so tells what the latter sentence means. In this sense of "truth-condition," to say that *p* (the state of affairs, not the sentence describing the state of affairs) is the truth-condition for *S* is to say that "*p*" *logically entails S*; and if "truth-condition"

---

[17] Cf. above, pp. 157-61.

is further used as an essentially singular term, such that if " *q* " likewise logically entails *S*, then the disjunctive state of affairs *p or q* is called the truth-condition for *S*, then to state the truth-condition for a sentence *S* in a nontrivial way is to assert a *logical equivalence* between *S* and some other sentence. But then the analysis of " meaning " in terms of " truth-condition " is implicitly circular: how else are we to distinguish the sentences logically entailed by *S* from the sentences factually implied (i. e. implied on the basis of empirical laws) by *S* except by determining whether they are derivable from *S* just by reflecting on its *meaning*, without supplementary information? Loose talk about the " consequences " of a statement as determining its meaning has indeed been responsible for futile debates about the dictum " the meaning of a statement is the method of its verification." Thus C. I. Lewis has persistently defended the paradoxical thesis that statements about the past mean present and future facts as an iron corollary of the pragmatists' theory of " meaning." But it is clear that while there may be laws of succession relative to which a statement about what happened at some past time *factually* implies a statement describing a *present* fact—and if it were not for such regularities of succession of events, it would indeed be impossible to verify any statements about the past except such as describe a remembered experience— no statement about what happens at one time could *logically entail* any statement about what happens at any other time. It is not self-contradictory to suppose that the entire succession of events which afforded evidence to Caesar's posterity for the proposition that he was stabbed by Brutus had been different and that nevertheless Caesar *was* stabbed by Brutus; hence it is confusion to say the historical statement means all this subsequent evidence for its truth.

Once this distinction between logical and factual consequences [18]

[18] It was, indeed, argued in Chap. 11 that this distinction is vague as applied to a natural language with " intensionally vague " class terms (cf. secs. C and D). But to *deny* a distinction because of its vagueness is, of course, a semantic naiveté of the first order. To say of the given distinction that it is vague is quite compatible with saying that there are cases to which one and only one side of the distinction clearly applies. Thus, one could consistently hold that the implication " if *x* is an apple, then *x* does not taste like a pear " is a borderline case with respect to the *L*-consequence—*F*-consequence distinction, but that the implication " if Caesar was stabbed by Brutus, then Brutus killed Caesar " is clearly a case of *L*-consequence, and that the implication " if Brutus stabbed Caesar, then Brutus was a man thirsting for political power " is clearly a case of *F*-consequence.

is made, the verificationist conception of analysis will be seen to be caught in a dilemma. Either it amounts to the advice to clarify the meaning of a statement by stating its " truth-condition," where " truth-condition" is defined in terms of " logical entailment." [19] In that case all that is asserted is that the meaning of a statement is expressed by the latter's logical consequences, but according to any ordinary use of the term " verification" one may know the logical consequences of a statement without having the slightest idea as to how the statement could be verified.[20] Or what is meant is that any statement describing evidence in terms of which S could be verified in the ordinary sense of " evidence" and " verified" expresses part of the meaning of S. In that case the verificationist conception obliterates completely the distinction between logical and factual implication, and is committed to such paradoxical consequences as that statements about other minds are statements about behavior, statements about the past are statements about the present, and indeed all empirical statements are reports of the speaker's sense experience. This dilemma is clearly visible in D. Rynin's attempt to clarify and defend Schlick's theory of meaning, in his critical essay on A. B. Johnson's *A Treatise on Language* (University of California Press, 1947). To explain the meaning of a statement, says Rynin, is to describe the condition under which the statement would be true. This condition, or fact (where " fact" is obviously meant in the sense of " possible state of affairs "), says Rynin, is what " we normally call ' evidence' for the statement; but we must distinguish between direct and indirect evidence. Direct evidence for a statement ' S ' is the F (read: fact) from which its truth *directly* follows, while all other facts which bear on the truth of ' S ' we call ' indirect evidence' " (*op. cit.*, p. 337). But it is not at all " normal" to say that the fact of Hitler being dead is " evidence " for the statement " Hitler is dead "; it would be a joke to try to satisfy the quest for evidence expressed by the question " how do you know that Hitler is dead " by replying " because it is a fact that he is dead." Anything that one would normally call

[19] " Logical entailment " is here meant as a contrast to " causal " entailment, if there be such a relation. It does not mean an entailment statement which is logically true; on the contrary, entailments by which the truth-condition of a sentence is specified contain the analysandum expression *essentially*.

[20] For a development of this line of criticism see my book *Analytische Erkenntnistheorie* (Springer, Vienna, 1955), chap. 1.

" evidence " comes under Rynin's title " indirect evidence," e. g. " the Reichskanzlei was destroyed by bombs at 3:10 A. M. and Hitler spent the night in the Reichskanzlei and it was practically impossible for him to get out of it before or during the raid." This is " indirect " evidence simply in the sense that " Hitler is dead " does not *logically* follow from the stated evidence,[21] though the latter bestows a high probability on this hypothesis. Rynin's criterion of meaning thus reveals its circularity the moment the intended meaning of his expressions " the truth of *S directly follows* from *F*," " the existence of *F* would *conclusively establish S* as true " is clarified.

It could hardly be said in defense of the verificationist conception of analysis that the distinction between logical and factual implication, on which the above criticism rests, is not clear. For this distinction is identical with a distinction presupposed by all verificationists, viz. the distinction between analytic and factual statements. The weakness of the argument from method of verification to meaning is that it overlooks that it may be by virtue of implicit belief in an empirical law that a person accepts evidence *E* as *establishing* statement *S*. Thus we accept behavioral evidence as verification of statements about other minds because we tacitly assume psychophysical laws. Before we could safely conclude that *S means E* for the person who accepts *S* on the basis of *E*, we would have to make sure that he regards it as *logically impossible* that *S* should be false even though *E* exists. And no amount of observation of procedures of verification can tell us what states of affairs

[21] Says Rynin: "*F*, (the dead Adolf Hitler), alone constitutes direct evidence for the statement 'Adolf Hitler is dead'" (p. 337). What could this mean? That the fact that Adolf Hitler is dead constitutes direct evidence for the statement "Adolf Hitler is dead"? But then Rynin's guide to statement meaning, leading merely to the tautology that a statement means what it means, is hardly useful. If the intention behind the quoted statement is that the *sight* of Hitler's corpse constitutes direct evidence for the statement, the following comment is in order. " Somebody saw Hitler dead " does indeed entail, in ordinary usage, " Hitler is dead." But if *E* is evidence for *S* in any ordinary sense of " evidence," then it must be possible to establish " *E* " independently of establishing " *S* "; hence " somebody saw Hitler dead " cannot be said to describe evidence for " Hitler is dead." If, on the other hand, it is supposed to be the visual experience as such, properly described by " so-and-so seemed to see Hitler dead " (" so-and-so had sense data which he interpreted as sense data of Hitler's corpse "), which constitutes evidence, this would not be direct evidence in Rynin's sense, since " Hitler is dead " does not logically follow from this sense statement.

are considered logically possible and what states of affairs logically impossible by a given thinking animal.

As to the question whether the " criterion of epistemic adequacy," pronounced by Moore, should be adopted by analytic philosophers— a question on which I may justly be accused of having avoided a commitment in spite of all the discussion of the problems raised by the criterion, especially in Chapter 10—I may venture these concluding remarks. If Moore's requirement is put in the formal mode of speech, it amounts to nothing else than the requirement that " B " must be *universally* interchangeable with " A " if the analysis " $A = B$ " is to be acceptable, in particular in such non-extensional contexts as " so-and-so knows that x is an instance of A." And since this requirement leads, as we have seen, straight to the paradox of analysis, it had better be dropped. To prescribe to analytic philosophy any precise degree of similarity between explicandum and explicatum, measured roughly by degree of inter-changeability, is perhaps no wiser than it would be for an inductive logician to prescribe to scientists that they should not accept a generalization until a certain minimum number of confirming tests have been made. The dissimilarity between explicandum and expli-catum will be the greater the more analysis of concepts antecedently used gives way to *construction* of new, more precise, concepts. And it is no surprise that those analytic philosophers who devote themselves to such construction pay little attention to either the introspectionist or the verificationist requirements of adequacy. Introspection of " intentions " and observation of procedures of verification would be dismissed as equally irrelevant tests of explica-tions by the members of this school. Let us call this school, whose creative center is Carnap, the school of " systematic explication." And let us, in the concluding chapter, take a close look at one of its characteristic theses, viz. that logical concepts, in particular the concept " logical consequence," are *relative to a language*.

CHAPTER 14. *Systematic Explication*

A. *Carnap's Relativization of "Explication" to Language Systems*

CARNAP holds that both the central concept of deductive logic, " *L*-implication " (variously called " logical entailment," " logical consequence ") , and the central concept of quantitative inductive logic, " degree of confirmation," are *vague* unless they are relativized to a language system. Statements of the form " S_1 logically entails S_2," " evidence *e* highly confirms hypothesis *h*," would be relegated by him to the inexact language of " explicanda "; in the exact language of " explicata " we must replace them by " S_1 logically entails S_2 in language system *L*," " *e* highly confirms *h* in language system *L*." If we look at the semantic framework laid by Carnap in recent years for both deductive and inductive logic, we perceive a common source of this relativization: both concepts are explicated in terms of the concept " state description " and the latter concept is relativized to a language system. Before raising critical questions about Carnap's *logical relativism*, as it might be called, let us see what apparent advantages are gained by such relativization, especially in connection with the explication of " degree of confirmation " (or logical probability, probability$_1$) in terms of a relativized concept of state description.

The fatal defect of Laplace's well-known measure of probability was that the equiprobability of all mutually exclusive and jointly exhaustive alternatives had to be determined by invoking a " principle of insufficient reason " which notoriously led to contradictions (as demonstrated especially by Keynes, who called it " principle of indifference ") . These contradictions easily arise if the disjunction of alternatives has the form " either *p* or not-*p* "; for by constructing a similar disjunction on the basis of a subalternative of " not-*p*," say " *q* or not-*q* " (where *q* entails not-*p*) , and so on, probabilities exceeding the maximum probability (unity) can easily be derived. As Keynes pointed out, in order to avoid such trouble we must

405

make sure that the enumerated alternatives are absolutely specific, indivisible. Thus we must not enumerate, as equally possible ways in which the event " making two successive throws of a coin " may happen, the three alternatives " two heads coming up, two tails coming up, one head and one tail coming up," because the latter alternative can be split up into " a head first and a tail second " and " a tail first and a head second." The difficulty with the suggested replacement of the requirement of equiprobability with the requirement of *indivisibility* of the enumerated alternatives, however, is that propositions seem to be infinitely divisible, by virtue of the law of propositional logic: $p \equiv (p \cdot q \vee p. -q)$. For example, consider the classical urn problem, and let p, one of the enumerated alternatives, be: the drawn marble is blue. This is a pretty indeterminate description of the object; it does not specify, e. g., the precise shade of blue. But even if we used a more specific color predicate, there remain innumerable determinable predicates with respect to which the object has not been described, such as shape, size, weight, temperature, etc. Even if the number of determinable qualities of an object should be finite, we could hardly ever be sure that our description had reached the limit of exhaustiveness, and hence Laplace's measure would remain inapplicable.

Carnap preserves the spirit of Laplace's measure of probability, the idea of probability as measuring the relative number of equipossible realizations of a state of affairs (or kind of event). But he avoids the difficulty connected with the indefinite divisibility of alternatives by formulating the definition of probability semantically and thereby relativizing the defined concept to a language. The language is of the artificial type called " molecular," i. e. its sentences are either atomic or truth-functional compounds of such sentences (e. g. " Pa or not-Qa "), and since the language contains only a finite number of individual constants, any general sentence is translatable into such a truth-functional compound.[1] The semantical counterpart of the concept " indivisible alternative " is the concept " state description in L ":[2] the individuals for which there are names in L are described as exhaustively as the stock of primitive predicates in L permits, i. e. a state description is a description of

[1] For a detailed discussion of the concept " molecular language " see " Testability and Meaning," sec. IV, 23, in *Philosophy of Science*, 1937.

[2] Cf. *Logical Foundations of Probability*, § 18.

such a kind that it tells us with respect to any individual that has a name in L and with respect to any simple property of individuals that is designated by a primitive predicate in L, whether or not the individual has the property. The *range* of a sentence of L is defined as the class of those state descriptions of L in which the sentence holds. Then the degree of confirmation of h relative to e in L is defined as the ratio of a stipulated measure of the range of " h and e " divided by the corresponding measure of the range of " e." Notice that state descriptions are absolutely complete, not disjunctively divisible, descriptions of possible states *in the given language.*

Now, as mentioned above, this semantical concept of state description is used by Carnap not only for the explication of " degree of confirmation " but also for the explication of " L-implication " and " L-true." [3] " S is L-true in L " simply means that S holds in all the state descriptions of L. Hence " ' p ' L-implies ' q ' in L " means that the range of " p " in L is included in the range of " q " in L, whereas probability implication consists in an overlap of the respective ranges. The conceptual unification of deductive and inductive logic thus achieved is surely admirable. However, a question which inevitably arises if the logical (or " metalogical ") concepts are thus relativized to a language is: just what is the best linguistic reference-frame to use in order to arrive at adequate explications? And I want to show that in the process of choosing what we may call an *adequate linguistic reference frame* we must make use of *absolute* concepts of " possibility " and " necessity." Indeed, these concepts must be used, and are used by Carnap himself, in defining " adequate linguistic reference frame "; if, therefore, these concepts be inexact, then the corresponding semantical concepts, being defined via " adequate linguistic reference frame," will themselves be infected with inexactness. I have in mind especially a requirement stated by Carnap which languages relative to which " state description " is defined must satisfy: the requirement of logical independence.[4]

A state description is a description of a *possible world*—though this is to be regarded, according to Carnap, not as a definition within the precise language of explicata but rather as an " informal " identification of the explicandum. But then we must make sure

---

[3] " L-true " is the more fundamental concept, since " L-implication " is definable in terms of it: " p " L-implies " q " if and only if " $p \supset q$ " is L-true.

[4] Cf. the earlier discussions of this requirement, pp. 16-17, 225-8.

that the worlds described by our state descriptions are really possible. In other words, a language L is an adequate reference frame for a definition of " state description," and indirectly for definitions of semantical concepts defined in terms of " state description " (such as " degree of confirmation " and " L-truth "), only if " S is a state description in L " entails " S is a description of a possible world." Hence judgments as to what worlds are possible must precede the construction of the linguistic reference frame. In particular, Carnap noted that if we selected two primitive predicates " P " and " Q " of such a kind that the property P, being complex, entails the property Q (e. g. " square " and " equilateral "), then some state descriptions would be inconsistent, viz. those containing conjunctions of the form " Px and not-Qx." Hence the requirement of logical independence, which really reduces to the requirement that the properties designated by the primitive predicates should be *simple*.[5] But the concept of entailment, or alternatively the concept of possibility, must be used in stating this requirement: for any two primitive properties P and Q, it is possible that something have P without having Q, and it is possible that something have Q without having P—or alternatively, it is not the case that " (x) $(Px \supset Qx)$ " is necessary, and it is not the case that " (x) $(Qx \supset Px)$ " is necessary.[6] There is a related requirement of *compatibility* of primitive predicates, which Carnap lays down in the form " select no more than one primitive predicate per family of related predicates," [7] which is again based on a modal judgment outside the linguistic framework: for any properties P and Q which are designated by primitive predicates, it is possible that a thing have both P and Q. Thus it is insights into relations of compatibility and incompatibility between properties which determine the choice of primitive predicates and therewith of the linguistic framework.

B. *Meaning Postulates*

In a recent paper, referred to above, Chap. 8, Carnap suggests indeed that the requirement of logical independence be abandoned

[5] As Carnap seems to admit in " On the Application of Inductive Logic," cited above, p. 16.

[6] I disregard here the difficulty created for this requirement by *determinable* predicates, like " colored," " having weight," on account of such entailments as " being red entails being colored." See above, pp. 154-6.

[7] Cf. the discussion above, p. 226.

for language systems containing primitive *relational* predicates, like "warmer," and that instead "meaning postulates" describing the logical structure of the designated relations be incorporated into the language system. But the underlying insight into logical relations which determines the adoption of this rather than that meaning postulate cannot be concealed by the gratuitous application of the term "(semantic) rule" to meaning postulates. In what sense is the proposition that the relation *warmer* is necessarily (not contingently) asymmetrical—a "nonsemiotic" mode of speech which Carnap himself has sanctioned—a *rule*? It is an intelligible use of the word "rule" to say "let us observe the rule to designate the relation here-now experienced by the word 'warmer.'" But once we have adopted this semantic rule (which in Carnapian semantic systems is written in the form "'*P*' designates *P*"), we are no longer free to rule that the relation *warmer* is to satisfy such and such axioms—or rather it is senseless to speak of ruling about the properties of a relation. According to Carnap (cf. "Meaning Postulates," p. 68) it "is not a matter of knowledge but of decision" whether the properties Bachelor and Married are incompatible and whether, accordingly, the postulate "$(x) (Bx \supset -Mx)$" ought to be incorporated into a semantic system containing "B" and "M" both as primitive predicates. He holds that one can significantly say "I know that the English words 'bachelor' and 'married' are usually understood in such a way that they are incompatible," but not "I know that the properties Bachelor and Married are incompatible." But surely Carnap's implicit translation of "B and M are incompatible properties" into "the English words 'bachelor' and 'married' are used incompatibly" is no more plausible than its translation into "the German words 'Junggeselle' and 'verheiratet' are used incompatibly." Further, it is indeed permissible to speak of *stipulations* of incompatibilities and entailments where the relevant words are vague in relevant respects. For example, that "x is a bachelor" entails "x is older than 25" can only be a stipulation, not an insight. But this vagueness of the word "bachelor" is surely irrelevant to the question whether "x is a bachelor" entails "x is unmarried."

The Carnapian relativization of the basic semantical or logical concepts, which includes the concept of necessary truth ("*L*-truth") itself, to a constructed language amounts either to arbitrary or to circular definition. It amounts to the former if no restriction at all is imposed on the choice of the linguistic framework. If, for example, the chosen L contains the definition " man = immortal bird," then we can say " all men are birds " is L-true relative to this L. Or, if the language contains both " blue " and " red " as primitive predicates, we can say that " some individuals are both blue and red " is not *necessarily* false (relative to this language). Indeed, this procedure would be strikingly analogous to purifying the laws of mechanics of the allegedly meaningless concept " absolute motion " by substituting for " uniformly moving " the term " moving uniformly relative to some arbitrary reference frame ": just as statements intuitively recognized as necessarily true could be made to lose this character by a suitable choice of linguistic reference frame, so the first law of motion could be turned into an obvious falsehood by a suitable choice of material reference frame for the definition of " uniform motion." As for the other horn of the dilemma: it is well known that if we want to describe an observable reference-frame R such that the law of inertia is exactly valid relative to R, we have to describe R as a reference frame relative to which particles move in accordance with the law of inertia (" inertial " reference-frame). The analogous circularity involved in the relativization of " L-truth " consists in defining an " adequate " linguistic framework as one such that all state descriptions in it are descriptions of a *possible* world.

It should further be noted that any empirical law could, by an arbitrary choice of " meaning postulates," be turned into an L-truth if we take seriously Carnap's most recent definition of " L-true in L ": " A statement S_i in L is L-true with respect to $P =_{df} S_i$ is L-implied by P (in L) " (*loc. cit.*, p. 69), where P is a set of meaning postulates. For, obviously any meaning postulate is, according to this definition, itself L-true in the language in which it occurs. If we rule that only sentences expressing necessary propositions are eligible as meaning postulates, we presuppose again the absolute concept of necessity which Carnap apparently wishes to avoid. It seems that Carnap attempts to escape between the horns of this dilemma by saying that the system builders' choice of meaning postulates is " guided not by their beliefs concerning facts of the world but by their intentions with respect to the meanings, i. e. the ways of use of the descriptive constants." But is it not clear that my honest assertion of, e. g., the proposition " the relation *warmer* is transitive " cannot be due *solely* to my intention to use the word " warmer " as a designation for the relation *warmer*, but must moreover express my belief that this relation is transitive? And is not, then, the question left open whether the proposition believed is contingent or necessary? To be sure, I might make this assertion, along with several others about the same relation, in order to communicate to somebody what relation I mean by " warmer," but this purpose can be served by uttering sentences expressing true *contingent* propositions about the relation as well.[8] For example, in order to communicate verbally what I mean by " red," I might begin by saying " red is, at any rate, a color " and then continue with the more specific information " red is a property shared by all the flags now on this building." Presumably the former proposition is necessary and the latter contingent. This shows that the restriction which Carnap imposes upon the *motivation* of a choice of a meaning postulate is insufficient to rule out the possibility that contingent statements might be elected as meaning postulates.

C. *Logical Relativism, Sentences and Propositions*

That *absolute* modal concepts are indispensable for the very construction of those language systems that are to enable precise definitions of modal concepts may be illustrated further by asking what is meant by saying that a given sentence *holds* in a given state description. If this were defined as " the state description *L*-implies the sentence," the definition of " *L*-true " sentences as those that hold in all state descriptions would, of course, be circular. But Carnap carefully avoids such circularities. Instead of giving an explicit definition he constructs a recursive definition (see *Logical Foundations of Probability*, +D18-4, pp. 78-9) which really amounts to an enumeration of the cases of entailment from the state description to the sentence which is said to " hold " in it, e. g. if the sentence is a component of the state description, or if it has the form " $j \vee k$ " and either j or k satisfies the aforementioned condition, etc. Obviously, Carnap has constructed just this recursive definition and no other because he already knows, prior to any state description

[8] Cf. above, p. 170.

test of L-implication, various entailments, such as that "p and q" entails "p," "p" entails "p or q," etc.

A similar comment applies to, formally unobjectionable, recursive definitions of "logical consequence" relative to a logical calculus in terms of a set of rules of derivation. Here it is the question of *deductive completeness* which cannot be discussed without employing the very *absolute* concept of entailment which is to be disposed of by such definitions. To say that a logical calculus is deductively complete [9] is to say that any sentence constructable with the means of expression of the calculus which *really* follows from, or contradicts, the primitive sentences, can be shown to stand in this logical relation to the primitive sentences with the help of the rules of derivation explicitly formulated. Hence the logician's endeavor to lay down as complete as possible a set of rules of derivation is guided by his intuitive knowledge that certain forms of argument are valid. For example, we know intuitively that a consoling subsumptive syllogism like "all men are mortal, McCarthy is a man, therefore McCarthy is mortal" is valid; that the conclusion, in other words, is entailed by the premises. Now, if our rules of derivation comprised only rules referring to unanalyzed elementary propositions (that is, the rules of the propositional calculus), we could not show formally that such an argument is valid. To obtain a more complete system of logic, therefore, the rule of specification "'Fz' (where 'z' represents an individual constant) is derivable from '$(x) Fx$'" is added, which together with the *modus ponens* rule suffices to demonstrate the validity of the subsumptive syllogism: "$(x) (fx \supset gx)$" entails "$fa \supset ga$," which together with "fa" entails "ga."

---

[9] This concept of completeness is different from the concept of completeness used in the theory of extralogical axiomatic systems, i. e. axiomatic systems containing non-logical terms, where a system of the latter kind is called complete if every sentence constructable on the basis of the primitive terms of the system is either derivable from the axioms or contradicts the axioms. Only the concept of syntactic derivability, not the concept of absolute entailment, enters into the definition of this concept. It is clear that if a logical calculus is of such a kind that the normal interpretation of its constants turns all the axioms into *logical truths*, then it cannot be complete in this syntactic sense: e. g. the formula "$p \supset q$" neither is derivable from the axioms of *Principia Mathematica*, nor does it contradict them. The concept of completeness which is applied in particular to a *propositional* calculus is very similar to the concept of "deductive completeness" as above defined: the calculus is complete if every *tautology* (provable as such by the truth-table test—cf. above, p. 144) is derivable from its axioms.

The sort of " logical relativism " here criticized might be given an air of plausibility by pointing out that surely the semantical and logical properties of an expression depend on the language to which it belongs. Thus the graphic sign " hut " designates one kind of object in German (called " hat " in English) and a different kind of object in English (called " hütte " in German). Similarly, what a sentence entails and is incompatible with depends on what proposition it expresses, and what proposition it expresses depends on the language to which it belongs. Thus in a language containing the rule that " all A are B " is to be considered true only if there are A's, " all A are B " would not be the contradictory of " some A are not B." However, the thesis that logical properties thus vary with lingustic rules loses its plausibility once it is admitted that logical relations hold primarily between *propositions*, not sentences. That it depends on linguistic conventions what proposition is expressed by a given sentence is a commonplace. And if " S_1 entails S_2 " is elliptical for " S_1 designates (in L) p, and S_2 designates (in L) q, and p entails q," it is no surprise that relations of entailment between *sentences* vary with linguistic rules. But to claim such relativity for the logical properties of the propositions is to use time-independent predicates as time-dependent predicates, which error was sufficiently exposed in Chapters 5 and 7. Carnap himself is ambivalent on this important point, since he seems, on the one hand, to frown on absolute entailment statements as " inexact," or at least elliptical, but recognizes, on the other hand, absolute modal concepts corresponding to semantical (language-relative) modal concepts. When critics took Carnap to task for speaking, in the *Introduction to Semantics*, of *absolute* modal concepts applicable to extralinguistic propositions, charging him with a commitment to Platonism, he decided to placate them by abandoning the term " absolute ": in *Meaning and Necessity* he speaks of the *transferred*, or *nonsemantical* use of such terms as " L-true," " L-implies," " equivalent." However, Carnap has not emancipated himself sufficiently from his early logical relativism to state clearly and boldly that entailment and other logical relations hold primarily between designata and are transferred to the designators, rather than the other way around. To consider an analogy, if John is taller than Peter, it follows that the names " John " and " Peter " stand in the derived relation expressed by the semantic statement " ' John ' designates a taller individual than ' Peter.' " If John and Peter happened to be nameless, the first statement would still be true; but the second statement presupposes the existence of these names and hence would in that case be meaningless (or at least false).[10] So, we cannot at any rate regard the two sentences as synonymous. For a similar reason, we cannot regard the statements " 4 is a square number " and " ' 4 ' is a square-number-numeral " as synonymous. And for just the same reason, an absolute entailment-statement is not translatable into a semantic entailment-statement.

Carnap does not unambiguously commit himself on this question, but one gathers that he favors such a thesis of translatability from " nonsemantic " to " semantic " formulations from the following criterion of adequacy he lays down for definitions of *absolute concepts*:

> *Convention 17-1.* A term used for a radical semantical property of expressions will be applied in an absolute way (i. e., without reference to a language system) to an entity u if and only if every expression A_i which designates u in any semantical system S has that semantical property in S. Analogously with a semantical relation between two or more expressions [*Introduction to Semantics*, § 17].

A clear illustration of this convention, for the case of the *absolute use of L-terms,* follows: " Thus a proposition p will be called *L-true* if and only if every sentence designating p in some system S is *L*-true in S." That is, the definition of the absolute term " *L*-true " must be so constructed that this equivalence becomes demonstrable. But if the definition is to be a reconstruction of the absolute concept of *L*-truth ordinarily used (in science and in everyday life) —which, I should say, is equivalent to supposing that the definition has philosophical relevance—then this criterion of adequacy ought to express an intuitively (or " pre-analytically ") *necessary* equivalence. But that it does not, it is easy to see. Its formalization yields: *L*-true $(p) \equiv (x)\ (S)\ [\text{Des}\ (x, p, S) \supset L\text{-true}\ (x, S)\ ]$.   Suppose that p is a factual proposition which nobody has ever thought of

---

[10] Which of these alternatives is accepted depends on whether one takes the existence of the subject which a statement is about as a significance-condition or as a truth-condition of the statement. This question is important (see my article " Logic, Existence, and the Theory of Descriptions," *loc. cit.*) , but need not be settled in connection with the above argument.

and nobody will ever think of, such that there exists no sentence x which designates p in some language S. Then the right-hand side of our equivalence would be vacuously true, but the left-hand side would be, *ex hypothesi*, false.[11] The attempt to save the equivalence as itself *necessarily* true by replacing material implication on the right-hand side with strict implication, would be unsuccessful for the reasons already given in Chapter 7. Let us restate one of those objections and add one which is based on the *NN* thesis.

(1) The semantic use of *L*-terms is supposed to have the virtue of saving the thesis of extensionality by enabling translations of modal statements into an *extensional* metalanguage, which advantage would of course be lost if nonextensional connectives were used.

(2) Suppose we consider the analogous translation of " true (p) ": (S) (L) $[\text{Des}(S, p, L) \dashv \text{true}(S, L)]$. In accordance with the *NN* thesis, any proposition of the form of the definiens would, if true, be necessarily true (remember that " $p \dashv q$ " is definable as " $N(p \supset q)$ "). But then " true (p) " would likewise be necessarily true, for any value of " p " that satisfies the definiens, which means that all true propositions are necessary! On the other hand, if the universal implication in the semantic metalanguage were an inductive generalization, then the following state of affairs would have to be logically possible:

$$(\exists S) \ (\exists L) \ [\text{Des}(S, p_1, L) \cdot \text{true}(S, L)]$$
$$\cdot (\exists S) \ (\exists L) \ [\text{Des}(S, p_1, L) \cdot -\text{true}(S, L)],$$

where p_1 is a given proposition. But this state of affairs is self-contradictory!

The relativization of modal concepts to language systems is obviously connected with the thesis of extensionality which Carnap has not abandoned yet, though his confidence in it seems to have weakened since the days of the *Logical Syntax of Language*. After all that has been said already in this book in defense of " intensional " modes of speech,[12] little needs to be added to indicate its untenability. For the reasons given, statements of belief and modal

---

[11] A similar criticism of the special case of convention 17-1 for the absolute concept of truth is contained in my " Note on the Semantic and the Absolute Concept of Truth," *loc. cit.* See also B. Robbins, " Remarks on Semantic Systems," same journal (Feb. 1953) , and my " Rejoinder to Mrs. Robbins," same journal (June 1953) .

[12] Cf. above, Chaps. 3, 5, 7, 10.

statements are not translatable into a metalanguage containing names of sentences instead of names of propositions. If, however, an indefatigable adherent of the thesis of extensionality should reply that it is unwarranted to conclude that such translations are impossible from the evidence that those offered so far are unsatisfactory, it must be countered that the grounds for rejecting it are not just inductive. It has been shown that to say of a sentence " q " that it expresses adequately the meaning of a sentence " p " is not to make an empirical generalization about usage but is to assert such *modal propositions* as " it is impossible that p and not q," " it is necessary that if p, then q." Suppose, now, that " p " were a nonextensional sentence like " I believe that Hitler is dead " and " q " an extensional sentence which is offered by an extensionalist as a translation of " p," such as " I am disposed to an affirmative response to some sentence synonymous with ' Hitler is dead.' " Then we would have to use a nonextensional language anyway in discussing the question whether the translation is adequate, e. g., we would have to raise the question " *is it possible that* a man should believe a proposition p, yet not be disposed to an affirmative response to some sentence synonymous with ' p '? " It follows that the very question of the correctness of the thesis of extensionality cannot be discussed except in terms of absolute modal concepts, in a nonextensional language. Even if an extensional language were adequate for all empirical science and for mathematics, it would be inadequate for philosophical analysis as actually practiced even by the critics of " intensional " ways of speaking.

D. *Intuitive Necessity and Convention*

It was stated at the opening of the preceding chapter that the *absolute* use of the concepts of entailment and self-contradiction is frowned upon without justification by the practitioners of systematic explication who wish to minimize the role of intuition in philosophical analysis. What I wish to emphasize here is that, whatever the merits of this Carnapian method of analysis may be, it must be conceded that it is *intuitive* perception of necessity of propositions which guides the selection of the material criteria of adequacy for a given explication, and that if this is denied, explication appears either as circular or as philosophically irrelevant. As an illustration of this dilemma facing a radical formalist we might consider the criterion of adequacy relative to the analysis of the contrary-to-fact conditional,[13] viz. that " if it were the case that p, then it would be the case that q " and " if it were the case that p, then it would not be the case that q " are *incompatible* statement forms (at least for self-consistent values of " p "). Suppose somebody who was asked whether he accepted this criterion of adequacy refused to commit himself on this question of incompatibility *until* the analysis of the subjunctive " if-then " is actually produced. In other words, suppose he took the position that one can decide whether two formally compatible statements are incompatible *relative* to explicitly stated definitions, but that it does not even make sense to speak of *absolute* incompatibility. This would surely amount to asking that the analysis be produced before the goals to be reached by the analysis are identified. It would amount to saying, in one breath, " the criterion of adequacy is acceptable if the analysis is acceptable, and the analysis is acceptable if the criterion of adequacy is acceptable." If, on the other hand, the position is taken that the act of laying down such a criterion is not a cognitive act at all, an act of recognizing a proposition intuitively (pre-analytically) as necessary, but simply a *convention* ("let us construct an explicatum of T which will satisfy the following requirements "), then one must face the consequence that explication is wholly unrelated to clarification of actually used concepts, that it is a self-contained game in much the same way in which the construction of scientific theories from which no antecedently verified or subsequently verifiable empirical laws are deducible would be a self-contained game.

It is true that the meanings of philosophically interesting terms of everyday language and even of scientific language are sufficiently inexact to allow considerable leeway in the choice of criteria of adequacy. But, on the other hand, they are also sufficiently definite to *impose* some criteria of adequacy as statements which cannot be denied without changing the ordinary meanings of their terms. The situation may be illustrated in terms of the explication of " probability." All inductive logicians seem agreed that an adequate explication of probability must satisfy the axioms of the calculus

[13] Cf. above, p. 382.

of probability, such as the axioms of addition and multiplication; it is said to speak for the adequacy of the frequency interpretation, e. g., that it satisfies the axioms in the sense of turning them into theorems of arithmetic. But why is it that no interpretation of "probability" is adequate unless it satisfies such axioms as "if e entails h, then the probability of h relative to e is a maximum," "if e contradicts h, then the probability of h relative to e is a minimum"? Obviously because these statements are implicitly analytic, i. e. true by the ordinary meaning of "probability." A definition of probability must "satisfy" these axioms not only in the sense of turning them into *true* propositions but in the sense of turning them into *necessarily true* propositions. Nevertheless it could not be said that any modification of the specifically *metrical* axioms (those constituting probability as a magnitude whose values can be calculated) would do violence to the ordinary meaning of "probability," and to this extent the adoption of the axioms is partly conventional. Consider the axiom of addition, in the special form: if h and h' are incompatible relative to e, and $P(h/e) = x$, and $P(h'/e) = y$, then $P(h \text{ or } h'/e) = x + y$. This axiom entails that the probability of a disjunction of two hypotheses, each of which is finitely probable, is greater than the probability of each hypothesis. Analogously the multiplication axiom entails that the probability of a conjunction of finitely probable, and mutually independent, hypotheses is smaller than the probability of each hypothesis. These consequences of the axioms, I should say, are necessary statements relative to the ordinary meaning of "probability." On the other hand, there are infinitely many functions of x and y, other than the sum and the product, which would have the same consequences, e. g. the double sum, the square of the product (assuming the further convention that probability is measured by fractions between 0 and 1 inclusive). Therefore the choice of a particular function is partly conventional and partly dictated by the ordinary meaning of "probability."

Carnap himself has, in his recent work in probability theory, adopted as material criteria of adequacy for the explication of logical probability not only the customary axioms of the calculus of probability but also customary rules of inductive inference, e. g. "on the basis of the evidence that the relative frequency of a property in a long initial segment of a· series is high (say, r), it is very *probable* that it will likewise be high (approximately equal to r) in a long continuation of the series " (*Logical Foundations of Probability*, § 41). The question of how such a rule could be *justified* is one of the perennial problems of philosophy; it is the venerable " problem of induction." However, before we can hope to solve this problem we must solve the problem of what this problem is: what does it mean to " justify " induction? Carnap himself suggests (*loc. cit*) that to justify such a rule of inference is to construct an explicit definition of " probability " on the basis of which the rule is deductively provable. A hardened skeptic might sneeringly ask Carnap: " Are you not begging the question? Why should I accept your definition? Because it leads to the rule to be justified? But you must first convince me of the validity of the rule before you can expect me to accept a definition which enables a demonstration of the rule. Another inductive logician might come along and produce a definition which entails the falsehood of the rule. How am I to choose between such incompatible definitions if I don't know whether the rule of induction is valid? " But to ask that an explication be justified without presupposing the necessity of some statements involving the explicandum, is to ask for " justification " in an utterly obscure sense of this trenchant word. The axioms of the probability calculus and the commonly observed rules of inductive inference *implicitly determine* the meaning of " probability " (allowing for the conventional components noted above), and to ask that a definition of probability be justified without presupposing their necessary truth is simply unreasonable. The skeptic overlooks that if we understand, though in a " pre-analytic " way only, the meaning of " probability," then we must be able to accept prior to any explication some probability statements as valid by the very meaning of " probability." The maxim " hold all truths contingent until they are *proved* to be necessary," which is implicitly adopted by many analytic philosophers, overlooks that any such proof of necessity presupposes definitions which themselves cannot be justified without assuming the *intuitive* necessity of some statements involving the defined terms.

E. *Conclusion: Analytic Philosophy and the Appeal to Intuitive Evidence*

The practitioners of systematic explication would probably agree with Schlick that analysis is a process of clarification of concepts which does not terminate in assertion of a distinctively philosophical kind of necessary proposition.[14] It is a mistake, on this view, to speak of analyses, or explications as though they were *propositions* (or " assertions," as Carnap is fond of saying). When a precise " explicatum " for a vague " explicandum " is proposed, Carnap would say, no identity of concepts is asserted at all; and he might add (though he has not expressed himself to this effect) that the paradox of analysis (which was discussed in Chap. 10), therefore, is a curse arising from a wrong conception of analysis. However, I am not impressed by an argument which systematically explicating philosophers sometimes use to discredit analysis in the sense of a process terminating in such identity assertions: to assert an identity of concepts, or propositions, is simply to express an alleged *intuitive* apprehension of a necessary equivalence. What, then, is one to do if a fellow philosopher professes a conflicting intuition? Now, this distrust of intuitive apprehension of logical relations is best reduced to absurdity by a *tu quoque* argument: what would become of empirical science if there were no agreement among sensory intuitions of observers? If, say, 40 out of a sample of 100 laboratory observers reported to have observed a different pointer coincidence from that observed by the other 60, is there any other " objective " criterion for deciding who observed the true state of affairs than the democratic criterion " let the majority decide "? It is just a brute fact (and for empirical science a fortunate one) that visual perceptions, specifically perceptions of pointer coincidences, are highly correlated within the class of scientific observers. At this point the anti-intuitionist will probably exclaim: " Precisely! But there is no similar agreement among various philosophers' intuitions as to which propositions are necessary, which entail which, and which are compatible with which. That's why an analytic philosophy based on alleged intuitions of logical necessity and possibility is really built on quicksand."

In my concluding reply to this charge I first wish to repeat that the surely commendable method of guiding an explication toward a specific goal, and at the same time rendering it testable by laying down criteria of adequacy to be satisfied by it, does not dispense with the appeal to intuitive evidence but merely displaces

[14] Cf. Chap. 10, p. 269.

it from the explication itself to the criteria of adequacy. Thus
the only condition on which Tarski's explication of the concept of
truth can be regarded as an explication of the concept ordinarily
associated with the word " truth," rather than as a construction of
a concept which is arbitrarily named " truth," is that the equivalences of the form " ' p ' is true if and only if p " which he stipulates
as material conditions of adequacy express necessary propositions
according to the ordinary usage of " true." If their necessity were
not pre-analytically evident,[15] their selection as adequacy criteria
would be arbitrary and unrelated to the aim of clarifying a concept
already in use. Now, what if a disagreement breaks out over the
adequacy criteria? I do not mean a disagreement as to which of
various propositions involving the explicandum should be selected
as contexts in which the explicatum must prove interchangeable
salva necessitate, or at least *salva veritate,* with the explicandum.
Such disagreements are to be resolved by agreeing on the purpose
to be served by the explication, and thus are philosophically unproblematic *practical* disagreements concerning a choice of means (e. g.
a philosopher of mathematics might disagree with Russell's adoption
of contexts of applied arithmetic as adequacy criteria for explications
of arithmetical concepts because he is not interested in the clarification of applied arithmetic but only in the clarification of pure
arithmetic). I mean the case where two philosophers disagree
about the eligibility of a given proposition as a context in which
the explicatum should be interchangeable *salva necessitate* with the
explicandum, because they disagree about the modality of the
proposition: one, e. g., holds it to be necessary, the other believes
it is contingent. If, in particular, it can be expressed as a conditional sentence, the issue might be whether one proposition
really entails a certain other proposition. Now, the answer (which
has already been given in the preceding chapter) is simply that a
disagreement about an entailment, or about a relation of logical
compatibility, of the intuitively evident variety is bound to be
verbal because such entailments (or incompatibilities) are constitutive of the explicandum. In other words, such a disagreement
simply manifests a difference of explicanda. Such disagreements,
therefore, may serve the good purpose of making philosophers

---

[15] For a detailed discussion of this question of pre-analytic necessity see my article
" Propositions, Sentences, and the Semantic Definition of Truth," *Theoria* (1954).

aware of ambiguities and thereby cutting verbal disputes short.
To be sure, in some cases we may consider the hypothesis that the
disagreeing philosophers associate different concepts with the *nonlogical* terms involved as so improbable that we may begin to wonder
whether they mean the same by the modal terms "entailment,"
"logically possible," etc. For example, if they disagree whether the
proposition expressed by "anything which is red is colored" is
analytic, it is more likely that they attach different meanings to
"analytic" than that "red" or "colored" are the ambiguous terms.
Yet, since it is only *by means of* modal judgments that we can clarify
concepts—e. g. "is it logically possible that a man should be wholly
devoid of reasoning ability?" we ask, in order to make clear to
ourselves the meaning of "man"—faith in mutual understanding
of basic modal terms is indeed an indispensable presupposition of
all analytic philosophy. To him who does not grasp the sense of
"possible" in which the existence of immortal men is possible yet
the existence of round squares not possible, no analytic philosophy
can be taught. No more than we can begin to teach logic to a
student who, while satisfying most of the usual tests of familiarity
with the English language, simply does not see that "q" follows
from "p and q," or that "p" and "not-p" cannot both be true.

Let it be added, however, that just as the empirical sciences,
beginning with crude concepts, formulate crude laws which in turn
enable them to precisify the concepts, which precisification in turn
leads to more precise laws (a dialectic process which has been called
"successive redefinition"), so there is no vicious circle in the
attempt to clarify modal concepts by means of themselves. We do
just that in logic when, starting out from "primitive" judgments of
entailment and incompatibility such as "p is incompatible with
not-p," "(p and q) entails p," "(p or q) is incompatible with (not-
p and not-q)," "(a is f) entails (something is f)," "(everything is
f) entails (a is f)" we construct a proof technique and definitions
of logical constants which then enable us to define the modal concepts themselves systematically and generally. The distrust of the
"intuitional" basis of analytic philosophy, therefore, is rooted in
nothing less than an imperfect understanding of scientific method—
in the broad sense of "scientific" in which analytic philosophy
can be scientific.

GLOSSARY

Absolute concepts	contrasted, by Carnap, with *semantical* concepts in that they are not relative to a language (e. g. *L-implication* as a relation between propositions, not sentences)
Analysandum	concept which is (or is to be) analyzed
Analysans	concept expressed by a complex expression and claimed to be identical with analysandum (e. g. brother = male sibling)
Analytic	
broadly	true by virtue of the meanings of constituent terms (*a priori*)
explicitly	substitution instance of a logical truth (*logically true*)
implicitly	not explicitly analytic, but translatable into an explicitly analytic statement with the help of adequate explicative definitions
incompatibility	p and q are analytically incompatible if " if p, then not q " is strictly analytic
strictly	explicitly or implicitly analytic
trivially	statement synonymous with a statement of the form " if p and q, then p," or " all AB are A "
Antecedent	if-clause of a conditional statement
A priori proposition	proposition expressed by a broadly analytic statement; can be known to be true without experience of confirming instances, by just thinking about the proposition
Atomic statement	singular statement which contains no statements as components; ascribes a simple quality to an individual or a simple relation to a set of individuals
Classificatory concept	concept effecting a simple division of things

	into those to which it applies and those to which it does not apply (e. g. " hot " in contrast to " warmer " and " degree of temperature ")
Codeterminate predicates	predicates designating determinate forms of the same determinable quality, e. g. color predicates. Any two codeterminate predicates are incompatible.
Cognitive	
meaning	a sentence is said to have cognitive meaning if it is used to express a proposition
question	question capable of being answered by a sentence that has cognitive meaning
Comparative concept	concept expressing a comparison, like " harder," " warmer "
Conditional	statement of the form " if p, then q "
Conjunct	statement conjoined with others
Connective	word used to form a compound statement, like " or," " if-then "
Connotation	a predicate is said to connote those properties which a thing must have in order for the predicate to be applicable to it; contrasted with *denotation*
Consequent	then-clause of a conditional
Contingent proposition	p is contingent if p as well as not-p is logically possible
Contradictory	the contradictory of p is that proposition which must be false if p is true and true if p is false
Converse relation	see *relation*
Coordinate language	language in which qualities and values of magnitudes are ascribed to space-time positions or regions
Counterfactual conditional	conditional which asserts what *would* be the case if a condition, which in fact is not realized, *were* realized
Decision procedure	procedure for deciding a logical question,

	e. g. whether a sentence is a consequence of, or contradicts the axioms of, a system
Deductively valid	an argument is deductively valid if the conclusion follows with logical necessity from the premises; in other words, if it is a contradiction to assert the premises and at the same time to deny the conclusion
Definiendum	expression which is defined
Definiens	complex expression by which the definiendum is defined
Definientia	plural of *definiens*

Definition

circular	the definiendum occurs in the definiens, or a part of the definiens is defined in terms of the definiendum
coordinative	as used by Reichenbach, interpretation of the terms of a formal deductive system by means of expressions denoting observable objects or processes (e. g. definition of " length " in terms of a standard rod)
eliminative	enables elimination of definiendum from any sentence in which it occurs (" to define a term is to show how one can get along without it ")
explicative	analysis of the meaning of the definiendum
explicit	definiendum can simply be replaced by definiens in any sentence without changing the remainder of the sentence (e. g. father = male parent)
implicit	a set of postulates (axioms) is said to implicitly define the primitive terms in it, i. e. it delimits their denotations to objects and relations that satisfy it
in use (contextual)	rule for translating sentences containing definiendum into synonymous sentences that do not contain it; but while being eliminative, it is not explicit (e. g. x is brother of $y = x$ is male and has the same parents as y)

ostensive	explaining the meaning of a term by pointing at, or inducing experience of, instances denoted by it
recursive	rule for eliminating definiendum in a finite number of symbolic transformations from expressions in which it occurs together with constant arguments (e.g. " $+$ " from " $3 + 2$ ")
Denotata	objects of which a term is truly predicable (e.g. individual men are denotata of " man ")
Denotation	class of all the denotata of a term; also called *extension* of the term; also used in the sense of *denotatum*
Designator (designative expression)	expression referring to objects, events, relations, properties, etc.; contrasted with " syncategorematic " words, like " of," " or," " the," also with purely emotive words
Designatum	Carnap: that which is designated by a designator; C. W. Morris: connotation
Descriptive	
predicate	word designating a sensory quality or relation, or a characteristic whose presence can be inferred from what is observed
semantics	empirical study of the meanings of expressions of natural languages
term (constant)	descriptive predicate, or name of a concrete entity, or description in terms of descriptive predicates of a concrete entity
Dichotomous concept	classificatory concept
Dispositional property	tendency to react in a certain way to a certain kind of stimulus (in a generalized sense of " stimulus ") ; e.g. " soluble," " fragile," " irritable "
Domain (converse domain) of a relation	see *relation*
Empty predicate (concept)	predicate of which there are no denotata, e.g. " unicorn," " man who is 30 ft. tall "

Equivalence

    extensional — two predicates are extensionally equivalent if they have the same extension though they may differ in connotation

    logical (strict) — see *logical*

    material — two statements are materially equivalent if they materially imply each other

Essential occurrence — nonvacuous occurrence

Existential

    generalization — the inference of "something has property P" from "x has P" where x is a particular entity (e. g. cruelty is hated, therefore something is hated)

    quantifier — the expression "there is an x"—or its idiomatic equivalents "something," "somebody," etc.

    statement — statement asserting that something (one or more) has a specified property, without saying which it is (they are)

Explicandum — concept to be explicated (analyzed) in terms of a more precise concept

Explication — process of analyzing (explicating) a concept already used in everyday or scientific discourse, sometimes within the framework of a "language system"

Explicating (or analytic) synonym — definiens of an explicative definition

Explicatum — correlative to "explicandum" the way "analysans" is correlative to "analysandum"

Explicit contradiction — a conjunction of statements is an explicit contradiction if at least two conjuncts are contradictories of each other (e. g. "p and q and not-p," but not "p and (if p, then q) and not-q")

Explicitly analytic — see *analytic*

Extension — see *denotation*

Extensional

    connective — connective used to form compound statements which are truth-functions of the component statements (e. g. " and," but not " if-then " in most ordinary uses)

    context — a sentence is an extensional context for a constituent predicate, if replacement of the latter with a predicate of equal extension does not change its truth-value; it is an extensional context for a constituent sentence, if it is a truth-function of the latter; and for a constituent name (or description) if replacement of the latter by one that denotes the same object does not affect the truth-value of the sentence

    language — language whose compound statements, i. e. statements containing parts which are themselves statements, are truth-functions and whose noncompound statements have a truth-value which depends only on the extensions of the predicates they contain (excludes, e. g., sentences of the forms " it is necessary that p," " A believes that p ")

    sentence — sentence which is an extensional context for all constituent expressions

Extralinguistic — outside of language

Extralogical axioms (postulates) — axioms which are not logical truths in their intended interpretation, e. g. the axioms of a system of geometry, or of mechanics

Factual

    content — a statement is said to have factual content, by logical empiricists, if it is neither self-contradictory nor analytic (it " says something about the world ")

    implication — see *implication*

    truth — true contingent proposition

Factually empty — devoid of factual content (not to be confused with Carnap's term " F-empty ": a predicate which is empty though it is logically possible that it should denote)

Formal

contradiction	negation of a logical truth, i. e. false by sole virtue of the meanings of logical constants
entailment	*p* formally entails *q* if " if *p*, then *q* " is a logical truth
deduction	deduction without attention to the meanings of nonlogical constants
implication	see *implication*
mode of speech	speaking about words in discussing a philosophical problem; contrasted with *material* mode of speech
postulate	postulate whose nonlogical constants are given no particular interpretation in making deductions from it

Formation rules	rules specifying what sequences of what kinds of symbols are sentences (formulae)
Functional logic (calculus)	logic as including not only the propositional calculus but also the theory of quantification (see *quantifier*); includes syllogism theory as well as the theory of relations
Functor	expression designating a magnitude, mathematical or physical, e. g. " sum," " length "
Higher functional calculus	see *lower functional calculus*

Implication

factual	implication by virtue of an empirical law, e. g. " if a block of ice is exposed to 90° F, then it melts "
formal	a propositional function *Fx* formally implies a propositional function *Gx* if the universal statement " for every *x*, if *Fx* then *Gx* " is true and extensional
logical (strict)	implication which is logically true
material	*p* materially implies *q* if either *p* is false or *q* is true—though *p* and *q* may be wholly unrelated in meaning
probability	a probability implication from *p* to *q*

obtains if q has a certain probability relative to p (a formal implication is an extensional probability implication of the highest degree)

Implicit contradiction

conjunction from which an explicit contradiction is deducible though it is not itself an explicit contradiction

Indicator term

term whose reference constantly changes with the context in which it is used, like "this," "now," "here," "I"

Individual

    constant

name of a particular

    variable

variable whose substituends are individual constants

Intension

of a predicate: connotation; of a sentence: proposition expressed by it

Intensional vagueness

a predicate or common noun is intensionally vague if the set of connoted properties is not fixed (e. g. would a human being with female reproductive organs but otherwise masculine body be a man or a woman?)

Interpreted language

language whose expressions are not only connected by syntactic rules but also have semantic meaning (reference to something outside of language)

L-determinate

L-true or self-contradictory

L-equivalent

logically equivalent (see *logical*)

L-true

logically true (see *logical*)

Language system

language defined by an explicit listing of primitive (undefined) vocabulary, both logical and descriptive, and by the following kinds of rules: rules of sentence formation, rules of deduction (transformation), semantic rules

Level of a predicate

predicates connoting qualities or relations of individuals belong to the first level, predicates connoting properties or relations of such qualities or relations belong to the second level, and so on (e. g. " is a color," " is a desirable quality " are second-level predicates)

Logical

construction

an entity A is said to be a logical construction out of a specified set of entities S, if the expression " A " which denotes A is contextually definable by reference to members of S (in this sense physical objects are, according to phenomenalism, logical constructions out of sense data)

equivalence

p and q are logically equivalent if they logically imply each other

independence

two propositions are logically independent if they are compatible and none logically implies the other; in a derivative sense, predicates are said to be *l. i.*

possibility

state of affairs which is conceivable without self-contradiction

truth (principle)

necessary proposition which contains only logical concepts (for the meaning of " logical concept—or constant," see Chap. 6)

type

two expressions a and b are of the same logical type if for any sentential function " Fx," " Fa " and " Fb " are either both meaningful or both meaningless sentences; the logical type of an expression is the class of expressions of the same logical type as itself. In a parallel sense, one speaks of the logical type of an *entity*

Logically

proper name

name which is meaningless unless it denotes something; contrasted with proper names which are abbreviations for descriptions which may or may not denote something, e. g. " Apollo "

true

a necessary statement which contains only logical constants essentially; in a narrower sense, substitution instance of a logical

	truth, but not itself a logical truth (principle)
Logicist	the Frege-Russell philosophy of mathematics according to which mathematics is a branch of logic
Logistic language	language using the symbolism and syntax of symbolic logic
Lower functional calculus	that part of functional logic in which only *individual* variables are employed; contrasted with the *higher* functional calculus in which also variables ranging over abstract entities, like properties and classes, are used
Material	
criterion of adequacy	implicitly analytic statement containing a term whose meaning is to be explicated in such a way that the statement becomes explicitly analytic
entailment	entailment expressed by a conditional which is not logically true
mode of speech	contrasted with *formal* mode of speech: discussing a philosophical problem in the object language, talking about extralinguistic entities
Meaning postulate	postulate of a language system which is broadly but not strictly analytic; serves to delimit possible interpretations of descriptive primitive terms
Mention of an expression	contrasted with *use* of an expression, i. e. speaking about the expression itself, not about its denotata (e. g. " ' men ' is the plural of a noun " vs. " men cannot live without women ")
Metalanguage	language used to talk about language
Metalogical	discourse about logic (e. g. the statement that the propositional calculus as axiomatized in *Principia Mathematica* is complete, is metalogical)
Mentalistic term	term designating a subjective, not publicly

	observable, state of consciousness; contrasted with *behavioristic*
Metrical concept	concept of a magnitude, like velocity, temperature, degree of blood pressure
Modal	
logic	logic using modalities, i. e. concepts like "possible," "necessary," and therefore containing nonextensional statements
statement	nonextensional statement using modalities
Modalities	see *modal logic*
Model of a set of postulates	an ordered set of entities which satisfies all the postulates, in other words, of which all the postulates are true ("entities" in the broadest sense, including relations)
Modus ponens (*ponendo ponens*)	the principle that whatever proposition is implied by true propositions is itself true
Modus tollens (*tollendo tollens*)	the principle that whatever proposition implies a false proposition is itself false
Molecular statement	singular statement composed of atomic statements
Natural language	contrasted with *language system*; the rules of a natural language are implicit in the use of the expressions, but most of them are not explicitly formulated; further, a natural language is characterized by ambiguity and vagueness
Necessary proposition (truth)	proposition which cannot possibly be false
Nominalistic language	contains in its primitive vocabulary no names except names of individuals, and no variables except individual variables (such languages are extensional, but an extensional language need not be nominalistic)
Nomological implication	implication expressing an intensional connection, logical or causal, unlike material and formal implications, which are extensional sentences

Non-natural (property, entity)	not given in sense experience, or capable of being so given; e. g. propositions, as distinguished from sentences, are usually held to be thinkable but not sensible
Object language	contrasted with *metalanguage*: language used to talk about extralinguistic objects. In a relative sense, however, a metalanguage may itself be object language relative to a meta-metalanguage which is used to talk about it
Occurrent concept	concept referring to occurrences (events); usually contrasted with *dispositional concept*
One-place predicate	nonrelational predicate
Pragmatic	
contradiction	sense (1): proposition which must be false if it is asserted, but could be true if it were not asserted; sense (2): proposition whose falsehood may be inferred with high probability from the fact that it is asserted
meaning	states of the sign user or sign interpreter which are causally connected with the occurrence of the sign (e. g. " it will rain " pragmatically means that the speaker believes that it will rain, also that he does not believe that it rains at the time of utterance of the sentence)
Pragmatics	the science of pragmatic meaning
Pre-analytic	before analysis; e. g. pre-analytic understanding of a predicate = understanding of the predicate before having analyzed its meaning
Predication	statement ascribing a predicate to something, e. g. " he is a general " is a predication of " is a general "
Primitive predicate	predicate which is not defined, except ostensively
Principle of deduction	statement as to which propositions are

deducible from which, referring only to the forms of propositions (e. g. *modus ponens*)

Proposition

anything which is not a sentence and can significantly be said to be true or false; state of affairs which may or may not be actual (if it is actual, it is a fact, or a true proposition) ; anything which can be the meaning of a declarative sentence; anything which may be believed or disbelieved

Propositional

function

sense (1) : expression containing one or more free variables such that a meaningful sentence (true or false) results when suitable constants are substituted for the variables;

sense (2) : that which is expressed (designated) by a propositional function in sense (1). In this sense a propositional function seems undistinguishable from a property, in the broad sense including relations

logic (calculus)

that part of logic in which nonmolecular statements are treated as units, and are not further analyzed (in traditional terminology, only relations between *propositions*, not between *terms*, are dealt with)

variable

variable whose range consists of propositions

Psychologism

the tendency to confuse *logical* issues with *psychological* issues; e. g. if one tried to answer a question of logical validity by investigating actual beliefs (however, the meaning of this deprecatory word is unclear to the extent that the meaning of " logical " is unclear)

Psychophysical law

statement of a correlation between a mental and a bodily (or behavioral) state

Qualitative predicate

predicate designating a quality, and not defined in terms of names of particulars (e. g. " solar," " higher than Mt. Everest " are not qualitative predicates)

Quantifier	expressions like " some," " all," " for every," " there is," by means of which general statements are constructed
Range	
of a proposition (sentence)	class of state descriptions (states) in which the proposition (sentence) is true; the greater the range of a proposition, the more possibilities are left open by it
of significance	the range of significance of a predicate " P " is the class of values of " x " for which " Px " is true or false (e. g. numbers are outside the range of significance of " blue ")
of a variable	class of entities whose names are substitutable for the variable
Realistic language	as contrasted with *nominalistic* language, it contains variables ranging over abstract entities, and possibly also names of such
Relation	
asymmetrical	for all x and y, if xRy, then not-yRx
converse	the converse of R is the relation $\breve{R}$ such that " xRy " is equivalent to " $y\breve{R}x$ "
domain	class of objects having a given relation to something
converse domain	class of objects having the converse relation to something
field	sum of domain and converse domain
intransitive	for all x, y, z, if xRy and yRz, then not-xRz
irreflexive	relation which nothing has to itself
many-one	if $(xRy$ and $uRz)$ implies $y = z$
many-many	neither many-one nor one-many
one-many	if $(xRy$ and $uRz)$ implies $x = u$
one-one	one-many and many-one
reflexive	R such that if x has R to something, then xRx (sometimes distinguished from *totally reflexive*: R which everything has to itself)
symmetrical	for all x and y, if xRy, then yRx
transitive	for all x, y, z, if xRy and yRz, then xRz
Relational predicate	predicate designating a relation

Reduction

    basis — set of primitive predicates on the basis of which other predicates are introduced into a language either by definitions or by reduction sentences

    sentence — sentence which is not an eliminative definition but describes a kind of test for deciding empirically whether a given property which is not directly observable is present

Self-consistent — not self-contradictory

Self-contradictory — proposition from which a contradiction is deducible without presupposing any contingent propositions

Semantic

    concept — concept referring to semantic meanings of expressions (e. g. truth as ascribed to sentences)

    meaning — of a sentence: the state of affairs which must exist if the sentence is to be true; of a predicate: connotation, intension

    rule — specification of the semantic meaning or the denotation or the denotatum of a designative expression (definitions are semantic rules if the terms constituting the definientia are already understood)

Semiotics — theory of signs (Morris)

Sense — Frege's term for connotation, intension; but Frege applies it also to names and definite descriptions, e. g. if " Shakespeare is the author of *Hamlet* " is an informative statement, then " Shakespeare " and " the author of Hamlet " differ in sense

Sense-data statement — statement about sensations, not about physical events or objects

Sentential

    function — *propositional function* in sense (1)

    variable — variable whose values are sentences (and whose substituends are names of sentences)

Singular statement — statement containing no quantifiers

State description	as a term of semantics, complete description, in the form of a conjunction of atomic statements or of atomic statements and negations of atomic statements, of a possible world
Substituend	term which is substitutable for a variable, name of a value of a variable
Substitution instance	statement derivable from a universal statement by substituting the same constant for each occurrence of a variable bound by the same universal quantifier (" for every x," " (x) ") ; also statement derived by substitution from a propositional function
Syntactic rule	rule governing manipulation of symbols without regard to semantic meaning
Synthetic	not (strictly) analytic but self-consistent
Tautology	sense (1) : compound statement which is true regardless of the truth-values of its components; sense (2) : propositional function all of whose instances are tautologies in sense (1) ; sense (3) : logically true statement
Theoretical concept	concept referring to something which is postulated in order to explain the observed, but is not directly observable; e. g. electron, gravitational potential, unconscious wish
Thing language	the prescientific language of everyday life in which we speak of things and their observable qualities; contrasted with both sense-data language and theoretical languages of quantitative sciences
Time independent	a property P or relation R such that it is meaningless to say " x has P at time t " or " x has R to y at time t "; e. g. equality as a relation between numbers, entailment as a relation between propositions
Transformation rule	principle of deduction; in a wider sense, also definitions conceived as rules of substitution of symbols

Truth

condition	semantic meaning of a sentence
function	propositional (sentential) function constructed by means of connectives such that the truth-values of its instances are uniquely determined by the truth-values of the component propositions (sentences); instances of truth-functions (to which "truth-function" is sometimes also applied), therefore, are extensional with respect to the component sentences
table	table constructed in order to define an extensional connective in terms of possible combinations of truth-values of the connected statements, or in order to decide on the basis of such tables whether a given truth-function is tautologous, self-contradictory, or neither
value	truth or falsehood

Two-valued logic   logic assuming that every proposition is either true or false

Type vs. token   repeatable pattern of a linguistic expression, as distinguished from different instances of the same pattern (e. g. an ambiguous word is a type such that not all tokens of the type are synonymous)

Use of an expression   see *mention*

Vacuous occurrence   a term occurs vacuously in a sentence S if the truth-value of S remains unchanged under replacements of that term by any other grammatically admissible term; a term occurs vacuously in an argument if the validity or invalidity of the argument does not depend on its meaning

Value of a variable   member of the range of the variable

Variable

bound	variable occurring in a sentential function to which a quantifier containing it is prefixed
free	variable which is not bound

BIBLIOGRAPHY OF CITATIONS

BOOKS AND MONOGRAPHS

A. Ambrose and M. Lazerowitz, *Fundamentals of Symbolic Logic*, New York, Rinehart and Co., 1948.

A. J. Ayer, *Thinking and Meaning* (inaugural lecture), London, 1947.

————— *Language, Truth and Logic*, 2d ed. New York, Dover Publications, 1950; esp. chaps. 3, 4.

————— *Philosophical Essays*, New York, St. Martin's Press, 1954.

M. Black, *Language and Philosophy*, Ithaca, Cornell University Press, 1949.

————— ed. *Philosophical Analysis*, Ithaca, Cornell University Press, 1950.

B. Blanshard, *The Nature of Thought*, 2 vols., New York, Macmillan, 1940; esp. chaps. 28-30.

P. W. Bridgman, *The Logic of Modern Physics*, New York, Macmillan, 1927; esp. chap. 1.

R. Carnap, *Logical Syntax of Language,* New York, Harcourt Brace, 1937.

————— "Foundations of Logic and Mathematics," in the *International Encyclopedia of Unified Science, 1*, No. 3, 1939.

————— *Introduction to Semantics*, Cambridge, Mass., Harvard University Press, 1942.

————— *Meaning and Necessity*, Chicago, Chicago University Press, 1947, 2d enlarged ed. 1956.

————— *Logical Foundations of Probability*, Chicago, Chicago University Press, 1950.

L. Couturat, *La Logique de Leibniz, d'après des documents inédits*, Paris, 1901.

C. J. Ducasse, *Nature, Mind and Death*, La Salle, Ill., Open Court Publishing Co., 1951; chaps. 4, 5.

H. Feigl and M. Brodbeck, *Readings in the Philosophy of Science*, New York, Appleton-Century-Crofts, 1953.

H. Feigl and W. Sellars, *Readings in Philosophical Analysis*, New York, Appleton-Century-Crofts, 1949.

G. Frege, *The Foundations of Arithmetic*, trans. J. L. Austin; New York, Philosophical Library, 1950.

N. Goodman, *The Structure of Appearance*, Cambridge, Mass., Harvard University Press, 1951; chap. 1.

C. G. Hempel, "Fundamentals of Concept Formation in Empirical Science," in the *International Encyclopedia of Unified Science, 2,* No. 7, Chicago, 1952.

D. Hume, *Enquiry into Human Understanding,* 1748; esp. sec. 4.

────── *Treatise of Human Nature,* 1739; Bk. I.

A. B. Johnson, *A Treatise on Language,* ed. D. Rynin, Berkeley and Los Angeles, University of California Press, 1947.

I. Kant, *Critique of Pure Reason,* 2d ed. 1787.

────── *Prolegomena to Any Future Metaphysic,* 1783.

────── *Vorlesungen zur Logik,* in E. Cassirer ed., *Immanuel Kants Werke,* Berlin, 1921-23.

W. Kneale, *Probability and Induction,* Oxford, Clarendon Press, 1949; secs. 16-19.

S. Körner, *Conceptual Thinking,* Cambridge, Cambridge University Press, 1955; Pt. I.

M. Lazerowitz, *The Structure of Metaphysics,* London, Routledge and Kegan Paul, 1955; last chapter.

G. W. Leibniz, *New Essays Concerning Human Understanding,* New York and London, Macmillan, 1896; esp. Bk. IV.

C. I. Lewis, *An Analysis of Knowledge and Valuation,* La Salle, Ill., Open Court Publishing Co., 1946; chaps. 3-8.

────── *Mind and the World Order,* New York, Scribner's, 1929.

C. I. Lewis and H. Langford, *Symbolic Logic,* New York and London, Century Co., 1932; esp. chap. 8.

L. Linsky, ed., *Semantics and the Philosophy of Language,* Urbana, University of Illinois Press, 1952.

J. Locke, *Essay Concerning Human Understanding,* 1690; esp. Bk. IV.

H. Margenau, *The Nature of Physical Reality,* New York, McGraw-Hill, 1950.

J. S. Mill, *System of Logic,* 1887; esp. Bk. II.

C. W. Morris, "Foundations of the Theory of Signs," in the *International Encyclopedia of Unified Science, 1,* No. 2, Chicago, 1938.

────── *Signs, Language and Behavior,* New York, Prentice Hall, 1946.

A. Pap, *The A Priori in Physical Theory,* New York, King's Crown Press, 1946.

────── *Elements of Analytic Philosophy,* New York, Macmillan, 1949; esp. chaps. 1, 6, 13, 14, 16, 17.

────── *Analytische Erkenntnistheorie, Kritische Übersicht über die neueste Entwicklung in USA und England,* Vienna, Springer Verlag, 1955; esp. chaps. 1, 6.

W. V. Quine, *From a Logical Point of View,* Cambridge, Mass., Harvard University Press, 1953; esp. chaps. 1, 2, 8.

———— *Mathematical Logic*, Cambridge, Mass., Harvard University Press, rev. ed. 1951; intro.

F. P. Ramsay, *The Foundations of Mathematics and Other Logical Essays*, London, 1931.

H. Reichenbach, *Elements of Symbolic Logic*, New York, Macmillan, 1948; chaps. 7, 8.

———— *The Rise of Scientific Philosophy*, Berkeley and Los Angeles, University of California Press, 1951.

R. Robinson, *Definition*, Oxford, Clarendon Press, 1950.

B. Russell, *A Critical Exposition of the Philosophy of Leibniz*, Cambridge University Press, 1900; esp. chap. 2.

———— *The Problems of Philosophy*, New York, Oxford University Press, 1943; first pub. 1912; chaps. 7-11.

———— *Introduction to Mathematical Philosophy*, London, Allen and Unwin, 1948; 1st ed. 1919; esp. chaps. 1, 2, 13, 14, 18.

———— *The Principles of Mathematics*, 2d. ed., New York, Norton, 1938; esp. chaps. 1, 3.

———— *Human Knowledge, Its Scope and Limits*, New York, Simon and Schuster, 1948; Pts. II, IV.

———— *An Inquiry into Meaning and Truth*, New York, Norton, 1940; esp. chaps. 5, 12, 13, 19.

P. A. Schilpp, ed., *The Philosophy of G. E. Moore* (Library of Living Philosophers), Evanston, 1942.

———— *The Philosophy of Bertrand Russell* (Library of Living Philosophers), Evanston, 1944.

M. Schlick, *Gesammelte Aufsätze*, Vienna, 1938.

C. L. Stevenson, *Ethics and Language*, New Haven, Yale University Press, 1944; chap. 3.

A. Tarski, *Logic, Semantics, Metamathematics*, Oxford, Clarendon Press, 1956.

G. H. von Wright, *Form and Content in Logic* (inaugural lecture), Cambridge University Press, 1949.

———— *Treatise on Induction and Probability*, London, Routledge and Kegan Paul, 1951; chap. 6.

A. N. Whitehead and B. Russell, *Principia Mathematica*, 3 vols. Cambridge, Cambridge University Press, 1910-13, 2d ed. 1925-27; intro. to both eds.

L. Wittgenstein, *Tractatus Logico-Philosophicus*, New York, Harcourt Brace, 1922.

ARTICLES

A. Ambrose, "Linguistic Approaches to Philosophical Problems," *Journal of Philosophy* (1952).

A. J. Ayer, "Basic Propositions," in *Philosophical Analysis*, ed. M. Black, rep. in A. J. Ayer, *Philosophical Essays*.

J. Bar-Hillel, "Bolzano's Definition of Analytic Propositions," *Methodos*, 2, (1950).

G. Bergmann, "The Logic of Psychological Concepts," *Philosophy of Science* (April 1951).

M. Black, "The Semantic Definition of Truth," *Analysis* (March 1948); rep. in M. Black, *Language and Philosophy*.

———— "Vagueness," *Philosophy of Science*, 1937; rep. in M. Black, *Language and Philosophy*.

K. Britton, "Are Necessary Truths True by Convention?" *Proceedings of the Aristotelian Society*, Supplementary Volume *21* (1947).

C. D. Broad, "Are There Synthetic A Priori Truths?" *Proceedings of the Aristotelian Society, Supplementary Volume 15* (1936).

———— "Leibniz' Predicate-in-Notion Principle and Some of Its Alleged Consequences," *Theoria*, *15* (Lund, Sweden, 1949).

H. Brotman, "Could Space be Four-dimensional?" *Mind* (July 1952).

R. Carnap, "On the Application of Inductive Logic," *Philosophy and Phenomenological Research* (Sept. 1947).

———— "Truth and Confirmation," in Feigl and Sellars, *Readings in Philosophical Analysis*.

———— "Testability and Meaning," *Philosophy of Science* (1936-37); lithographed by the Graduate Philosophy Club, Yale University (Whitlock's Inc., New Haven, Conn.).

———— "Meaning and Synonymy in Natural Language," *Philosophical Studies* (University of Minnesota, April 1955).

———— "On Some Concepts of Pragmatics," *ibid.* (Dec. 1955).

———— "The Problem of Relations in Inductive Logic," *ibid.* (Oct. 1951).

———— "Meaning Postulates," *ibid.* (Oct. 1952).

———— "Semantics, Empiricism and Ontology," rep. (from *Revue Internationale de Philosophie, 11*, 1950) in L. Linsky, ed., *Semantics and the Philosophy of Language*.

———— "Logical Foundations of the Unity of Science," in Feigl and Sellars, *Readings in Philosophical Analysis*.

———— "The Methodological Character of Theoretical Concepts," in *Minnesota Studies in Philosophy of Science*, Minneapolis, University of Minnesota Press, 1956; Vol. *1*.

R. Chisholm, "The Problem of Empiricism," *Journal of Philosophy* (1948).

———— "A Note on Carnap's Meaning Analysis," *Philosophical Studies* (Dec. 1955).

A. Church, "On Carnap's Analysis of Statements of Assertion and Belief," *Analysis* (April 1950).

A. C. Ewing, "Philosophical Analysis in Ethics," *Philosophical Studies* (Oct. 1950).

———— "The Linguistic Theory of A Priori Propositions," *Proceedings of the Aristotelian Society*, new ser. (1940).

R. Firth, "Radical Empiricism and Perceptual Relativity," *Philosophical Review* (April and July 1950).

G. Frege, "On Sense and Nominatum" (trans. from the German), in Feigl and Sellars, *Readings in Philosophical Analysis*.

N. Goodman, "On Likeness of Meaning," in Linsky, *Semantics and the Philosophy of Language*.

———— and W. V. Quine, "Steps towards a Constructive Nominalism," *Journal of Symbolic Logic, 12* (1947).

W. Hay and J. Weinberg, "Concerning Allegedly Necessary Nonanalytic Propositions," *Philosophical Studies* (Feb. 1951).

C. G. Hempel, "The Concept of Cognitive Significance: a Reconsideration," *Proceedings of the American Academy of Arts and Sciences, 80* (1951).

———— "Problems and Changes in the Empiricist Criterion of Meaning," reprinted (from *Revue Internationale de Philosophie, 11*, 1950) in Linsky, *Semantics and the Philosophy of Language*.

———— "Geometry and Empirical Science," in Feigl and Sellars, *Readings in Philosophical Analysis*.

———— "A Logical Appraisal of Operationism," *The Scientific Monthly* (Oct. 1954).

A. Kaplan and H. F. Schott, "A Calculus for Empirical Classes," *Methodos* (1951).

W. Kneale, "Are Necessary Truths True by Convention?" *Proceedings of the Aristotelian Society*, Supplementary Volume *21* (1947).

———— "Truths of Logic," *ibid.*, new ser. 47.

S. Körner, "On Entailment," *ibid.*, new ser. 47.

———— "Are Philosophical Questions, Questions of Language?" *ibid.*, Supplementary Volume *22* (1948).

H. Langford, "Moore's Notion of Analysis," in *The Philosophy of G. E. Moore*.

———— "A Proof that Synthetic A Priori Propositions Exist," *Journal of Philosophy* (1949).

C. I. Lewis, "Professor Chisholm and Empiricism," *Journal of Philosophy* (1948).

C. Lewy, "Entailment and Necessary Propositions," in Black, *Philosophical Analysis*.

―――― "Is the Notion of Disembodied Existence Self-contradictory?" *Proceedings of the Aristotelian Socity,* new ser. *43.*

P. Marhenke, "Phenomenalism," in Black, *Philosophical Analysis*.

B. Mates, "Synonymity," *University of California Publications in Philosophy, 25* (1950); reprinted in Linsky, *Semantics and the Philosophy of Language.*

G. E. Moore, "Russell's Theory of Descriptions," in *The Philosophy of Bertrand Russell.*

―――― "Reply to My Critics," in Schilpp, *The Philosophy of G. E. Moore.*

N. Malcolm, "Are Necessary Propositions Really Verbal?" *Mind, 51* (1942).

K. Marc-Wogau, "Kants Lehre vom analytischen Urteil," *Theoria* (1951).

E. Nagel, "Logic without Ontology," in Y. H. Krikorian, ed., *Naturalism and the Human Spirit,* New York, Columbia University Press, 1944; reprinted in Feigl and Sellars, *Readings in Philosophical Analysis.*

D. J. O'Connor, "Pragmatic Paradoxes," *Mind* (July 1948).

―――― "Pragmatic Paradoxes and Fugitive Propositions," *Mind* (Oct. 1951).

A. Pap, "Indubitable Existential Statements," *Mind* (July 1946).

―――― "Ostensive Definition and Empirical Certainty," *ibid.* (Oct. 1950).

―――― "Synonymity and Logical Equivalence," *Analysis* (March 1949).

―――― "Reduction Sentences and Open Concepts," *Methodos, 5* (1953).

―――― "Reduction Sentences and Disposition Concepts," in *The Philosophy of Rudolf Carnap,* ed. P. A. Schilpp (Library of Living Philosophers), forthcoming.

―――― "Other Minds and the Principle of Verifiability," *Revue Internationale de Philosophie* (1951).

―――― "The Philosophical Analysis of Natural Language," *Methodos, 1* (1949).

―――― "Synonymy, Identity of Concepts, and the Paradox of Analysis," *ibid., 7* (1955).

―――― "Logic and the Concept of Entailment," *Journal of Philosophy* (1950).

―――― "Necessary Propositions and Linguistic Rules," in *Semantica,* issued by *Archivio di Filosofia,* Rome, 1955.

———— "Logic, Existence and the Theory of Descriptions," *Analysis* (April 1953).

———— "Note on the Semantic and the Absolute Concept of Truth," *Philosophical Studies* (Jan. 1952).

———— "Propositions, Sentences and the Semantic Definition of Truth," *Theoria, 20* (1954).

———— "Once More: Colors and the Synthetic A Priori," *Philosophical Review* (Jan. 1957).

K. Popper, "Logic without Assumptions," *Proceedings of the Aristotelian Society,* new ser. *47.*

———— "New Foundations for Logic," *Mind* (July 1947).

H. Putnam, "Reds, Greens and Logical Analysis," *Philosophical Review* (April 1956).

———— "Reds and Greens Again: a Rejoinder to Arthur Pap," *ibid.* (Jan. 1957).

W. V. Quine, "Designation and Existence," in Feigl and Sellars, *Readings in Philosophical Analysis.*

———— "Truth by Convention," *ibid.*

———— "Two Dogmas of Empiricism," *Philosophical Review* (Jan. 1951) ; reprinted in Quine, *From a Logical Point of View.*

F. P. Ramsay, "The Foundations of Mathematics," in F. P. Ramsay, *The Foundations of Mathematics and Other Logical Essays.*

C. Rollins, "Are There Indubitable Existential Statements?" *Mind* (Oct. 1949).

B. Russell, "On the Notion of Cause," in B. Russell, *Mysticism and Logic,* New York, Norton, 1929; reprinted in Feigl and Brodbeck, *Readings in the Philosophy of Science.*

D. Rynin, "Probability and Meaning," *Journal of Philosophy, 44* (1947).

———— "Critical Essay on A. B. Johnson's *A Treatise on Language*"; in A. B. Johnson, *A Treatise on Language,* ed. D. Rynin.

M. Schlick, "Is There a Material A Priori?" trans. in Feigl and Sellars, *Readings in Philosophical Analysis.*

———— "Meaning and Verification," *ibid.* (originally in *Philosophical Review, 45,* 1936).

A. F. Smullyan, "ϕ-Symbols," *Analysis* (Jan. 1951).

P. F. Strawson, "Necessary Propositions and Entailment-Statements," *Mind* (April 1948).

A. Tarski, "Über den Begriff der logischen Folgerung," in *Actes du Congrès International de Philosophie Scientifique,* Paris 1936; trans. in A. Tarski, *Logic, Semantics, Metamathematics.*

F. Waismann, "Was ist logische Analyse?" *Journal of Unified Science* (continuation of *Erkenntnis*) (1939-40).

――― " Analytic-synthetic," *Analysis* (Dec. 1949, Dec. 1950, Jan. 1951, and June 1951) .

M. G. White, " Analytic-synthetic: an Untenable Dualism," in Linsky, *Semantics and the Philosophy of Language.*

J. Wisdom, " Logical Constructions," *Mind* (1931-33) .

REVIEWS

A. Church, Review of M. G. White vs. M. Black, " The Paradox of Analysis," *Journal of Symbolic Logic* (Dec. 1946) .

C. Lewy, Review of Carnap's *Meaning and Necessity, Mind* (April 1949) .

G. Ryle, Review of Carnap's *Meaning and Necessity,* in *Philosophy* (England) (1949) .

P. F. Strawson, Review of G. H. von Wright's " Form and Content in Logic," *ibid.* (Oct. 1951) .

INDEX

A priori: concepts, 41; knowledge, and analyticity, 69-72, 94 ff., 202 ff., and conceptual analysis, 274, and factual knowledge, 61-2, in Kant, 22-6, in Locke, 47-53; Propositions, *see* Necessary propositions

Absolute: concepts (Carnap), 153, 366, 413-14, 423; entailment and contradiction, 381 ff., 414, 417

Abstract: entities and nominalism, 51-3, and Platonism, 163, 173, 185 ff.; ideas, 294

Abstractions, 81, 190-1, 221

Adequacy criteria (for analyses), 119, 156, 160, 218 ff., 252, 278-82, 400

Agreement of ideas (Locke), 47 ff.

Ambiguity, 192, 311, 314-16, 365-6

Ambrose, A., 95, 100, 270, 440, 443

Analysis of Knowledge and Valuation (Lewis), 95, 97, 101, 286, 322, 441

Analysis: correctness of, 12, 46, 156 ff., 269 ff., 381 ff.; and definition, 64-6, 239 ff.; and demonstration, 11-12, 278; and existential statements, 389 ff.; and explication, *see* Explication; and formal validity, 159-61; and introspection, 398-9; and ordinary usage, 271 ff., 292-4, 397; paradox of, *see* Paradox; and psychology, 240 ff.; and synthetic a priori, 46

Analytic: definitions of various senses, 128, 423; implicitly, 218 ff., 234, 388, 419, 423; philosophy, v, 3, 85, 92, 273, 381, 419-22; synonyms, 290 ff.; syntactic vs. semantic, 259; systematically, 60, 107, 274

Analytic statements: and a priori knowledge, 94 ff.; and arithmetic, 43 ff.; and factual content, 306-10, 428; and implicit definition, 202 ff., 375; and logical truth, 106-8; and ostensive definition, 249 ff.; and reduction sentences, 307-10, 335-6; and simple predicates, 101-3, 224 ff.; and theoretical language, 318-21; triviality of, 178, 230, 275 ff.

Analytic-Synthetic: and a priori—empirical, 94 ff.; and analyses, 46, 232-3, 237 ff.; and changes of meaning, 231-4; and "gradualism," 299, 325 ff., 344-6, 352 ff.; in Hume, 70-2; in Kant, 27 ff., 39-42, 60, 154, 246; and the linguistic theory, 210 ff.; and open concepts, 112, 306 ff.; and partial interpretation, 213; and self-contradiction, 46, 96, 367-8

Aristotelian: logic, 18, 49; 112; physics, 230; theory of real definition, 271, 279; theory of scientific knowledge, 278

Aristotle, 13, 32, 271, 278-9

Arithmetic: and experience, 396, 421; Kant and Frege on, 43-6; and the linguistic theory, 182; logicist reduction of, 131, 141-3, 160, 224, 295-6, 387, 396, 421

Association of ideas, 25, 29

Atomic statements, 145 ff., 251 ff., 423

Axiom: of infinity, 45, 131, 296, 387; of reducibility, 140

Axioms: in geometry, 35 ff., 60, 203-7; role in demonstration (Leibniz), 10-11

Ayer, A. J., 163, 171, 192, 199, 260, 344, 354, 400, 440, 443

Bain, A., 38

Bar-Hillel, J., 128, 358, 443

Basic sentences, 260

Becker, O., 368

Behavior theory, 342

Behaviorism, logical, 285, 325, 330, 332 ff., 347 ff. *See also* Physicalism

Belief sentences, 173 ff., 149, 285, 328-9, 416. *See also* Propositions and belief

Bergmann, G., 337-40, 343-4, 443

Berkeley, 81, 162, 245, 349, 393, 395

Bernouilli, J., 10

Black, M., 125, 152, 260, 276, 327, 440, 443

Blanshard, B., 154, 162, 178, 440

Braithwaite, R. B., 320

Bridgman, P. W., 309, 315-16, 440

THE YALE PAPERBOUNDS